The Premodern Condition

The Premodern Condition

Medievalism and the Making of Theory

BRUCE HOLSINGER

The University of Chicago Press   Chicago and London

BRUCE HOLSINGER is professor of English and music at the University of Virginia. His previous book, *Music, Body, and Desire in Medieval Culture: Hildegard of Bingen to Chaucer,* won the First Book Prize of the Modern Language Association.

The University of Chicago Press, Chicago 60637
The University of Chicago Press, Ltd., London
© 2005 by The University of Chicago
All rights reserved. Published 2005
Printed in the United States of America
14 13 12 11 10 09 08 07 06 05   1 2 3 4 5

ISBN: 0-226-34972-1 (cloth)
ISBN: 0-226-34974-8 (paper)

Appendix I was originally published as Georges Bataille, "La litérature française du Moyen-Age, la morale chevaleresque et la passion" in *Oeuvres completes* vol. 11 (Paris: Editions Gallimard, 1988), 502–518. © 1988 by Editions Gallimard, Paris.
Appendix II was originally published as Pierre Bourdieu's postface to Erwin Panofsky, *Architecture gothique et pensée scolastique.* Reprinted by permission of Éditions de Minuit.

Library of Congress Cataloging-in-Publication Data

Holsinger, Bruce W.
    The premodern condition : medievalism and the making of theory / Bruce Holsinger.
        p. cm.
    Text in English; Appendix I and II translated from French.
    Includes bibliographical references and index.
    ISBN: 0-226-34972-1 (cloth : alk. paper)—ISBN: 0-226-34974-8 (pbk. : alk. paper)
        1. Criticism—France—History—20th century. 2. Medievalism.
    I. Title

PN99.F8H65 2005
801'.95'0944'0904—dc22   2005011953

For Anna

You know the crazy story, the one that arouses my delirious admiration? I roll on the floor laughing when I read Saint Thomas Aquinas, because it's awfully well put together. For Aristotle's philosophy to have been reinjected by Saint Thomas into what one might call the Christian conscience, if that had any meaning, is something that can only be explained by the fact that Christians—well, it's the same with psychoanalysts—abhor what was revealed to them. And they are right. JACQUES LACAN, *SEMINAR XX*

As for the Text, it reads without the inscription of the Father. Here again, the metaphor of the Text separates from that of the work: the latter refers to the image of an *organism* which grows by vital expansion, by "development" (a word which is significantly ambiguous, at once biological and rhetorical); the metaphor of the Text is that of the *network;* if the Text extends itself, it is as a result of a combinatory systematic (an image, moreover, close to current biological conceptions of the living being). Hence no vital "respect" is due to the Text: it can be *broken* (which is just what the Middle Ages did with two nevertheless authoritative texts—Holy Scripture and Aristotle); it can be read without the guarantee of its father, the restitution of the inter-text paradoxically abolishing any legacy. ROLAND BARTHES, "FROM WORK TO TEXT"

Contents

Acknowledgments

"French theory is an American invention." So reads the opening salvo in a recent collection titled *French Theory in America,* which dedicates itself to unpacking some of the baggage accompanying the transatlantic migrations of postwar French thought into American institutions and disciplines over the last thirty years. Though the collection markets itself under the name of the category it rejects, its contributors usefully remind us of the strange intellectual metamorphoses these migrations have brought about. One of the many results of the Anglo-American calcification of a diverse field of francophone critical dialects under the category of "theory" has been a general (though by no means ubiquitous) reluctance to examine some of the more eccentric affiliations of those who spoke them. The events of 1968 continue to distort the work of the generation that in part precipitated them—less in a political sense, though, than in an intellectual one. Even when proven chimerical, the originality of this particular avant-garde must always be sacrificed to the originality of another—the generation of Sartre and Beauvoir, the surrealists, the denizens of pre–World War I French modernism—or to the insights of certain individuals who anticipated its projects in a finite trajectory of historical regression: Bergson, Freud, Nietzsche, Marx . . . and now, of course, Hegel, who in his post-Žižekian incarnations subsumes every glimmer of twentieth-century originality within an *avant*-avant-garde Spirit suffusing the critical work of modernity. As Suzanne Guerlac warns, however, those wishing to discern the more complex genealogies of the postmodern must "dig back into layers of the modern, and seek out old fault lines," for such fault lines have everything to do with the intellectual and institutional habits of segregation that continue to define contemporary regimes of periodization and disciplinarity. The decades of knowledge production, stargazing, and canonization that gave us what we know, teach, and practice as *theory*, then, should not blind us to the curious processes of speciation that produced mutant forms of critical practice from the very beginning.

This book traces the shaping force of the medieval in that decade most responsible for the emergence of "French theory," one of the great reifed formations of academic modernity. It is a formation eternally ripe for defamiliarization, and I cannot claim to have studied this particular aspect of it with anything approaching the care or comprehensiveness it deserves. In fact, the closer this project came to completion, the more clearly I could see the extent of its blind spots, and thus the extent of my reliance throughout on the works of those with real expertise in the intellectual history of twentieth-century France; here I would single out François Dosse's indispensable histories of French structuralism and of the *Annales* school (two works which, when read side by side, would make many of the same points belabored in what follows), Tony Judt's books on the modern French Left, and the dozen-odd intellectual biographers of the central figures studied in these five chapters. Nor can the notes reflect the influence of other scholars I have never met—particularly Margaret Cohen, Patrick Ffrench, Suzanne Guerlac, Rosalind Krauss, and Michael T. Saler—on my ways of thinking about the intricate and often surprising inner workings of modern avant-garde subcultures, both the one studied here and others. I have benefited as well from the growing genre of books scrutinizing the impact of medievalism and medieval studies on modern (mostly French) thought, in particular R. Howard Bloch and Stephen G. Nichols's *Medievalism and the Modernist Temper*, of which this book might be understood as a later chapter; Katherine Bergeron's *Decadent Enchantments*, which approaches related issues from a musicological angle; and Amy Hollywood's *Sensible Ecstasy*, which appeared as the manuscript was nearing completion and which I have tried to note where appropriate.

I owe a special debt to the late Pierre Bourdieu, who shortly before his death granted me permission to include a translation of his postface to Erwin Panofsky's *Gothic Architecture and Scholasticism* as an appendix to this project. Emily Steiner encouraged me to expand what was a long and unwieldy essay into a short book. Brainstorming sessions with William Kuskin and Mark Winokur helped me to reframe some of the central questions I have tried to ask, while Jessica Rosenfeld's sharp reading of the second chapter clarified what I was trying to say about Lacan. The book has its distant point of origin in a deceptively simple question Caroline Bynum asked me more than ten years ago; I hope I have begun to answer it here. Jennifer Jahner and Kat Rutkowski furnished able research and fact-checking assistance in the final stages. Others providing helpful comments, invitations, readings, and responses included Barbara Nolan, Helen Solterer, Michelle Warren, Barbara Newman, David Wallace, Rita Copeland, Jody Enders, Catherine Sanok, Eugene Vance, Vance Smith, Michael Uebel, Andrew Cole, Kellie Robertson, Erin Labbie, Sarah Kay, Andy Stafford, John Caputo, Sarah Beckwith, David Aers, and Ann Williams-Gascon; and, at the University of Colorado, Karen Jacobs, Jeffrey DeShell, Christopher Braider, Andy Cowell, Jeff Cox, Timothy Morton, Katherine Eggert, Elizabeth Robertson, John-Michael Rivera, Joe Amato, Katherine Millersdaughter, Charlotte Sussman, Valerie Forman, Brendan O'Kelly, and John Stevenson.

At the University of Chicago Press, Alan Thomas's early interest in this project yielded a contract and several extensions, while Randy Petilos has been a model of editorial patience and precision; both have made working with the Press an absolute joy. I have been particularly fortunate in the Press's choice of external reviewers: an anonymous reader helped me sharpen and define the project at a much earlier stage, while Amy Hollywood and Kevin Hart crucially stressed the importance of turning the book more explicitly toward the theological issues that now dominate several of the chapters. All three saved me from a number of embarrassing errors and oversights.

Laurence Petit has proven an indefatigable ally throughout the course of this project: as a translator, a fact-checker, and a patient respondent to innumerable uninformed questions about French intellectual culture, university organization, and so on. She has been a collaborator in the best sense of the word, and I owe her an enormous debt of gratitude.

Two budding avant-gardistes in my life, Campbell and Malcolm, have helped me maintain perspective and sort priorities at nearly every turn, and I thank them for their eternal lack of patience. The book is dedicated to Anna Brickhouse, both for lending this book her legendary skills as a reader and commentator and for sharing the gifts of her intellect, her humor, her time, and her love.

Introduction: The Avant-Garde Premodern

In the winter of 1922, a young French medievalist defended his thesis for a postgraduate diploma in paleography at the École Nationale des Chartes, the great Parisian training center for would-be editors, archivists, and librarians. The thesis, an edition of a thirteenth-century Old French poem, the *Ordene de chevalerie,* sought to provide the first modern text of a work the editor regarded as an important literary testament to the chivalric culture of sacrifice. Unfortunately for the aspiring scholar (only twenty-five at the time), another edition of the *Ordene de chevalerie,* by University of Chicago medievalist Roy Temple House, had appeared in print just before he began his own, and House's would go on to become the standard edition of the text— despite our young scholar's efforts to the contrary: as he asserted somewhat defensively in the opening pages of his introduction, House's edition "is difficult to obtain." Though the scholar's edition was indexed in the 1922 volume of the "Position des thèses" (the rough French equivalent of Dissertation Abstracts International), it appears not to have survived his death; the École des Chartes does not archive theses completed before 1961, and the Bibliothèque Nationale does not possess a copy.[1]

Nevertheless, the rigorous training he received at the École des Chartes quickly earned him a job at the Biblio-

1. *Position des thèses soutenues ...,* 21–24; the comments on House's edition (*L'Ordene de Chevalerie: An Old French Poem*) appear on 21.

thèque Nationale as an assistant curator in the antiquities section, where he would work until 1942 as a numismaticist and archivist. From the 1920s through the late 1950s, our scholar made numerous contributions to French medieval studies, publishing articles on the medieval apocalypse, chivalry, and mysticism as well as book chapters on feudalism and medieval kingship; toward the end of his career, he produced a lengthy edition of legal documents, depositions, and other materials relating to the life of a fifteenth-century French nobleman. Though his publications ranged at times far afield from the Middle Ages, his early professional interest in the era's cultural forms—chivalric literature, Gothic architecture, scholasticism, feudalism, and many others—remained a constant source of intellectual and imaginative energy until his death in 1962. The name of this medievalist—a paleographer of Old French by training, with considerable expertise in medieval numismatics, codicology, editorial practice, and romantic philology, and whose main source of income from 1922 through the early 1950s came from his employment as an archivist in Paris, Orléans, and Charpentras—was Georges Bataille.[2]

The twentieth century knew the same Georges Bataille as a prolific "anti-philosopher" (his own term) of economics, violence, and death, an author of brainy pornographic fiction, and an intellectual polymath whose writings are today regarded as among the most influential strands in the emergence of modern literary and cultural theory. For Michel Foucault, who was instrumental in launching Bataille's twelve-volume *Œuvres complètes* in 1970, Bataille was one of the most significant intellectuals of the twentieth century.[3] Philippe Sollers would go so far as to dub Bataille the "godfather" of the *Tel Quel* circle and its eponymous journal, and the very conceptual divide separating structuralism from poststructuralism was often described in this era as deriving from Bataille's differentiation between restricted and general economies.[4] Maurice Blanchot, Jacques Derrida, Jacques Lacan, Julia Kristeva, Roland Barthes, and Pierre Bourdieu are just a few among the subsequent generation of French intellectuals who credited him with inspiring significant turning points or departures in their thought. That Bataille did so as a practicing medievalist, however, has been all but forgotten, the casualty of a presen-

---

2. The details of Bataille's biography given here derive in large part from Mattheus's exhaustive *Georges Bataille: Eine Thanatographie* and Surya's more episodic *Georges Bataille, la mort à l'oeuvre* (translated as *Georges Bataille: An Intellectual Biography*).

3. Foucault's assessment of Bataille as "one of the most important writers of the century" appears in his preface to volume 1 of Bataille's *Oeuvres complètes* (5).

4. Guerlac, *Literary Polemics*, 12. On Sollers and Bataille, see Kauppi, *The Making of an Avant-Garde*, 66.

tism that continues in large part to define the historiography of modern critical thought.

Viewed from a certain angle, though, Bataille's professional dedication to the culture of the European Middle Ages appears less anomalous than it might seem, and indeed the intimacy between his lifelong vocation as a scholar of medieval culture and his *a*vocation as a critic of such foundational influence on the intellectual avant garde of 1960s France provides an intriguing lens upon other aspects of this subculture's eccentrically diachronic historical sensibility. For Sollers, too, found in the Middle Ages a constant source of revisionist engagement with tradition. His obsession with rewriting the text of Dante inspired his experimental fiction and essays from his earliest work through *Paradis* (1981); it was Sollers, too, who engineered the serial translation and publication of Umberto Eco's *Le moyen âge de James Joyce* in the eleventh and twelfth issues of *Tel Quel,* as well as the cluster of essays on Dante in the twenty-third. When *Tel Quel* was launched in 1960, Jacques Lacan was just completing his seventh seminar, *The Ethics of Psychoanalysis,* at least a third of which is devoted to the residual effects of the medieval literature of "courtly love" within modern regimes of subjection. Later in the decade, in 1967, Les Éditions de Minuit published Derrida's *Of Grammatology,* with its extended critique of Rousseau's fantasy of medieval decadence in his *Essay on the Origins of Language.* That same year Minuit released Pierre Bourdieu's French translation of Erwin Panofsky's classic study of medieval systems of thought, *Gothic Architecture and Scholasticism,* the postface to which included the sociologist's first extended elaboration of the *habitus*—leading Michel de Certeau, thirteen years later, to hail a "return to the medieval order" in "contemporary technocracy."[5] And in a May 1970 issue of *Le Monde,* Raymond Jean's review of *S/Z* praised Roland Barthes for deliberately reviving a medieval hermeneutic practice by appropriating the roles of *auctor, compilator, scriptor,* and *commentator* in relation to the text of Balzac. So wide-ranging and energetic was the French avant garde's preoccupation with medieval formations during this decade that it merits recognition as one of the most significant epiphenomena accompanying the emergence and consolidation of so-called French theory as a meta-discourse of posthumanistic inquiry. This epiphenomenon—let us call it *theoretic medievalism*—embraces a spectrum of approaches and attitudes toward the Western Middle Ages shaping postwar French critical discourse in its myriad forms: from the straightforward appropriation of medieval philosophical texts and an

---

5. Certeau, *The Practice of Everyday Life,* 215 n. 29.

enthusiastic affiliation with modern medievalist scholarship to a range of abnegations, elisions, and denials of the premodernities at the heart of the modern.

The Premodern Condition explores the critical impact of medievalism in the writings of Bataille and the French avant garde of the 1960s and its implications for current understandings of theory, history, and the difficult relation between the domains of the theoretical and the historical. Drawing on an array of philosophical, literary-critical, sociological, and other writings produced within this milieu, *The Premodern Condition* proposes that the critical discourse of postwar France be reconceived in part as a brilliantly defamiliarizing amalgamation of medievalisms that together constitute the domain of the avant-garde premodern. The diachronic imagination of the *nouvelle critique* reaches across a millennium to embrace a distant epoch as a foundation for its own intellectual work while elaborating a diverse and often perplexingly self-contradictory vision of the Middle Ages and their legacy to modern theoretical reflection. In this sense, the archaeology of medievalism uncovered here has important bearing on the stories that modernity's own critical tradition continues to tell and to leave untold about its past.

One of these stories, of course, is that narrated in Jean-François Lyotard's widely influential 1979 treatise on what he termed the "postmodern condition," a phrase I have adapted as the title for this book. This appropriation is less polemical than it might appear, for in the eschewal of *grands récits* he imputes to postmodern views of history, Lyotard captures the historical sensibility that, with some exceptions, also defined the diverse practices of medievalism among the avant garde, though not always in the ways we might expect. One of the ironically recursive effects of the "incredulity toward metanarratives" postulated in *The Postmodern Condition* has been the growing demand in recent years to "historicize theory," to subject the ostensibly universalizing rhetorics of psychoanalysis, structuralism, and so on to the same analytic rigors they themselves claimed to exercise upon their subjects.[6] These injunctions have yielded two complementary models of historicism in regard to the languages of theory: first, synchronic accounts of the aesthetic practices and cultural institutions that accompanied the rise of theory and of the influence of these practices and institutions on particular thinkers (Benjamin's relation to Paris surrealism of the 1930s, for example, or the involvement of the structuralist generation in the institu-

6. Lyotard, *The Postmodern Condition*, xxiv.

tional and cultural politics of postwar France and the events of 1968); and second, diachronic perspectives on theory's relation to earlier strands of intellectual history and its complex debts to numerous philosophical and literary progenitors, from Hegel and Marx to Valéry and Breton.[7] As the following chapters collectively demonstrate, historicizing the medievalism of the theoretical avant garde entails an awareness of the pressures exerted on these writers by contemporaneous institutions and schools of thoughts (French Thomism, the *Annales* school) as well as an approach to intellectual history that recognizes strands of influence between thinkers separated by as little as a decade (Panofsky and Bourdieu) and as many as sixteen centuries (Augustine and Derrida). While thick description and old-fashioned source study have thus both lent themselves to this book's historical argument, neither is capable of explaining this coterie's recurrent fascination, even obsession with the historical period that modernity most consistently abjected as its temporal other. In its variegated assault on the legacy of the Enlightenment, the critical generation of this era turned to the Middle Ages not in a fit of nostalgic retrospection, but in a spirit of both interpretive and ideological resistance to the relentless inevitability of modernity.

Crucially, however, the premodern condition is far from a condition of "mourning," with all the displaced emotionalism and sentimentalized pseudo-politics that Michel de Certeau and others have identified as symptomatic of much modern historical reflection. Nor does it entail a fetishistic preoccupation with detached fragments of a vanished past, though in its tendency to piece together far-reaching critical paradigms from seemingly minor shards of premodern history, the medievalism of the avant garde in part confirms Lyotard's view of postmodern historical knowledge as willfully fragmentary, invested in "a pragmatics of language particles" that discerns in the past the same heterogeneity experienced in the present.[8] Yet the medieval fragments inspiring the critical work of the avant garde function less as detached objects for the fetishist's sterile delectation than as productive sacraments of creative ingenuity, partial remains from an unknowable past invested nevertheless with a transformative capacity in the critical present. In this sense, the premodern condition entails a stridently secularized historicism that is nevertheless reminiscent of the sacramental sensibility motivating much medieval historiography, which finds in discrete past events and

---

7. On both of these modes in various incarnations, see Cohen, "*Critical Inquiry, October,* and Historicizing French Theory."

8. Lyotard, *The Postmodern Condition,* xxiv.

surviving relics the wondrous promise of an invisible totality it can only occasionally glimpse in the lived present.[9] As we shall see, this idiosyncratic medievalist historicism—promoting neither an unbroken continuity with the medieval past nor the epistemic ruptures implied in modernity's disavowal of the Middle Ages—provides in turn a powerful mechanism for questioning traditional schemes of periodization and temporality in the Western tradition. As theory continues its steady migration from critical provocation to the hallowed status of the primary source, we may find new and unexpected answers to many of the current disputes over the historical shape of our disciplines in the very historical preoccupations that informed some of theory's own most pressing engagements with the past.

———

The history of theoretic medievalism is a truly international one, though this history must be written differently from the perspectives of the various linguistic and national traditions in which it unfolded (and thus forces a certain modesty in any attempt to account for its particular implications within one). Its Germanic genealogy has fertile roots in the work of Martin Heidegger, easily the most significant twentieth-century philosophical influence on theoretical discourse after Freud. Like Bataille, though, Heidegger began his career very solidly in medieval studies, with a *Habilitationsschrift* entitled "Duns Scotus's Theory of the Categories and of Meanings," which he defended in a public lecture in July 1915. (The central text studied in the thesis, *De modis significandi sive Grammatica speculativa*, has since been attributed to Thomas of Erfurt.) As he was completing the thesis, in fact, Heidegger was planning an academic life dedicated to studying medieval theology and what he regarded as its vital anticipation of Husserlian phenomenology— scholasticism's "theoretical content," as he saw it. Had he not been denied a vacant chair in the history of Catholic philosophy at the University of Freiburg, it is likely that we would know Heidegger today as one of the great twentieth-century exponents of medieval thought. Though his subsequent training obviously took him in other directions, medie-

9. Here I am thinking of Gabrielle Spiegel's sense of medieval historiography as centrally motivated by "a vast range of material systematically excluded from the precincts of modern historical realism: miracles, resurrections, saints, myths, and visions inter alia"—phenomena that would assume central roles in the historiographical writings of, for example, Suger of St. Denis, to whom, in Spiegel's words, "the recollection of the past was not only a memory; it was also, and perhaps more important, the promise of the future" (*The Past as Text*, xii, 177); see especially the chapter "History as Enlightenment," 163–177.

val mysticism, scholasticism, and theological hermeneutics remained a crucial part of the philosophical apparatus he would bring to bear on the broader questions he grappled with throughout his life.[10]

Heidegger was preceded in his medievalist obsessions by, among others, Max Weber, the prime mover of modern sociology, who wrote his dissertation and first book on the medieval Italian merchant economy; and by Hegel himself, who dedicated a significant portion of his *Lectures on the History of Philosophy* to medieval thought in an enterprise that reads Maimonides and al-Kindi alongside Aquinas and Jean Gerson. The lectures elaborate an expansive vision of premodern philosophy in which the Renaissance figures as little more than an afterthought separating medieval thinkers from the moderns who built on their foundations.[11] Later significant Germanic instances of theoretic medievalism include, to name just three, the early work of Walter Benjamin on the *Trauerspiele,* the subject of an (ultimately failed) *Habilitationsschrift* that emphasized "the affinity between the baroque drama and the religious drama of the Middle Ages" by quoting liberally from Vincent of Beauvais, Otto of Freising, and the medieval mysteries; the critical theory of Max Horkheimer, who more than once expressed his exasperation at the "superficiality" of medieval-modern periodization; and the work of Hans Robert Jauss, whose extensive inquiries into medieval genres shaped the diffusion of the *Rezeptionsästhetik* of the Constance school in Anglo-American literary studies.[12]

An Italian genealogy, on the other hand, might begin with the great aesthetician Benedetto Croce's *La poesia di Dante* (1922), which sought to dismantle the "parasitic vegetation" of nineteenth-century mystifications of the national poet by postulating a synthesis of the lyrical and

10. On the significance of Heidegger's early work in medieval theology, see van Buren, *The Young Heidegger,* esp. 70–75; Kisiel, *The Genesis of Heidegger's Being and Time,* 108–111; the many essays in Esposito and Porro, eds., *Heidegger e i medievali,* which prints the proceedings of a 2000 colloquium at Cassino in the subject; and, from a medievalist's perspective, Shoaf, "Medieval Studies after Derrida after Heidegger," esp. 11–13. The thesis itself is available in Heidegger, *Frühe Schriften,* 189–411.

11. Hegel, *Medieval and Early Modern Philosophy;* Weber, *The History of Commercial Partnerships in the Middle Ages.* As Andrew Cole suggests, moreover, Hegel's so-called master/slave dialectic may be read in part as a distillation of his views on medieval European feudalism; see Cole, "What Hegel's Master/Slave Dialectic Really Means." On Weber's medievalism and *The Protestant Ethic,* the best place to begin is Kaelber, "Weber's Lacuna: Medieval Religion and the Roots of Rationalization." As Michel Zink remarked in his inaugural lecture for the Collège de France, "It is no accident that the first person to truly conceive of the Middle Ages within a philosophy of history and an aesthetics was Hegel" (Zink, *Enchantment of the Middle Ages,* 7).

12. Benjamin, *The Origin of German Tragic Drama,* 76; Horkheimer, *Critical Theory,* 48. On Jauss, see the discussion below. Relevant too is Nietzsche's early career in classical philology and what James I. Porter has shown was its important bearing on his later philosophical investigations, beginning with *The Birth of Tragedy;* see Porter, *Nietzsche and the Philology of the Future.*

the political in the *Divine Comedy*.[13] Antonio Gramsci's *Prison Notebooks*, by contrast, turned to the texts of Dante for their unique linguistic perspectives on both semiotic and political representation, perspectives that would figure significantly in Gramsci's more overtly theoretical reflections on hegemony and resistance.[14] The most familiar case of an informing theoretical investment in the Middle Ages is of course the oeuvre of Umberto Eco, which combines semiotics, narrative, theory, and intellectual history into a simultaneously popular and academic medievalism that has made itself felt in the pages of *Tel Quel* and, much later, on the Hollywood screen.[15] The European Middle Ages provide a virtually inexhaustible source of intellectual provocation to the critical imagination of modernity, from Mikhail Bakhtin's influential vision of the medieval culture of carnival to Slavoj Žižek's investigations of the libidinal investments enabling courtly love; from Charles Sanders Peirce's founding of the Anglo-American school of semiotics on the shoulders of Duns Scotus to Emmanuel Levinas's antimystical investments in the rationalism of Moses Maimonides.[16]

Even with regard to twentieth-century France alone, many alternative trajectories might be imagined that would yield a picture very different from the relatively limited one presented in this book. A study of the role of premodernity in the New Novel and modern French experimental writing would have to embrace the extended dialogue between Thomas Aquinas and Hegel in Blanchot's *L'Entretien infini* (1969) alongside Sollers's *Paradis* and the immortal medieval nobleman at the center of Simone de Beauvoir's *Tous les hommes sont mortels* (1946).[17] Medievalism played a complex role as well within the twentieth-century fortunes of Bergsonism, from the neo-Thomist philosopher and theologian Jacques Maritain's first book, *La Philosophie Bergsonienne* (1913), through Gilles Deleuze's *Bergsonisme* (1966); both books had an enormous influence on their respective intellectual milieus, yet Maritain and the entire history of Thomist Bergsonism go all but unmentioned in the post-Deleuzian revival of Bergson's thought (despite Deleuze's own longstanding inter-

13. Caserta, "Croce's Essay on Dante."

14. Bové, "Dante, Gramsci and Cultural Criticism."

15. See especially Coletti, *Naming the Rose,* a book unjustly neglected in the last decade's metatheoretical discussions among medievalists.

16. For a fascinating study arguing that "the genuine English avant-garde of the interwar period were the medieval modernists," see Saler, *The Avant-Garde in Interwar England* (citation from 173).

17. Such a study, though, could only gesture at a figure such as Alain Robbe-Grillet, whose manifestos for a *nouveau roman* through the 1950s and 1960s seem almost obsessively opposed to the sorts of historical complexities evident in the metafictional writings of a Roland Barthes or, for that matter, a Jean-Paul Sartre (see the 1956 essay "A Future for the Novel," in Robbe-Grillet, *For a New Novel*, 15–24). On Blanchot's *L'Entretien infini*, see Taylor, *Altarity*, 222–23.

ests in medieval romance and scholasticism). And studies such as Peter Tracey Connor's *Georges Bataille and the Mysticism of Sin*, Alexander Irwin's *Saints of the Impossible*, Amy Hollywood's *Sensible Ecstasy*, and Kevin Hart's *The Dark Gaze* are demonstrating the diverse reception of pre-Enlightenment mysticism in modern French thought. I have thus been constantly aware throughout the writing of this book both of its selectiveness and of the resultant distortions its chronological focus has inevitably introduced into the treatment of particular writers and texts. Narrowness possesses advantages too, of course: the concentration here on a single intellectual trajectory highlights Bataille and the generation of the 1960s both for the especially dense constellation of theoretic medievalisms these writers produced and, more generally, for their founding impact upon the subsequent trajectory of literary and critical theory (whether in fact or in legend).

Indeed, given Lyotard's social-scientific stress on the emergence of new networks of global capital, the rise of "technocracy," the performative dimensions of recent scientific inquiry, and the collapse of metanarrative across the fields of human knowledge, it is often forgotten that *The Postmodern Condition* explicitly singled out "the end of the 1950s," specifically in France, as the moment that heralded the beginning of the "postmodern age": an age born with the founding of *Tel Quel*, the death of Bataille, the eclipse of Sartre—and with the rise of the last recognizable avant garde of twentieth-century France.[18] It was largely due to the influence of Lyotard's book, in fact, that the denizens of French theory came to be retroactively associated with the postmodern as its most significant intellectual progenitors. The transmission of these French intellectual projects into Anglo-American academic circles led to the peculiar hypostatization of *theory* as a distinct institutional formation and mode of critical engagement whose practitioners were not always willing to address honestly their debts to even their most immediate precursors. Similarly, the premodern condition as it emerged during the 1960s witnessed widely varying degrees of commitment to and knowledge of its appropriated subject—and, as a corollary, a wide range of methodological and interpretive practices. Bataille spent much of his career practicing medieval studies; his paleographical, codicological, and philological skills rivaled those of the most accomplished medievalist scholars of his day. Others spent extended periods of time in their writ-

18. For contrasting but equally provocative discussions of avant-garde "dissolution," which almost seems to represent a kind of trope in contemporary writing about theories and practices of avant gardes, see Lehman, *The Last Avant-Garde*, 283–303; Perloff, *The Futurist Moment*, 195–238; and Lorau, *Autodissolution des avant-gardes*, esp. 15–77.

ings reflecting on specific medieval works or problems and, while making no claim to disciplinary expertise, nevertheless immersed themselves in the relevant scholarship with an ingenuous fervor. Still others turned to the medieval at important moments in the development of their thought while leaving unaddressed the consequences and implications of their extended forays into medievalist domains. Perhaps we might understand the rise of French theory as at heart a revival of Greek *theoria*, with all the participatory wonderment and sacralized rapture implied in the term. As Hans-Georg Gadamer once remarked, *theoria* "is a true sharing, not something active, but something passive (pathos), namely being totally involved in and carried away by what one sees."[19] This passive sense of awe in the presence of the medieval will be a frequent theme in what follows; if nothing else, theoretic medievalism in twentieth-century France remained honest to the philological origins of "theory" as both perspective and affliction.

––––––––

The task of excavating the avant-garde premodern seems especially urgent at a moment that is more and more often being imagined as "posttheoretical." "Literary theory has been dead for ten years," Stanley Aronowitz laconically remarked to *The New York Times* in 2001, a claim ostensibly supported by a spate of books and articles over the same decade greeting the news of theory's passing with everything from retrospective nostalgia to urbane dismissal to undisguised delight; a very partial list would include titles such as *After Theory, Reading after Theory, What's Left of Theory?* and, for the early periods, David Scott Kastan's *Shakespeare after Theory*, which seeks to describe and perform "the almost inevitable practice of Shakespeare studies after theory, no longer chasing after it but working powerfully and productively in its wake." Since theory's own "day has passed," Kastan contends, in its place we are now to pursue "history" and "facts" while armed with its insights: "theory has now brought us to the point where we must begin to respond to its significant challenges, not by producing more theory but more facts, however value-laden they will necessarily be, that will reveal the specific historical conditions that have determined the reading and writing of literature."[20] These facts and historical conditions will emerge most clearly through the practice of textual criticism, the principles of biblio-

19. Gadamer, *Truth and Method*, 111; see Jay, *Downcast Eyes*, 31.
20. Kastan, *Shakespeare after Theory*, 31.

graphical and editorial study that will reveal the "historicity" of the text as a material, social artifact. It is "only by turning to history from theory," Kastan argues, "that the particular forms and particular effects of a text's 'worldliness' can be discovered and demonstrated."[21] The jarring prepositional shift in this formulation—"*to* history *from* theory"—does an enormous amount of rhetorical work, though it is hard to accept its logic. Like many of those writing in this vein, Kastan here forces himself into the uncomfortable position of theorizing the death of theory.

Reports of theory's demise are thus both greatly exaggerated and, more often than not, self-defeating. Coming as they do from a scholar of the early periods, such confident proclamations are symptomatic of a growing tendency in medieval and early modern studies to construct "theory" as a presentist, formalist, and inherently external formation which, while it may have taught important interpretive lessons for a few decades, must now be recognized as a discursive effect of modern intellectual history. If theory's presence in Anglo-American literary scholarship is not as explicit as it once was, this logic runs, then the continuing reflection on theory qua theory can safely be consigned to specialists in modernism and postmodernism (who themselves like to recall, with a barely ironized nostalgia, those "heady days" when we all agreed upon what theory was).[22] The recent publication of François Cusset's *French Theory: Foucault, Derrida, Deleuze & Cie et les mutations de la vie intellectuelle aux États-Unis* only confirms that many contemporary French intellectuals are similarly engaged in a large-scale jettisoning of formative parts of their own recent intellectual history in the wake of "l'effet Sokal" and in reaction to "la 'menace' postmoderne."[23] This anxiety of philosophical influence couples the rejection of the generation of the 1960s with the triumph of a moralizing humanism that has no use for the solipsisms of theory and its culture of self-promotion.

Yet theory might more enablingly be envisioned as a series of hermeneutic practices fully integrated and (to lift an appropriately sacramental term from medieval theology) consubstantial with the historicist practices of literary and cultural study. To proclaim the demise of theory as an enduring problematic in itself, to metaphorize its continuing presence in literary studies as a "wake," is to risk once again privileging a pu-

21. Kastan, *Shakespeare after Theory*, 42.

22. See, for example, Culler, "The Literary in Theory," 272. Cusset (*French Theory*, 110–17) provides an amusingly detached overview of the Americanization of "theory" as a "nouvel objet transdisciplinaire façonné par les littéraires à partir du poststructuralisme français" (110).

23. Cusset, *French Theory*, 323–41 (citation from 140); and, from a very different position, see Judt, *Past Imperfect: French Intellectuals, 1944–1956*, 299–301. A devastating overview of this agonism can be found in Jay, "Lafayette's Children: The American Reception of French Liberalism."

tatively discrete discourse of theory over the disciplines and methodologies in which it emerged, that it continues to inhabit, and apart from which it is ontologically unthinkable. It is thus to accept, as Cusset puts it, perhaps the most dire consequence of the Americanization of French theory: its devolution to the "intransitive," the objectless elaboration of a metaphysical discourse concerned only with itself. At least among medievalists and early modernists, serious work on perhaps the most complex and difficult dimension of our relationship to theory—the excavation of and accounting for its diverse intellectual genealogies and their intercalation with those of our own disciplinary pasts—has just begun. If Fredric Jameson is correct in his assessment of "the constitutive impurity of all postmodernism theory,"[24] the particular impurity this book will be pursuing through various theoretical languages is the trace of the medieval: the deep, sustaining, and constitutive role of the European Middle Ages and European medieval studies in the last half-century's theorization of language, culture, and society.

———

I have chosen the term *archaeology* to circumscribe the aims and methods of this inquiry for several reasons. First, I mean to evoke the obvious sense in which critical discourse has long been engaged in a project very much in the spirit of the original Greek sense of *archaiologia,* meaning simply the study of the archaic, the distant past. It goes without saying that the literatures and philosophies of classical antiquity pervade the most influential texts of the French avant garde; one thinks of Derrida on Plato's *pharmakon,* Lacan on *Antigone,* or the second and third volumes of Foucault's *History of Sexuality.* The European Renaissance, too, looms powerfully in this diachronic imagination, which makes Hölderlin and *Hamlet* frequent reference points in its excavation of the past. Such classical and Renaissance archaeologies, though, are both more familiar and (I would argue) much easier to explain. In the Western tradition's clichéd narratives of intellectual and cultural progress, the modern begins in the Renaissance, which in turn reanimates the intellectual and literary heritages of the ancient world as horizons for our own. The Middle Ages, by contrast, persist imaginatively as the dark age preceding the Renaissance discovery of the individual postulated by Burckhardt, whose legacy can still be perceived in such quaint forms as Harold

———

24. Jameson, *Postmodernism, or, The Cultural Logic of Late Capitalism,* xii.

Bloom's vision of the "invention of the human" in the works of Shakespeare, or Nancy Armstrong and Leonard Tennenhouse's postulation of the "origins of personal life" in the seventeenth century.[25] Such tired narratives remain all too familiar and—except among medievalists themselves, who have created a veritable subgenre of criticism dedicated to their dismantling—rarely questioned.

This enduring notion of the Renaissance as the birthplace of the modern continues to lead many contemporary critics into a glib homogenization of the medieval epoch, their teleologies entirely unaffected by the last fifty years of medievalist scholarship. Thus, Homi Bhabha can knowingly evoke "the sacral ontology of the medieval world and its overwhelming visual and aural imaginary," while Jean Baudrillard can get away with the odd proposal that, in feudal societies, "signs are limited in number and their circulation is restricted."[26] These and many other caricatures of the period have understandably led medievalists to bemoan the misrepresentations of the Middle Ages perpetrated in the name of postmodernism and its critical apparatus. "In some very influential theoretical and critical work developing out of postmodernism," Carolyn Dinshaw argues in a critique of Bhabha's writings on nationalism, "the Middle Ages is still made the dense, unvarying, and eminently obvious monolith against which modernity and postmodernity groovily emerge."[27] For Paul Strohm, who takes Baudrillard to task, "most postmodernist practitioners indulge a furtive and dishonest relation to the medieval past. This relation consists in a shifty double move, according to which the Middle Ages are debunked as static, hieratic, and unchanging, even while these same accusations are called repeatedly into service in order secretly to nourish the illicit relation between most postmodern cultural analysis and the idea of the social 'totality' or whole."[28]

Yet for Bataille and the critical generation that followed him, the European Middle Ages represented anything but a static era of unchanging hierarchies and social uniformity.[29] As I have already suggested, many of these writers found in the thousand years before the Renaissance an extraordinary cultural variety and an enabling source of heuristic models

25. Bloom, *Shakespeare: The Invention of the Human;* Armstrong and Tennenhouse, *The Imaginary Puritan.*

26. Bhabha, "DissemiNation: Time, Narrative, and the Margins of the Modern Nation," 308; Baudrillard's comments are cited and discussed in Strohm, *Theory and the Premodern Text,* 158.

27. Dinshaw, *Getting Medieval,* 16.

28. Strohm, *Theory and the Premodern Text,* 158.

29. As it so clearly had for Sartre; see the comments on medieval writing as a "means solely of preserving and transmitting Christian ideology" in Sartre, *What Is Literature?* 84.

for their own critical practice. Far from simply an object of nostalgic longing or an occasional source of metaphorical exempla, the medieval epoch was continually mined by these thinkers for specific philosophical vocabularies, social formations, and systems of thought that would inspire some of theory's most recognizable lexicons and problematics, from Bataille's model of "transgression" to Pierre Bourdieu's notion of the *habitus*. The medieval presence in theory is in this sense both performative and citational: an investment in medievalism gives critical discourse myriad lessons in the nature of ethical inquiry, the historical processes of subject formation, the social implications of scriptive technologies, and the ideological consequences of periodization itself. [30]

It is particularly ironic, then, that so many medievalists have described their disciplines' relations to the allegedly antihistorical languages of theory as marginalized, subservient, or belated (let alone anachronistic). The generation of French medievalists that came of age in the 1960s was surely aware on some level of the central role played by medievalists and medieval culture in the development of, for example, historical anthropology, Russian formalism, semiology, and structuralism. Yet if "the greatest paradox of nineteenth-century medieval studies was that it created a modernist canon in a medieval setting," as Stephen G. Nichols has eloquently argued, perhaps the greatest paradox of twentieth-century medieval studies was its curious refusal to examine its own role in shaping the critical languages of modernity: a refusal captured in that century's very rhetorics of medievalist inquiry, from the "suspicion of modernity" that characterized even the most innovative work of Joseph Bédier around 1900 to the ascetic sense of theoretical belatedness suffusing the disciplines of medieval studies from the early 1970s through the 1990s.[31]

This sensibility became an unexamined yet ubiquitous disposition in medieval studies during the years immediately following the era studied in this book, and it is nowhere more apparent than in the influential 1979 special issue of *New Literary History* on the topic of "Medieval Literature and Contemporary Theory." The volume is dedicated in particular to what was then a wide-ranging and generally collegial debate among medievalists concerning the "alterity and modernity" of medieval culture, a debate that arose largely in response to Paul Zumthor's *Es-*

30. The observations of Fradenburg, "'So That We May Speak of Them': Enjoying the Middle Ages," 211, are especially pertinent here.

31. Nichols, "Modernism and the Politics of Medieval Studies," 50; Corbellari, "Joseph Bédier, Philologist and Writer," 284.

sai de poétique médiévale (1972) and Hans Robert Jauss's *Alterität under Modernität der mittelalterlichen Literatur* (1977; the book's introduction is translated as the first essay in the *NLH* volume). Despite considerable differences in approach and assumptions separating the two critics, this compelling exchange on the topic of medieval alterity sets a certain tone for the succeeding decades concerning the status of theory in the disciplines of medieval studies—a tone adumbrated in Jauss's opening paragraph: "The study of the literature of the European Middle Ages has at the present time a peculiar advantage. It has lost its place in the educational canon, and therefore it hardly shows up in courses of study or curricula. It stands far from the modern trend of the development of theory [*Theoriebildung*] and began its reorientation almost without notice; it is therefore still more strongly challenged in terms of its universality and public reputation than are the neighboring historical disciplines."[32] Zumthor agrees, citing two habits of mind that have led medievalists to deny the fundamental alterity of the Middle Ages. The first is "naïve historicism," which coerces a "presupposition . . . of the continuity of history, considered as a regular evolving process."[33] This mode of historicism was particularly prevalent among the nineteenth-century "fathers of medieval studies," who bequeathed to their disciplines "immense amounts of knowledge on which we still draw today" yet "never questioned the ideological and philosophical implications of their manner of working."[34] Zumthor's second species of denial concerns something like what Edward W. Said would later term "traveling theory": the unmooring of theoretical paradigms from the specific political and social circumstances that produced them and gave them their initial meaning and critical purchase.[35] As Zumthor puts it:

By "blind modernism," I mean a more subtle phenomenon, resulting from conceptual tools and methods at our disposal in 1978, following the extensive use of analytical perspectives in the last twenty or thirty years. On the one hand, it would be impossible to renounce recourse to these tools and methods, since they are, for us, as academics dedicated to texts, the essential of *our* culture. It is only with their aid that we succeed in knowing the Other. . . . But, on the other hand, these critical tools have generally been perfected in the course of reflecting upon modern texts (most often

32. Jauss, "The Alterity and Modernity of Medieval Literature," 181; German cited from Jauss, *Alterität under Modernität*, 9.
33. Zumthor, "Comments on H. R. Jauss's Article," 370.
34. Zumthor, "Comments on H. R. Jauss's Article," 371.
35. See Said, "Traveling Theory," in *The World, the Text, and the Critic,* 226–47.

contemporary), answering to our own universe; such texts do not pose the problem of an intercultural relationship. In fact, most often, their study concerns history only . . . insofar as it constitutes the depth and breadth of the present and not insofar as it gives rise to the presence of the Other. Almost all research (more or less heterogeneous), which today forms what is called "the theory of the literary text," is thus historically marked. Generated by Western culture of the mid-twentieth century, it is tied in every way to the specificity of the latter, and nothing appears more dubious than the universality of its possible applications.[36]

Again, while Jauss and Zumthor approach the problem of medieval alterity from distinctive angles, the supposed implications of this historical otherness for the contemporary self-identity of medieval studies lead to an identical premise: that medieval studies "stands far from the modern trend of the development of theory," in Zumthor's words; and, for Jauss, that the "theory of the literary text" is "tied in every way to the specificity" of "Western culture of the mid-twentieth century."

What interests me about this exchange is not so much its consensus on theory's blindness to medieval culture and its concordantly unimpeachable modernity, though it should become clear in the course of the following chapters that this consensus was both profoundly misguided and somewhat perverse. The much more remarkable aspect of this dialogue, rather, is the disjunction it highlights between the intellectual biographies of its participants and the rhetoric through which these two critics abnegate their own considerable contributions to the "modern trend of the development of theory." How can it be that Hans Robert Jauss and Paul Zumthor, two of the twentieth century's greatest theorists of medieval literary culture, could so thoroughly deny themselves and their fields the considerable impact they exerted on the rise and consolidation of theory during the very era in which they were producing their most influential work?[37] This, of course, is a story in itself, tied inti-

36. Zumthor, "Comments on H. R. Jauss's Article," 371.

37. A measure of Jauss's theoretical influence can be found in Paul de Man's introduction to a 1982 collection of Jauss's essays, *Toward an Aesthetic of Reception*, vii–xxv, which closes thus: "His work confonts us with the enigma of the relationship between the aesthetic and the poetic and, by so doing, it demonstrates the rigor of its theoretical questioning" (xxv). Writing in 1973 in a review of Zumthor's *Essai*, Eugene Vance evoked a number of examples of what I have been calling theoretic medievalism (including Barthes's work in premodern rhetoric and Kristeva's discussions of *Le petit Jehan de Saintré*), avowing that Zumthor's earlier *Langue et techniques poétiques à l'époque romane* (1963) "had already enunciated in its own terms many fundamental premises that the so-called 'structuralist' critics and semioticians would subsequently elaborate for themselves" (Vance, "Modernity of the Middle Ages," 142). In 1993, Alexandre Leupin's *Fiction et incarnation* came at the question of the medievalism of modernity in a different way, though his unexamined dismissal of the "alterity/modernity" debate as "untenable" strikes me as wishful thinking (see Leupin, *Fiction and Incarnation*, xxiv). Among the many recent efforts of literary and intellectual historians to trace medi-

mately to what Rita Copeland identifies as "one of the common (and crippling) forms of self-representation within medievalist communities, that medievalists do not 'produce theory'."[38] In fact, the so-called marginalization of medievalists from disciplinary change in the humanities results from a quite recent ghettoization of medieval studies that is international in origin yet largely self-imposed.[39] *The Premodern Condition* seeks in part to correct such misperceptions—not, however, by tracing the influence of an externalized theory upon medieval studies, but by returning to a slightly earlier milieu in which the nature of "theory" as an archaeological and always historical enterprise becomes most clearly visible. The millennium separating Saint Augustine from Saint Teresa, late antiquity from the Age of Exploration, serves as perhaps the most vital, dazzling, yet egregiously overlooked object of avant-garde appropriation.

Archaiologia has a distant etymological cousin in *archeîon*, which originally denoted a government building housing official documents and has since become our *archive*. French theory's medievalist archaeology was an intensely archival one: Bataille spent most of his career as a medieval archivist; Foucault's obsession with the political consequences of archival knowledge is well known; and, as we shall see, Lacan's desire for archival authority led him to go so far as to lecture at some length on a specific medieval manuscript that never actually existed. Fantasies of archival recovery work in strange ways in theoretical discourse, granting empirical weight to critical languages dedicated precisely to resisting empirical certainty. The premodern archive in particular is continually freighted with a symbolic capital that confers a kind of materialist prestige upon those who plumb its depths.[40] The paradoxes of the archive, Derrida warned, create unique pathologies inseparable from the techniques of memory and preservation enabling archival accumulation.[41]

---

eval origins of modern science, literature, and philosophy and/or to theorize the "modernity" of the Middle Ages, see (in addition to Leupin) Colish, *Medieval Foundations of the Western Intellectual Tradition;* Cazelles, ed., *Modernité au Moyen Âge,* particularly Cazelles's introduction (9–32) and Stock, "Tradition and Modernity"; and the works cited in reference to Stock's discussion of "medieval modernity," 34 n. 2.

38. Copeland, "Gender, Space, Reading Histories," 3. Jauss clearly saw himself as more of a literary historian than a theorist, as evident in the title of his 1970 *NLH* essay, "Literary History as a Challenge to Literary Theory" (actually a translation of several chapters of his 1967 book, *Literaturgeschichte als Provokation der Literaturwissenschaft*).

39. Compare the comments in Patterson, "On the Margin: Postmodernism, Ironic History, and Medieval Studies," 105–8; Fradenburg, "'So That We May Speak of Them'," 211–12; and Frantzen, preface to *Speaking Two Languages,* xii–xv.

40. See the remarks of Certeau, *The Writing of History,* 74–77: "'Going to the archives' is the statement of a tacit law of history" (77).

41. Derrida, *Archive Fever: A Freudian Impression.*

This book is archival as well. Translated in the appendices are two essays—both drawn from the voluminous archive of theoretic medievalism, and presented here in translations by Laurence Petit—that speak in various ways to the strange persistence of medieval studies in French postwar avant-garde writings. I have chosen these two very different essays, by Georges Bataille and Pierre Bourdieu, both for their individual illumination of particular modes of theoretic medievalism and for their testimony to the diverse and often contradictory critical interests the Middle Ages could be recruited to serve. While the essays by Bataille and Bourdieu thus provide in a sense case studies of medievalism's durable role in the formation of certain languages of critique, they are also intended as separate contributions to broader, ongoing critical discussions to which they are most relevant.

Finally, the ultimate project of this book is more archaeological than genealogical in the well-worn Foucauldian senses of the terms.[42] If a Foucault-inspired archaeology of a particular cultural moment might seem hopelessly quaint by this point, there is a lingering appeal in Foucault's sense of archaeology as providing a lens upon the peculiar modes of locatedness that embrace the very conditions of rupture, of originality, of avant-gardisme in its many forms. *The Archaeology of Knowledge* (1969) begins with its own medievalist performance, a seldom-remarked rumination on the *nouvelle histoire* of the *Annales* school and the effort among historians of the premodern epoch to discern "the movements of accumulation and slow saturation, the great silent, motionless bases that traditional history has covered with a thick layer of events."[43] I quote at length from the *Archaeology* what is perhaps Foucault's most explicit description of the methodological aims of archaeological inquiry:

Archaeology is not in search of inventions; and it remains unmoved at the moment (a very moving one, I admit) when for the first time someone was sure of some truth; it does not try to restore the light of those joyful mornings. But neither is it concerned with the average phenomena of opinion, with the dull grey of what everyone at a particular period might repeat. What it seeks in the texts of Linnaeus or Buffon, Petty or Ricardo, Pinel or Bichat, is not to draw up a list of founding saints; it is to uncover the regularity of a discursive practice. A practice that is in operation, in the same way, in

42. While genealogy became Foucault's preferred approach to cultural study with *Discipline and Punish* and the introductory volume of *The History of Sexuality*, an archaeological analytic remained a central component of his genealogical diagnoses: or, as two of his most influential commentators once put it, "*There is no pre- and post-archaeology or genealogy in Foucault*"; see Dreyfus and Rabinow, *Michel Foucault*, 104 (emphasis in the original).

43. Foucault, *The Archaeology of Knowledge*, 3.

the work of their predecessors; a practice that takes account in their work not only of the most original affirmations (those that no one else ever dreamt of before them), but also of those that they borrowed, even copied, from their predecessors. A discovery is no less regular, from the enunciative point of view, than the text that repeats and diffuses it; regularity is no less operant, no less effective and active, in a banal as in a unique formation. In such a description one cannot admit a difference in nature between creative statements (which reveal something new, which emit hitherto unknown information, and which are "active" in the same way) and imitative statements (which receive and repeat information, and remain, as it were, "passive"). The field of statements is not a group of inert areas broken up by fecund moments; it is a domain that is active throughout.[44]

Particularly useful in this micro-manifesto is its insistence upon the banal and the imitative as the very ground of the original and the revolutionary—a central tenet of the New Historicism, of course, but an axiom less frequently invoked within our disciplines' variegated reception of the continental critical traditions that enabled new historicist inquiry in the first place. The originality of the avant garde, to adapt Rosalind Krauss's polemically circular formulation, will always be invoked as a founding presumption of any intellectual or artistic movement that disdains looking back in favor of looking ahead but fails to look very carefully around.[45]

The primary impulse underlying this book, then, might be characterized as a desire to look around in a different way at the critical insights that continue to define our understanding of French theory as it emerged at a particular cultural moment: a reluctance to accept at face value the stories this avant garde liked to tell regarding the sources of influence and inspiration deemed most crucial to its own formation. An obvious subtext to such investigations will be what Vincent Descombes describes as the "concentric, highly centralized formation" of the French educational system since the Third Republic, and the regularization of syllabi, examination reading lists, institutional expectations, and so on that such centralization demanded.[46] Educated at elite schools such as the École Normale Supérieure (and, in the cases of Bataille, Lacan, Foucault, and Sollers, in Jesuit primary schools) yet inhabiting during the 1960s mostly marginal positions vis-à-vis the official university system, the figures treated here absorbed as an integral part of their pedagogical

---

44. Foucault, *The Archaeology of Knowledge*, 145.
45. Krauss, *The Originality of the Avant-Garde and Other Modernist Myths*.
46. See the discussion in Descombes, *Modern French Philosophy*, 5–8.

lives both the canonical texts of medieval culture and, later, the innovative and synthetic works of premodernists: the historical writings of
Marc Bloch, Lucien Febvre, and the early *Annales* school, the literary
comparativism of Ernst Robert Curtius and Erich Auerbach.[47] Medievalism was part of the everyday fabric of the intellectual culture of
twentieth-century France, its diffusion coextensive with the emergence
of structuralism, post-Freudian psychoanalysis, poststructuralism, and
French feminism. In this sense, the avant garde's most triumphant moments of originality can be understood to exist in sedimented relation to
the workaday productions of medieval philologists, paleographers, and
historians within a field of "enunciative regularity," in Foucault's apt
phrase, that embraces a diversity of archaeological projects dedicated in
very different ways to the excavation of the medieval.[48] Other facets of
this centralized climate of inquiry include a durable fondness for rigorous if less formalized exchanges across discipline and period, as exemplified by the regular interdisciplinary mini-conferences initiated by
Paul Desjardins that have taken place since 1910 at Pontigny, Royau-
mont, and, beginning in 1952, Cerisy, which during these decades
brought medievalists and modernists together under numerous thematic rubrics; or, from another direction entirely, by the annual colloquium of French Jewish intellectuals (initiated in 1957), where Levinas
presented his Talmudic Lectures starting in 1960.[49] Among the many attributes of this French colloquial disposition were the voraciously poly-
mathic reading habits that led the postwar avant garde to absorb and incorporate into their own epistemes medievalist works such as Marc
Bloch's *Feudal Society* (cited several times over the course of Lacan's seminar), or more fantastical treatises such as Denis de Rougement's *Amour
et L'Occident*.

Just as crucial as these various modes of intellectual centralization to
the formation of the premodern condition—and an occasional preoccupation of this book—is the seldom acknowledged but often momentous pressure of Catholic theology on various avant-garde aspirations
from the end of World War II through the 1960s. From the perspective

47. On the complex legacy of Auerbach to twentieth-century criticism, see the essays collected
in Lerer, ed., *Literary History and the Challenge of Philology.*

48. The archaeological *mentalité* of the avant garde might be contrasted in this respect with
Zumthor's literal-minded archaeological metaphor in *Speaking of the Middle Ages,* 27.

49. On the latter, see Gibbs, *Correlations in Rosenzweig and Levinas,* 175. This is not to impute a
friendly collegiality to gatherings that could often provoke heated disagreements; on the national
and disciplinary politics of the September 1963 colloquium organized by *Tel Quel* ("Une nouvelle littérature?"), for example, see Marx-Scouras in *The Cultural Politics of Tel Quel,* 64–66.

of France's dominant institutional religion, the decade of the 1960s was remarkable not for the ascendancy and increasing popularity of a small group of urban avant-gardistes (the "French intellectual nobility," as one chronicler has termed this post-Sartrian subculture), but for the global ecclesiological and theological paroxysms that culminated in the Second Vatican Council of 1962–65.[50] The arguments of several of the chapters that follow are animated by some of the same theoretical concerns with medieval and early modern religiosity central to postmodern theology and the so-called religious turn in critical-theoretical studies (the long-standing role of apophaticism in Derrida, for example, or the thematic persistence of mysticism in the writings of Bataille). Of equal interest, though, are the sorts of synchronic intellectual affinities that might be identified between, say, the *nouvelle critique* of Bataille and Barthes and the *nouvelle théologie* of Henri de Lubac and Jean Daniélou in the moments of their efflorescence, moments in which bellicose conflicts within French Catholic theology over the modern reception of medieval theology can be heard as subterranean echoes under the ground of Parisian avant-garde engagements. Similarly, historians of the *nouvelle critique* have made much of the momentous 1966 colloquium at Johns Hopkins on the "Languages of Criticism and the Sciences of Man," at which Derrida first presented "Structure, Sign, and Play," and where Barthes, Lacan, and other of the French critical generation's luminaries were present; virtually unmentioned in the relevant literature, by contrast, are appearances by Barthes, among others, at small colloquia on subjects like the history and practice of biblical exegesis, such as the 1969 gathering in Chantilly of the Association catholique française pour l'étude de la Bible.[51] The defamiliarizing points of view such gatherings afford on avant-garde intellectual affiliations can approach the sublime in their seeming incongruity: in a living room in occupied Paris in 1944, Georges Bataille went head to head over a chapter draft from *On Nietzsche* with Jean Daniélou, the future cardinal and prolific scholar and editor of Origen, Gregory of Nyssa, and other Christian writers of late antiquity. Premodern religiosity sediments itself within the avant garde in numerous ways, arguing against the tendency among historians of twentieth-century French philosophy to deemphasize the centrality of Catholic philosophies and theologies in the shaping of modern critical

50. The term comes from Kauppi, *French Intellectual Nobility: Institutional and Symbolic Transformations in the Post-Sartrian Era.*

51. On the Hopkins gathering, see the lively discussion in Rabaté, *The Future of Theory,* 36–46; on the Chantilly colloquium, see chapter 5 below.

thought.[52] To put it another way, we might learn something important about the avant garde's broader cultural milieu by accounting for an actuality that a lapsed Catholic such as Georges Bataille knew quite well (and indeed exploited throughout his career): that the issue of "modernity" burned as hotly for the editors of *La Revue Thomiste* as it did for the collective running *Tel Quel*.

This book, then, attempts an archaeological reading of an inherently archaeological pursuit. Such a project will more than once entail reading the claims of the avant garde against themselves, especially those claims regarding the seeming bursts of inspiration founding particular keywords, modes of analysis, and ways of reading. In the brief moment of intellectual efflorescence studied here, theoretic medievalism forms an active domain underlying the field of French critical inquiry more generally.

––––––––

The argument proceeds in a roughly chronological order. The first chapter treats the medievalisms of Georges Bataille, the avatar of theoretic medievalism whose early and rigorous training in medieval studies has been virtually obliterated from recent accounts of his intellectual production yet has vast implications for his larger oeuvre. While Bataille's "canonization" by the Tel Quel circle, in Suzanne Guerlac's characterization, led to severe distortions of his intellectual production, it also gave him status as the *éminence grise* of the *nouvelle critique,* a status that renders his medievalism an ideal point of departure for this study as a whole.[53] I consider Bataille's early work in materialist medieval studies not as a recherché preoccupation that he would abandon for more avant-garde pursuits, but as the very impetus of his subsequent intellectual trajectory, from his magnum opus, *La somme athéologique,* through the three volumes of *The Accursed Share* (a trajectory that includes a 1949 essay on chivalry and ethics, published in *Critique* and translated here as Appendix I). Bataille's career as a medievalist has important bearing as well on the work of his successors, and in particular that of Michel Foucault; the chapter concludes by considering the unexpected light Bataille's medievalism sheds on Foucault's much-discussed appropriations of the Middle Ages.

52. Witness the cursory section on the Neo-Thomists in Gutting, *French Philosophy in the Twentieth Century,* 94–98.
53. Guerlac, *Literary Polemics,* 24.

Chapter 2 turns to the seventh seminar of Jacques Lacan, *The Ethics of Psychoanalysis,* delivered beginning in the fall of 1959. A longtime friend of Bataille's, Lacan centers the seminar around an extended psychoanalytic foray into the Middle Ages that clearly evokes the transgressive potential of medieval forms of sovereignty and love postulated by Bataille. Lacan's specific focus is on the psychic machinations of "courtly love," which he invests with a formative role in the history of subjectivity and desire. Yet the historical commitments of the seventh seminar are undermined by the strangely empiricist authority Lacan vests in medievalism, an authority embodied in a phantom manuscript that paradoxically grounds the archaeological project of the *Ethics.* While the Middle Ages precede what Teresa Brennan has identified in Lacan as the "era of the ego" beginning in the seventeenth century, Lacan's own medievalism exposes the limits of his attempt to construct a psychoanalytic archaeology of modernity. At the same time, Lacan here hints at the important sense in which the clinical situation provides an analogy for the writing and remembering of history writ large, however eccentrically this analogy might be drawn, and it is in this sense that ethics and history are most intimately related over the course of the seminar.

Pierre Bourdieu's relations to Bataille were primarily sociological rather than literary-philosophical; in his *Outline of a Theory of Practice* (1972) Bourdieu acknowledges with obvious admiration the importance of Bataille's theory of sacrifice and its role in the general economy. Yet Bourdieu's direct intellectual debt to the Middle Ages was perhaps second only to Bataille's among the figures studied in this book. As chapter 3 explains, Bourdieu derived what would become a central term in his sociology from his own brief excursion into medieval studies. The long essay translated as Appendix II is Bourdieu's postface to his French translation of Erwin Panofsky's *Gothic Architecture and Scholasticism.* A fascinating if now virtually unread document, the postface contains Bourdieu's first extended elaboration of the *habitus,* which he claims here to have derived from Panofsky's own inquiry into the intellectual and artistic culture of Gothic France. Bourdieu's self-proclaimed affiliation with the numerous medievalists cited and discussed in the postface will likely come as a surprise to most of his readers, especially given Marcel Mauss's deployment of the *habitus* much earlier in the twentieth century. Yet it demonstrates as clearly as any other example of theoretic medievalism the full extent of theory's conceptual debts to a certain mode of medievalist inquiry.

Chapter 4 addresses a less explicit but equally powerful elaboration of theoretic medievalism in Jacques Derrida's *Of Grammatology.* Though an avid reader of Bataille (to whom he devoted a full chapter of *Writing and Difference,* published the same year as *Of Grammatology*), Derrida never addressed the Middle Ages or its cultural production as primary objects of scrutiny during the 1960s. Instead, as I argue in a reading of his own critique of Rousseau, Derrida organizes the second half of this most influential book around the practices of periodization that came to define the medieval in the imagination of the Enlightenment. Medieval decadence and linguistic barbarism haunt Rousseau's *Essay on the Origin of Languages,* which Derrida critiques in part for its anti-teleological vision of linguistic decline over the course of human history. Even as Rousseau assaults the Middle Ages for its Gothic barbarism, Derrida identifies a corrosive *différance* in the anti-mimetic "spacing" Rousseau posits between music and language in the era preceding the invention of writing. And Derrida articulates his most devastating critique of the *Essay* by turning to Rousseau's fantastical vision of the mimetic immanence of the medieval liturgy. *Of Grammatology* thus emerges not as the founding text of an "antihistorical" deconstructive enterprise, but rather as a sustained critique of the ideological consequences of the very practice of historical periodization.

The final chapter engages a text that represents in many ways the apotheosis of the premodern condition, Roland Barthes's *S/Z* (1970). The chapter begins by situating Barthes's medievalism among the Tel Quel group's broader archaeological endeavors, including Philippe Sollers's important essay on Dante and the "traversal of writing" and Julia Kristeva's *Le Texte du roman,* which takes up a fifteenth-century "proto-novel" for its founding perspectives upon the formation of genre and the workings of the ideologeme. I then turn away from the urban avant garde of 1960s Paris to consider a crucial intellectual context for the Protestant Barthes's textual machinations in *S/Z:* the culture of biblical exegesis in the climate of Vatican II Catholicism. Central to my argument is the imaginative impact of Henri de Lubac's massive *Exégèse médiévale* on the interpretive apparatus elaborated in *S/Z:* a shared preoccupation between these two defining but very different works of postwar French intellectual culture with the multiplicity of the text as the boundless object of hermeneutical delectation.

The Epilogue takes up Bruno Latour's recent reflections on modernity in order to consider the difficult relationship between the premodern and the antimodern, concluding with some thoughts on Lyotard's final project on Augustine.

A final clarifying word: I am not by profession an intellectual historian, and what follows is not a work of intellectual history that attempts in any responsible way to explain the motivations of its human subjects and the writings they generated as responses to their specific institutional circumstances, social pressures, or political affiliations. Books like François Dosse's *Histoire du structuralisme* and *Histoire en miettes,* Martin Jay's *Downcast Eyes,* and others provide magisterial surveys of much wider intellectual and cultural milieus out of which the French avant garde emerged; for at least three of the five central figures treated in these chapters, thorough intellectual biographies are available, and the critical literature on all of them is vast. I have regarded the subject of this book, rather, as a series of interrelated conversations and acts of cultural translation that collectively illuminate certain rather eccentric facets of this era's intellectual character. While this introduction has outlined some of the book's more general propositions concerning the difficult relationship between history and theory, just as central to the intended purpose of *The Premodern Condition* are the discrete interventions the individual chapters seek to make within ongoing discussions in the relevant metatheoretical subfields concerning the nature and fate of history in the age of theory.

It is my hope that these particularized contributions will help to excuse the extended engagements here (several of them highly critical and perhaps distracting) with certain models of historical understanding inspiring some of the more influential recent work on these thinkers. Chapter 2, for example, includes a detailed response to Teresa Brennan's *History after Lacan,* a book that has done much to solidify prevalent understandings of Lacan's historical project at the considerable expense of the medieval subjects whose desirous habits he spent so much time pondering in the early 1960s. And chapter 4 confronts the theologians of the so-called Radical Orthodox school, who have made it part of their mission to expose an ahistorical nihilism as the motivating force of Derrida's entire oeuvre. Though more than one reader has (probably wisely) recommended that these discussions be moved to the notes, I have decided to retain them in the main text for reasons that I hope will become clear at the proper time. Medievalism once breathed strong wind into the sails of avant-garde polemic; *mutatis mutandis,* these sails remain full of air both cold and hot.

ONE

Para-Thomism: Bataille
at Rheims

Vae mihi, si non thomistizavero.

JACQUES MARITAIN (AFTER 1 CORINTHIANS 9:16)

The year 1922 marked a turning-point both personal and professional in the life of Georges Bataille. After his stellar performance at the École Nationale des Chartes (he graduated second in his class), he won a fellowship for study at the School of Advanced Hispanic Studies in Madrid.[1] Traveling widely in Spain over the course of the next year, Bataille happened to witness the death-by-goring of the bullfighter Manolo Granero in early May; as his later writings suggest, the convergence of sexuality, ritual, and sacrifice registered in Granero's spectacular demise was a crucial factor in his subsequent renunciation of Catholicism and its psychological demands.[2] A sudden passion for Nietzsche

1. See the brief account of Bataille's matriculation at the École des Chartes in Mattheus, *Georges Bataille: Eine Thanatographie*, 1: 55–56. A 1962 obituary by his old friend André Masson may be unique in its recollection of Bataille's time at the ENC; see Masson, "Georges Bataille." Jean-Pierre La Boulier has demonstrated compellingly that Bataille's work on the *Ordene* represented one of two editorial "failures" stemming from his medievalist editorial training at the ENC; the other was apparently to be an edition of the Old French *Roman de Berinus* that Bataille never completed. See La Boulier, "Georges Bataille et la Société des anciens textes français: Deux 'échecs sinistres' (1925–26)," cited in a coda on Bataille in Warren, "Joking with the Enemy," 293.

2. See the discussion in Champagne, *Georges Bataille*, 6–7; and Bataille's own remarks in his fragments on the "limits of utility," *Oeuvres complètes* [hereafter OC] 7: 223–24, where a bullfight figures curiously in a comparison of the medieval cathedral to the imagined cityscape of New York.

upon his return to Paris sealed Bataille's spiritual fate; the succeeding months included an embrace of atheism, a new life of debauchery, and immersion in the culture of 1920s Surrealism.

As is well known, Bataille's relationship with the surrealists would remain difficult, unsettled, and often fiercely polemical.[3] It is strangely fitting, then, that his first published contribution to the growing body of surrealist literature would return him to the French Middle Ages for what he seems to have imagined as a poetic anticipation of the movement's aesthetics of nonrationalism. For the March 1926 volume of *La révolution surréaliste,* Bataille modernized from the Old French a series of "fatrasies," a medieval genre of "nonsense poetry," most of it anonymous. Bataille's brief introductory comments speak to a kind of interventionist medievalism that would characterize many of his future contributions to the avant-garde aesthetics of the twentieth century: "Most *fatrasies,* incoherent poems, composed in the thirteenth century, are anonymous. Only Philippe de Beaumanoir, the renowned poet and jurist, is known as the author of two among them. Numerous poets of the same era must have written *fatrasies* that have not survived: those of which a few fragments follow here have escaped the contempt of succeeding generations as they had escaped the brain of those whom a burst of laughter blinded one day."[4] Bataille includes five *fatrasies* in the collection, which is followed directly in the 1926 volume by four pages of aphoristic "Textes Surréalistes" composed by André Breton. The choice of these centuries-old poems was a curious one for the aspiring writer of erotic fiction; Bataille's roughly contemporaneous erotic novella, *Histoire de l'oeil* (1928), matched the best efforts of the 1920s generation toward a surrealist aesthetic, and it is easy to find in his own poetry or prose many examples that he could have chosen to contribute to the volume. Yet the juxtaposition of Bataille's translated medieval poems and Breton's surrealist productions reveals a cynical, almost irreverent stance on Bataille's part toward the movement's often inflated claims to originality. The *fatrasies* suggest the extent to which Bataille would seek to ground all "revolutions" in which he participated—aesthetic, theoretical, religious, and ideological—within a long historical view, eschewing easy generalizations and manifestos extolling the exceptionalism of the present.

3. See, among many others, Krauss, *The Originality of the Avant-Garde,* and Jay, *Downcast Eyes,* esp. 211–62.

4. Bataille, "Fatrasies"; edited in *OC* 1:103–6. Bataille apparently translated and published the *fatrasies* in response to a letter from Michel Leiris; see the chronology in Surya, *Georges Bataille: La mort à l'oeuvre,* 474–75.

The *fatrasies* translated in the 1926 *La révolution surréaliste* originated within the same thirteenth-century French milieu that produced the *Ordene de chevalerie*. This 490-line poem (in House's edition) narrates the capture in battle and imprisonment of Hughes of Tabarie by the Saracen leader Saladin, who asks his noble captive to teach him how to become a knight.[5] Hughes responds with the admonition that true knighthood is limited by definition to Christian men—though upon further pleading, Saladin convinces Hughes to demonstrate at least its outward rituals for his own edification. Hughes proceeds with an orderly and patiently glossed performance of the material signs of chivalry that occupies the middle third of the poem: the knight's bath represents Christian baptism, the scarlet gown the blood willingly shed for Ecclesia, the *chaint* girding his loins the chaste lifestyle demanded by chivalry, and so on.

The performance stumbles, however, upon Hughes's refusal to indulge Saladin's thirst for chivalric knowledge: not only will Hughes refrain from granting his Muslim captor the "stroke" of knighthood (the distinction being denied to non-Christians), but he will not answer Saladin's plaintive question regarding its meaning: "Pour coi ne le m'avés donnée / Et dite la senefianche?" (244–45). Knowledge is belonging, Hughes implies in his moralizing response, and Saladin's continued pursuit of both constitutes a demand for a non-material ransom from his Christian captive that gives way to an excessive, nearly comic display and exchange of material wealth between the two men—an exchange that anticipates the most extravagant expenditures Bataille will ponder in *The Accursed Share* (see below). Like many contemporaneous chivalric works, of course, the poem weds its celebration of knightly virtue to an austere Christian clericalism that demands of the aspiring knight penitence, liturgical obedience, and self-denial. Yet the poem concludes with a spectacular ritual of gift-giving—approaching the hyperbole of potlatch in its excessiveness—that belies Hughes's chivalric aesthetic of austerity.

On one level, the *Ordene de chevalerie* finds Bataille working within the best traditions of nineteenth-century positivist philology. As Georges Duby once wryly described the École des Chartes, "It excelled—and still excels today—at teaching the methods that confer upon history the appearance of an exact science."[6] Yet Bataille's editing of the *Ordene de*

---

5. The following commentary on the poem follows House's edition, the *Ordene de Chevalerie*, and cites line numbers internally; there is some confusion in the literature on *L'ordre de chevalerie* stemming from the similarly titled work by Ramon Llull.

6. Duby, *History Continues*, 23.

chevalerie speaks as well to the forms of social and economic organization that his later work locates in the European Middle Ages. Though the
thesis edition represents his earliest scholarly work, Bataille's first publication had appeared several years before his matriculation at the ENC,
probably in the summer of 1918. "Only today, mutilated, she rises in
desolation." The phrase appears in a pious encomium entitled "Notre-
Dame de Rheims"; unknown to Bataille's readers until its recovery in the
early 1970s by Denis Hollier (the general editor of Bataille's twelve-volume *Œuvres complètes*), "Notre-Dame de Rheims" is a brief panegyric to
the war-torn ruins of the medieval cathedral in the shadow of which
Bataille spent his early years.[7] The text exhibits the sober Catholic piety
that Hollier sees as a crucial foil to the "anti-architectural" impulse
evident elsewhere in Bataille's writings. Indeed, for Hollier, the rigid aesthetic of the Gothic cathedral is the aesthetic that Bataille most soundly
rejects—even "obliterates"—in and through his post-conversion writings; in the shattered vaults of Rheims, it seems, the Middle Ages reso-
nate with an architectural and historical authority antithetical to the
subsequent trajectory of Bataille's intellectual production.[8]

Written in the wake of the Great War, "Notre-Dame de Rheims" registers an undeniable nostalgia. Bataille imagines the structure's medieval
past as a promise of restoration: of the lost childhood that he had spent
in the cathedral's long shadow, of the shattered ruin that the great
edifice has become. Bataille reaches back through the past of the cathedral to a triumphant Middle Ages in which Joan of Arc herself makes a
memorable appearance: "Now the Saint never forgot the good welcome;
she said she would have liked to go to her eternal rest next to her good
people of Rheims, who were so Christian and so devout. And when
she—who lived in the sunlit garden of her own voices—rode off again
on new missions, she must often have fondly recalled this memory of
the coronation: the people exultant with pious joy and hope, the cathedral white and immense as victory, and the whole city open like the or-
nate portals of Notre-Dame to anyone coming in the name of the Lord."
For Bataille, those who did not come "in the name of the Lord" included
especially the Germans, who had bombed the cathedral almost beyond
repair just before he wrote the words above: "on September 19 shells tore
through, killing children, women, and old people...Then the Germans
set the cathedral on fire." The distant memory of a pristine, whole cathe-

7. The text is unavailable in its original form; Hollier's translation in *Against Architecture* is followed here.
8. Hollier, *Against Architecture*, 162.

dral that now lay in ruins inspires a meditation on the unrecoverable losses of history: "I thought that corpses themselves did not mirror death more than did a shattered church as vastly empty in its magnificence as Notre-Dame de Rheims."

Yet Bataille's momentary medievalist nostalgia in "Notre-Dame de Rheims" is hardly a prelude to unproductive or inertial longing. The bombed-out shell of Rheims embodies an era to which Bataille will spend his career returning in an array of works and in an astonishing number of guises. Already in his earliest writings—his paean to the cathedral at Rheims, his thesis edition of a thirteenth-century chivalric poem, and his irreverent contribution of medieval verse to one of the manifestos of surrealist innovation—we are glimpsing a dimension of Bataille's intellectual biography that has been virtually ignored in the burgeoning scholarship on his legacy to the subsequent development of theory.[9] *Pace* Hollier, I propose that we read "Notre-Dame de Rheims" as symptomatic of a sustained, rigorous, and remarkably productive engagement with the medieval: its texts, its mentalities, its social formations and material cultures, and its literary politics. If the legacy of nineteenth-century medievalism to subsequent generations of medievalists is in part a melancholic inability to mourn an epoch lost forever,[10] Georges Bataille's oeuvre and its significant influence upon the subsequent trajectory of theory are as deeply implicated in this dialectic of mourning and melancholy as are the staunchest productions of nineteenth-century philology.

9. This was already true in the August-September 1963 commemorative volume of *Critique* prepared shortly after his death by Bataille's friends, including Michel Leiris, Raymond Queneau, Maurice Blanchot, Pierre Klossowski, and others, only one of whom—Michel Foucault, in "Préface à la transgression"—gestures toward Bataille's life-long vocation as a medievalist (though see Leiris's reminiscence of his first meeting with Bataille, to whom he was introduced by Jacques Lavaud, an *ancien chartiste* and the author of a thesis on the sixteenth-century poet Philippe Desportes [Leiris, "De Bataille l'impossible," 685]); and remained so during the 1972 Cerisy-la-Salle colloquium, "Vers une révolution culturelle: Artaud, Bataille," organized by Philippe Sollers and published as Sollers, ed., *Bataille*. For overviews of the Cerisy colloquium, see in particular Lotringer, "Artaud, Bataille, et la matérialisme dialectique"; Roudiez, "Présentation du Colloque Artaud/Bataille"; Sollers, "Pourquoi Artaud, pourquoi Bataille?"; and August and Liddle, "Beyond Structuralism." Bataille's formative two-plus years of work at the École des Chartes provide an especially glaring case in point. To read Surya's chapters in *Georges Bataille: La mort à l'oeuvre* is to encounter an almost willful refusal to grant any significance to Bataille's paleographical and archival training; for Surya, Bataille's second year at the training institute "presents no special interest" aside from the fact that his mother moved to Paris the same year (*Georges Bataille: An Intellectual Biography*, 34).

10. See the germane discussions in Biddick, *The Shock of Medievalism*, esp. 19–57.

Para-Thomism and La somme athéologique

Bataille published "Notre-Dame de Rheims" at the end of the First World War and began what many consider to be his greatest work in the early years of the Second.[11] As its title indicates, Bataille intended *La somme athéologique* to work self-consciously with the intellectual legacy of Thomas Aquinas's *Summa theologiæ*. With few exceptions, though, the scholars who have addressed Bataille's curious titular revision of Aquinas have seen it as a symbolic swipe at Catholic tradition; for Nick Land, one of Bataille's most recent commentators, it is simply anti-Christian "parody."[12] The most exhaustive and respected intellectual biography, Michel Surya's *Georges Bataille, la mort à l'oeuvre,* finds ample room for philosophical forebears such as Hegel, Nietzsche, and Bergson in the author's discussion of Bataille; Thomas Aquinas does not appear in the index. Even those who have begun to explore Bataille's sustained and considerable debts to the Western mystical tradition have little to say about the thirteenth-century Dominican whose life's work provided Bataille with the organizing metaphor and, as we shall see, the raison d'être of his own magnum opus.

For predetermining Bataille's stance toward Aquinas as one of resistance, dismissal, or even parody ignores the historical status of the *Summa theologiæ* as an integral part of French intellectual culture during the years Bataille conceived and wrote his *Atheological Summa.* Since Leo XIII's 1879 papal encyclical, *Aeterni Patris,* Thomas Aquinas's philosophical teachings had been the basis for instruction in Roman Catholic schools worldwide; Pius XII's *Humani Generis,* confirming the continuing doctrinal centrality of Thomism to Catholic thought, was circulated in 1950, four years before the reissue of Bataille's three-volume *La somme athéologique.*[13] Not surprisingly, then, Aquinas's magnum opus inspired immense cultural production in France from the 1920s through the 1950s, a period that saw some fifteen new editions and translations of the *Summa theologiæ* and *Summa contra gentiles* as well as an unprece-

11. The publication history of the three-volume *La somme athéologique* presents a somewhat confusing picture, as Bataille himself acknowledges more than once. Bataille began *Guilty,* the eventual second volume, in 1939, though it would not be published until 1944; the first volume, *Interior Experience,* appeared in 1943, followed by *On Nietzsche* two years later. It was only in 1954 that Gallimard would reissue the three volumes together as *La somme athéologique,* though Bataille had the unifying title in mind almost from the beginning.

12. Land, *Thirst for Annihilation,* 99.

13. A brief but helpful discussion of the enduring influence of *Aeterni Patris* can be found in FitzGerald, "Gilson, *Aeterni Patris* and the Direction of Twenty-First-Century Catholic Philosophy."

dented outpouring of Thomistic scholarship from leading intellectuals, clerical and non-clerical alike. Though the late-nineteenth-century Leonine Aquinas remained the standard edition of the *Summa theologiæ*, more popular among the French Catholic intelligentsia was the Latin text with facing-page translation by A. D. Sertillanges and others, a sixty-volume behemoth published by Desclée for the Revue des Jeunes beginning in 1925 and advertised in its preface as the vernacular answer to *Aeterni Patris*.[14] Published under the French title *La somme théologique*, the first of a fifty-one-volume reissue of the Desclée translation came out in 1943—the year that the first volume of Bataille's *La somme athéologique* appeared in print.

Serendipity aside, Bataille's creative struggle with the intellectual and religious legacy of Aquinas was rigorous, sustained, and brilliant; it was also carefully researched. The records of Bataille's transactions at the Bibliothèque Nationale from 1922 through 1950 find him reading widely in the history of medieval theology and spirituality; it seems clear that his approach to the religiosities of the Middle Ages was based upon an extensive grounding in primary text and contemporary scholarship.[15] Bataille's intellectual open-mindedness vis-à-vis the tradition of Catholic theology can be discerned in many ways; one of its most direct exemplifications survives in the form of his extended 1944 exchange with Jean Daniélou, the prolific Jesuit theologian, liturgist, and historian who had recently edited Gregory of Nyssa's *Life of Moses* as the inaugural volume of Sources chrétiennes in 1941 (and had just completed his first monograph, *Platonisme et théologie mystique: Doctrine spirituelle de saint Grégoire de Nysse*, which would appear the same year from Aubier). This exchange took place at the home of Marcel Moré in Vichy Paris, and was one in a series of occasional gatherings organized by Moré since the first year of the war that brought together numerous French urban intellectuals of widely varying political and religious persuasions. This particular gathering, for example, included such luminaries as Maurice Blanchot, Jean-Paul Sartre, Simone de Beauvoir, Jean Hyppolite, and Maurice Merleau-Ponty, in addition to Dominican and Jesuit intellectuals such as

14. M. S. Gillet, O.P., "Préface," in Thomas Aquinas, *Dieu*, 5–9.

15. Bataille's transactions at the BN are printed in *OC* 12: 551–621; see, among other examples, entries 760, 786, 814, 818, 823, and 835. Yet Bataille also favored more eccentric collections of medieval religious arcana even in his youth, as indicated in the provocative discussion by Michel Surya of his "bedside reading" in 1918–19, Rémy de Gourmont's *Le Latin mystique* with its catalogue of torturous martyrdom (*Georges Bataille: An Intellectual Biography*, 26–30). The implications of this reading have also been discussed in Weingrad, "Parisian Messianism: Catholicism, Decadence, and the Transgressions of Georges Bataille," 117–18, in reference to Bataille's debts to fin-de-siècle Decadents.

Augustin Maydieu and Daniélou: all together for the purpose of responding to Bataille's current thinking on Christianity, sacrifice, and the philosophy of communication.[16] What I am questioning, then, is the received view of Bataille as a non- or anti-Thomist jettisoning several generations' worth of neo-Thomist theology with little or no reflection.[17] At this point in his career, Bataille is, rather, a *para*-Thomist: an energetic student of the discourses of Thomism intent upon contributing in his own weird way to shaping Aquinas's intellectual *Nachleben* in modern France.

At first glance, Bataille's mode of engagement with the medieval *summa* appears transparent. Aquinas argues in the ostensibly inflexible symmetries of scholasticism, posing questions, responses, counter-responses, and (often provisional) resolutions in the rigid progression that led Erwin Panofsky to draw his famous analogy between the medieval philosophical *habitus* and the architecture of the Gothic cathedral—and leads Hollier, in turn, to envision *La somme athéologique* tout court as a rejection of the architectonics of Thomistic theology.[18] More specifically, Bataille's philosophical style is aphoristic rather than appositive; the *Somme* consists largely of a long series of self-reflective, sometimes gnomic utterances presented as the product of the author's haphazard scribblings in his journal. Nevertheless, Aquinas serves Bataille as much more than a rhetorical and formal foil. From the opening passage of *Guilty*—the first words Bataille wrote in *La somme athéologique*—it becomes clear that the theological work accomplished in the text will depend not solely upon the raw materials provided by the *Summa theologiæ* itself, but also upon the visionary writings of one of Thomas Aquinas's Franciscan contemporaries:

It's so impossible to read—most books anyway. I've lost the urge. What's depressing is the amount of work I have to do. I'm always on edge, I get drunk often. I'm true to life if I eat and drink what I want. Life's a delight, a feast, a celebration, it's an incomprehensible and oppressive dream with charms I'm hardly blind to. Being conscious of chance lets me see a difficult fate for what it is. And chance wouldn't stand a chance if it weren't for sheer craziness.

16. The transcript of this colloquium, which includes Daniélou's prepared response to Bataille's chapter, is now available in English translation in Bataille, *The Unfinished System of Nonknowledge*, 26–74.

17. A view that informs one of the most influential French readings of Bataille in recent years, Jean-Claude Renard's *L''Expérience intérieure' de Georges Bataille ou la négation du Mystère*, in particular the chapter "Le mystère et l'espérance," 120–21.

18. Hollier, *Against Architecture*, 36–46.

On a crowded train standing up, I began reading Angela of Foligno's *Book of Visions.*

I'm copying it out, uncontrollably excited—the veil's torn in two (*le voile ici se déchire*), and I'm emerging from my fog of flailing impotence.[19]

In a double gesture of futility and empowerment, Bataille registers in this passage the impossibility of reading "most books" even as he opens the *Book* of a medieval visionary whose mystical voice finally allows him to see beyond an *integumentum* of intellectual inertia and spiritual impotence. Indeed, as Amy Hollywood has explored in rich detail, despite the almost arbitrary tone of the work's opening, Bataille's turn to Angela of Foligno at the chronological beginning of *La somme athéologique* is a gesture of immense significance for the project's aim of cultivating a new form of personal life.[20] An Italian tertiary born in 1248, Angela underwent a life-changing conversion experience in 1285 and began having visionary knowledge of God's love roughly six years later; her popular *Liber de vere fidelium experientia,* dictated to her Franciscan uncle and others between 1290 and 1296, consists of three discrete treatises (in the edition cited by Bataille) relating her spiritual journey, visionary life, and theological teachings.

I would propose, in fact, that Bataille modeled his three-part *Somme athéologique* deliberately on Angela of Foligno's tripartite *Liber de vere fidelium experientia.* Despite its seeming anti-Christian and anti-mystical argument—Part I of *Interior Experience* begins with a "critique of dogmatic servitude (and of mysticism)"—the work as a whole bears a formal and thematic resemblance to Angela's *Liber* too compelling to be coincidental.[21] Just as Angela's first treatise details her conversion, penitence, and resistance to temptation as she took on the ascetic life of the tertiary, Bataille's first volume inscribes a penitential journey to a new form of "torment," what he calls a "New Mystical Theology" that will "have

19. Bataille, *La coupable, OC* 5:245; trans. Boone, *Guilty,* 11.
20. Compare the riveting discussion in Hollywood, *Sensible Ecstasy,* esp. chapter 2, "Mysticism, Trauma, and Catastrophe in Angela of Foligno's *Book* and Bataille's *Atheological Summa,*" 60–87.
21. My argument assumes that Bataille was working with the edition of Angela's *Book* by M.-J. Ferré, published as *Le livre de l'expérience des vrais fidèles* (1927), which included a facing-page French translation done with the assistance of L. Baudry. In this edition, the book is clearly divided into three main parts, as it is not in the more recent editions and translations based on a different redaction of Angela's thirteenth-century text (and none of which would have been available to Bataille in the 1940s when he wrote *L'éxperience intérieure*). At various points in the writing of the *Somme,* Bataille suggested that it would be a four- or even a five-part work, though he seems most consistently to have planned it in three parts; see the discussion in Stuart Kendall's introduction to Bataille, *Unfinished System,* xi–xii.

only the unknown as object"[22]; Angela's self-sacrifice to a new form of spiritual living comes to twentieth-century fruition in Bataille's giving over of himself to the new *a*-theology, a final "anti-conversion" that is immediately followed in the pages of *Interior Experience* by another long citation from Angela's *Liber*. Positioned between brief expositions of Meister Eckhart and Descartes, Bataille's post-conversion return to Angela focuses upon the visionary's last words: "O nihil incognitum!" ("O Unknown Nothingness!"), Angela cried before dying, a phrase Bataille appropriates as the model for his own mystical descent into the fiery pleasures of eroticism: "burning experience (*l'expérience brûlante*) takes little heed of limits received from the outside."[23]

Angela's second treatise moves from her penitential life and initial search for God to the visions themselves, which embrace seven stages of mystical illumination culminating in her merging with Christ at the crucifixion. As we have seen, Bataille opens *Guilty* with the first-person account (quoted above) of his initial reading of Angela of Foligno's text. The passage that follows reveals that the portion of Angela's *Liber* Bataille was reading on the train in 1939 as he began his second volume came from the beginning of her own second treatise, at which point Angela initiates the account of her mystical anguishes and ecstasies: "The Holy Ghost speaks to the Saint, 'I'll speak to you all along your way. There won't be any interruption in the flow of my words and I defy you to listen to anyone else's, since I've bound you to me and won't release you till you've come here again. And then I'll only free you relatively—relative to this joy today. But relative to everything else, never never—if you love me.' The next few pages express a love so rapturous only torment could fuel it."[24] "The next few pages": Bataille signals very clearly that the second stage of Angela's mystical life foretells the second stage of his own, which will constitute a gradual descent into *Guilty*'s solipsisms of nonbelief and self-negation. As he writes near the conclusion, "The idea of God, affection, acts of sweetness associated with him—these are preparations for God's absence. In the night of this absence, these insipid delights and signs of affection have disappeared, reduced to the inconsistency of childish memory. The element of terrifying grandeur in God heralds an *absence* in which we are stripped bare (*l'absence où l'homme est mis à nu*)."[25] The absence of God here and elsewhere in the *Somme* reg-

22. Bataille, *L'expérience intérieure*, OC 5: 120; trans. Boldt, *Inner Experience*, 102.
23. *OC* 5:123; trans. Boldt, 104.
24. *OC* 5:245; trans. 11.
25. *OC* 5: 363, trans. 116.

isters Bataille's Nietzschean atheism, true; but as he acknowledges, the "gaping wound" of divine nonexistence posited here is terrifyingly proximate to the wound in Christ's side that defines the goal of Angela's spiritual pilgrimage.

The proposed relation of Christian theology and Nietzschean atheology becomes clearest in volume three of *La somme athéologique*. Here again the correspondences between Bataille's text and Angela of Foligno's are uncanny. Unlike the first two parts, the third and final portion of Angela's *Liber*, dictated to a variety of unnamed scribes, is doctrinal, consisting largely of Angela's teachings to her spiritual students. Combining personal anecdote with theological instruction, Angela ranges over a variety of religious topics in an extended effort to penetrate to the difficult truths of evangelical Christianity. In *On Nietzsche*, the final volume of the *Somme*, Bataille too assumes the role of teacher: his tutor-text is not the Bible or the matter of personal visions, but the writings of Nietzsche, which he had begun to study voraciously beginning in 1923 and continued to read in depth during the writing of *La somme athéologique*.[26] As we would expect, Bataille's quasi-expositions of the philosopher in *Sur Nietzsche* are far from systematic; they *are* doctrinal, however, and in their mixing of autobiographical reflection and philosophical argument they read remarkably like Angela of Foligno's personalized and self-negating teachings of Christian doctrine. As Allan Stoekl has put it in a convincing consideration of Bataille's agonistic and diverse encounter with the philosopher, "'Nietzsche . . . in Bataille is a radical self-forgetting, a loss; 'Bataille' is the agent of that loss, just as Nietzsche is the agent of the 'loss' to Christianity, the remembering of the definitively unrecuperable loss."[27]

"I suffer from not being like her and coming near death, coming to close quarters with death and inhaling it like a lover's breath."[28] Angela of Foligno's are the first words Bataille cites in *La somme athéologique*—before those of Nietzsche, Gogol, Blanchot, Blake, Stendhal, and the numerous other modern forebears crucial to the work's intellectual project (which Bataille typically presents throughout precisely as a rejection of "project" in any form).[29] Unlike these post-Enlightenment writers, from

26. See especially Mattheus, *Georges Bataille: Eine Thanatographie*, vol. 1.

27. Stoekl, *Agonies of the Intellectual*, 281.

28. Guilty, *OC* 5: 246; trans. 12

29. See, for example, *OC* 5: 18: "L'opposition à l'idée de projet—qui prend dans ce livre une part essentielle—est si nécessaire en moi qu'ayant écrit de cette introduction le plan détailleé, je ne puis m'y tenir." On this aspect of Bataille's thought as it relates to his engagements with Hegel, see Taylor, *Altarity*, 121–24.

whom Bataille derives much of the philosophical and literary energy that sustains him throughout, Angela's religious life and its inscription in her *Liber* serve as direct exempla: both for the alternative, personalized mystical theology Angela propounds and for the paradigmatic self-negations Bataille found in her life and death. In its revisionist stance toward Thomas Aquinas, then, Bataille's *Somme athéologique* is not a simple or simplistic rejection of the systematic theology of the *Summa theologiæ*, as critics such as Hollier have contended. Again, while Angela's *Liber* is aphoristic in a way that the *Summa* of Aquinas is not, Bataille's implicit juxtaposition of the two texts seems intended in part to expose the architectonics of the theological *summa* itself as illusory; however rigid its theological architecture, that is, no *summa* can successfully claim the completeness and omniscience to which it aspires. Enlisting Angela of Foligno into its extended meditation on the futility of such a project, *La somme athéologique* reaches back to Aquinas's own century—indeed, to the spiritual world of late medieval Italy from which Thomas emerged as a theological prodigy—to rewrite his greatest work. Bataille's project is thus not to construct an anti-systematic, experiential theology radically opposed to the Dominican's religious world-view, but to ally himself with Angela of Foligno as Thomas's theological Doppelgänger. Angela allows Bataille to expose both the hilarity and the tragedy of Aquinas's attempt to systematize Christian knowledge in the face of the inevitable *non*-knowledge of God that terrifies Angela yet provides the mystical foundation for her visionary life. Angela thus reigns for Bataille as the most provocative and theoretically useful of the many mystical writers who, as Peter Tracey Connor shows, provided him a means of both postulating and experiencing "the moment at which thinking . . . comes up against its limit, and opens onto the possiblity of 'violent thinking.'"[30]

More specifically, what Bataille found in Angela of Foligno's text in particular was for him an almost ideal form of "inner experience," a self-negating mode of spiritual existence for which *La somme athéologique* continually longs. Angela's life entailed a seamless merging into the Crucifixion, the supreme Christian event Bataille detheologizes as the ultimate form of erotic torture: "In its cruelty," Bataille writes in Part I of *Guilty,* "eroticism brings indigence, demands ruinous outlays (*ruineuses dépenses*). . . . 'God,' says Angela of Foligno, 'gave his Son whom he loved a poverty such that there never has been nor will ever be a poor man like

---

30. Connor, *Georges Bataille and the Mysticism of Sin,* 158. Connor's book provides a convincing rejoinder to Sartre's notoriously pejorative denigration of Bataille as a "New Mystic"; see also Hollywood, *Sensible Ecstasy,* and Irwin, *Saints of the Impossible,* 124–68.

him.'"[31] The opening section of *Inner Experience* reveals the theological tradition in which Bataille's empathetic meditations on Angela's life will hereafter be situated:

I read in Denys l'Aréopagite: "Those who by an inward cessation of all intellectual functioning enter into an intimate union with ineffable light . . . only speak of God by negation" (*Noms divins,* 1, 5). So is it from the moment that it is experience and not presupposition which reveals (to such an extent that, in the eyes of the latter, light is "a ray of darkness"; he would go so far as to say, in the tradition of Eckhart: "God is Nothingness [*néant*]"). But positive theology—founded on the revelation of the scriptures—is not in accord with this negative experience. Several pages after having evoked this God whom discourse only apprehends by negating, Denys writes, "He possesses absolute dominion over creation . . . , all things are linked to him as to their center, recognizing him as their cause, their principle and their end. . . ."[32]

Here again Bataille is negotiating between knowledge and ignorance, between a shattering proximity to the Divine and a painful distance between himself and the always unknown—a dialectic articulated in this instance through the writings of Dionysius the Areopagite, the early medieval neoplatonist who provided the religious philosophers of the Middle Ages with one of the most influential early accounts of apophatic or negative theology. Apophaticism, the theology of the "negative way," takes on numerous guises in medieval Christianity, from the metaphysical speculations of the Areopagite to the mystical self-negations of thirteenth-century visionaries such as Angela to the hybrid mystical theology of Meister Eckhart (another medieval theologian regularly cited by Bataille).[33] Apophaticism is perhaps the primary theological inspiration for *La somme athéologique,* crucial to Bataille's presentation and systematization of his vision of a self-annihilating eroticism. Appropriating the spiritual breath of the negative way from Angela of Foligno and the desire to "erase" himself and his knowledge from Dionysius the Areopagite, Bataille constructs a negative theology with the neg-

31. *La coupable, OC* 5: 257–58; trans. 22–23.
32. *OC* 5: 16; trans. 4.
33. The general neglect of Bataille's reliance on the medieval apophatic tradition throughout *La somme athéologique* has resulted in more than one misreading of the project's stance toward the history of Christian thought. For Champagne, Bataille's ostensibly revolutionary "atheology" in the *Somme* "values individual contingency, loss, and fragmentation," even though these "values" were inherent in the medieval apophatic tradition (*Georges Bataille,* xxiii); Land sees a "heresy of annihilation" inspiring Bataille's self-negations in the work—without recognizing what Bataille himself knew to be the securely orthodox roots of the desire for mystical annihilation (*Thirst for Annihilation,* 102).

ative theologians of the Middle Ages as its unattainable objects: Bataille suffers not from being unable to attain knowledge of God, but from his distance from Angela and *her* mystical experience: "I suffer from not being like her."

Bataille concludes *Guilty,* however, not with another self-annihilating lament, but with a theological gesture we would least expect after the apophatic experiment of the preceding treatise: a catechism—or, as he titled it, *Alleluiah, catéchisme de Dianus,* included as an appendix to the 1954 edition (though dating from a decade earlier). Far from a manifesto of theological truths, Bataille's catechism performs a credo of delirium, obscenity, laceration, and vertigo: "Lovely and an offering, a silence, presentiment of unfathomable skies, your nakedness can be compared to the horror of nighttime, whose infinity it points to. This is what can't be defined and what raises to our faces a mirror of infinite death."[34] Yet here, too, Bataille is struggling with the theological legacy of Aquinas— perhaps with Thomas Pègues's breathtaking *La somme théologique de Saint Thomas d'Aquin en forme de catéchisme pour tous les fidèles* (1920), a 574-page tome commissioned by Pope Benedict XV that sought to present Aquinas's systematic theology in an easily digestible form. While it is difficult indeed to imagine *tous les fidèles* turning to Pègues on any kind of regular basis, the massive catechism, confident in its doctrinal teachings, provides a convenient foil for Bataille's own refusal to become an unquestioning Thomistic catechumen: his inscription in the *Alleluiah* of an oxymoronically apophatic catechism that can know its object only by negation. *Guilty*'s catechetical conclusion signals not a final rejection of medieval theology in the form of the *Summa,* then, but an embrace of the insecure mystical theology of an Angela of Foligno, an insistence on the *anti*-catechetical elements of the era's religiosity. As Bataille writes, "The more inaccessible the object of desire, the more it communicates a feeling of vertigo. The greatest vertigo comes from the beloved's uniqueness (*Ce qui donne le plus grand vertige est l'unicité de l'être aimé*)."[35] This is an apophatic sentiment Meister Eckhart would have understood well; writing in his eighty-third German Sermon, Eckhart imagines the unspeakable Divine as "ein vber swebende wesen vnd end vber wesende nitheit" ("an over-soaring being and an over-being Nothingness")—a vertiginous presence a catechism could never touch.[36]

34. *Guilty,* OC 5: 408; trans. 156. On the biographical and historical resonances of the *Catéchisme,* see Mattheus, *Georges Bataille: Eine Thanatographie* 2:142–45.

35. *OC* 5: 409; trans. 158

36. See the seventh chapter of Sells, *Mystical Languages of Unsaying.*

Before leaving Bataille's *Atheological Summa,* it is crucial to emphasize the extent to which this para-Thomist project resonated with the polemics internal to contemporaneous Thomistic theology in postwar France. For *l'expérience intérieure,* as it turns out, is the precise terrain on which many Catholic theologians of the 1940s and 1950s were struggling for dominance in the pre–Vatican II world. There were two central factions in this battle for the intellectual soul of the Church: the proponents of the so-called *nouvelle théologie,* including, most prominently, Henri de Lubac and Jean Daniélou; and the traditionalist Thomists centered around the venerable periodical *Revue Thomiste,* and in particular the Dominican theologian Marie-Michel Labourdette.[37] What infuriated Labourdette and his coterie of neo-Thomists about the *nouvelle théologie* was what they perceived as its historical relativism, which in turn derived from its guiding spirit of *ressourcement,* the more general movement within the Church to recover lost or little-known patristic and medieval theological traditions and make them newly vital to religious life in the present. (I shall have much more to say about Henri de Lubac and *ressourcement* in chapter 5, which considers the influence of his scholarly work in the history of biblical exegesis upon the late structuralism of Roland Barthes.) Even seemingly innocent editorial projects, such as the series *Sources chrétiennes* (initiated in 1942), threatened to undermine the centrality of Thomas Aquinas and scholastic theology to the spiritual and intellectual mission of the Church, which was to seek the "time-transcending truth" in the harmonizing discourse of the *Summa.* Thus, according to this logic, every edition of the works of figures such as, say, Gregory of Nyssa, Origen, or Gertrude of Helfta, while perfectly fine in its own right, represented the potential erosion of the unquestionable truth of the Angelic Doctor's theological foundation. Never had archival work posed such a grave threat to the very survival of Christian truth, or so Labourdette and the Dominicans contended, and the only solution was papal disapproval of these spiritualist tendencies toward historicism. As Labourdette's ally and mentor, the great Jacques Maritain, wrote in an unpublished essay, it was as if de Lubac and his ilk were "setting the Fathers of the Church to the music of Hegel."[38]

For Labourdette, moreover, the extreme subjectivism of the *nouvelle théologie* led to a variety of relativism that was anathema to the Christian truths systematized in Aquinas. And one of this relativism's most perni-

37. The observations in this paragraph follow closely the discussion in Nichols, "Thomism and the Nouvelle Théologie."

38. Donneaud, "Une vie en service de la théologie," 25. See the remarks in Nichols, "Thomism," 7.

cious symptoms, he believed, was its dissident promotion of "personal spiritualism," of "inner experience" (*l'expérience intérieure*) divorced from rigorous theological inquiry, as he would put it in a 1946 essay in the *Revue Thomiste* treating theology and "sources."[39] Maritain himself, perhaps the most influential French Thomist of the twentieth century, had of course followed Étienne Gilson in arguing for the authentic existentialism at the heart of Thomism, illustrating the extent to which both factions in this debate often treaded dangerously in the waters of Modernism.[40] Yet for Maritain, "inner experience" was emphatically not a pathway to a glum Sartrean subjectivism, but an informed mystical fusion deeply embedded in the liturgical and theological rigors of the Christian life. As early as 1932, just after publishing his manifesto on Aquinas, *Le Docteur Angélique* (1930), Maritain had described true mystical experience as "a vast movement of thought with a practical finality carrying with it all speculative effort of a theological and liturgical reflection which itself serves as the vehicle for powerful metaphysical energies."[41] Maritain's "practical mysticism" and "the interior experience to which it corresponds" were rooted indelibly in the material realities of service to God, or so his idiosyncratic brand of Thomistic mysticism continually insisted—in large part by defining Thomism itself as *philosophia perennis*, a "perennial philosophy" that holds true "for all times and places."[42] As these examples begin to suggest, the phrase *l'expérience intérieure* appears ubiquitously in French Thomistic writings of the twentieth century, reflecting a fundamental ambivalence within neo-Thomism in all its permutations regarding the relative spiritual worth of the individual's experiential encounter with the divine and the implications of this encounter for recognizing the limits of what the human being can become. In promoting the inaugural volume of *La somme athéologique* under the brash title *L'expérience intérieure*, then, Bataille was not simply reacting to an emergent existentialism embodied in Sartre's *Being and Nothingness* (first published in 1943, the same year as *Interior Experience*), but also exploiting with a delighted irreverence the central-

39. See Labourdette, "La théologie et ses sources."

40. This despite Maritain's own longstanding objections to modernist tendencies as exemplified most vociferously in *Antimoderne* (1922), discussed in the Epilogue. For an assessment of Maritain's contributions to modern French philosophy and the seeming limitations of his influence, see Gutting, *French Philosophy in the Twentieth Century,* 94–98.

41. Maritain, "Commentaire au livre de G. Dandoy, *L'Ontologie du Vedânta*," 1061; cited in Arraj, *Mysticism, Metaphysics and Maritain,* ch. 3.

42. See Dennehy, "The Philosophical Catbird Seat," 65. The strongest objections to Maritain's version of a changeless and eternal Thomism have come from McCool, *From Unity to Pluralism;* compare the more appreciative treatment in McCool, *The Neo-Thomists,* 75–92.

ity of "inner experience" to the contemporary legacy of St. Thomas Aquinas.[43]

Finally, this discernible sense of a *positive* return to the medieval embodied in *La somme athéologique* must also be read as a response to the denigrated status of Thomas Aquinas in the rhetorics of the twentieth-century avant garde, most notably those of the surrealists. Bataille's modernization of the thirteenth-century *fatrasies* for *La révolution surréaliste* was only one element within a wider medievalist riposte to André Breton and his followers, who more than once yoked their avant-gardiste aspirations to a rejection of a representational tradition stretching back to the Middle Ages. Here, of course, I am referring most especially to Breton's blistering attack on the "realist" tradition from the first "Manifesto of Surrealism" (1924), which named the Angelic Doctor among a pantheon of dogged anti-intellectualists: "the realistic attitude, inspired by positivism, from Saint Thomas Aquinas to Anatole France, clearly seems to me to be hostile to any intellectual or moral advancement. I loathe it, for it is made up of mediocrity, hate, and dull conceit. . . . It constantly feeds on and derives strength from the newspapers and stultifies both science and art by assiduously flattering the lowest of tastes; clarity bordering on stupidity, a dog's life."[44] As a medievalist, Bataille would surely have rejected this surrealist flattening of centuries of intellectual production in the name of avant-garde programmatics, and he would likely have dismissed the conflation of scholastic dialectics and the realism of Anatole France (also a prominent biographer of Joan of Arc) as an absurdity. It is one of the great intellectual virtues of *La somme athéologique* that it never once directs its revisionist agonism in a heavy-handed or simplistic way against the thirteenth-century *Summa* it reimagines.

An Archaeology of Antiproductivity: The Accursed Share

If *La somme athéologique* represents Bataille's multifaceted response to the encyclopedic productions of medieval scholasticism, the three volumes of *The Accursed Share* assimilate the Middle Ages into a systematic theorization of a political economy of expenditure. The elusive yet ubiquitous subject of *The Accursed Share* is what Bataille terms "excess energy";

43. On Bataille's quite exceptional openness to the category of experience in general (an openness that distinguished him from Derrida, Althusser, and others), see Jay, *Cultural Semantics*, 62–78.
44. Breton, *Manifestoes of Surrealism*, 6.

the study as a whole is meant to be a vast critique of economic theory from the neglected vantage point of expenditure, loss, and waste as opposed to production and utility. Bataille is fascinated by "that glorious operation . . . useless consumption (*consommation inutile*),"[45] the pursuit of unproductive labor—the erection of vast burial pyramids for a single corpse, the sacrifice of victims in the prime of life, entire economies devoted to the building and sustaining of monasteries—as well as the deliberate and seemingly willful expenditure of resources at the expense of utility. The "accursed share" represents that in any society which is "destined for violent consumption (*promise à la consommation violente*)," including even victims of human sacrifice.[46] Bataille's examples include, among others, the sacrificial society of the Aztecs, in which "an extreme value placed on consumption" led to an economy that "put nothing in reserve"; the "ritual prodigality" of potlatch among Indians in the American Northwest, whose "industry of archaic luxury" had been famously analyzed in Marcel Mauss's *The Gift*; and the monastic civilization of Tibetan Lamaism, a religious system whose continued sustenance of tens of thousands of Buddhist monks clearly fascinated Bataille as perhaps the most glorious paradigm of "pure expenditure."[47]

A central plank of Bataille's argument in *The Accursed Share*—the exemplary bridge in the book between "archaic" and western European civilizations—is the "generous squander" of pre-seventh-century Arab societies and its fate after the Hegira. With the spread of Islam, new spiritual strictures "replaced this gift-giving for the sake of pure vainglory with the socially useful giving of alms." Though Islam's renunciation of "wasteful" exuberance met with widespread success, the tension between ancient expenditure and Muslim ascesis left a crucial cultural legacy to the European Middle Ages:

[W]hat we ourselves have from Islam does not partake of Mohammed's contribution, but precisely of those condemned values. It is curious to recognize an Arab influence in our chivalrous "religion" so different from the institution of chivalry revealed in the *chansons de geste,* the latter being quite foreign to the Moslem world. The very expression, *chivalrous,* took on a new meaning during the time of the Crusades, a poetic meaning tied to the value of passion. In the twelfth century, in the West, the ordinary interpretation of the ritual of armament was Moslem. And the birth, in the South of

45. *OC* 7: 31; trans. 23.
46. *OC* 7: 64; trans. 59.
47. *OC* 7: 60, 78; trans. 55, 76. On Bataille's reading of Mauss, see Métraux, "Rencontre avec les ethnologues."

France, of the poetry of passion apparently extended a tradition going back, via Andalusia, to those poetry competitions of the tribes that provoked the austere reaction of the Prophet.[48]

The obvious subtext is Denis de Rougemont's thesis on the "Arabic" origins of courtly love in *Love in the Western World,* an influential study of the Western love tradition that will also figure prominently in the vision of courtly love set forth in Lacan's seventh seminar, *The Ethics of Psychoanalysis* (see chapter 2 below). Yet Bataille may also have had in mind here the *Ordene de chevalerie,* the thirteenth-century poem he had edited more than a quarter of a century earlier. Near the end of the text, as Hughes longs for his Christian homeland, Saladin grants him an excessive "advance" on his *raënchon* or ransom, and the gathered nobles "fall to giving" ("commenchent a donner") in an excessive display of mutual largesse (346–49). Upon Hughes's return to France an even more lavish exchange ensues, with Hughes sharing the jewels he has brought back from the East with each and every man in his retinue, all of whom become rich themselves.[49] The anonymous poet's account of this extravagance includes a polemic against miserliness, a proverbial injunction directed at those who would cast their jewels before swine (411–16). The poem's desire to see its riches "spent" parallels the literary strategies of the troubadours, whose poetics of "personal expenditure" Bataille opposes to the militaristic, "useful" economics of the *chansons de geste.*

For Europeans, then, it is the Middle Ages that represent the quintessential era of expenditure. As the first volume of *The Accursed Share* (the only volume published in Bataille's lifetime) progresses, the medieval era begins to emerge as a society of limitless expenditure constantly in tension with the demands of religious ascesis and self-denial. Though always aware of the dangers of medievalist nostalgia, Bataille posits medieval economic organization as a powerfully "nonproductive" mode of excess that capitalist accumulation had to resist: "What differentiates the medieval economy from the capitalist economy is that to a very large extent the former, static economy made a nonproductive consumption of the excess wealth (*des richesses excédantes une consommation improductive*), while the latter accumulates and determines a dynamic growth of the production apparatus. . . . In the economic system of the Middle Ages wealth was unevenly distributed between those who manifested the ac-

---

48. *OC* 7: 91–92; trans. 90–91.
49. "Dont departi l'or et l'argent / K'il avoit od lui aporté / Si en a maint homme donné / Ki en est riches devenus," ll. 402–5.

cepted values, in the name of which wealth was wasted, and those who furnished the wasted labor."[50] Medieval Europe becomes in Bataille a civilization of glorious wastefulness: cathedrals, monasteries, castles, and fortresses embody the extravagant expenditures demanded by the medieval sovereign. Only with the "complete adequation of man to production (*l'adéquation achevée de l'homme à la production*)" entailed by industrial capitalism is feudalism's ethics of "nonproduction" finally abandoned.[51]

The second and third volumes of *The Accursed Share* survived only in manuscript until their editing for the *Oeuvres complètes* in 1976. They are perhaps the least familiar of Bataille's major works, and their relationship to the first volume is more difficult to discern than it would be had the author completed and published them. In volume two, *The History of Eroticism* (not to be confused with *Erotism,* published in 1957), Bataille clearly has medieval modes of erotic life on his mind as he theorizes eroticism's function as the most personal—and thus most horrifying— "accursed share" within human relations. Discussing the incest taboo with Lévi-Strauss while questioning its universality, Bataille notes how often the "arbitrary boundary between permitted and prohibited kin" has been violated—in particular during the long history of "divorce proceedings of the Middle Ages" (55), when sanctioned degrees of consanguinity were imposed, contested, and revised with mind-numbing regularity.[52]

The History of Eroticism arrives ultimately at the nature of "individual love," "those strong and obsessive feelings that attach an individual being to another whom he has chosen."[53] What follows is an extended account of the relationship between love and literature, a relation embodied not in literature's slavish "expression" of love, but in love's temporal resort to fiction for its very perpetuation: "The incompatibility of love and duration is so general (even if duration is its principle) that love's privileged domain is fiction."[54] The relationship between love and literature is not reciprocal, then, but one-sided, for "Love does without literature (which may even be responsible for the prevailing mistrust toward it), but literature cannot avoid joining its own wealth of possibilities to that which love has in abundance but cannot realize." This unbalanced dynamic between human love and literary production receives its most

50. *OC* 7: 112, 133; trans. 116, 139.
51. *OC* 7: 133; trans. 140
52. *OC* 8: 46; trans. 55.
53. *OC* 8: 135, trans. 157.
54. *OC* 8: 141; trans. 165.

spectacular form in medieval romance, which Bataille envisions as "a festival of individual love" founded on an "opulent" display of chivalric ritual and desirous festivity (165–66). The "final lesson of these captivating displays," Bataille argues, is a spectacle of individual love "whose purpose seems to have been betrayed as much as it was served":

From this episodic entry of individual love into history there clearly emerges the incompatibility of meanings of a historical event on the one hand, and on the other, of the lovers' absorption in the universe engendered by their embrace. On the side of the event there is the manifest need of discourse (*la nécessité du discours*), of formulas that convey values in keeping with limited ends. On the side of the universe, secrecy and silence are essential, where nothing takes place that doesn't signify the totality of being affirmed at one go, compared with which all the rest, whose meaning is definite, has no meaning ultimately but that of the void.[55]

The chivalric "event" produces discourse, ritual, formula: the antitheses of the silent world in which love's private performance takes place.

Dirty Immanence

At this point in his analysis of individual love, Bataille cites a closely related essay, published just as the first volume of *The Accursed Share* came into print, that greatly clarifies the force of his medievalism in *The History of Eroticism*. "La Littérature française du Moyen Age, la morale chevaleresque et la passion," translated for the first time in Appendix I, appeared in the 1949 volume of *Critique*, the journal Bataille had launched three years earlier with Blanchot and others.[56] One of his very few publications in this immediate postwar period devoted exclusively (and "academically") to a medieval social formation, this essay explores the "strange institution" of chivalry and its remarkable synthesis of various modes of medieval life. The writings of Chrétien de Troyes, John of Salisbury, and Ramon Llull as well as the *Song of Roland* and (most familiar to Bataille, for obvious reasons) the *Ordene de chevalerie* are located within a sacrificial economy of courtly love indispensable to the medie-

---

55. *OC* 8: 143, trans. 166.
56. See Michelle Warren's illuminating comments on this review essay in "Joking with the Enemy," 294–296.

val Church, which finds in knighthood's "dialectic of personality and consummation" a supremely useful "man of passion" even while allowing chivalry to retain its sovereign form.

The essay is most fascinating, however, for the peculiar theory of chivalry it proffers in response to a recently published book by Gustave Cohen, *Histoire de la chevalerie en France au Moyen Age.* One of the book's inevitable shortcomings, Bataille avows, is that even its learned author is unable to tell his audience "about the origin of chivalry," an origin at which Cohen can only hint but that Bataille confidently locates in the misty violence of the Teutonic past: "The origin of chivalry is certainly Germanic, and radically foreign to the origins of Christian or Roman institutions. One may also assume that it is the survival, in the Christian world, of a secret society of a relatively primitive nature. . . . The (strictly speaking) savage and frantic character has at least subsided, if not disappeared, but it must be noted that even though the quality of knight was not lost with age, the meaning, or rather the prestige, of the word remains closely associated with the idea of youth."[57]

Yet Germanic "savagery," intimately familiar though it was to a French readership in the late 1940s, can explain only part of the cultural dynamic of medieval chivalry, which achieved a spiritual prestige via its absorption by the one premodern institution that most needed a human mechanism to justify its own inhumanity. If for Cohen and so many other scholars of chivalry the knight embodies a noble spirit of unwilling but necessary violence, Bataille insists on the culpability of the medieval Church in forgetting the conditions of evil that enable knightly prestige, instead masking its sanctioning of chivalric triumphalism as moral theology:

[T]he paradox of war prestige . . . was belatedly tied, in the Middle Ages, to the moral attitude defined by Christianity. It was difficult for the Church to sanctify a condition that was so little in keeping with the spirit of the Gospel. A scholastic saying cited by Cohen (p. 173) indeed identified chivalry with evil: *militia malitia,* as people would say (in medieval Latin *miles* is often the translation for knight). However, the seduction of such evil was so great that, instead of cursing it, the clergy decided to redefine it as good. Not, it goes without saying, in the sense of an exaltation of the life that the knights actually led, but by discerning, in the seductive character of their condition, the sign of an ideal vocation. This shift is not ordinarily given the attention that it de-

57. Rather than citing each quotation from the essay by page number of the original, I simply refer readers to the full translation in Appendix I.

serves, and yet it reveals the innermost forces at work in the judgments that found good and evil. The position of good is inherently given in a determination of worldly life (*sacred* life). Consequently, if such determination is contrary to good as defined rationally, it becomes necessary to lie. Although what is *sacred* is not in the least identical with good, it must nonetheless now become good. Hence the possibility of a *sacred* status from the other world defined by its identity with good, or that of a *sacred* essence from this world which is being substituted by an *ideal.* In both cases, lying is inevitable, and it is introduced at the moment of a transcendence.

Christianity absorbs the sacral evil generated by the ancient cult of barbaric and indiscriminate violence, and its moral theology must thereafter continually lie about this originary appropriation in order to justify its ethical construction and defense of the sacred life. This foundational deception sullies the entire tradition of chivalric literature with its ostensibly rational code of ethics, leading the Church in turn to "identify blatant opposites: fighting and good, violence and reason," that would even give rise to "religious chivalry: Templars, Hospitallers" in the age of the Crusades. Thus Bataille's chilling invocation of the "dirty immanence," as he terms it, "that no command can dominate": the condition of post-chivalric man in his sovereignty and nobility, conferred by a traumatic refusal to subject the rapacious archaeologies of these institutions to the scrutiny of the very moral theology that constructed them in medieval romance.[58]

Like the prestigious knighthood that serves as its historical embodiment, Bataille's theory of chivalry is strangely seductive, and not only for its foundational theoretical status in relation to many of the themes that will characterize his wider scrutiny of forms of sovereignty throughout *The Accursed Share.*[59] For perhaps the most provocative passage in "Medieval French Literature, Chivalric Morals, and Passion" concerns Bataille's vision of the nature of human desire as the pursuit of transcendent and impossible things—or, to be more precise, *the* transcendent and impossible *thing:*

God is not the *sacred* given in worldly life in the form of contagion, immanence, or more exactly active immanence, dangerous and ruinous for the personal (and sepa-

---

58. Albeit in the greatly compressed form of this essay, Bataille's sense of the theology of violence at the heart of the chivalric institution anticipates some of the best revisionist work on chivalry in recent years; see, for example, Kaeuper's assessment of some of the same issues in *Chivalry and Violence in Medieval Europe.*

59. See Guerlac's discussion of the "paradoxical proximity of Bataille to Hegel—or of sovereignty to mastery" evident in the *History of Eroticism* in "'Recognition' by a Woman!" 93.

rate) being. What is *sacred* is what denies and destroys the separation to which we cling in the fear of death, what merges us directly (mystical fusion is an example of this) into the immanence of man and the world. On the contrary, it is the *thing* that is transcendent, this particular object that presents itself from the start as a limit to any possibility of fusion (God is the *sacred,* or infinite, character, granted to the transcendence of the finite object, of the separate object).

"[I]t is the *thing* that is transcendent": it would surely be too much to suggest that Jacques Lacan was thinking of this essay when, in December 1959, less than a month into his seventh seminar, he first introduced his own rendition of "The Thing," the "absolute Other of the subject." As Lacan announces at the opening of that day's lecture, "I am going to try to speak to you about the thing—*das Ding,*" a German term resonant in its Freudian incarnations with more mystery than the French *chose* (the word Bataille uses here) could be. Yet as we shall see in chapter 2, Lacan asks that the Thing be understood in part as an *effect* of courtly love, indeed as one of courtly love's primary and lasting effects in the archaeology of Western desire.[60] For those familiar with the vision of courtly love as outlined in the *Ethics,* then, there is something utterly compelling about the immanent relation that Bataille, writing in 1949, posits between the sacred character of chivalric love and this other *thing,* this "object that presents itself from the start as a limit to any possibility of fusion." For Bataille, the chivalric ethic of the Middle Ages is the responsibility of a religion that crafted courtly love as constraint, without recognizing that the sacrifice of the loving subject's desire would become inextricable from the *thing* as impossible object of an annihilating passion:

This religion could even be subtly presented as being the profound betrayal of passions: for does it not reduce pride and original frenzy to the geometric point? Does it not have as its ultimate goal to annihilate and annul precisely what it seems to defend? And has the *evil* in it not taken on the saddest form, that of the defense of a reserve no longer justified, against the law, by any surpassing of the self or outburst of passion?

And yet, we all know the reason why we cannot renounce this survival, within us, of a moral ethic that was formed by no intellectual speculation and came down to us merely as a fire, the result of the naïve ardor of a timeless passion.

The reason is that, through a considerable attenuation, by means of brakes opposed to the animality of our most common violent impulses, passion reached, in one

60. For an extended analysis of The Thing in Lacan, see Žižek, "Much Ado about a Thing," in *For They Know Not What They Do,* 229–78.

fixed point, its preferred object, which is, for man, a woman, or for woman, a man. There is no doubt that this woman or this man did not have the power to condense in themselves the promises that the world brings, at birth, to the being in the process of coming to life. But luckily, for a man, a particular woman suddenly has the power to be an opening onto the totality of the world.

Here, cast in miniature, is Lacan's theory of courtly love as anamorphosis, a formation of desire seen from two radically different angles: one that assumes the ultimate desirability and perhaps even the ultimate conquest of the beloved, and another that posits the courtly lady as "vacuole," as that which the loving subject not only will never possess but which, by virtue of that non-possession, will organize the subject's own relationship with the symbolic. The perpetual "fire" of chivalric love thus burns an effigy of its own fantastical making, and the "totality of the world" that the lady opens up for the lover is an apocalypse, promising annihilation.

Bataille leaves the wider implications of this courtly Thing unaddressed in this essay, which soon turns to the "brawls, knife fights, and foul crime" that the knight commits in common with the criminal. Yet the post-Lacanian reader is left with a provocative glimpse at the immediate intellectual genealogy of Lacan's vision of courtly love, and in particular his revelation in the seventh seminar of "that final demand to be deprived of something real" that defines the courtly lover in his poetic excess.[61] So, too, did medieval orthodoxy strategically allow for the ecstatic excesses of Christian mysticism, the subject of Bataille's final excursus in *The History of Eroticism* on divine love and the limitlessness of religious experience. While evoking the "ravished" St. Theresa familiar from his earlier *Erotism*, Bataille firmly resists an obvious conflation of the *Brautmystik* of the Middle Ages with the specific erotic form of individual love: "It seems to me no more legitimate to reduce mysticism to sexual eroticism than to reduce the latter, as people do, even without saying it, to animal sexuality."[62] Mystical love was nevertheless an ideal form of expenditure for a society eager to squander its excessive passion: "Whatever one makes of the erotic language of the mystics, it must be said that their experience, having no limitation, transcends its beginnings and that, pursued with the greatest energy, it finally retains only eroticism's transgression in a pure state, or the complete destruction of

61. Lacan, *The Ethics of Psychoanalysis*, 150.
62. *OC* 8: 147; trans. 170.

the world of common reality, the passage from the perfect Being of positive theology to that formless and modeless God of a 'theopathy' akin to the 'apathy' of Sade."[63] Apophatic theology returns as mysticism's destructive anticipation of Sade, whose "limitless eroticism" "gave this negation its logically consistent form, so much so that one cannot dream of surpassing it."[64]

The third and final volume of *The Accursed Share* (also left incomplete) proposes an overarching category that will embrace the various forms of expenditure Bataille has theorized thus far. The societies of excess mined throughout the project—in their economic organization and values, their erotic life and arrangements, the relations they organize between power, wealth, and desire—are "sovereign" societies for Bataille, who now seeks to shake the word free of its sacred connotations. Sovereignty itself is to be defined as "the use of resources for nonproductive ends," whether in the "detestable" sumptuousness of Versailles or the erection in the Middle Ages of "churches, castles, palaces whose purpose was *to evoke wonder* (qui avaient pour fin d'*émerveiller*)."[65] Medieval forms of sovereignty are once again the historical paradigm; though Bataille acknowledges Marxian attempts to broaden the working notion of feudalism to include pre-bourgeois societies worldwide, the "feudality" of premodern Europe clearly functions as the ground of his critique.[66] The "sovereign attitude," Bataille proposes, "is exemplified by the use of the surplus for nonproductive ends," ends that include the expropriation of peasant labor into the production of limitless spectacle: "Only the king crowned under a cathedral's majestic and sacred vaults, resounding with the millennial and tragic tones of the liturgy, satisfied the desire to gaze upon the miraculous image of an unlimited existence. It seemed out of the question to look for this miracle within."[67]

This "unlimited" medieval sovereign rules as the apotheosis of expenditure, consuming the architectural space of the cathedral, the musical strains of the liturgy, and the desiring gazes of his subjects. We can see Bataille recasting here the thematics of "Notre-Dame de Rheims," for Rheims, as Bataille knew very well, served as the coronation church for the medieval kings of France; as he notes at the opening of the early

---

63. *OC* 8: 147, trans. 171.

64. *OC* 8: 149, trans. 174. On Sade in Bataille's *History of Eroticism*, see the illuminating discussion in Dean, *The Self and Its Pleasures*, 187–88.

65. *OC* 8: 321–22, trans. 280-81 (emphasis in the original)

66. On the paradoxical status of *le communisme* in *Sovereignty*, see Stoekl, *Politics, Writing, Mutilation*, 97–98.

67. *OC* 8: 326, 279, trans. 284, 233.

essay, "Clovis the barbarian, baptised by Saint Remi, gave a pious renown to the good Christian city, and there the kings of France were crowned."[68] Bataille's vision of the medieval sovereign in *The Accursed Share*, the king "crowned under a cathedral's majestic and sacred vaults," transports him back to the shattered cathedral of his youth, which has now been reconstituted into an all-consuming exemplum sustaining his revision of political economy. In *Sovereignty*, then, Bataille returns to Rheims to pay secret homage to what he had mourned in his youth as the "formerly living stone" and "skeleton's rictus" of the cathedral— but not to mourn again. The cathedral, restored to its former glory during the intervening decades, now serves as concrete testimony to the endurance of the medieval society of consumption that laid its foundations.

After Bataille: Foucault's Middle Ages Redux

Bataille's career-long engagement with the social, literary, and psychic formations of medieval Europe forms one of the few threads of continuity and consistency in a greatly diverse oeuvre. At the same time, it provides us with the most complex theoretic medievalism of the twentieth century, an intermillennial consciousness so intimately entwined with the form and argument of Bataille's central theoretical works that it necessarily raises questions about the ramifications of his medievalism within the subsequent development of French avant-garde thought. If we consider, for example, Michel Foucault's Middle Ages through the lens of Bataille's, we can begin to understand why Foucault so often imagined the "liberatory potential" of a medieval era free of restraint, as Carolyn Dinshaw argues, and so often located his desire "for a realm of clearly apprehensible acts and legible surfaces" in a millennium whose juridical apparatus did not "know the truth" of sexuality as confidently as modernity's did.[69] As Dinshaw writes, "the Middle Ages Foucault most deeply desires is a time whose lack of unified sexuality is preferable to the present with its 'fictitious unity' of normative heterosexuality, a time whose sexual disaggregation is not to be feared but can for the future offer a creative, even liberatory, potential."[70]

68. "Notre-Dame de Rheims," trans. Hollier.
69. Dinshaw, *Getting Medieval*, 196, 201.
70. Dinshaw, *Getting Medieval*, 205. Contrast the assessment of Foucault's medievalism in Lochrie, "Desiring Foucault."

Bataille's most profound intellectual legacy to Foucault may have been precisely the Middle Ages that Dinshaw and others have credited to the author of *Discipline and Punish* and *The History of Sexuality*. Foucault articulates this imaginative debt most explicitly in the opening passage of "A Preface to Transgression," his 1963 homage to the recently deceased Bataille published in the commemorative volume of *Critique*:

> We like to believe that sexuality has regained, in contemporary experience, its full truth as a process of nature, a truth which has long been lingering in the shadows and hiding under various disguises—until now, that is, when our positive awareness allows us to decipher it so that it may at last emerge in the clear light of language. Yet, never did sexuality enjoy a more immediately natural understanding and never did it know a greater 'felicity of expression' ['*bonheur d'expression*'] than in the Christian world of fallen bodies and of sin. The proof is its whole tradition of mysticism and spirituality which was incapable of dividing the continuous forms of desire, of rapture, of penetration, of ecstasy, of that outpouring which leaves us spent: all of these experiences seemed to lead, without interruption or limit, right to the heart of a divine love of which they were both the outpouring and the source returning upon itself.[71]

As his references make clear, the direct source for Foucault's vision here of the Middle Ages and its felicity of sexual expression—written more than a decade before Foucault began his own history of the subject—is Bataille's *Erotism*. This theory of medieval sexual "felicity" would come to full fruition in Foucault's argument in volume 1 concerning the medieval confessional, though Foucault significantly complicated this aspect of Bataille's work on medieval eroticism by showing that the long history of truth-seeking practices in Western discourses of sexuality had an important point of origin in medieval ecclesiastical practices.

Yet there are important elements of Bataille's historical vision as a medievalist that were entirely lost on Foucault. *The History of Eroticism* was published for the first time in 1976, the same year as the first volume of Foucault's *History of Sexuality*. Had the former appeared just two or three years earlier, it is likely that Foucault's enormously influential treatise—with its stark periodizations, its vision of the proto–*scientia sexualis* performed in the medieval confessional, and its overweening focus on institutionally sanctioned discourse—would have looked very different indeed. Reading these works alongside one another, one cannot help but

---

71. Foucault, "Preface to Transgression," 1; the French is cited from "Préface à la transgression," 751. See the astute reading of Foucault's engagement with Bataille here in Guerlac, *Literary Polemics*, 14–16.

be struck by the vast conceptual differences between a history of eroticism and a history of sexuality. Bataille's vision of "sovereign love," for example, directly opposes a history of eroticism to a history of sexuality in Foucault's sense: the two modes of experience constitute entirely distinct domains for Bataille, who brings very different analytical tools to bear upon each. For Foucault, it often seems, they are indistinguishable. Moreover, Bataille's complex theorization of a sphere of love, eroticism, and secrecy that eludes utility—indeed, whose participants *devote* themselves to exceeding utilitarianism in favor of expenditure—points to the conceptual limitations of Foucault's notion of "biopower," the discursive form of "right of death and power over life" that preoccupies the final third of his introductory volume. Bataille's vision of an inescapably transgressive eroticism allows for a mode of love that "joins the lovers only in order to spend, to go from pleasure to pleasure, from delight to delight: theirs is a society of consumption, as against the State, which is a society of acquisition." [72] Foucault, despite his scrupulous avoidance of state power qua repression in the *History of Sexuality,* clearly wrote the history of the latter.

It is one of Bataille's final works, *The Trial of Gilles de Rais* (1959), that is most in the spirit of Foucault's inquiries into the historical relations of discourse, knowledge, and power. Published just three years before the author's death, Bataille's study of the notorious fifteenth-century French nobleman—comrade-in-arms of Joan of Arc, powerful knight, a child murderer conflated with Bluebeard in the popular imagination of Brittany—has generally been regarded as idiosyncratic even within Bataille's already diverse corpus. In form, I would suggest, it appears among the most traditional: an edited collection of material scoured from medieval archives—legal documents, trial transcripts, witness depositions, inquests, and so on—and presented with accompanying commentary. In this largely archival study, Bataille returns full circle to the skills that enabled him to produce the *Ordene de chevalerie* at the École des Chartes and formed his earliest intellectual identity as archivist, paleographer, and editor of medieval texts.

In stark contrast to the pious medievalism of "Notre-Dame de Rheims," however, *Gilles de Rais* envisions a Middle Ages of "ruinous expenditure," [73] a time when the lives of dozens of children could be squandered for the sake of one man's narcissism. Gilles de Rais's theology of murderous expenditure perhaps explains the constant allure of

72. Bataille, *OC* 8: 140, trans. 162–63.
73. *OC* 10: 279, trans. Robinson, 10.

medieval religiosity for Bataille; even in its rejection, it furnishes him with myriad instances of unaccountable extravagance:

It does not seem to me that Christianity above all requires the rule of reason. It may be that Christianity would not want a world from which violence was excluded. It makes *allowances* for violence (*Il fait* la part *de la violence*); what it seeks is the strength of the soul without which violence could not be endured. Gilles de Rais' contradictions ultimately summarize the Christian situation, and we should not be astonished at the comedy of being devoted to the Devil, wanting to cut the throats of as many children as he could, yet expecting the salvation of his eternal soul. . . .[74]

Bataille's bitter humor here points to an unspoken awareness that the same Christian civilization that wrote the *Ordene de chevalerie* and built the cathedral at Rheims found other, more unsettling modes of expenditure on which to squander its excess. A quintessentially "medieval" murderer, Gilles de Rais exemplifies the category of premodern sovereignty, a way of life that the fifteenth-century mass murderer brings to its apogee: "For Gilles, as for the barbarians of the past, the goal was in breaking bounds; it was a question of living sovereignly (*de vivre souverainement*)."[75]

The Trial of Gilles de Rais likely served Foucault as the most immediate model for *I, Pierre Rivière, having slaughtered my mother, my sister, and my brother . . . : A Case of Parricide in the Nineteenth Century* (1973), a collaborative project that brought a similar collection of legal documents, transcripts, memoirs, and critical commentary to bear on a single case of mass murder in French history. More intriguingly, Foucault may well have taken from Bataille the historical inspiration and logic for the gruesome and now notorious scene of public execution that begins *Discipline and Punish;* as Bataille writes of Gilles de Rais's theatrical demise: "It is only recently that the judicial execution of men ceased to be a spectacle intended for the entertainment and anguish of the crowd. There was no corporal punishment in the Middle Ages that was not spectacular. Death by corporal punishment was then, in the same capacity as tragedy is on the stage, an exalting and significant moment in human life . . . Before being judged and consequently executed, Gilles de Rais was thus destined for the crowd at the instant of his arrest; he was promised to them as is a choice spectacle on a theater bill."[76] When Foucault gleefully

74. *OC* 10: 281–82, trans. 13.
75. *OC* 10: 304, trans. 30.
76. *OC* 10: 337, trans. 57–58.

narrated the bone-cracking, theatrical display of "the body of the condemned" that crystallized monarchical power in the "spectacle of the
scaffold,"[77] perhaps he was paying homage to the "spectacle" of Gilles
de Rais' death—and thus to the frank periodization of bodily practices
for which Foucault was fundamentally indebted to Bataille.

―――

When Georges Bataille died in 1962, he had just completed the novella
Ma Mère, which Roland Champagne has called his "erotic masterpiece."[78] The book was published posthumously in 1966 under the pseudonym and in the first-person narrative voice of Pierre Angélique,
a name that Bataille also adopted for several other of his erotic novels.
The story focuses on the erotic initiation of Pierre, who endures and
eventually enjoys the rites of sexual passage demanded of him by a
pornography-plying father, an overly interested mother, and a series of
prostitutes—one of whom turns out at the end also to be his *mère* (hence
the book's title). Aside from Bataille's characteristic swipes at Catholic
sexual guilt and ritual, there is nothing particularly "medieval" about *Ma
Mère*—with the important exception of young Pierre himself. By select-
ing Pierre Angélique as his pseudonym and protagonist, Bataille was enlisting into the excessive erotic world of his fiction Pierre's homonymic
double. As Bataille's French audience knew very well, Pierre Angélique
resurrects the medieval theologian known to French Catholicism as
"Père Angélique"—the "Angelic Father" or "Angelic Doctor" with whom
Bataille had forged and enjoyed a life-long creative relationship: Thomas
Aquinas.

77. Foucault, *Discipline and Punish,* chapters 1 and 2. Denis Hollier has pointed to similarities between Bataille's treatment of Gilles de Rais's death and Artaud's "theater of cruelty" in "La tragédie
de Gilles de Rais."
78. Champagne, *Georges Bataille,* 23.

TWO

Apocalypse and Archaeophilia: Lacan's Middle Ages and the Ethics of History

If we carefully consider also all the occasions where actions seem to come under a commandment or a prohibition, these must be taken to refer to the will or the consent to actions rather than to the actions themselves, otherwise nothing relating to merit would be put under a commandment and what is less within our power is less worthy of being commanded.   PETER ABELARD, *SCITO TE IPSUM*

I propose then that, from an analytic point of view, the only thing of which one can be guilty is of having given ground relative to one's desire.
JACQUES LACAN, *SEMINAR VII*

Ethical Chic

Over the last twenty years, *ethics* has devolved into one of those nearly meaningless words populating the lexical field of modern critical thought. Histories of ethical philosophy appear saturated with mutually contradictory claims about the nature and genealogy of ethics, which now includes in its compass a host of durable as well as newly familiar ethical models: Kant's categorical imperative and its numerous twentieth-century revisions and rejections by Heidegger, Levinas, and others; neo-Aristotelian models of ethical moderation; Charles Taylor's so-called ethics of authenticity; a spectrum of feminist and postfeminist ethical criticism, ranging from Mary Daly's radical feminist ethics of the 1970s to the lesbian ethics of Sarah Hoagland; and the postmodern ethics of Zygmunt Bauman and others, which achieves an oxymoronic vitality by exposing the moral parochialisms obtaining in much of the history of ethics.[1] A measure of the term's cultural capital can be found in the recent edition of the essays of Michel Foucault, one volume of which markets itself under the title *Ethics,* a rubric that hardly does justice (and in fact does much injustice) to most of the book's contents.[2] The New Ethical Criticism, as one overview has prominently dubbed it, promotes both a rigorous accounting for the varieties of modern ethical thought and a programmatic effort to propagate new ethical practices of reading, thinking, and living.[3]

In its omnivorous search for historical precedents and problematics, contemporary ethical thought has taken a recent turn toward an array of premodern moral philosophies as agents of revisionism. The ethical thought of St. Augustine alone has been resurrected over the last several years by Jacques Derrida, whose *Circumfession* warps a series of autobiographical meditations across the woof of his fellow North African's *Confessions;* by the late Jean-François Lyotard, whose final book (published posthumously and in fragments) was to be a frankly devotional treatise revealing Augustine's shaping influence on his own intellectual trajectory; and by several theologians of the Radical Orthodox school, for example Graham Ward, who calls for a neoaugustinian rethinking of urban activism as the building of new Cities of God.[4] Augustine has rarely been read so diversely as he has in the last decade. Medieval hagiographical practice, too, provides a virtual script for new ethical criticism, as in Edith Wyschogrod's *Saints and Postmodernism,* with its breathless call for fostering a new morality grounded in the sacrificial economies of sainthood; David Halperin's *Saint Foucault,* which (purposefully mocking Sartre's *Saint Genet*) discerns an activist ethic inspiring much of Foucault's œuvre and biography; and Cristina Mazzoni's *Saint Hysteria,* which locates European mysticism as a frequent obsession for twentieth-century medical ethics.

It seems possible, in fact, to identify a diverse field of ethical production oriented (if clearly not unified) along a particular historical axis

---

1. Taylor, *The Ethics of Authenticity* ; Daly, *Gyn/Ecology: The Metaethics of Radical Feminism;* Hoagland, *Lesbian Ethics: Toward New Value;* Bauman, *Postmodern Ethics.*

2. See Foucault, *Ethics.*

3. Buell, "In Pursuit of Ethics." For wider views of the reemergence of ethics in the wake of postmodernity, see Dosse, *History of Structuralism,* 2: 282–87; and Booth, *The Company We Keep,* esp. 3–48.

4. Ward, *Cities of God.*

that turns more often than not around antecedents in late classical and medieval traditions. Premodernity clarifies the ethical imaginings of modernity from a variety of viewpoints and along a spectrum of intellectual-historical trajectories. Much twentieth-century ethical thought is rigorously archaeological in its approach to its subject: it favors ancient ethical models over modern, and it energizes old and sometimes forgotten writings in its tradition as defamiliarizing agents of moral revisionism.

On a certain level, then, we should find it hardly surprising that one of the more ambitious attempts over the last half century to articulate an ethics of psychoanalysis—Lacan's Seminar VII, *The Ethics of Psychoanalysis*—represents as well one of the most historically minded endeavors of its author's career. Despite the increasingly copious study of Lacanian ethics, however, there has been little mention of the historical lineaments of this ethical model, let alone of the particular historical trajectory in and by means of which Lacan locates his ethical project in the course of the seminar. Conversely, despite a proliferation of work addressing Lacan and history, even the best writing in this vein has left largely unaddressed the extent to which the master's historical vision was self-consciously an ethical one—or, to put it more bluntly, to recognize that ethics *is* history for Lacan, who elaborates a history of ethics that promotes itself simultaneously as an ethics of historical understanding.[5]

Lacan befriended Georges Bataille in the mid-1930s while both were attending Alexandre Kojève's influential lectures on Hegel and *The Phenomenology of Spirit.* The two were constant interlocutors over the next twenty-five years, sharing connections both intellectual and personal (Lacan married Bataille's ex-wife, the actress Sylvia Maklès, shortly after her divorce).[6] The extent of the psychoanalyst's debt to Bataille is becoming increasingly evident in the literature on Lacan; *pace* Simone de Beauvoir, Bataille's writing on violence and sexuality in *Erotism,* for example, must now be now regarded as the impetus behind Lacan's sudden interest in the Marquis de Sade beginning in the late 1950s.[7] In *The Ethics*

---

5. The work on Lacan's ethics that I have found most helpful includes Zupančič, *Ethics of the Real;* Ragland, *Essays on the Pleasure of Death;* Rajchman, *Truth and Eros;* and especially Fradenburg, *Sacrifice Your Love.*

6. On the intellectual and personal implications of this friendship, see Roudinesco, *Jacques Lacan,* 121–39.

7. See the extensive discussion of Lacan's various conceptual debts to Bataille (most of them unacknowledged and often begrudged) in Borch-Jakobsen, *Lacan: The Absolute Master,* 91–93 and elsewhere.

of Psychoanalysis, Lacan attributes to his longtime friend the recognition of the "true value" of Sade's writings, "their power to open up the possibility of the assumption of being on the level of immorality."[8] Sade furnished Lacan as well with a non-Freudian theory of pleasure located in the "transgressive," the realm that Bataille did so much to fashion as an urgent thematic beginning in the 1950s. *Erotism* appeared in 1957, as Lacan was completing Seminar II (on the ego) and beginning Seminar III (on psychosis). At the time Bataille was working in the library at Charpentras, and he would not relocate to Paris until 1961, the year before his death. Yet Lacan's omnivorous medievalism in the seventh seminar can be read as a kind of *hommage* to his tubercular friend, an archaeology of ethics that finds its most vibrant historical exemplars in the textual cultures of the Middle Ages. A subcurrent running throughout the following discussion is my sense that it was the inspiriting influence of Georges Bataille that prompted Lacan to ground such a large portion of his ethical project in a certain medievalism, a field of desire and transgression that modeled the salient distinction between morality and ethics—a distinction of course fundamental for Lacan's ethical thinking (and for much postmodern ethical thought in general).[9] As we saw in chapter 1, Bataille's "other" Middle Ages was productive of the most amoral (not *im*moral, but *a*moral) ethics imaginable, an ethics of sovereignty and expenditure that Lacan sought to instill as the very core of psychoanalytic practice. As Lacan had made clear in introducing the *Nom du Père* during his 1955–56 seminar on the psychoses, the "attribution of procreation to the father can only be the effect of a pure signifier, of a recognition, not of a real father, but of what religion has taught us to refer to as the Name-of-the-Father": a declaration that has been read as a "semi-facetious allusion to the Christian liturgy" clearly indebted to Bataille's *Inner Experience.*[10]

Lacan's biography, both intellectual and personal, yields some intriguing clues as to the direction his medievalism would take in his later life. As recounted with some amusement by Elizabeth Roudinesco, Jacques was twenty-five years old when his younger brother Marc-Marie made his final decision to join the monastic order in 1926: "The call

---

8. Lacan, *The Ethics of Psychoanalysis,* 201; page numbers hereafter will be cited parenthetically in the text, as in a few cases will Lacan's French from *L'éthique de la psychanalyse.* The influence on Lacan of Bataille's writings on Sade have been discussed in Dean, *The Self and Its Pleasures,* 194–95, though with some important qualifications.

9. This is of course one of the main theses defended in Bauman, *Postmodern Ethics.*

10. Lacan, *Écrits,* 199 and 225 n. 40; see Bowie, *Lacan,* 108, and Bible and Culture Collective, *The Postmodern Bible,* 203.

came to him on May 13, as he was reading the Rule of St. Benedict. He wrote down the word *Benedictine,* and the sight of it acted on him like a revelation. Jacques was furious when he heard of his brother's decision and advised him to wait and go on with his law studies." [11] Lacan had already turned against his family's tradition of devout Catholicism, favoring newly vogue postwar models of rational, aristocratic Catholic inquiry and (like Bataille) turning to Nietzsche as a source of a nihilist skepticism. As his brother's de facto guardian, Lacan experienced the enlistment as a keen betrayal that was only made worse when, in 1931, Marc-Marie took his vows and changed his middle name to François as an homage to St. Francis of Assisi. Yet Lacan's intellectual maturation included formative contacts with premodernist philosophers and theologians: at the Collège Stanislas, for example, he was trained by Jean Baruzi, a Catholic scholar writing a doctoral thesis on St. John of the Cross; Baruzi in turn had been deeply influenced by the philosophical and pedagogical methods of the great medievalist Étienne Gilson, whose vigorous approach to textual explication would in part shape Lacan's own lifelong devotion to the texts of Freud. Like Bataille, then (and, one suspects, the preponderance of twentieth-century non-clerical French intellectuals), Lacan's youthful anti-Catholicism coexisted alongside an intensive and longstanding absorption of the premodern religious culture that made it possible.

This chapter examines the premodern archaeology of the seventh seminar, suggesting that Lacan's truly bizarre understanding of the nature and purpose of ethical reflection cannot be fully understood apart from its historical rootedness in the courtly, theological, and philosophical cultures of the European Middle Ages. My aim here is not to explicate Lacan's idiosyncratic elaborations of courtly love poetry in the seminar as a means of better understanding *fin'amor* and the Middle Ages themselves, nor am I claiming responsible coverage of Lacan's medievalism as a whole.[12] The present chapter, much narrower in scope and ambition, pursues two guiding questions. First, why was it *here,* in this most ethically directed of the seminars, that the medieval (and for reasons that will become clear, I will be taking Lacan's medievalism as metonymic of his historicism writ large) would figure so prominently, even audaciously, as the evidentiary and artifactual core of the master's ana-

---

11. See Roudinesco, *Jacques Lacan,* 13ff. for this account.

12. The former project has been performed by Sarah Kay in *Courtly Contradictions: The Emergence of the Literary Object in the Twelfth Century;* the latter is the subject of a forthcoming study by Erin Labbie, *Phoné Sex.*

lytic?[13] Second (and conversely), what was it about the medieval cultures treated in *The Ethics of Psychoanalysis* that inspired Lacan toward the topic of ethics, and how might the seminar's axioms and arguments have been shaped by Lacan's invocation and elaboration of (his understanding of) medieval modes of ethical praxis?

This narrowness of scope will admittedly allow me to dodge some of the more difficult exegetical issues one must confront when reading the seventh seminar in the order of its delivery (e.g., whether to treat it as early, middle, or late period Lacan; how to understand it in relation to Lacan's continually evolving understanding of the real; and so on). More simply, and in keeping with the spirit of this book, I want to consider the *Ethics* as an exemplary text for the premodern condition at the opening of the 1960s. Like the present one, this book's subsequent chapters will assay their archaeological queries largely through close readings of single texts: Bourdieu's postface to Panofsky, Derrida's *Of Grammatology*, Barthes's *S/Z*. As I understand it here, the historical argument propounded in Lacan's *Ethics* places the medieval at the service of an ethical interventionism with interesting parallels in *Of Grammatology* and Bourdieu's contemporaneous reflections on the *habitus*. For all of these thinkers, medievalism represents less a reserve of isolated historical artifacts for occasional delectation than a spectrum of historical variety casting multi-hued beams on the cold surfaces of modernity.

Honey and Blade: Lacan's Ethical Stylistics

The Ethics of Psychoanalysis begins with one of Lacan's typically conflative performances of modest narcissism. The master had just pre-

---

13. One possible answer to this question (which I will not be exploring here) may be that the subject of Seminar VII was not, in fact, the *ethics* of psychoanalysis, as Lacan claimed, but the *asceticism* of psychoanalysis, if Geoffrey Harpham's useful distinction is followed: "Ethics implies closure and decision, an end to temptation; asceticism repudiates such a possibility. Ethics honors the distinction between 'being tempted' and 'resisting'; asceticism acknowledges no such distinction. Ethics worries the differences between *what* you might resist; asceticism demands only *that* you resist. Asceticism, then, is the resistance to ethics as well as the basis for ethics. On its ambivalent imperative all critical theory, and much else, is founded" (*The Ascetic Imperative*, 269). Though *The Ethics of Psychoanalysis* appeared in English translation several years after Harpham's book, which mentions Lacan only in passing, the distinctions drawn between ethics and asceticism in *The Ascetic Imperative* may do much to explain the appreciative reception of the slippery rhetoric of Lacanian ethics within cultural criticism over the last decade. See in particular Harpham's prescient comments on the critic's traditional distrust of the language of moral philosophy: "However admirable and necessary ethical judgments are, they appear to the professional literary critic somehow anti-intellectual in their binary decisiveness and decidedly anti-fictional or anti-aesthetic in their worldliness. Literary criticism becomes professional partly through the insistence that it is not ethics" (243).

sented the outline of the seminar a week earlier, on November 18, 1859; now, he gestures back across the central issues covered during the preceding year, alluding to the themes that had preoccupied him then while building a case for the importance of the work to be done in the months ahead. In this case, though, Lacan figures the seminar's new beginning in terms of the daunting culinary challenge it will present to his auditors:

Honey is what I am trying to bring you, the honey of my reflections [*le miel de ma réflexion*] on something that, my goodness, I have been doing for a number of years and which is beginning to add up, but which, as time goes by, ends up not being that much out of proportion with the time you devote to it yourselves.

If the communication effect here sometimes presents difficulties, reflect on the experience of honey. Honey is either very hard or very fluid. If it's hard, it is difficult to cut, since there are no natural breaks. If it's very liquid, it is suddenly all over the place—I assume that you are all familiar with the experience of eating honey in bed at breakfast time. (19; 27)

In its vision of pedagogical transmission as a sensual incorporation of the "honey" of the master's teachings "in bed," the seminar's opening passage evokes the beginning of Bernard of Clairvaux's *Sermons on the Song of Songs.* For Bernard, the twelfth-century Cistercian abbot, scripture was textual "food" to be chammed, digested, and absorbed in the exegetical process: if the preacher "who desires to follow St. Paul's method of teaching" to the "people of the world" gives them "milk to drink rather than solid food," Bernard's monks are sufficiently learned to "feed on bread rather than milk . . . the bread of that book called the Song of Songs." [14] Employing the traditional pedagogical language of *ruminatio,* the abbot enjoins his auditors to incorporate the sacred words as part of their very beings through a kind of theological osmosis that the modern Cistercian scholar Jean Leclercq had described as a "repeated mastication of the divine words." [15] At the time Lacan spoke the introductory words above, Leclercq had only recently located the twelfth-century monk as the seminal *auctor* of monastic theology in his *L'Amour des lettres et le désir de Dieu* (1957), a study of the language of monastic learning that became an academic bestseller in France in the years immediately preceding Lacan's seventh seminar. The hermeneutic process set forth in Bernard's *Sermons* promotes a life of devotion, patience, and

14. Bernard of Clairvaux, *Sermons on the Song of Songs,* 1.1, 1.
15. Leclercq, *The Love of Learning and the Desire for God,* 73.

charity in the face of biblical mysteries, and honey is one of his favored metaphorical vehicles: "As food is sweet to the palate," Bernard writes in sermon 7, "so does a psalm delight the heart. But the soul that is sincere and wise will not fail to chew the psalm with the teeth as it were of the mind, because if he swallows it in a lump, without proper mastication, the palate will be cheated of the delicious flavor, sweeter even than honey that drops from the comb. . . . As honey flows from the comb so should devotion flow from the words; otherwise if one attempts to assimilate them without the condiment of the Spirit 'the written letters bring death.'"[16] Bernard's sermon to his Cistercian community models an appropriately reverential reading aesthetic for absorbing the text of Freud, Lacan's own lifetime object of exegetical devotion. In retroping this medieval commonplace for psychoanalysis, Lacan casts his own wisdom as the biblical "honey" that will present numerous difficulties for his students' ingestion and digestion; the payoff, though, will be a more thorough and indeed visceral articulation of psychoanalytic ethics than any previously available.

If an enlistment of monastic *ruminatio* registers Lacan's reflective familiarity with his audience, the violent rhetoric of scholastic *disputatio* propels the seminar into its central argument about the ethics of "the real": "for the moment I will not attempt to polish further the blade of my argument [*à fourbir autrement le tranchant de ce que j'apporte ici*], since what will likely constitute the thrust of my purpose has precisely to do with the meaning to be given to the term real—within that system of categories that I profess as a function of our practice as analysts" (20; 28–29). Here the guiding metaphor comes from the writings of Bernard of Clairvaux's older contemporary, Peter Abelard, who opens his autobiographical *Historia calamitatum* by narrating his abandonment of a military life in favor of the violence of dialectic:

For my part, the more rapid and easy my progress in my studies, the more eagerly I applied myself, until I was so carried away by my love of learning that I renounced the glory of a soldier's life, made over my inheritance and rights of the eldest son to my brothers, and withdrew from the court of Mars in order to kneel at the feet of Minerva. I preferred the weapons of dialectic to all the other teachings of philosophy, and armed with these I chose the conflicts of disputation instead of the trophies of war.[17]

16. Bernard of Clairvaux, *Sermons on the Song of Songs*, 7.5, 41–42.
17. Peter Abelard, *Historia Calamitatum*, 58.

Lacan's tongue-in-cheek phallicism foregrounds the obvious parallels between the twelfth-century maverick scholastic and the twentieth-century rogue psychoanalyst: both were metropolitan intellectuals questioning the methodological and analytical orthodoxies of their respective fields; both would reject the official pedagogical institutions that had sponsored their earlier careers; and both would abscond with dozens of devoted auditors to establish an alternative forum within the same city in which to stage their intellectual dissent: Abelard at the abbey of Ste. Geneviève outside the city limits, Lacan in the amphitheater of the Hôpital Saint-Anne and, later, at the École freudienne de Paris, which he would found three years after the conclusion of the seventh seminar. This emergent spirit of doctrinal dissidence held a particular resonance in 1959–60, a period during which Lacan's relations with the International Psychoanalytic Association were growing increasingly tense and disputatious.[18]

Though Bernard and Abelard were perhaps the two best-known intellectuals of their early twelfth-century generation, their pedagogical styles, as Lacan knew quite well, could not have contrasted more vividly; nor would their contributions to the history of ethical thought. As Leclercq had described it, Bernard's theology entailed an ethics of textual fidelity that was inseparable from the loving of God's humanity and sacrifice. All ethical human acts fall within the devotional compass of *lectio divina,* which makes of sacred texts the living script of human morality; for Bernard, it would have made no sense to carve out a discrete sphere of "ethical philosophy," when in fact all philosophy is already (or already should be) theology, and all theology inherently (even mystically, as Gilson had argued) concerns the practice of ethical living.[19] For Abelard, by contrast (although he was writing in the Augustinian ethical tradition), the discrete roles of intention, will, and consent are crucial to the moral reckoning of human acts; acts in and of themselves are neither good nor evil, or at least only trivially so: "the will itself or the desire to do what is unlawful is by no means to be called sin, but rather, as we have stated, the consent itself. . . . The doing of deeds has no bearing upon an increase of sin and nothing pollutes the soul except what is of the soul."[20] In Abelard's understanding, consent *is* action for all intents and purposes, but consent is emphatically not synony-

18. See Roudinesco, *Jacques Lacan,* 250–59.
19. See Gilson, *The Mystical Theology of St. Bernard.*
20. Peter Abelard, *Ethics,* 15, 23.

mous with desire; the desire and even the will to sin may sustain themselves unproblematically and naturally within the ethical subject, whose soul functions as a hothouse of libidinal energy that only occasionally erupts into the sin of consent. This structuration of the ethical subject has an important corollary in the title of Abelard's ethical magnum opus: *Scito te ipsum* ("Know yourself"). Abelard's titular injunction to his readers to "know themselves"—to understand the tangled roots and obscure trajectories of the compulsions and *concupiscentiae* that have come to shape their souls—is clearly much more than a penitential rendering of the confessional. Read a certain way (a way Lacan might have been tempted to read it), the treatise in fact promotes a genealogy of permissible desire, pushing sin at times to the margins of ethical relevance in favor of a self-reflexive discernment of the *habitus* or *dispositio* shaping the path from suggestion to pleasure to consent to act. (How far may I go and to what extent may I desire without committing sin? Can I get away with certain ostensibly sinful acts if my intention was moral? Where and what are the boundaries between desire and consent, and how might I learn to manipulate these boundaries to the advantage of my desire?) Yet if disposition and intention determine utterly the moral valence of acts without regard to desire, desire is precisely what must be overcome if an ethical lapse is ultimately to be avoided. This paradox may be understood as the ethical dilemma at the heart of Lacan's seventh seminar.

I am not suggesting here that *The Ethics of Psychoanalysis* takes the moral theologies of the Middle Ages as models for its own theory of ethics, though the seminar does invoke these theologies more than a few times, and their influence on Lacan may be more than incidental. What I am proposing, rather, concerns what I would characterize as Lacan's ethical stylistics, which in this seminar can be understood as a peculiar confection of Bernardine textual devotion (to the writings of Freud) and an Abelardian combativeness (vis-à-vis his many targets of disagreement in contemporary psychoanalysis and behavioral psychology). These ultimately complementary pedagogical modes seem peculiarly suited to Lacan's vision of himself as a seductive preacher and an intellectual pugilist in the sphere of ethical thought.

At the heart of this medievalist concatenation of honey and blade is the pressure of Bataille. The gnomic kernel of Lacanian ethics, at least as this ethics is formulated in Seminar VII—"The only thing one can be guilty of is giving ground relative to one's desire"—distinguishes Lacanian ethics from those moral philosophies that make proscription into

the defining element of ethical understanding.[21] What Lacan propounds, by contrast, is an analytic accommodation of sovereignty, in its
purest Bataillean form.[22] Lacanian ethics, as John Rajchman characterizes it, demands "a sort of suspension or *epoche* of the analyst in the face
of the madness of another's desire, combined with a neutral 'listening.'
This stance makes possible the transference that structures the analytic
process of articulating this madness in speech."[23] A truly ethical analysis will find the analyst and analysand together engaging the realm of
the symbolic while the analyst scrupulously fends off the impulse "to
cure [the analysand] from the illusions that keep him on the path of his
desire" (219). "We make reality out of pleasure," Lacan insists, yet the
policing of the real is exactly what conventional psychoanalytic ethics
has taken as its mission, due in large part to a certain misreading of
Freud: the reading for the cure, for the "hard determinism" that undermines any search for "morality" in the clinical setting.[24] *The Ethics of
Psychoanalysis,* then, might be understood as a provisional distillation of
Bataille's notion of sovereignty into the sphere of ethical philosophy. In
this respect it is also an oblique (if rather twisted) revivification of
Abelardian ethics: the honest comprehension and pursuit of the subject's desire not into the realm of acts and desires to be suppressed or
redirected, but into an unconscious domain of a *jouissance* that can
speak only truth to power.

This is hardly the grounds for a coherent and workable ethical system,
however, at least not as the history of ethical philosophy would demand
that such a sytem be delineated, and this is of course part of Lacan's
point. Lacanian ethics is an ethics of negation: an apophatic ethics. In
the analytic situation, the analysand's successful comprehension of the
Real depends on the analyst's own abnegation of the will to cure through
ethical modeling in the realm of the Symbolic. Analysis itself, then, can
hope to achieve ethical purchase on the subject only through an eternal
process of dialectical negation. As Lacan puts it near the conclusion of
the seminar, "If analysis has a meaning, desire is nothing other than that
which supports an unconscious theme, the very articulation of that

21. The phrase has been much commented upon, perhaps most eloquently (if briefly) by Alain
Juranville, "Ethics with Psychoanalysis."
22. The ethical implications of Lacan's argument here might be contrasted with those implied in
Freud's distinction between "aim inhibition" and "sublimation"; see Wallwork, *Psychoanalysis and
Ethics,* 165–70.
23. John Rajchman, "Lacan and the Ethics of Modernity," 42.
24. Lacan, *Ethics of Psychoanalysis,* 225; the phrase appears in Wallwork, *Psychoanalysis and Ethics,* 291.

which roots us in a particular destiny, and that destiny demands insistently that the debt be paid, and desire keeps coming back, keeps returning, and situates us once again in a given track, the track of something that is specifically our business" (319). By expending its energies reifying "the delusion and deception of individuals by the collectivities to which they belong,"[25] this argument goes, traditional ethical philosophy stands no chance of intervening in the subject's most intimately internal ethical negotiations. Throughout *The Ethics of Psychoanalysis,* the Middle Ages not only play a central role in defining these engines of delusion in their historicity, but also model in crucial ways the specifically historical modes of resistance to such collectivities that the seminar's proposed ethical revolution must entail. It is in this sense that Lacan's initiating evocations of Bernard and Abelard register much more than a self-reflexive commentary on his own intellectual style. In a recent deployment of Lacanian ethics against the tenets of bourgeois ethical thought, Alain Badiou derives a number of impassioned rallying cries from the *Ethics,* among them the moral imperative to "seize in your being that which has seized and broken you."[26] In heuristic terms, this injunction could well serve as the organizing principle of Lacan's medievalist vision of ethical practice.

History after History after Lacan

Any serious study of Lacan's variegated appropriations of history must take at least an implicit position on the most influential treatment of the subject currently available. As I read it here, *The Ethics of Psychoanalysis* argues strongly against Teresa Brennan's widely cited theses on the historical dimensions of Lacan's project in *History after Lacan,* a book that has achieved a wide currency in recent Lacanian versions of literary historicism and (more surprisingly, as will become clear) in the burgeoning corpus of psychoanalytic medievalism.[27] At the same time, I think it safe to say that the seventh seminar adumbrates a historical argument that is somewhat idiosyncratic within Lacan's oeuvre and, as a result, exists in somewhat tenuous relation in any case to the psychic trajectory as postulated by Brennan. In particular, I want to suggest, while Lacan's his-

---

25. See Schaffer, review of Alain Badiou's *Ethics,* n.p.
26. Badiou, *Ethics,* 47.
27. See, for example, David Aers's preface to "Historical Inquiries/Psychoanalytic Criticism/ Gender Studies," 199–208. A very different though ultimately complementary study of Lacan's historical practice can be found in Copjec, *Read My Desire.*

toricism (on Brennan's reading) grounds itself in a more general diachronic periodization of the human subject and its drive toward containment, the *Ethics* powerfully undermines this periodizing impulse by
exposing the modes of premodern subjection that must be forgotten if
the modern subject is to claim its mythical status as a paragon of psychic
containment.

In order to avoid simplifying a dense and complex series of arguments, I want to concentrate here on the aspects of Brennan's thesis
most relevant to the subject of this chapter: the dimensions of *History after Lacan* that are most clearly and avowedly historical and thus have
most to do with Lacan's ethics. (What this means in practical terms is
that what I say here will be relevant to roughly the first half of the book,
with admittedly little bearing on Brennan's extension of her thesis into
the realm of political theory in the final two chapters). Brennan's guiding premise is that, in Lacan's vision of Western history as articulated in
the seminars, the psychosis of modernity "begins with an ego's era,
which in turn begins in the seventeenth century."[28] This Lacanian periodization of history, though more often assumed than explicit, illuminates the instantiation of the bounded ego as the foundational psychic
phenomenon of modern Western civilization, providing us "a lever for
thinking through the trajectory of modernity" (7). Prior to the "foundational fantasy" of the early modern, which ruptured the primal psychic
connections among human subjects and the physical environment, the
"conative, energetic force coursing through and activating individual subjects and their living environment" (81) was relatively uncon-
strained. Indeed, it has been the "escalating ego"—the evolution toward
dominance of the self-knowing subject, whose discrete relation to the
physical world has progressively hardened since the Renaissance—that
has been primarily responsible for the psychic severing of the subject
from the domain of materiality and the object. Though "subject/object
thinking . . . has been with us since the pre-Socratics," the point for Brennan is that "these ideas have hardened" (85) over the last several centuries, pointing to a "fundamental distinction" in Lacan which has important bearing on the subject's relation to the unfolding of time. "The
symbolic attributes of temporality, rewriting history and making consistent connections are *counterposed* in [Lacan's] argument to the totalizing,
objectifying trends of the ego" (38), which increases its dominance as
historical time passes, "leading to social psychosis" (49) more generally

---

28. Brennan, *History after Lacan,* 3; citations from this book will hereafter be parenthetical in
the text.

as the tragic flaw of the modern subject—so much so that we have even become resistant ourselves "to making the connections necessary to understanding the ego's era" (38).

The unwillingness of the modern subject to reconnect with the "conative, energetic force" that once bound subjects to one another and to their material world arises in part from the so-called master-slave dialectic, which Lacan had absorbed from Kojève's lectures on Hegel. For Brennan, the foundational fantasy of the modern subject is sustained by "the attempted destruction of the other consciousness, or other within, that the dialectic forestalls" (100). This unsatisfied desire for violence against objects and others constitutes perhaps the most destructive compulsion of psychic modernity—or, in Lacan's phrase (quoted by Brennan), the "most formidable social hell" of the ego's era (100). Imperialism, colonialism, commodity fetishism, the objectification of the past in modern historiography: the ideological pathologies of the modern era cannot be extricated from the psychic domain of the ego's era, and are in fact its most deep-seated productions. Lacan's vision of history is thus crucially and systematically gendered—not only in the sense that "the tendency to homogenize sexual difference is part of the course of the ego's era" (61), but in the related sense of this era's compulsion to totalize its objects: "far from being the means of preventing the social psychosis, the psychical fantasy of woman may be its trigger; it may help explain why the territorializing and totalizing imperative arose in the West" (52). In fact, Brennan avows, "the psychical fantasy of woman and the ego's era have a common source, in so far as both have their origin in the process of passification: the means whereby the ego maintains its self-image" (73).

As explicated by Brennan, Lacan's theory of the ego's era has far-reaching implications for psychoanalytic cultural study, let alone for prevalent understandings of Lacan himself as an ahistorical structuralist. If Lacan proffers a model of historical understanding that makes some psychic sense of the unfolding of modernity, this model may provoke an enabling return to the history of the individual: not the history of the bourgeois individualism of the Enlightenment, but the history of the suffering, desiring, pathological individuals whose psychic lives populate the Real of the ego's era. If there is a theory of history sustaining Lacan's oeuvre from beginning to end, then this oeuvre must itself be reconceived within the twentieth-century genealogy of French historiography, finding a place alongside (and in an often irresolvable tension with) historical schools such as *Annales* and the Collège de Sociologie in their various incarnations. If Brennan is right, in sum, the alleged chasm between psychoanalysis and historicism may continue to be bridged by a rigorous scrutiny of Lacan's historicizing comprehensions of the era of the ego.

For all the revisionary appeal it offers by virtue of its newly historical grasp of post-Freudian psychoanalysis, however, Brennan's study tells us very little about Lacan's strange and abiding investment in the epoch *preceding* the era of the ego, and in fact seems almost perversely unwilling to address the implications of this elusiveness. While Brennan may be correct to suggest that Lacan's historical genealogy of the modern subject makes its most direct case (as she makes hers) with the evidence of the last four centuries, it is also true that the seminar anchors its historical vision in a much more expansive archaeology of desire, from Sophocles' *Antigone* through the theological paroxysms of the Reformation. On one level this is a trivial complaint to level against a book that so self-consciously limits its historical optic (as well as its subject's) to the modern. Yet in building her theses concerning Lacan's "theory of the ego's era and perspective on history," Brennan forces herself into precisely the claims about the psychic life of premodernity which, as we shall see, *The Ethics of Psychoanalysis* itself compels us to reject. Brennan remains loftily skeptical throughout *History after Lacan* about "the power of the secondary source in structuring received views" (7); her own view of the Occidental history that allegedly generates Lacan's theory of modernity nevertheless bases itself entirely on an archive of secondary studies whose collective claims upon the nature of *pre*modern subjectivities determine her own formulation of the ego's era. The result is a tautological rendering of Lacan's historical project that leaves some of its most productive archaeological work frustratingly unexamined.

The fallacies start piling up at the opening of Part II of *History after Lacan,* where Brennan begins to explore a series of "historical shifts in contained and subject-object thinking" that preceded the era of the ego. This survey—in part historiographical, in part philosophical—seems intended "to show how we come to conceive of ourselves as individually contained, and thus come to resist thinking about energy in interactive terms"—or, to put it another way, to get at the historical interconnectivity among human subjects that the modern has largely abandoned: "A little investigation suggests that the notion opposed to psychical energetic connection, the notion of psychical containment, may be historically and culturally specific to the modern West." By "modern" Brennan means post-medieval, of course, and the timeline she proposes has its origins in the early seventeenth century, when the sorts of "interconnectivities" predominant for over a millennium began to give way to the "psychical containment" that would increasingly characterize the emergence of the modern subject.

At this point in the argument, Brennan begins a mass conscription of anthropologists, philosophers, and linguists, as well as historians of science, culture, literature, and art, all of whom serve to isolate the crucial transitional moment leading to the psychical containments endemic to modernity—and all of whom lend support to "the idea that the 'ego's era,' as a Western event, coincides with the advent of the contained individual" (83). Thus, Michèle le Doeuff's study of *Venus and Adonis* furnishes Brennan with a Renaissance "philosophical revolution" marking a decisive break with the "Avicennean tradition," in which "*my* imagination is not really *my* imagination" (83). Along with this abandonment of collective imagination comes "the hardening of the notion of individual containment" in "Renaissance thought" (85). Indeed, with the coming of the early modern period—embodied in the spheres of culture and philosophy by, respectively, Shakespeare and Hobbes—"each individual becomes a closed space in relation to their fantasmagoria: their desires and dreams are their business," business that in the Middle Ages, presumably, they invariably shared with their communities, for (and here Brennan is drawing on Norbert Elias's notion of the civilizing process) "Western pre-moderns did not have an 'invisible wall' dividing them one from another" (83). The cross-cultural work of Marilyn Strathern suggests to Brennan that the very notion of the individual is "culturally specific" to the West, and that "other cultures conceive of people as potentially divisible" just as they "eschew subject-object thought" (84). Charles Taylor's *Sources of the Self* confirms that the "condition of being an 'individual' with an 'inside' is born" in the early modern period, while Susan Bordo's work on Cartesianism and objectivity demonstrates how the post-premodern self "is aware of distance . . . in a way that pre-modern people were not; this modern self no longer thinks of itself as connected with the cosmos, but as dislocated" (85).

To be fair, Brennan is careful at several points to hedge her historical bets against the charge of nostalgia, for example in her discussion of the continuities marking the Western habit of sexual objectification: "The idea that the passification of women pre-dates the ego's era needs to be stressed in case this argument is read as nostalgia" (74). More generally, she points out, these continuities risk being taken as sources for contemporary political revisionism:

[T]he ego's era is born of patriarchy, a system of social life which moulds the foundational fantasy into an acceptable expression, at the same time as it fosters some of its fonder delusions. To the extent that this book contributes a theory of history and modernity, this notion is fundamental. It is basic to the political and ethical implications of my argument. For if the psychical affinity between modernity and its patriarchal sire is forgotten, it is relatively easy to mistake the constraints that feudal patriarchy imposed for solutions to the anomie and fragmentation that mark postmodernism. The longing for the past, the seeping nostalgia that characterizes key theories critical of the modernity that leads to postmodernism, is prompted and then justified by a limited insight, limited in that it sees the patriarchy that preceded the ego's era and kept it in check as its solution, not its precipitate.

The passage should be understood as a rejection of patriarchal melancholia for a simple past, and I am happy to appropriate it here as a salient critique of certain modes of theoretic medievalism, those modes that long for a return to the Medieval as a political corrective to the Modern while failing to account for the ideological baggage of the medievalism they proffer. It is a longing that populates the modern history of French medievalism, from Gaston Paris's invention of *amour courtois* to Georges Bataille's postwar meditation on the shell of Rheims cathedral to Simone de Beauvoir's *Tous les hommes sont mortels* (1946), with its medieval sovereign surviving through the centuries to become the plaintive companion of a modern actress.[29] The longing is perceptible, too, in Roland Barthes's will to take textual commentary "back to the Middle Ages" without addressing what this semiotic time-travel might imply for the post–Vatican II (and post-1968) intellectual culture he helped to define.[30]

To put it another way, modernity's utter confidence in its own discrete ontology is perhaps the most dazzlingly successful symptom of the historicist pathology Brennan seeks to circumscribe as fantasy. If Brennan claims that the "ethical implications" of her thesis depend on the break with "feudal patriarchy" that births the modern, her argument nevertheless elides Lacan's most extended treatment of ethics in the seventh seminar, which takes precisely the psychic mechanisms of "feudal patriarchy"—and in particular courtly love—as a key to the ethics of his psychoanalytic practice. *The Ethics of Psychoanalysis* goes almost entirely uncited in *History after Lacan,* a book that relies to the core on a historical rupture with the premodern while never turning to Lacan's extended engagement with premodern cultures themselves. So pervasive is this avoidance that, by the end of the book, Brennan can voice no hesitation

29. On Gaston Paris, see, most recently, Hult, "Gaston Paris and the Invention of Courtly Love."
30. See the discussion in chapter 5 below.

in reiterating her project's abiding investment in "the medieval times before subject-object thought" (171).

Medievalists have long since grown weary of responding to glib narratives about the communal, collective, unbounded, public nature of pre-Renaissance egos and subjectivities, so much so that the putting of one's name to such a response in print has to feel a bit embarrassing these days.[31] (And as Fredric Jameson has recently conceded, "We cannot not periodize," so perhaps we should stop complaining.[32]) What is so intriguing about Brennan's particular version of this Enlightenment teleology, though, is the uncharacteristic self-consciousness of its erudition as well as the confidence of its empiricism. The magisterial historiographical tone as well as the array of scholarly citations marking the properly historical argument of *History after Lacan* strangely recapitulate Lacan's own archaeological performance in the seventh seminar. Yet Brennan's claims for the empirical veracity of the historical shift she posits—the "contained individual" *really did* emerge in the seventeenth century, she avows—seem quite remote from Lacan's own historical recognition of the medievalism of modernity. While it may be true that much early modern philosophy deluded itself into believing in subject/object separation and contained individuals (Brennan's "foundational fantasy"), the notion of "interiority or inwardness, a condition of being an 'individual' with an 'inside',," was not "born in this period" (85), as Brennan suggests, but rather *served* this period as perhaps the most effective ideological instrument for the construction of a medieval past that (read: the abjection of medieval selves who) lacked the capacity to exist in this same condition.

This process of historical abjection is then the misrecognized ideological work of the foundational fantasy, and as such it exposes the devastating irony at the heart of *History after Lacan*. For even as Brennan posits containment as the social psychosis of the modern era, she misreads the modern era's most enduring historical fantasy about itself, a fantasy so deep-seated that it can be shared and reiterated endlessly by critics as diverse as Harold Bloom (as Shakespeare's "invention of the human"), Stephen Greenblatt (as an unprecedented capacity for "self-fashioning"), Charles Taylor (as the "birth" of individual self-consciousness), and Teresa Brennan: put crudely (as indeed its adherents so often put it), the fantasy that the bounded ego has its point of origin in the soliloquies of *Hamlet*. Perhaps it might be useful, then, to conceive of *History after La-*

---

31. For example, Aers, "A Whisper in the Ear of Early Modernists."
32. Jameson, *A Singular Modernity: Essays on the Ontology of the Present*, 29.

can more as a *symptom* than as a *diagnosis* of Lacan's view of history. Unknowingly constrained by a *pre*-Lacanian historicism, Brennan cannot put history on the couch without engaging in a transferential process of her own, imputing to Lacanian psychoanalysis a fantasy of premodernity that informs and sustains her own extensive analysis.

Archaeology of the Ethical Subject

The eclectic historical methodology of *The Ethics of Psychoanalysis*—which puts, say, Melanie Klein in conversation with the Cathars, Holbein with Bernfeld, St. Thomas Aquinas with Leopold von Sacher-Masoch—can often obscure the quite deliberate organization of the past Lacan uses to sustain his seminar's argument. While others have revealed the depth and extent of the seminar's formative interest in medieval discourses of courtly love within the history of desire, these discourses form just one component of a much broader engagement with the culture and civilization of the Western Middle Ages as an integral part of the seminar's ethical project.[33] Over the course of the year, Lacan grounds his treatment of psychoanalytic ethics in an array of written production spanning the 2,500 years of the literary and philosophical tradition, from Sophocles to Henry Miller. Yet Lacan remains keenly aware throughout the *Ethics* of the logic undergirding the seminar's temporal framework, and in particular of the tactical emplacement of the medieval in the archaeology of the ethical subject.

It would be tempting, in fact, to posit a will to periodize as one of the primary compulsions inspiring the seminar, which it is possible to read as an exercise in a psychoanalysis of the *longue durée*. First, the artifacts of the ancient world adumbrate the dilemmas that will preoccupy the long history of ethical thinking: *Antigone* is (famously) read by Lacan as embodying the essence of the tragic, revealing to us "the line of sight that defines desire" (247) ("the threshold of the symbolic," on Judith Butler's reading);[34] Aristotle is invoked as the first great theorist of catharsis—not simply the catharsis of *mousiké,* but that of subjection itself as "a crisis that sometimes threatens pleasure" (246); Plato registers the Hellenic psyche's synecdochal relation to urban disorder; and the

33. Lacan's work with courtly love is treated in Kay, *Courtly Contradictions;* Labbie, *Phoné Sex;* Žižek, "Courtly love, or, Woman as Thing," in *The Metastases of Enjoyment,* 89–112; and Maillet, "L'amour courtois."

34. Butler, *Antigone's Claim,* 29. On the role of Antigone in Lacan's *Ethics,* see (in addition to Butler) Rabaté, *Jacques Lacan,* 69–84; and Zupančič, "Ethics and Tragedy," 186–90.

books of the Old Testament lay down foundational laws whose language exceeds their own capacity to legislate (the Ten Commandments, for instance, "clarify[ing] that without which no speech is possible" [69]). Next, in New Testament Christianity and the theologians of late antiquity, Lacan seems to locate a transition to a certain form of ethical constraint that nevertheless remains keenly aware of perversion's potential to define the subject: Clement of Alexandria is mined for his "denunciatory references" to "pagan abominations" of the sort found in Hellenic religious ceremonies (299), while Augustine models the initial historical consciousness of the moral "pile of garbage" that mankind has left in its wake ("it is by the mental process of the subtraction of the good from the good that one ends up refuting the existence of anything else but the good in being, given that that which remains, since it is more perfect than that which previously was, can in no way be evil" [233–34]).

The reworking of ancient ethical thought that distinguishes the centuries of the Renaissance is also central to the historical account propounded in the *Ethics,* including, among many others, the *Heptameron* of Marguerite de Navarre (read through the lens of Lucien Febvre's short study of the author), in which the moral philosophies inspiring the "sauce" of the frame narrative (Lacan's metaphor) become inseparable from the main "dish" of the stories; Martin Luther, whose writings "renewed the very basis of Christian teaching when [they] sought to express our dereliction, our fall in a world where we let ourselves go" (92–93); the ethical dilemma of *Hamlet,* a drama which, on "the threshold of the modern period," "bear[s] witness to the special weakness of future man as far as action is concerned" (251); and even Galileo, whose telescope registers the "increasing power of symbolic mastery . . . consuming around it any reference that would limit its scope to intuited data" (122). The Age of Enlightenment furnishes Lacan with numerous moral-philosophical adumbrations of modernity—most obviously the ethics of Kant and the categorical imperative, a continuous point of resistance for Lacan's own ethical project. The œuvre of Friedrich Hölderlin, the eighteenth-century poet of moral renewal, comes to Lacan's attention in the seminar by means of Laplanche's dissertation (nearing completion at the time of the *Ethics*) for its exemplification of "a poetic experience which displays and which unveils" the psychotic process of symbolic substitution in the face of despair.[35] This is also the age of Sade, of course,

---

35. This was a work also known to Michel Foucault; see his review, "Le 'non' du père: Jean Laplanche, Holderlin et la question du père."

the Enlightenment's philosophical black sheep, whose avid readership among French and German postwar intellectuals (Beauvoir, Bataille, Adorno, and others) illuminates Lacan's insistence that Sade speaks the ethical truth of Kant's whole moral system.[36]

What, then, can the Middle Ages hope to contribute to this diachronic unfolding of the history of desire, this multimillennial archaeology that embraces such a vast expanse of philosophical, theological, and psychological thought? The question goes to the more general historical movement of the seminar across the terrains of premodernity. The *Ethics* maps an intellectual pilgrimage that first transports its auditors through the moral fields of Kant and Sade, lingers on St. Paul, takes up Marx through the lens of Augustine, and finally ascends through Hegel and Sade again to *Antigone,* the seminar's culminating artifact. Yet in fact, as we shall see, Lacan concludes *The Ethics of Psychoanalysis* with a meditation on the Book of Revelation that recasts the Bernardine honey of wisdom as an apocalyptic vision of the future of all ethical thought. This apocalyptic framing may help to clarify the argumentative function of the Middle Ages in the seminar, a function in which Catharism, the writings of Andreas Capellanus, the poems of the Minnesänger and troubadours will all play a part. In short, *The Ethics of Psychoanalysis* as a whole guides its readers and auditors through an interlocking series of ethico-historical arcs that extend from Aristotle to Freud, from Sophocles to Bernfeld—all invariably reaching their analytical apex in the epoch separating Augustine from Luther.

Here I want to isolate just one of these arcs in order to get at the rhetorical centrality of the Middle Ages in Lacan's ethical project. Following the early weeks of the *Ethics,* which move through Lacan's inaugural discussion of the Heideggerian/Freudian *Ding* as well as a skeptical appraisal of Kant's categorical imperative, comes an extended excursus on "The Problem of Sublimation," which for Lacan is in some sense a problem of periodization. "Read a little Luther," Lacan advises in his discussion of "drives and lures," for it is in the text of the German reformer that we find the residue of a monumental transition in the history of the human subject, a critique of the polymorphous drives that had held sway over the domain of Occidental subjectivity for at least a millennium and produced "the fundamentally bad character of the relations between men," "the essentially digestive and excremental schema forged by a thought that draws the ultimate consequences from the form of exile in

---

36. Also pertinent is Lacan's famous account in "Kant avec Sade."

which man finds himself relative to any good in the world whatsoever" (97, 93).[37] The argument in this segment of the seminar reflects the clear influence of Bataille, whose account of Luther and Calvin in *The Accursed Share* postulated a Reformation theology aimed at "the utter negation of a system of intense consumption of resources" that had characterized the Middle Ages (122). Lacan's initial engagement in the *Ethics* with the function of the real revolves around Bataille's *part maudite*, which by the late 1950s had emerged as an important element of the "morbidity" Lacan was positing within the psychical dimension of the real.

The seminar at this point becomes a virtual exercise in periodization: in Luther's historical moment, tensions building over the medieval centuries peak during "a crisis from which emerged our whole modern immersion in the world." The result is a moral theology of "erogenous zones . . . fundamental points of fixation" that will ever after problematize the "total, complete, epidermic contact between one's body and a world that was itself open and quivering" (93). Yet this "contact" is clearly not, as Brennan would have it, the "intersubjective," "uncontained" sphere of human relations under the sign of premodernity, but rather a fantasy sustained within an avowedly private domain of desire and its inscription.

The seminar is emphatic on this point, for "what interests us here," Lacan proposes, "very probably emerged in the middle or at the beginning of the eleventh century" (145). Lacan refers of course to "courtly love," the subject of a sweeping treatise at the heart of *The Ethics of Psychoanalysis;* as he asks his audience about courtly love, "How should we situate it as analysts?" The question will go to the heart of psychoanalytic ethics, provoking as it does a vigorously diachronic interrogation of ethical thought in relation to human desire and its frustration (148). Indeed, if "Freud placed in the forefront of ethical inquiry the simple relationship between man and woman" (84), the ethical genealogy of this relationship (for the modern West, at least) roots itself in the medieval discourse of courtly erotics. In the spirit of Lacan's own provocation to "look awry" at courtly love, though, we might begin scrutinizing his approach to this medieval formation through a particularly confounding moment in *The Ethics of Psychoanalysis* that occurs just after he launches his discussion of courtly love as anamorphosis. The "feminine object is emptied of all real substance" (149) in the courtly economy, Lacan contends, and what the male lover demands "is to be deprived of something

---

37. On Luther in the *Ethics of Psychoanalysis*, see Žižek, *Enjoy Your Symptom!* 179–80.

real" (150). Far from the lady herself, the true object of courtly desire is *das Ding*, the "vacuole" in the real that subjects us to the "ways of the signifier"; courtly narrative, in other words, constitutes an unfulfilled quest rooted in an experiencing of "unpleasure" around which courtly love organizes its significations (a process that Sarah Kay imputes in both Lacan and Occitan poetry to "the rigid and alien formalism of the Thing").[38]

This startling vision of the courtly dynamic—as a kind of secular apophaticism that never admits itself as such—entails in turn a mode of signification rooted in a particular cultural moment, the twelfth century in the south of France. It is here that the argumentative substance of Lacan's discussion begins to mirror its rhetoric: the pleasure of analysis in this seminar is an archaeophilic one, a love for the archaic as it embodies itself in the artifacts in which it perdures. Accordingly, the seminar soon comes around to a concrete archival discovery that helped produce a massive twentieth-century interest in the forms and expressions of medieval courtly love:

> The existence and operations of these tribunals devoted to the casuistry of love and evoked by Michel de Nostre-Dame are open to debate and often debated. Nevertheless, we do have certain texts, including especially the work by Andreas Capellanus that Rénouart discovered and published in 1917. The shortened title is *De Arte Amandi*, which thus makes it a homonym of Ovid's treatise—a work that was passed down to posterity by the clergy. This fourteenth-century manuscript that Rénouart discovered in the Bibliothèque Nationale gives us the text of judgments handed down by Ladies, who are well-known historical figures and include Eleanor of Aquitaine. (146)

De Arte Amandi provides unique evidence of a moment of profound importance in the relation between desire and the signifier. In the text of Andreas, Lacan suggests, courtly love receives its most extended formulation as a "scholastics of unhappy love" (146). Rénouart's archival discovery of a fourteenth-century text of Andreas, Lacan suggests, opened a modern window onto a fascinating period in the history of love.

But there was no such "discovery." Andreas Capellanus's *De arte honeste amandi* has had a continuous history of transmission since the twelfth century; there is nothing to suggest that the text was ever "discovered" at the Bibliothèque Nationale, least of all in 1917. Moreover, not a single mention of a scholar with the surname "Rénouart" (or its

38. Kay, *Courtly Contradictions,* 157.

more common homonym, "Rénouard") appears in the long editorial history and extensive scholarly literature on Andreas's text.[39] In the 1950s the standard text of the *De arte* was E. Trojel's edition, which was published in Copenhagen in 1892. Lacan seems to have fashioned this scholarly micro-narrative out of thin air.

Toward what end? Clearly Lacan was seeking in part to lend the seminar a sheen of historical erudition, and in this respect the ponderous invocation of Rénouart's codicological feat in the dusty BN manuscript room (less than a mile away from the Hôpital Saint-Anne) was a stroke of archaeological brilliance. One can easily imagine Lacan's audience nodding sagely at the erudition of the master, pretending knowledge of an important archival discovery that had never actually taken place. On one level, of course, this error comes as no surprise. As Elizabeth Roudinesco has shown, the transcription, distribution, and publication history of the seminars had been characterized from the beginning by a basic disregard for scholarly and bibliographical reliability that originated in Lacan's own unwillingness to standardize his seminar texts and grew only worse with the similar treatment of the master's legacy by his son-in-law and literary executor, Jacques-Alain Miller.[40] I want to stress here that this verdict does not reflect antipsychoanalytic empiricism: *The Ethics of Psychoanalysis* in particular is characterized throughout by a complete disregard for academic standards widely accepted within the contemporaneous French psychoanalytic community, including those shared by Lacan's immediate circle in the Société français de philosophie. Such lapses in this seminar include mistranslations of virtually every Greek word and phrase, numerous misattributions of quotations central to Lacan's historical arguments, and, with regard to the long medieval sections of the seminar, several serious misrepresentations of the arguments of twentieth-century scholars.[41] In the case of Lacan's medievalism, then, we are far from the laconic rigor of a Georges Bataille.

Ironically so, for Lacan's bizarre fabrication of Rénouart actually plays

39. The closest candidate is the great lexicographer François Raynouard, whose *Lexique roman, ou dictionnaire de la langue des troubadours* had appeared in six volumes in 1838–44. But Raynouard was a Romance philologist, not a latinist. As Jean-Michel Rabaté informed me, another candidate may be François Baynouard, an antiquarian who produced luxury facsimiles of early manuscripts with limited print runs, though I have had no luck tracking down any early twentieth-century facsimile of an Andreas manuscript.

40. Roudinesco, *Jacques Lacan*, 423–24.

41. According to Roudinesco (*Jacques Lacan*, 423), the great classicist Pierre Vidal-Naquet received a copy of the *Ethics* from Jacques-Alain Miller shortly after its publication in 1986; Vidal-Naquet was surprised to discover at least two errors in the Greek on every relevant page, and sent Miller a lengthy letter (apparently ignored) documenting them for future printings.

into the voracious and largely effective sweep of the seminar's medievalist ethics. While Lacan's own ultimate *objet* in Seminar VII is courtly love and its literary artifacts, his discussion takes detours through an overview of the moral teachings of St. Paul and their theological aftermath, the *Heptameron* of Marguerite de Navarre, the prophecies of Nostradamus, Dante's *Vita Nuova* and *Divine Comedy,* and Denis de Rougement's *Love in the Western World,* originally published in France in 1939. For Lacan, the text of Andreas captures that moment when giving ground relative to one's desire became an aesthetic and cultural imperative for perhaps the first time in the history of love literature. In this sense, courtly love models for Lacan the nature of sublimation and emerges as a powerful proving ground for the ethical practice delineated in the seminar.

Nowhere is the giving of ground relative to desire more powerfully illustrated for Lacan than in premodern ceremonies of potlatch as he comprehended them. Much later in the seminar, after he has moved away from the exemplarity of courtly love to teach the ethical lessons of *Antigone,* Lacan turns almost offhandedly to a medieval baronial ceremony in the south of France, which he holds up for his seminar as illustrative of the compulsions toward destruction and negativity at the origins of the courtly dynamic:

I couldn't find today the piece of paper on which I noted that at the beginning of the twelfth century—that through courtly love marked the rise to the surface in European culture of a problematic of desire as such [*avec l'amour courtois l'émergence à la surface de la culture européenne d'une problématique du désir comme tel*]—we see appear in a feudal rite the manifestation of something wholly analogous. The rite in question occurred at a festival, a meeting of barons somewhere in the region of Narbonne, and it involved huge destruction, not only of the goods that were consumed directly as part of the festivities, but also of animals and harnesses. Everything occurred as if the foregrounding of the problematic of desire required as its necessary correlative the need for ostentatious forms of destruction, insofar as they are gratuitous. Those who in the community claim to be privileged subjects, feudal Lords, those who set themselves up as such in this ceremony, throw down challenges to each other, rival each other in attempting to destroy the most. (235; 276)

The lackadaisical tone of this passage ("I couldn't find today the piece of paper . . .") contrasts vividly with the bibliographical certitude Lacan had adopted earlier in the seminar around the subject of Rénouart and the Andreas manuscript. In this case, however, Lacan seems to have cribbed his medievalist notes from a reliable source, most likely the first volume of Bataille's *Accursed Share,* with its long discussion of potlatch among a variety of nobilities, including those of the European Middle Ages.[42] Here as elsewhere in the seminar, the Middle Ages perform a complex function as both theoretical inspiration and artefactual exemplar, offering up a "problematic of desire as such" by which premodern cultural practice anticipates and embodies an entire domain of desire defining modernity.

Such deep-seated continuities crop up everywhere in Lacan's account of courtly love and its legacy in his own century, though he is careful throughout to convey to his auditors the (often unknowable) specificity of medieval cultures. Drawing on Lucien Febvre's history of unbelief and recent anthologies of medieval heretical writings by René Nelli and others, Lacan tests Rougement's famous thesis linking the dualism of the Cathar heresy to the emergence of courtly love against the primary sources themselves; the result is a skeptical reappraisal of the paradigm that exposes its fictionality while historicizing the medieval "style of thought" that produced it. The seminar assimilates some of the most influential works in French medieval studies of the preceding twenty years, as when Lacan speaks of society's "just emerging from the first feudal period," a chronological marker inspired by the great Marc Bloch's distinction between the first and second feudal ages in *Feudal Society.* At some points Lacan's historical method verges on a kind of dialectical materialism as he provides an earthly frame for courtly love, which he insists is the result of specific historical processes that objectified and sublimated "The Thing" as the unattainable object of desire:

The whole theory of the *Minne* or of courtly love has, in effect, been decisive. Although it has completely disappeared nowadays from the sociological sphere, courtly love has nevertheless left traces in an unconscious that has no need to be called "collective," in a traditional unconscious that is sustained by a whole literature, a whole imagery, that we continue to inhabit. . . . This mode was created deliberately. It was by no means a creation of the popular soul, of that famous great soul of the blessed Middle Ages. . . . The rules of polite conduct were articulated deliberately in a small literary circle and, as a result, the celebration of the object was made possible. . . . This moral code instituted an object at the heart of a given society, an object that is nevertheless completely natural. Don't imagine they made love in those days any less than we do.

In sum, argues Lacan, "courtly love is, in effect, an exemplary form, a paradigm, of sublimation," a social mechanism that "tends to locate in

42. See the discussion in chapter 1 above.

the place of the Thing certain discontents of the culture." A prime example of such sublimatory narrative is the œuvre of Chrétien de Troyes, whose romances embody the "extreme arbitrariness" of the ideology of courtly love. Yet the historical specificity of the origins of courtly love, and thus of modernity's habits of sublimation, are quite startling in Lacan's analysis: a "small literary circle" of elite nobles in the eleventh century deliberately founded a mode of veneration that continues to hold sway over the sexual relation and force its pathological investment in the Thing.

A Note on Arnaut

"I have for you today," Lacan announced to the seminar on March 9, 1960, "something curious and amusing." It will be "a text," or rather "a note, on the subject of what might be called the paradoxes of sublimation." The text in question is a spectacularly gynephobic poem by the twelfth-century troubadour Arnaut Daniel, "a piece of evidence from the file of courtly love" that "breaches the boundaries of pornography to the point of scatology." This poem—which, Lacan asserts, "even the specialists themselves literally don't know what to do with; they can't make head or tail of it" (161)—figures the sexual anatomy of a certain Lady Ena as an incarnate trumpet that only the most unworthy suitor would ever consent to blow. The bulk of the seminar for that day was to be taken up with a lecture by a participant (a certain Madame Hubert) on the subject of Hans Sperber's work on sexuality and the development of language; Lacan's discussion of the Arnaut poem serves as a quick prologue to the lecture, though he clearly sees the text as related in a complex way to the subject of the ensuing explication.

Lacan decides to read the poem to his seminar in modern French translation—not, mind you, because he doesn't have Provençal himself, but "because I don't think that any of you can understand that lost language which is the *langue d'oc,* a language that nevertheless has its style and its value." The material survival of the poem is remarkable in itself, Lacan notes; "all the poetic works of the trouvères and troubadours have not come down to us," and even in the case of Arnaut, we find some of his poems in only "two or three manuscripts." This poem, however, "whose literary merit goes far beyond what a translation is able to reveal, not only was not lost but is to be found in some twenty manuscripts." Once again codicological rigor lends archaeological prestige to the psychoanalysis of text, grounding the poem's specificity in the material culture of the medieval book. Following Lacan, I quote the poem in full:

Though Lord Raimond, in agreement with Lord Truc Malec, defends Lady Ena and her orders, I would grow old and white before I would consent to a request that involves so great an impropriety. For as to "put his mouth to her trumpet," he would need the kind of beak that could pick grain out of a pipe. And even then he might come out blind, as the smoke from those folds is so strong.

He would need a beak and a long, sharp one, for the trumpet is rough, ugly and hairy, and it is never dry, and the swamp within is deep. That's why the pitch ferments upwards as it continually escapes, continually overflows. And it is not fitting that he who puts his mouth to that pipe be a favorite.

There will be plenty of other tests, finer ones that are worth far more, and if Lord Bernart withdrew from that one, he did not, by Christ, behave like a coward if he was taken with fear and fright. For if the stream of water had landed on him from above, it would have scalded his whole neck and cheek, and it is not fitting also that a lady embrace a man who has blown a stinking trumpet.

Bernart, I do not agree in this with the remarks of Raimon de Durfort, in saying that you were wrong; for even if you had blown away gladly, you would have encountered a crude obstacle, and the stench would soon have smitten you, that stinks worse than dung in a garden. You should praise God, against whomsoever seeks to dissuade you, that he helped you escape from that.

Yes, he escaped from a great peril with which his son also would have been reproached and all those from Cornil. He would have done better to go into exile than to have blown in that funnel between spine and mount pubic, there where rust colored substances proceed. He could never have been certain that she would not piss all over his snout and eyebrows.

Lady, may Bernart never venture to blow that trumpet without a large bung to stop up the penile hole; then only could he blow without peril.[43]

This "quite extraordinary document," as Lacan terms it, provides a uniquely privileged perspective on the operations of sublimation. In figuring this musical body, the poem's loving subject (perhaps the speaker, perhaps the speaker's addressee, perhaps Arnaut himself) is

---

43. Lacan, *Ethics*, 162; the poem has been edited and translated in Arnaut Daniel, *Poetry*, 74–77.

"push[ing] desire to the extreme point of offering himself in a sacrifice that involves his own annihilation"; the lady "finds herself, suddenly and brutally positing, in a place knowingly constructed out of the most refined of signifiers, the emptiness of a thing in all its crudity."[44] Anatomical emptiness gives way to an emptiness of signification; the poem's explicit thematic of the physical body in turn yields to a "model of an emptiness at the core, around which is articulated that by means of which desire is in the end sublimated" (163). In the case of Arnaut's song, Lacan contends, we are witnessing "the paradoxes of sublimation" in action: as much as the lover wishes to honor Lady Ena, her request that he put his mouth to her anus and "blow in that funnel between spine and mount pubic" not only proves too arduous a test, but also promises to de-sublimate the very feminine object of desire by substituting for her the crude emptiness of the Thing—in this case, the "anal thing," in Richard Halpern's phrase. Halpern paraphrases Lacan's ethical argument here as Lady Ena's challenge to her abject suitor: "If, Bernart, you are afraid of the revolting pleasure of eating my shit, how can you help me on the path to my *jouissance?* How will you (filled with pity as you are) bring yourself to shit in my mouth, especially since I will not ask you to do it? How can I trust you not to betray your desire, to give way before it, and thus betray my desire as well?"[45] The poem, in other words, demands that the subject take a scatological test to determine his worthiness to serve and embrace the Lady; yet the taking of this test, whether successfully accomplished or not, will by its very nature render the subject unworthy to become the lover he seeks to be. As Halpern explicates it, this paradox speaks to the enduring intimacy between sodomy and sublimation, between nonprocreative sexual dissidence and the limits of aesthetic practice. These categories converge in the Arnaut poem with particular force: like the flute in the story of Pan and Syrinx, to which Lacan turns immediately after his discussion of Arnaut, the anal trumpet into which the poem morphs Lady Ena's body "incorporates the void around which creation occurs" (101).

To take the ethical argument of the poem seriously, though, is precisely to recognize its historicity, a recognition crucial for understanding the exceptional nature of Lacan's citation of the Arnaut poem. For this passage from the *Ethics* is one of the very few instances (and perhaps the sole instance) in the run of Jacques Lacan's seminar at which the master

44. Staten, *Eros in Mourning*, 177–79, discusses Lacan's seeming misconstrual of the speakers in the poem.

45. Halpern, *Shakespeare's Perfume: Sodomy and Sublimity in the Sonnets, Wilde, Freud, and Lacan*, 100.

recited an entire literary text, from beginning to end, before his Parisian audience. Albeit in modern French translation, a troubadour poem resounds in the amphitheater of the Hôpital Saint-Anne as a means of schooling the leading lights of the French intelligentsia in the archaeology of their desire. Lacan reads "Lady Ena" as a kind of ethical mirror in which his auditors are to view the alterity of the medieval even while recognizing in this trashy bit of medievalism the lingering Thing at the core of modernity.

It is in just this sense, I think, that the Arnaut interlude models the provocative homology between the historicism of *The Ethics of Psychoanalysis* and the analytic situation itself. For Lacan, as we have seen, ethical psychoanalysis will work to undermine proscription, to allow the analysand the opportunity to take back the ground he or she has given relative to the object of desire. Analysis itself, then, is a *historical* process: like the *Ethics,* its function is in large part an archaeological pursuit and recovery of an obscured past; it performs this archaeological work by surveying the recovered artifacts, cathected objects, and embedded memories of desire that constitute the Other of the subject. It has become commonplace in psychoanalytic literary study to proffer analogies between psychic formation and literary practice, to observe that an impulse toward narrativity underlies the subject's self-understanding (read self-delusion) of development; this is why Freudian case histories, say, can often resemble literary narratives. What *The Ethics of Psychoanalysis* seems to suggest is that the particular kind of narrative most intimately affiliated with the inscription of desire and its progression through time may be *historical* narrative, the myriad stories about individual and collective pasts that together constitute the Western archaeology of subjection.

Yet if, in Alain Juranville's words, "history is the essence of ethics" for Lacan, it is so only with an important qualification: by *history* Lacan often seems to imply not a coherent narrative progression of discrete historical events, but rather a sacramental unfolding of individual desire through the mechanism of sublimation (a mechanism embodied here in and as the Arnaut poem). In Juranville's difficult paraphrase, this process culminates in Seminar VII as a dissimulative recapitulation of Christian revelation:

For if the essence of religion is the relation between the sacred and the saint, in God himself and repeated from man to God, it is "naturally" dissimulated by its form, a specifically sacrificial confusion between, on the one hand, the sacred, which is total sublimation that undoes itself and results in the mere partial sublimation of social existence . . . and, on the other hand, the saint, who is totally pure sublimation to which even human beings are called beyond partial sublimation, whence the necessity . . . of a *revelation*. . . . [T]hrough politics and history, the Christian religion establishes the secular world where the truly ethical act is possible.[46]

It takes a real leap of faith to equate this Christian revelation with history tout court, and Juranville may be overemphasizing here the extent to which rupture inevitably defines historical change.[47] Nevertheless, Lacan's suggestion that the form of the medieval troubadour lyric provides a site of resistance to desire's narrativization encapsulates the seminar's larger argument concerning the complex relationship between history and ethics.

A kind of lyric archaeology thus emerges in the seminar as an ethical alternative to narrativizing, periodizing history, with Lacan subtly allying a poetic critique of narrative desire with an undermining of its historiographical counterpart.[48] This may finally explain what a troubadour poem is doing at this crucial juncture in the seminar. For Lacan, as I read this portion of the seminar, ethical *faute* ("transgression" in Dennis Porter's translation of the *Ethics*) is embodied in troubadour lyric *prior* to its historical subsumption within the dominant, romantic model of courtly love. Troubadour lyricism, that is, maintains an insistent tension with the ethically flattening contours of narrative, or what María Rosa Menocal identifies in the historiography of medieval lyric as "the distortions of time and history constructed as a narrative and as development." Because "the troubadours succeeded so well in their radical project," Menocal suggests, "they not only were assimilated into the mainstream narrative, but they were made part of the line of venerable ancestors."[49] This assimilation of troubadour lyric into the genealogy of the Western love tradition has had the unfortunate effect, Lacan avows, of blinding moral philosophy to the heuristic ethical outrageousness of the pornographic, the scatological, the obscene—in a word, the medieval.

46. Juranville, "Ethics with Psychoanalysis," 129.

47. Juranville, "Ethics with Psychoanalysis," 127: "Thus when the founding act of creation is repeated, outside of any desire for rupture, the rupture that is history itself is accomplished."

48. In this respect, I would suggest that Lacan is anticipating Michel de Certeau's critique of Freud's psychoanalytic negotiation of historiographical "style" in *The Writing of History,* 287–307 (a chapter originally published as an essay in *Annales* in 1970).

49. Menocal, *Shards of Love,* 38.

Ethics and Apocalypse

Throughout *The Ethics of Psychoanalysis,* as we have seen, Lacan is practicing a certain form of medieval studies, teaching for one school year as
a kind of ad hoc medievalist in an intellectual climate that also embraced
the careers of Georges Duby, Jacques Le Goff, Jean Frappier, and Paul
Zumthor. While inventing a mode of psychoanalytic medievalism, Lacan sought nothing less than an ethical demystification of the aura of
"courtly love"—not so much by exposing its historical status as a fictive construct of Gaston Paris's nineteenth-century medievalism, as E. T.
Donaldson, F. X. Newman, and others soon would in very different
ways, but by excavating its almost mythic hold on human subjectivity
and desire.[50] If Lacan's critique lacks the philological precision and bibliographical accuracy of those penned by strictly academic medievalists,
this should not prevent us from taking Seminar VII seriously for its value
as a critical overview of the whole "courtly love" revival and reification
that had been (and in many ways still is) taking place since the publication of Rougement's book. Lacan casts a cynical eye upon the mini-
industry of what we might call courtly love kitsch, including books by
authors such as René Nelli, "in which," Lacan snidely notes, "I find a certain philogenic moralism along with a lot of facts." Lacan's historicized
analysis of courtly love refuses essentialism and represents one of the
most fascinating critical assimilations of medieval texts among the
postwar avant garde.

What comes across most palpably in the few passages from the *Ethics*
I have examined here is the sheer formal force of archaeophilia in Lacan's ethical project. By means of an intricate scrutiny of a *longue durée*
of Western history, the seminar sorts innumerable shards of history into
an antinarrative of psychic change. The reassembly of these fragments
thus becomes (so the seminar argues) ethical in mapping out how we
have come to be what we are, how we have come to desire and love as
we do. Yet only alongside an accounting for its strange lapses and para-
praxes can *The Ethics of Psychoanalysis* be recovered for the future practice of psychoanalytic historicism. More illuminating than Lacan's bibliographical charlatanism, for example, is the extent to which his errors
serve ironically to facilitate the central purpose of the seminar as a
whole: to uncover the millennial reach of the ethical imperatives organ-

---

50. For recent contributions to the historiography of the "courtly love" debate, see the exchange
between Don Monson and William Paden, "The Troubadour's Lady," as well as Hult, "Gaston Paris
and the Invention of Courtly Love."

izing psychoanalytic inquiry. When Lacan invents Rénouart, the result is a dubious performance of erudition—an assertion that the text of Andreas Capellanus was "discovered" in the early twentieth century—that nevertheless serves to confirm Lacan's sense of the longstanding investment of the West in the courtly love ethic. It may be true that medieval courtly ideals "are to be found in subsequent periods, down to our own," and that "the influence of these ideals is a highly concrete one in the organization of contemporary man's sentimental attachments, and it continues its forward march" (148). Yet by artificially curtailing the transmission history of what was then regarded as one of the central texts of *fin'amor*, Lacan elides the crucial mediating role in this "forward march" performed by those same medieval artifacts he reads so provocatively throughout the seminar. Lacan demonstrates more than convincingly here and elsewhere that the "sentimental attachments" of courtly love continually animate the history of Western desire, whether in Chrétien de Troyes's "revivals" of Ovid's own ascetic discourse of desire; in Freud's theories of the "sphere of foreplay" in *Three Essays on the Theory of Sexuality*, which stages a ritual of unpleasure derived ultimately from the agonizing courtly wait for the *don de merci;* or in André Breton's surrealist meditations on *L'amour fou*, for "it is once again in the place of the Thing that Breton has the madness of love emerge" as an end in itself. More than ten years later, when Lacan returned to the subject in Seminar XX, his raw amazement with courtly love had only grown; he now defined it (his irony here only slightly detracting from his wonderment) as "a highly refined way of making up for the absence of the sexual relationship, by feigning that we are the ones who erect an obstacle thereto. It is truly the most amazing thing that has ever been attempted."[51]

With its counterintuitive working through of the courtly relation as a paradox of sublimation, Lacan's vision of courtly love has inspired a significant current of theoretic medievalisms over the forty years since its initial explication in the *Ethics*. Among other endeavors, *The Ethics of Psychoanalysis* inspired one of the major Tel Quel–affiliated medievalist projects, Julia Kristeva's 1983 *Histoire d'amour* (translated as *Tales of Love*), a book that reflects an intensive critical engagement with the sexual-political implications of Lacan's medievalism (and, as we shall see in the discussion of the Tel Quel group in chapter 5, recapitulates her earlier interest in working through her idiosyncratic semiotic theory through the lens of medieval textual culture). Like Lacan, Kristeva has read energeti-

---

51. Lacan, *On Feminine Sexuality*, 69. On the role of mysticism and sexual difference in Seminar XX, see Hollywood, *Sensible Ecstasy*, 146–70.

cally in medieval studies, enlisting the work of medievalists from Charles Homer Haskins to Paul Zumthor as she ranges across a medieval textual landscape that includes Bernard of Clairvaux's *Sermons on the Song of Songs,* which "imposed upon Europe the idea of man as an amatory subject"; the *Summa theologiæ* of Thomas Aquinas, which "completes the *sublimation* of narcissism within an ontology of the *good*" (in ethical counterpoint to Lacan's vision of courtly love); and the literature of *fin'amor,* including the poems of the troubadours and the *Romance of the Rose.*[52] Though clearly indebted to Lacan's theory of the significatory dimension of the courtly love dynamic, Kristeva is interested as well in the sacrificial economy of specifically *sacred* desire. Her own analysis of *fin'amor* focuses not on the object or "thing" around which the subject of courtly love organizes its significations, but rather on the narrative of desirous subjectivity this form of love produces (a very different narrative, to be sure, than that adumbrated in Lacan, the frequent subject of her critique). And the spirit behind her much-cited essay in mariolatry, "Stabat Mater," may well be Bataille's: "One might be inclined to attribute Bataille's erotic experience to a Catholicism that was taken on to the limit of its sin-laden logic," Kristeva argues.[53]

Kristeva's oeuvre thus registers the archaeo-historical aspects of Lacanian psychoanalytic criticism as they have played themselves out over the last four decades. Several years before delivering the *Ethics,* Lacan had published his translation of Heidegger's "Logos" in an issue of *La Psychanalyse* he was also editing; Heidegger's subject in this treatise was Heraclitus, the pre-Socratic philosopher whose writings adumbrated a model for the subject's "spokenness" in or displacement by language that proved immensely attractive to Lacan in the years immediately preceding the seventh seminar, when he was developing key parts of his more general theory of language in structural relation to subjection.[54] The post-*Ethics* rise of psychoanalytic historicism received a strong boost with the founding of Le Champ freudien, a series published by Seuil during the 1970s and 1980s in which several of Lacan's seminars themselves appeared. A number of Lacan's former and ongoing seminar auditors ensured through publication in this series that the master's methods would permeate French literary-critical studies in an era that marked the first explosion of post-Freudian psychoanalytic literary studies in France. The series regularly featured work by medievalists, early modernists, and

52. Kristeva, *Tales of Love,* 152, 181.
53. Kristeva, *Tales of Love,* 364.
54. Roudinesco, *Jacques Lacan,* 226–28.

even classicists such as Alain Grosrichard, whose *Structure du sérail: la fiction du despotisme asiatique dans l'Occident classique* appeared in Le Champ freudien in 1979. Among the many titles published in this series during these decades, two books by medievalists—Charles Méla's *Blanchefleur et le saint homme: ou, La semblance des reliques: étude comparée de littérature médiévale* (1979) and Roger Dragonetti's *La vie de la lettre au Moyen âge: Le conte du Graal* (1980)—anticipated the psychoanalytic medievalism practiced more forthrightly in Jean Ancelet-Hustache's *Littérature médiévale et psychanalyse* (1990), a devotedly Lacanian book that takes Seminar VII's axioms on courtly love as its raison d'être.[55] Whatever its limitations, then, Lacanian psychoanalysis has from its inception been an archaeological, committedly historical enterprise possessing strong and institutionally specific affiliations with French medieval studies; the much-touted rapprochement between historicism and psychoanalysis of the late 1990s was more a belated reckoning than a hallmark of intellectual maturity.

On July 6, 1960, Lacan delivered the concluding lecture of *The Ethics of Psychoanalysis*. Near the beginning of the day's proceedings he reiterates the gnomic utterance that has sustained the seminar's ethical argument from its opening, the claim that "the only thing of which one can be guilty is of having given ground relative to one's desire" (319). This is one of the propositions that Lacan here terms "paradoxes," arguing as they do against the entire history of ethical philosophy with a provocative deliberateness. This is not to say that the subject's giving of ground is in itself amoral in intention: in fact, "the good" is so often what inspires the sacrifice of desire on the part of the subject, who "has often given ground relative to his desire for a good motive or even for the best of motives." "Doing things in the name of the good," Lacan asserts, has always inspired such self-betrayals, for the self is at issue in an ethical field in which desire serves as "the metonymy of our being," a notion as true for Augustine and his Christian progeny as for Freud and his psychoanalytic heirs:

[G]uilt has existed for a very long time, and it was noticed long ago that the question of a good motive, of a good intention, although it constitutes certain zones of historical experience and was at the forefront of discussions of moral theology in, say, the time of Abelard, hasn't enlightened people very much. The question that keeps reap-

---

55. Huchet, *Littérature médiévale et psychanalyse*, 19–20, points to post-Lacanian work in medieval studies by Christine Maillet, Roger Dragonetti, Charles Méla, and others as resistant to "the positivist tradition" (19).

pearing in the distance is always the same. And that is why Christians in their most routine observances are never at peace. For if one has to do things for the good, in practice one is always faced with the question: for the good of whom? From that point on, things are no longer obvious. (319)

"[I]n, say, the time of Abelard": once again Lacan's offhanded but weirdly persistent medievalism speaks a larger truth about the seminar's ethical argument. Abelard's contribution to the history of moral theology, too, was to focus attention on the inner sphere of intent rather than the ostensible moral transparency of action.

If the banality of Christian moral relativism here seems to undermine Lacan's larger point, the seminar nevertheless concludes on a powerfully moralizing note. As the year's teaching winds up, Lacan comes as close as he has anywhere in the *Ethics* to polemic, directed here against the rush of science—of the empirical, lab-testing, Sokal-hoaxing variety—into the field of psychological inquiry and treatment (that is, into "the field that is ours by reason of the fact that we are exploring it" [324]). In our modern era, Lacan avows, science occupies "that place I have designated the place of desire," and it does so with a fair measure of the same guilt that will always accompany the giving of desirous ground: "It's a fascinating thing, but as far as those who are at the forefront of science are concerned, they are not without a keen consciousness of the fact that they have their backs against a wall of hate. They are themselves capsized by the turbulent swell of a heavy sense of guilt." But, Lacan points out with unaccustomed bitterness, "that isn't very important because it's not in truth an adventure that Mr. Oppenheimer's remorse can put an end to overnight. It is moreover there where the problem of desire will lie in the future" (325).

The future of desire, in other words, is apocalyptic. As the Oppenheimer reference reminds us, Lacan delivered this seminar at the end of a cold war decade that witnessed the massive proliferation of nuclear weapons across both hemispheres. Yet this global threat represents for Lacan less a confirmation of the self-correcting arrogance of scientific knowledge than the logical outcome of the steadily "anesthetized" course of human desire since the twelfth century and the emergence of courtly love. It seems eerily inevitable, then, that the seminar's final sentences will sustain Lacan's historical orientation toward the premodern by reviving his opening rhetoric of *ruminatio* in its apocalyptic guise:

The universal order has to deal with the problem of what it should do with that science in which something is going on whose nature escapes it. Science, which occupies the place of desire, can only be a science of desire in the form of an enormous question mark; and this is doubtless not without a structural cause. In other words, science is animated by some mysterious desire, but it doesn't know, any more than anything in the unconscious itself, what that desire means. The future will reveal it to us, and perhaps among those who by the grace of God have most recently eaten the book—I mean those who have written with their labors, indeed with their blood, the book of Western science. It, too, is an edible book [*un livre comestible*]. (325; 375)

At issue here is the failure of post-Enlightenment science to know its own desire. This failure leads to the constant production of yet more knowledge, knowledge inscribed in blood in the pages of a certain book: the book of Western science, a book conjured throughout *The Ethics of Psychoanalysis* from its central role in Revelation 10:10: "And I took the little book out of the angel's hand, and ate it up; and it was in my mouth sweet as honey, and as soon as I had eaten it, my belly was bitter." The critical facility of the medieval book of life allows Lacan to issue a truly scriptural jeremiad, the apocalyptic reckoning of the seventh seminar engaging what was perhaps the most pressing international political issue of Lacan's day. The sweet Bernardine honey, imaginatively consumed with perplexing delight as an initiating ritual for the seminar's auditors, has become by the end the bitter apocalyptic Book of Lacan. Lacan's disciples have lapped this book up (as they continue to do today) as a decipherment of the world as it is (via analysis) and was (via historicism), when in fact it may be more fitting to read this book, this oeuvre, as apocalyptic prophecy of a world to come. The end of desire is annihilation, as John, Arnaut, Freud, and others in Lacan's apocalpytic genealogy knew so well. Here the compulsion to repeat—to revive, to reread, to unearth long-buried archaeologies from the smothering ground of History—embodies what Lacan's medievalism has worked against throughout the seminar: the hopelessness of a future sadly bereft of the desire to misbehave.

THREE

Indigeneity: Panofsky, Bourdieu, and the Archaeology of the *Habitus*

The other four chapters of this book focus on a cluster of writings that emerged from the intellectual milieu of an identifiable, self-proclaimed, and at least somewhat discrete avant garde. Whatever their philosophical differences (and of course they are considerable), throughout the 1960s and into the 1970s Jacques Lacan, Jacques Derrida, and Roland Barthes formed part of a larger collective that published in some of the same journals, shared many of the same students and auditors, and became associated in the public imagination with a particular style of thought eventually hypostatized and Anglo-Americanized as "French theory." Georges Bataille, who died too early to become a physical presence in the Parisian intellectual culture of the 1960s, significantly influenced Lacan, Derrida, and Barthes, all of whom read, lectured, and wrote on his work as well as on one another's.

Though Pierre Bourdieu remained somewhat at the periphery of this more linguistically minded avant garde during the decade of the 1960s, his institutional affiliations with the Lacanians and the Tel Quel group were always strong, and he more than once credited Bataille's sociological writings on sacrifice and community with inspiring some of his own earliest critical insights.[1] A classmate

1. See the comments in Champagne, *Georges Bataille,* 94.

of Derrida's at the École Normale Supérieure, Bourdieu returned to France in 1960 after years studying and practicing ethnology in Algeria and, before that, serving in the French colonial army. After holding university positions in Paris and Lille, he joined the faculty of the École pratique des hautes études in 1964, becoming there a colleague of Fernand Braudel and Jacques Le Goff and arriving just as Barthes was beginning his seminar in ancient and premodern rhetoric. Though always seeking opportunities for collaborative inquiry and authorship, Bourdieu in many ways typified the institutional centralization of the elite French intellectual culture he would spend a good portion of his later career diagnosing: a centralization that of course did much to unify the archaeological field of the 1960s avant garde despite the movement's innovatory rhetoric.[2]

This chapter is intended to serve as a brief critical introduction to Appendix II, Bourdieu's afterword or *postface* to his 1967 French translation of Erwin Panofsky's *Gothic Architecture and Scholasticism*.[3] As I will suggest, the *postface* represents a strangely isolated piece of Bourdieu's intellectual production, a hallmark of the same autodidactical eclecticism that led him to take on such a bewildering range of social and political phenomena as subjects of intensive research (the Algerian peasantry, the French educational system in which he taught, bourgeois photography, and so on). Even within the context of this eclecticism, though, the Panofsky project seems unduly eccentric; perhaps as a result it has remained largely unexamined by all but the most exhaustive of Bourdieu's commentators, and even they have given it no more than cursory treatment.[4] Published in 1967, Bourdieu's translation of Panofsky appeared in the wake of his four monographs on Algeria and his collaborative book on photography, *Un art moyen* (1965); the *postface* was one of his longest critical writings preceding *Reproduction in Education, Society, and Culture* (1970) and *Outline of a Theory of Practice* (1972), the two monographs that would establish his reputation beyond the disciplines of anthropology and sociology. The Panofsky *postface* thus appeared at

---

2. On Bourdieu's institutional and intellectual affiliation with structuralism during this period, see Dosse, *History of Structuralism*, 2: 70–75.

3. Bourdieu, "*Postface*." Though eccentric, the translation did not go unnoticed by Bourdieu's wider avant-garde coterie; Michel Foucault's review of the translation and of Panofsky's work in general was published as "Les mots et les images."

4. Certeau, *The Practice of Everyday Life*, 215, evokes Bourdieu's reworking of Panofsky's *habitus* as one among many "indices for a possible reading, in contemporary technocracy, of a return to the medieval order"; see also Lefebvre, *The Production of Space*, 257–58; Schinkel, "Pierre Bourdieu's Political Turn?" 75; Dianteill, "Pierre Bourdieu et la religion: Synthèse critique d'un synthèse critique," 5–7; and Swartz, *Culture and Power*, 101–2.

something of a turning point in Bourdieu's career, shortly after his appointment to the EPHE and just before his founding of the Centre de Sociologie Européenne.

As anyone's reading of the *postface* will corroborate, moreover, Bourdieu's seemingly one-off Panofskian medievalism had a crucial bearing on the subsequent development of his critical lexicon, and in particular on the formation of that most quintessentially Bourdieuan term, the *habitus*. For it is here, in the obscure translator's afterword to a long essay written by another, that Bourdieu develops for the first time what will become his central theoretical category for relating human subjects to the forces, histories, and structures that determine their forms of life and thought. The Panofsky *postface* does much to explain what this fourth declension Latin noun formed on the perfect passive participle of *habeo, habere* is doing at the center of one of the most influential sociological projects of the twentieth century. In Bourdieu's own words, Panofsky "developed a preexisting concept to account for the effect of scholastic thought," a concept that would thereafter be stripped of its medieval indigeneity to become a working dimension of Bourdieu's social criticism.[5]

It should be acknowledged here that Bourdieu himself would have disdained the empirical search for intellectual and lexical origins pursued in this chapter (and indeed throughout this book as a whole) as a conservative impulse antithetical to his own critical aims, if not outright pernicious. In a 1986 essay treating the genesis of the concepts of *habitus* and field, he distanced himself with barely disguised contempt from what he termed "theoretical theory," and in particular from its love of genealogy: "it never seemed to me that it is indispensable to trace the genealogy of concepts which, not having been born of theoretical parthenogenesis, don't gain much by being resituated in relation to previous usages."[6] In a late work, *Pascalian Meditations* (1997), he went further, condemning "the theoreticist derealization associated with the scholastic view of the *lector*." This was a habit Bourdieu particularly associated with those critics who attempt to trace "sterile genealogies" of theoretical vocabularies "so as to gloss them, by relating them to other texts," rather than actually applying the concepts in question "in order to do something with them, to bring them, as useful, perfectible instruments, into a practical use."[7] In this chapter, then, which supplements Bour-

---

5. Bourdieu, *In Other Words*, 12.

6. Bourdieu, "The Genesis of the Concepts of *Habitus* and of *Field*," 12.

7. Bourdieu, *Pascalian Meditations*, 61–62: "The lector's reading strives to find sources, always partial, often imaginary . . . with the intention, so typical of *academica mediocritas*, of explaining the

dieu's earliest conception of the *habitus* with a number of contextualizing observations regarding its affiliations and mode of explication, I will not pretend to be allowing the *postface* to "speak for itself" even as I violate its author's critical sensibilities. Instead, I hope readers will agree that the risk of such a violation may be worth the reward of making this text newly available and at least somewhat comprehensible to Bourdieu's posthumous audience.

Principium importans ordinem ad actum: *Erwin Panofsky*

Accompanying Bourdieu's French translation of Erwin Panofsky's *Gothic Architecture and Scholasticism* was a thirty-two-page *"Postface"* or epilogue, which presents Bourdieu's extended reflections on Panofsky's contributions to the sociology of knowledge. In the *postface*, Bourdieu engages in a critical contextualization of Panofsky's work within a tradition of "historical totality" embracing the sociology of Max Weber and the art history of Emile Mâle. (For convenience's sake, in what follows I simply refer readers to the appended translation rather than footnoting each individual citation of the *postface*.) What Panofsky has done, Bourdieu argues, is to initiate in our time a "history of sensibilities," a study of visual culture that transcends the "methodological circle" (also a "vicious circle" for Bourdieu) that traditional iconophilic art history continually traverses. Again, though his work up to this point had been directed primarily toward a number of anthropological monographs on the Algerian peasantry, Bourdieu's knowledge of medieval art history far exceeds what one would expect from an interloping dilettante. The *postface* finds Bourdieu reading diligently in the relevant art-historical bibliography, including the work of Robert Branner, Emile Mâle, Louis Grodecki, and Jean Bony, as well as more general works in medieval religion and philosophy, including studies by Gordon Leff and Martin Grabmann. In order to prepare and annotate his translation responsibly, he studied and absorbed Panofsky's major methodological statements in such works as *Iconography and Iconology* and *Meaning in the Visual Arts,*

---

unknown in terms of the already known, the academic variant of the slogan 'nothing new under the sun,' a favourite theme of conservative thought, and of demonstrating that 'known' authors are, like everyone else, simply readers of other known authors. (I am thinking of those who have applied themselves to cataloguing the earlier uses of the notion of *habitus*, not with a view to showing the originality of the latest usage—though that usage is the principle of their intervention—but with the aim of destroying it . . .)."

read numerous reviews of his work, and corresponded with the German art historian on a number of occasions.[8]

Gothic Architecture and Scholasticism began life as the 1948 Wimmer Lecture at the Benedictine St. Vincent College in Latrobe, Pennsylvania, and was published three years later as a short book copyrighted by the Archabbey of St. Vincent. Though known as a scholar of iconography, an expert on Low Countries book illustration, and a prolific generalist in early European art history (medieval, Renaissance, and baroque alike), Panofsky achieved some of his greatest renown in international humanistic circles for this pamphlet-length, speculative set of musings on the "connection between Gothic art and Scholasticism," a connection "more concrete than a mere 'parallelism' and yet more general than those individual (and very important) 'influences' which are inevitably exerted on painters, sculptors, or architects by erudite advisers."[9] Between about 1130 and 1270, Panofsky argued, this "astonishingly synchronous development" determined the very *modus operandi* of Gothic architecture: not so much in the theological content it reflected (the domain of the "representational arts" rather than architecture), but in the "peculiar method of procedure" that distinguished scholasticism as an intellectual practice (28). Like scholasticism on parchment, the Gothic cathedral sought to write in stone "a permanent peace treaty between faith and reason" (28–29), a treaty promoting two fundamental tenets. The first was *manifestatio,* or the "postulate of clarification for clarification's sake" (35), exemplified in the subdividing and other organizing schemes of the classic theological *summa* and in the "progressive divisibility," the explicit revelation of function, characterizing the Gothic style. For the "man imbued with the Scholastic habit," Panofksy avowed, "the panoply of shafts, ribs, buttresses, tracery, pinnacles and crockets was a self-analysis and self-explication of architecture much as the customary apparatus of parts, distinctions, questions, and articles was, to him, a self-analysis and self-explication of reason" (59).

The second tenet of Panofsky's treaty between faith and reason was *concordantia,* or "the acceptance and ultimate reconciliation of contradictory possibilities" (64). If the scholastic theologians of the university sought to harmonize the conflicts they found between and among scrip-

---

8. Panofsky's correspondence with Bourdieu will likely be included in the edition of Panofsky's voluminous letters currently being prepared by Dieter Wuttke, of which three volumes have appeared or will shortly appear; see Panofsky, *Korrespondenz 1910–1968: Eine kommentierte Auswahl in fünf Bänden.*

9. Panofsky, *Gothic Architecture and Scholasticism,* 20; references hereafter will be given parenthetically in the text.

tural citations and the *auctoritates* who first interpreted them (through the "technique of reconciling the seemingly irreconcilable"), the architects of the High Gothic cathedrals worked according to the same principles of reconciliation in order to solve the many structural and aesthetic "problems" (following the practice of the medieval *summa*, Panofsky actually calls them *quaestiones*) bequeathed to them by the *auctoritas* embodied in the "great structures of the past" (69). More than a stale Hegelianism, the habit of mind inspiring the architectural practice of this period was a direct counterpart to the rigorous quodlibetal debates and dialogical structures providing the framework for scholastic theology. In Panofsky's memorable concluding sentence, "Scholastic dialectics has driven architectural thinking to a point where it almost ceased to be architectural" (88).

At the time Pierre Bourdieu began translating *Gothic Architecture and Scholasticism* in the mid-1960s, the so-called Panofsky Thesis had already come in for some heavy criticism, much of it concerned with modifying, correcting, or rejecting outright the speculative elegance of his argument by focusing on particular architectural examples that belied his often sweeping claims.[10] Though his Wimmer Lecture would become a staple of undergraduate courses in English and American universities, few professional art historians now count it among his most important contributions to the field. What was it about *Gothic Architecture and Scholasticism*, then, that inspired Bourdieu to take a medievalist break from his sociological inquiries and work so exhaustively in an unfamiliar field, one that he would have had to learn practically from scratch? The translation project may have been provoked in some way by Bourdieu's more general interest in visual culture during these years, as exemplified in such coauthored books as *Un art moyen* (1964), an inquiry into the nature of bourgeois photography as an affirmative practice of mass culture; and *The Love of Art* (1966), a collective sociological study of European art museums and their construction of the public.

As the *postface* makes clear, a more compelling explanation for Bourdieu's sudden interest in Panofsky lies in the art historian's own analytic negotiation between the individual "creator" and the scholastic *habitus*. Though the architects and designers responsible for the great Gothic cathedrals were surely creative and even ingenious as individuals, their creativity cannot be separated from the forms and dispositions of a

---

10. See the reviews of the book cited in Bourdieu's *postface* in Appendix II. On Panofsky's broader significance to twentieth-century art history and philosophy of art, see Lavin, ed., *Meaning in the Visual Arts;* Ferretti, *Cassirer, Panofsky, and Warburg: Symbol, Art, and History;* Holly, *Panofsky and the Foundations of Art History;* and the Festschrift edited by Meiss, *Essays in Honor of Erwin Panofsky.*

collective unconscious that produced it—or, as Bourdieu puts it in the *postface:*

To contrast individuality with community so as better to safeguard the rights of creative individuality and the mystery of individual creation is to forego discovering community at the very heart of individuality in the form of culture—in the subjective sense
of *cultivation* or *Bildung*—or, to speak the language used by Panofsky, in the form of
the *habitus* through which the creator partakes of his community and time, and that
guides and directs, unbeknownst to him, his apparently most unique creative acts.

A thorough survey of Bourdieu's 1960s writings reveals that this passage
contains his first extended working definition of the term *habitus,* which
he here adapts directly from Panofsky's own numerous references to
the medieval "habit of mind" that enabled the interpenetrating influences of scholastic philosophy and Gothic architecture in the twelfth
and thirteenth centuries.[11] Panofsky justifies his own examination of the
scholastic-Gothic relation in the analytic language of scholasticism itself, and specifically in a passage from the *Summa theologiæ* of St. Thomas
Aquinas:

In contrast to a mere parallelism, the connection which I have in mind is a genuine
cause-and-effect relation; but in contrast to an individual influence, this cause-and-
effect relation comes about by diffusion rather than by direct impact. It comes about
by the spreading of what may be called, for want of a better term, a mental habit—
reducing this overworked cliché to its precise Scholastic sense as a "principle that regulates the act," *principium importans ordinem ad actum.* Such mental habits are at work
in all and every civilization. (21)

The Latin phrase comes from *Summa theologiæ* I-II, question 49, article 3,
paragraph c, where Aquinas is exploring the nature of *habitus* as "principles of action," as potentialities with respect to the operational disposition of the subject (*Summa theologiæ* I-II q. 49 art. 3c). Aquinas devotes
two dozen articles of the *Summa* to various questions concerning *habitus*
and their capacities: their subject; their cause; their increase, decrease,
and corruption; their multiple nature within human communities.[12]
Panofsky is thus finding within the precise intellectual milieu he examines the terminology necessary for understanding its most deeply en-

11. Bourdieu had used the term in earlier writings, though without development (Swartz, *Culture and Power,* 100).
12. See the numerous relevant entries in Deferrari and Barry, *A Lexicon of St. Thomas Aquinas,*
477–480.

grained principles. Gothic architecture and scholasticism are united not only in their forms of organization and harmonization, but in their *habitus,* the disposition that regulates the mental and bodily actions of their medieval practitioners. When Bourdieu elects in the *postface* "to speak the language used by Panofsky," then, he speaks the language of scholasticism, which provides him, through Panofsky, with a term and an idea that will suffuse his analytic lexicon for the next thirty years.

Bourdieu's frank acknowledgment of this particular conceptual debt may come as a surprise to many of his readers, accustomed as we generally are to affiliating Bourdieu's *habitus* with the earlier inquiries of Marcel Mauss, whose own precedents for the term included a long list of philosophers and social theorists, from Kant to Hegel to Weber to Durkheim.[13] Mauss's most direct statement on his methodological enlistment of the *habitus* occurs in a chapter entitled "Body Techniques," which appeared in his influential 1934 collection *Sociologie et anthropologie.* Devoted to exploring "the ways in which, from society to society, men know how to use their bodies," the chapter proposes a series of approaches to those everyday bodily activities—digging, marching, running, swimming, exercising, and so on—pushed outside the purview of traditional ethnology as somewhat embarrassing "miscellaneous" activities. Even the simplest bodily dispositions and behaviors change from one society to another, Mauss observes; thus, the corporeal *habitus* is inherently social in nature:

Hence, I have had this notion of the social nature of the habitus for many years. Please note that I use the Latin word—it should be understood in France—"*habitus.*" The word translates infinitely better than "*habitude*" (habit or custom), the "*exis,*" the "acquired ability" and "faculty" of Aristotle (he was a psychologist). It does not designate those metaphysical *habitudes,* that mysterious memory, the subject of volumes or short and famous theses. These "habits" do not vary just with individuals and their imitations; they vary especially between societies, educations, properties and fashions, types of prestige. In them, we should see the techniques and the work of the collective and individual practical reason rather than, in ordinary ways, merely the soul and its repetitive faculties.[14]

As Bourdieu will later argue in *The Logic of Practice,* this particular view of the *habitus* leaves the ethnologist caught in the trap of a prestruc-

---

13. A very useful historical overview of the "pre-history" of the sociological *habitus* before Bourdieu can be found in Camic, "The Matter of Habit."

14. Mauss, "Techniques of the Body," 458.

turalist ethnography. Mauss's classic study *The Gift*, for example, found its author "placing himself at the level of a 'phenomenology' of gift exchange," as Lévi-Strauss had also observed; yet in order to comprehend the concrete instantiations of the *habitus* in any given society, the science that studies it "must break with native experience and the native theory of that experience."[15] Mauss's confidence in the modes of "collective and individual practical reason" constituting the social life of human societies, by contrast, corrodes the Maussian *habitus* with the fallacy of self-consciousness.

Far from a knowing manifestation of "practical reason," for Bourdieu the *habitus* should be understood as both a "feel for the game" shared by those living within a certain cultural moment or sphere, and a collective disposition that in turn generates social practices, modes of human subjection, and symbolic forms. As a paradigm of social analysis, it has been argued, the *habitus* allowed Bourdieu to elude both the objectivist models offered by the structuralist anthropology of Lévi-Strauss and the extreme subjectivism found within the phenomenology of Merleau-Ponty. As he writes in *The Logic of Practice*, it provides a system of "principles which generate and organize practices and representations . . . without presupposing a conscious aiming at ends or an express mastery of the operations necessary in order to attain them."[16]

The Iconology of Knowledge

None of this is to deny Mauss's influence on Bourdieu's critical practice and lexicon; Bourdieu cites Mauss with an admiring regularity throughout his career. In fact, it is precisely the intellectual pressure of Mauss and his ethnological legacy on Bourdieu's generation that renders all the more surprising the rhetoric of intellectual indebtedness that suffuses the *postface*. It would be hard to exaggerate Bourdieu's enthusiasm for Panofsky's theoretical contributions to the sociology of knowledge, his perceived negotiation between subjectivism and objectivism, between the individual creator and the cultural collectivity. If traditional iconography is satisfied with the easy discernment of the symbols transparently embedded in the historical artifact, Panofsky insists that the "intrinsic meaning of the work" will emerge only from extensive historical inves-

15. Bourdieu, *The Logic of Practice*, 98.
16. Bourdieu, *The Logic of Practice*, 53.

tigation drawing on "the largest possible number of cultural documents historically connected with this work or group of works." What Panofsky offers, too, is an escape from intentionalism. "It is not the crowds who create, but the individuals," the great historian of medieval art Emile Mâle had said in a gnomic fallacy cited by Bourdieu; for Panfosky, by contrast, the medieval work of art is anything but a "mere allegory," the "sensory translation of a concept or an 'iconographical program.'" This gravely mistaken assumption about the meaning of the artwork "would boil down to the conscious intention of its creator: it would not convey anything that its author had not expressly meant to convey, or meant for it to convey." And the "epistemologically founded intuition of iconological science" as practiced by Panofsky, Bourdieu insists, has nothing to do with the "hasty and uncontrolled intuition of intuitionism," which conjures its totalities from the mystical realm of hunch and suspicion.[17] In a revealing analogy, Bourdieu goes so far as to assert that "iconological interpretation . . . is to iconography what ethnology is to ethnography."

More than an iconologist, though, Bourdieu's Panofsky is a sociologist of knowledge and a cultural critic of the first order. Like Durkheim and Mauss with their attention to "primitive forms of classification," but with a vastly greater analytic acuity, Panofsky teaches the human sciences how to uncover the meaning-generating core of cultural production:

Panofsky shows that culture is not just a common code, or even a common repertoire of answers to common problems, or a set of particular and particularized forms of thought, but rather a whole body of fundamental schemes, assimilated beforehand, which generate, according to an art of invention similar to that of musical writing, an infinite number of particular schemes, directly applied to particular situations. This *habitus* could be defined, by analogy with Noam Chomsky's "generative grammar," as a system of internalized schemes which have the capacity to generate all the thoughts, perceptions, and actions characteristic of a culture, and nothing else. What Panofsky is trying to draw from these concrete and particular discourses that Gothic cathedrals or general theological summas represent is perhaps, at the end of the day, this "interior form," to speak the language of Wilhelm von Humboldt, that is to say the *modus operandi,* capable of generating both the thoughts of the theologian and the schemes of the architect, that founds the unity of thirteenth-century civilization.

17. By "intuitionism" Bourdieu is likely referring to Bergsonism, the subject of Deleuze's widely read and at the time hot-off-the-presses *Le Bergsonisme* (1966).

The invocation of Chomsky in this passage is particularly suggestive, implying as it does an innate *habitus* structured into the biological inheritance of a given society without risking the full determinism of Chomskian generative grammar.[18] Later in the *postface,* Bourdieu pushes this analogy further, imputing to the *habitus* an almost biological propensity to generate the diction and syntax of human behavior, "as if the *habitus,* this grammar that generates behaviors, tended to produce all the concrete sentences whose virtuality it contains, and that no conscious program, especially if imposed from the outside, would ever be able to fully predict."

Bourdieu becomes most direct about his methodological and conceptual debt to Panofsky during an extended discussion of a 1963 article by the French paleographer Robert Marichal.[19] Here the *habitus* appears to connote what the Annalistes would call the *mentalité* of the medieval scribe, the unknowing will to obey within a scribal system of temporal and spatial organization. The Marichal article, published in a volume titled *L'Écriture et la psychologie des peuples,* sought to apply Panofsky's famous theory of division, clarity, and "manifest design" in the Gothic cathedral to the labor of the medieval scribe, who, following the university masters themselves, repeated the same tendency to divide and subdivide the material product of his work to reveal the underlying habitual logic of reconciliation beneath. As Marichal asks, "When a scribe has copied this pattern some ten thousand times, how could he not, however absent-minded or stubborn as one may like to imagine him, have acquired the habit of thus conducting his own thought?" Bourdieu's extended citation of this Panofsky-inspired essay clarifies the act of large-scale intellectual borrowing that marked his initial appropriation of the *habitus* into his own theoretical lexicon:

Marichal's analysis reveals not only how, in the copyist's daily activity, the *habitus,* defined by the interiorization of the principles of clarification and reconciliation of contraries, is constituted, but also how this *habitus* is concretely actualized in the specific logic of a particular practice:

> It can be assumed that the "masters" collaborated with the booksellers in the elaboration of a bookish architecture that so clearly "showed" their thought processes, but the booksellers and the copyists are imbued with the same methods: within the sentence, they carried the "division" of the text to the smallest logically conceivable unit by separating words from each other permanently . . . to the point of re-creating veri-

---

18. See Swartz, *Culture and Power,* 102.
19. Marichal, "L'Écriture latine et la civilisation occidentale du Ier au XVIe siècle."

table ideograms. What is more—and it is most unlikely that the "masters" intervened in these technical details—within the very words, inside each letter, prompted by an inveterate habitus, *they highlighted irreducible elements: the Gothic break, indeed, "divides" the letter while "composing" it. To substitute one or several acute angles for a curve is to decompose a movement into its "elementary" stages as do military rules for the use of weapons.*

The citation from Marichal in this passage occurs near the end of a series of extended quotations from the paleographer's 1963 article over six pages of Bourdieu's thirty-two-page *postface*. Bourdieu was clearly taken with this extension of the Panofsky thesis into the realm of writing practices, and Marichal seems to have inspired his speculative turn in the second half of the *postface* toward the generative capacities of the *habitus* beyond its immediate institutional domain.

Yet Bourdieu's extensive borrowing from Marichal at this point is confusing on several levels, and here it may be worth risking a bit of editorial pedantry in order to clarify its implications for the rhetoric of the *postface* as a whole. The longest quotation from the article begins in the middle of one of Bourdieu's paragraphs with the sentence "Anybody who has once opened any *Summa* has noticed that the author always took great care in leading his readers from proposition to proposition and in enabling him to have present in his mind the progression of his reasonings" (on page 154 in the original *postface*); it concludes three pages later with an observation about filigreed initials and their organizing attractiveness to the reader's eye. The four full paragraphs constituting the bulk of this quotation are not indented, nor are they set off from Bourdieu's prose with quotation marks signaling the continuity of the citation.[20] Without tracing back very carefully over the punctuation of this quotation (only a portion of which I have included here, and which represents several pages of Marichal's original article), one would have to take the following paragraphs as Bourdieu's own observations on the visual *habitus* of medieval Latin manuscripts:

[I]f an uninformed reader compares a manuscript from the ninth, tenth, or eleventh centuries, a beautiful manuscript, it goes without saying, of a work in prose, to a manuscript equally as neat of the *Summa theologiæ,* he will have the impression, I think,

20. It is true that French academic publishing conventions in the 1960s differed from Anglo-American standards, and this could be a result of editorial carelessness at Minuit. I compared ten other books published by Minuit in the years surrounding Bourdieu's Panofsky translation, however, and found no other similar treatments of extended quotations from contemporary scholarly sources.

that the former is clearer and less daunting than the latter, and yet if he takes a closer look at them, he will notice that the latter enables one to follow the author's thought much better.

In the manuscripts of the ninth, tenth and eleventh centuries, he will find sometimes a full page, sometimes two compact columns, without any white space; no division, a punctuation blended in the text; discrete capital letters that do not stop the gaze, even if, at a few major breaks, they stick out slightly in the margin; in short, a layout that is remarkably regular, dense, and yet attractive, open thanks to the delicate handwriting, the independent letters and the large space between the lines. The page has the cold elegance and the beautiful trappings of those large blind arcades of the steeple of the Abbaye-aux-hommes, in Caen, or those "Lombard stripes" on the façade of Marmoutier. It is, as it were, this "impenetrable space" that the Romanesque edifice represents; in no way does it express the order of discourse.

Admittedly, a few, less numerous, manuscripts, as well as some technical books (Cicero's *Partitiones,* for instance) that are sometimes in the form of dialogues, such as the *De Oratore,* also by Cicero, present, like our modern printed books, pages divided into small paragraphs whose last line is more or less blank. They are easy to read and even study.

What is most provocative about the inclusion of this sloppily punctuated citation is the tone of archaeological authority it lends to Bourdieu's explication of Panofsky. Like Lacan with his invocation of a phantom manuscript of Andreas Capellanus, Bourdieu in the *postface* enlists medieval manuscripts for the prestige they lend to his broader theoretical explication (and reproduces them visually as well: Bourdieu includes several manuscript plates that illustrate the unconscious obedience of the scribe to the Gothic *habitus*—all of which have been poorly reproduced from Marichal's article in their original order, though without shelf-marks).[21] Most readers of the *postface* since its publication in 1967 have thus received the impression (as I did until working through it sentence by sentence) that Bourdieu himself had performed the archival work necessary to extend Panofsky's thesis to the domain of codicology, unearthing just the manuscripts necessary to demonstrate the inherence of the Gothic-scholastic *habitus* in the collective unconscious of medieval scribal culture.

As Bourdieu clearly recognized, Marichal's Panofskian choice of this term was particularly appropriate for the twelfth- and thirteenth-century context he was analyzing, for *habitus* appears ubiquitously in the

21. See Marichal, "L'Écriture latine," esp. 238–39.

period's theology as a term denoting the disposition of a human subject within a field of moral, intellectual, or social practice. Again, Aquinas himself employs the term hundreds of times and in a range of argumentative contexts, from the *habitus intellectus,* the habitual knowledge of first principles, and the *habitus iustitiae,* the moral virtue of rendering to each his due, to the *habitus politicus,* the disposition within public life, and the *habitus factivus,* productive human practice directed to useful activity which results in some exterior work.[22] We find the same term employed in much the way Bourdieu intends it in monastic customals from the eleventh century onward, where it connotes the whole system of clerical rules, bodily disciplines, temporal regulations, and other "structures of feeling" (in Raymond Williams's loosely related term) that embrace the individual and communal life of the liturgical institution. In Middle English, the sartorial "habit" is often indistinguishable from the more generalized "habit" that connotes a subject's corporeal, mental, or moral condition. There are numerous instances in which writers deliberately seem to be conflating the two, as in the Wycliffite "Of feigned contemplative life," which rails against "thes ypocritis that han rentes and worldly lordischipis and parische chirches approprid to hem ayenst holy writt . . . for sytynkynge gronyngys and abite of holynesse"; or the opening lines of *Piers Plowman:*

In a somer seson, whan softe was the sonne,
I shoop me into shroudes as I a sheep were,
In habite as an heremite unholy of werkes.[23]

Will begins his journey "In habite as an heremite," in the habit or dress of a hermit, initiating an eremitical discourse that gains increasing purchase on the poem through the process of Langland's revisions.[24] Yet the eremitical "habit" that Langland's dreamer dons at the beginning of the prologue is also the eremetical *habitus:* a disposition, a form of subjection, a mode of relation to the dreamer's material and discursive world in which the dreamer bodily and intellectually participates as an agent but which he can never fully know as a subject.

In the *postface,* I have suggested here, we are witnessing Bourdieu's initial discernment of the *habitus.* From the scholarship of a medieval

22. Deferrari and Barry, *A Lexicon of St. Thomas Aquinas,* 477–480.
23. "Of feigned contemplative life," in Wycliffe, *The English Works,* 187–96; Langland, *Piers Plowman,* Prologue lines 1–2, 1.
24. See Hanna, "Will's Work."

paleographer working to assimilate Panofsky's theory into his own scholarship, Bourdieu adopts a term and an idea that will profoundly influence the course of his subsequent sociological writings for the next thirty years. In fact, the *habitus* as elaborated by Panofsky is almost too enchanting for Bourdieu, too ideal as a mode of critical inquiry into the historical milieu treated in *Gothic Architecture and Scholasticism.* As Bourdieu asks, "does not the philosophy of art that is implied in the notion of *habitus* as generative grammar adjust itself only too well, and therefore too exclusively, to those periods in which a style achieves its own perfection . . . ?" The medieval era, in other words, provides a kind of limiting case for the *habitus:* because the *habitus* as a model for critical social thought itself originates in the medieval context Panofsky analyzes, it feels somehow too "indigenous" to be useful as theory, a point Bourdieu makes more explicitly elsewhere.[25] Yet in Panofsky's hands, Bourdieu insists in his concluding sentences, the indigenizing pitfalls of the *habitus* become instead opportunities for a critical self-consciousness rivaled only by the greatest theoretical minds of the twentieth century:

[O]ne cannot help recalling a sentence from *Iconography and Iconology:* "The art historian differs from the 'naïve' spectator in that he is conscious of what he does." One should, Saussure wrote likewise, "show the linguist what he does," that is to say, as Emile Benveniste comments, highlight "what preliminary operations he engages in unconsciously when he tackles the linguistic facts." Just as much as and undoubtedly better than he did in the theoretical writings to which we have referred in order to justify our analysis of the epistemological presuppositions involved in this book, Erwin Panofsky reveals here, in a striking manner, that he can do what he does only on the condition that, at any given moment, he should know what he is doing and what it takes to be doing it, because both the most humble and the most noble scientific operations are worth the full value of the theoretical and epistemological conscience that accompanies these operations.

Bourdieu thus concludes this 1967 *postface* by likening Erwin Panofsky to Saussure and Benveniste, linguists who shared with this great art historian a methodological self-consciousness that allowed them, like Panofsky, to make explicit the *habitus* that guided their disciplines in the pursuit of knowledge.

---

25. Bourdieu, "Genesis of the Concepts of *Habitus* and of *Field.*"

Indigeneity

Despite its ancient lineage in classical writings and its twentieth-century deployment in Maussian sociology, then, the *habitus* as Bourdieu elaborates it derives from an intellectual genealogy rooted most strongly in the scholastic philosophy of the high Middle Ages. It is absorbed into Bourdieu's theoretical apparatus from the scholarship of medievalists whose work he was reading while translating one of the modern classics of medieval art history—and, in turn, from medieval lexicons favored by scholastic theologians and monastic writers in their own era. For Bourdieu, Panofsky's intellectual achievement in *Gothic Architecture and Scholasticism* was to take practices of cultural analysis beyond the exposure of homologies or structural similarities between social and aesthetic practices to a deeper, "antidisciplinary" understanding of the logic of cultural practice itself.[26] It is surely no accident that Bourdieu begins his remarks on *Gothic Architecture and Scholasticism* by lauding it as "undoubtedly one of those books that most effectively challenges positivism."

It was a challenge that Bourdieu would take up in writing his next book, which allows us to begin tracking what seem to be Panofsky's steadily declining fortunes over the course of Bourdieu's post-1967 oeuvre. The particular *habitus* unearthed by Panofsky, Bourdieu argues in the *postface,* is an excrescence of the medieval (and of course specifically French) schools, the institutional forebears of the contemporary Parisian academies that will figure so significantly in Bourdieu's subsequent sociological writings, from *Reproduction* to *Distinction* to the *Pascalian Meditations:*

Panofsky endeavors to discover the "concrete . . . connection" that will account, completely and concretely, for the logic and existence of these homologies. And, with this end in view, he is not content with invoking a "unitary vision of the world" or a "spirit of the time" and thus giving as an explanation the very phenomenon that needs to be explained, nor even the concrete individual—in this particular case, such-and-such architect—as the site for the coincidence or coexistence of structures, which often plays, in such a case, the role of refuge for ignorance. He offers the apparently most naïve explanation (simply perhaps because it takes some of their mystery from these correspondences). In a society in which the transmission of culture is monopolized by

26. On the resonances of "antidisciplinarity" among the 1960s French avant garde, see Mowitt, *Text: Genealogy of an Antidisciplinary Object.*

a school, the profound affinities that bind together human works (and, obviously, behaviors and thoughts) find their principle in the scholastic institution vested with the
function of transmitting, consciously and also, in part, unconsciously, a subconscious
knowledge, or, more exactly, of producing individuals endowed with this system of
subconscious (or deeply buried) schemes that constitute their culture or, better yet,
their *habitus;* in short, of transforming the collective heritage into an individual and
collective subconscious. To relate the works of a period with practices derived from a
school of thought is to give oneself one of the means to explain not only what they
claim, but also what they *betray* in so far as they partake of the symbolics of an epoch
and a society.

For Bourdieu, then, the homologies undergirding Panofsky's historical
thesis are the product of a univocal pedagogical apparatus. The medieval
university system that (on Bourdieu's view) "monopolize[s]" the "transmission of knowledge" also transmits a "collective heritage," in effect
creating individual and collective "subconsciousnesses" that will in turn
channel their knowledges into the façades, vaults, and piers of Gothic
cathedrals.

This emphasis in the *postface* on "school practices" importantly anticipates the pedagogical axioms outlined in the early chapters of *Reproduction in Education, Society, and Culture,* co-written with Jean-Claude
Passeron and published, like Bourdieu's Panofsky translation, by Minuit.
Here Bourdieu is concerned with assessing the productivity of what he
terms "pedagogic work," defined as "a process of inculcation which must
last long enough to produce a durable training, i.e. a *habitus,* the product of internalization of the principles of a cultural arbitrary capable of
perpetuating itself after [pedagogical authority] has ceased and thereby
of perpetuating in practices the principles of the internalized arbitrary."[27] In other words, once the institution embodying pedagogic authority loosens its hold on its subjects, "pedagogic work" will assume responsibility for the generation of *habitus,* internalizing mechanisms that
will ensure the subsequent reproduction of the authorizing "arbitrary"
in the practices of everyday life. The "specific productivity" of pedagogic
work will in turn be measured "by the degree to which the habitus it produces is *transposable,* i.e. capable of generating practices conforming
with the principles of the inculcated arbitrary in a greater number of different fields."[28] It is just this transposability of the *habitus* from field to

27. Bourdieu and Passeron, *Reproduction in Education, Society, and Culture,* 31.
28. Bourdieu and Passeron, *Reproduction in Education, Society, and Culture,* 33.

field that lends it a particular usefulness in cultural analysis, as Bourdieu's explanatory "gloss" on this axiom suggests: "Thus, the hold of a religious power is measured by the degree to which the habitus produced by the PW [pedagogic work] of the corresponding pedagogic agencies generates practices conforming with the inculcated arbitrary in areas remote from those expressly regulated by doctrine, such as economic conduct or political choices. Similarly, the 'habit-forming force' (Panofsky) of Scholastic education may be seen in the effects it produces in the structure of the medieval cathedral or the graphical layout of manuscripts."[29]

Reproduction appeared in 1970, and in this book Panofsky maintains his status as a generator of cultural theory, *Gothic Architecture and Scholasticism* remaining an exemplary text in the articulation of innovative antidisciplinary analysis. Two years later, by the time Bourdieu comes to publish his *Outline of a Theory of Practice,* Panofsky has been reduced to a whipping-boy for art-worshipping empiricism. In the book's opening paragraphs, Bourdieu indicts the "practical privilege in which all scientific activity arises" as resulting in large part from "neglect of the social conditions in which science is possible." This "epistemological choice" constitutes a devastating refusal to account for the critic's institutional and intellectual locatedness, a refusal nowhere more evident, Bourdieu bafflingly contends in the book's opening pages, than in the writings of art historians such as Panofsky:

It is instructive to glance at the case of art history, which, never having really broken with the tradition of the *amateur,* gives free rein to celebratory contemplation and finds in the sacred character of its object every pretext for a hagiographic hermeneutics superbly indifferent to the question of the social conditions in which works are produced and circulate. Panofsky, for example, writing on Abbot Suger and the "invention" of Gothic architecture, only exceptionally and almost accidentally abandons the point of view of the interpreter who, more concerned with the *opus operatum* than the *modus operandi,* represses the question of artistic production under the concept of the "objective intention" of the work and reduces immediate comprehension to a decoding that is unaware that it *is* a decoding.[30]

Panofsky's *Gothic Architecture and Scholasticism* now symptomatizes an anthropological mentality "condemned to adopt unwittingly . . . the

---

29. Bourdieu and Passeron, *Reproduction in Education, Society, and Culture,* 34.
30. Bourdieu, *Outline of a Theory of Practice,* 1.

representation of action which is forced on agents or groups when they lack practical mastery of a highly valued competence."[31] In the *Outline*, Bourdieu finds Panofsky "more concerned with the *opus operatum* than the *modus operandi*," more invested in the conscious intention of the artist (the *operator*) than the workings of the *habitus*. Yet just five years earlier in the *postface*, Bourdieu had enthusiastically credited Panofsky with discerning precisely this "*modus operandi*, capable of generating both the thoughts of the theologian and the schemes of the architect, which founds the unity of thirteenth-century civilization."[32]

While nothing in Bourdieu's writings directly explains this puzzling reversal vis-à-vis the argument of *Gothic Architecture and Scholasticism*, its ambivalence should hardly surprise us. Bourdieu wrestled throughout his career with what he understood as the objectification of his own critical vocabulary by his critics and followers alike: the meta-analytic solipsism that would come to form one of the most recognizable aspects of "theory" as it emerged from the writings of the avant garde to become a "programmatic discourse which is its own end," as he put it in a 1985 essay treating the "genesis" of the concepts of *habitus* and of field.[33] It is here that Bourdieu became most explicit about just what he was up to in translating Panofsky and adapting his art-historical vocabulary to his own sociological ends. "I introduced this notion [of *habitus*]," Bourdieu explains, "on the occasion of the publication in French of two articles by Panofsky which up to that point had never been looked at together; one on gothic architecture where the word *habitus* was used as an 'indigenous' concept, to explain the effect of scholastic thinking in the area of architecture, the other article on the abbot Suger, where one could also make it work." This lexical intervention was meant in a contemporary spirit of revisionism, Bourdieu claims, and indeed as a deliberate reaction "against structuralism and its odd philosophy of action which, implicit in the Levi-Straussian notion of the unconscious, was expressed in all clarity among Althusserians, with their agent reduced to the role of bearer—*Träger*—of the structure."[34] Given Bourdieu's oft-cited specification of *habitus* as "structuring structures," this retrospective disavowal of structuralism rings somewhat false: the language of high structuralism clearly suffuses the 1967 *postface*, and there is no reason to think that (at

---

31. Bourdieu, *Outline of a Theory of Practice*, 2.
32. Contrast here Bourdieu's remarks in *Language and Symbolic Power*, 166, which (if I am taking the antecedents correctly) put Panofsky back in the *opus operatum* camp.
33. Bourdieu, "Genesis of the Concepts of *Habitus* and of *Field*," 11.
34. Bourdieu, "Genesis of the Concepts of *Habitus* and of *Field*," 13. See also Bourdieu, *In Other Words: Essays Towards a Reflexive Sociology*, 12–13.

the time, at least) Bourdieu perceived in *Gothic Architecture and Scholasticism* a means of coherent resistance to an intellectual movement in which he himself played such a central role during the mid-1960s.

Moreover, before *Gothic Architecture and Scholasticism* could become theoretically useful for Bourdieu, Panofsky himself had to be "remov[ed] . . . from the neo-Kantian philosophy of 'symbolic forms,' in which he had remained imprisoned (even if to do it meant taking a rather forced advantage of the use, unique in his work, that he made there of the notion of *habitus*)."[35] For Bourdieu, then, the enlistment of the Panofskian *habitus* demanded a strict segregation of Panofsky from the philosophy of symbolic forms engendered by his University of Hamburg colleague Ernst Cassirer, whose neo-Kantianism led to what Bourdieu clearly regarded as an idealization of the work of art as a dialectical resolution of intention and materiality. What Bourdieu found most provocative in Panofsky instead were those forms of apperception (which Panofsky, years earlier, had termed the "connection of perceptions") that transform the artistic field itself into a visual archaeology merging past and present in a process of cultural interiorization.[36] If the *postface*, Bourdieu's mini-outline of a theory of practice, develops a "rather forced" version of the *habitus* based on Panofsky's grounding of certain speculative homologies in the language of high scholasticism, its ascription to *Gothic Architecture and Scholasticism* of such boundless insight regarding the social status of art signals once again what Bourdieu perceived as the power of medievalist indigeneity in its avant-garde capacity as cultural critique.

35. Bourdieu, "Genesis of the Concepts of *Habitus* and of *Field*," 13.
36. On the neo-Kantianism of Panofsky and its relationship to the work of Cassirer, see Sylvia Ferretti, *Cassirer, Panofsky, and Warburg*, 182.

FOUR

Gothic Invention: Liturgy, History, *Of Grammatology*

But we are already speaking Latin.

JACQUES DERRIDA, "FAITH AND KNOWLEDGE"

Pierre Bourdieu's translation of Panofsky appeared in 1967 from Les Éditions de Minuit, the Parisian publisher that had by then become a virtual clearinghouse for postwar avant-garde writings. Minuit specialized in critical and formal experimentalism to such an extent that the house became known during the 1960s as the Vatican of the Nouveau Roman, perhaps second only to Seuil (the principal publisher of Philippe Sollers and Roland Barthes) in its sponsorship of the urban theoretical subculture centered around *Tel Quel, Critique,* and other leading avant-gardiste journals.[1] Also included in Minuit's catalogues in 1967 was one of the first three books of Jacques Derrida, *De la Grammatologie,* which was intended to complement his other two books published that year (*L'Écriture et la différence,* a collection of previously published essays, and *La Voix et le phénomène,* an intricate study of Husserl that Spivak has termed "a philosophical companion-text to the study of Rousseau in Part II of the Grammatology").[2] While they shared the same avant-garde publisher, however, Bourdieu's Panofsky project and Derrida's *Of Grammatology* appear remote from one

1. See the discussion in Ffrench, *The Time of Theory,* 50–51.
2. Spivak, preface to Derrida, *Of Grammatology,* liv.

another in style, genre, and motivation: the one a translation of a modest tract by a medieval art historian accompanied by a short critical epilogue, the other a massive and parasitic critique of the metaphysics of presence in Western thought from Plato to Lévi-Strauss. Yet the insights elaborated in these two books work toward ultimately complementary ends, engendering an archaeology of the premodern that both Bourdieu and Derrida discern specifically within the sacred sounds and spaces of liturgy. If Bourdieu's *postface* uncovers the hidden structures generating the philosophical and architectural *habitus* of Gothic cathedrals, *Of Grammatology* devotes some of its most illuminating pages to the "Gothic" liturgies that breathed musical and spiritual life into their cavernous depths.

This chapter takes as its focus a certain medievalism developed largely in the second half of *Of Grammatology*. An inconspicuous yet momentous part of the book's argument, Derrida's medievalism aims to dismantle the theological scaffoldings of Enlightenment historicism, and in particular the Rousseauist fantasy of a Dark Age of linguistic barbarism. I emphasize the theological here and throughout this discussion in order to highlight the long-neglected centrality of religion to *Of Grammatology*, a text largely overlooked in the awakening of interest in Derridean religiosity among scholars such as Kevin Hart, Mark Taylor, and John Caputo. Despite the *cordon sanitaire* of secularism that the dominant tradition of Derridean scholarship has constructed around the philosopher's oeuvre, these and other commentators have demonstrated the many forms taken by Derrida's enduring concern with the sacred and the theological.[3] Derrida's most prevalent mode of speaking of divinity is avoidant, a habit of unsaying that has led many to associate the deconstructive project with the tradition of apophatic theology. In his own most explicit pronouncement on the subject, "How to Avoid Speaking: Denials" (1987), Derrida accounts for his alleged affiliation with negative theology by stressing its historical multiplicity: "Is there *one* negative theology, *the* negative theology? In any case, the unity of its legacy (*archive*) is difficult to delimit. One might try to organize it around certain attempts that are considered exemplary or explicit, such as the Divine Names of Dionysius the Areopagite (Pseudo-Dionysius). But as we shall see, for essential reasons one is never certain of being able to at-

---

3. See the discussion in Caputo, *The Prayers and Tears of Jacques Derrida*, 18–19, citing the observations of Hart, *The Trespass of the Sign: Deconstruction, Theology and Philosophy*. In addition to the relevant scholarship cited below, Caputo's useful "Select Bibliography on Derrida and Religion," 371–74, provides a list of just some of the work in this area over the last fifteen years.

tribute to anyone a project of negative theology as such."[4] The defensiveness here registers Derrida's sense of negative theology as a metalanguage that often defeats the best efforts of its proponents, leading to "simplistic interpretations" that miscomprehend the "ontological wager" implied in apophaticism itself.[5] We must remember, he puts it elsewhere, that "negative theology 'consists,' through its claim to depart from all consistency, in a language that does not cease testing the very limits of language, and exemplarily those of propositional, theoretical, or constative language."[6] Suffused with close readings of the Pseudo-Dionysius, Meister Eckhart, Thomas Aquinas, and Augustine, Derrida's writings on the apophatic mode nevertheless resist drawing clear lines of filiation linking his own corpus with such premodern theologies. At the same time, as Hart has put it, Derrida "know[s] full well that a denial of God conceived as an elevated mode of presence is no less metaphysical than an affirmation of the same deity."[7]

A tenuous analogy might thus be drawn between Derrida's medievalism and his religious sensibility, both of which achieve a kind of presence in his work by virtue of their negation. *La carte postale* (*The Post Card*, 1980) captures something of this ambivalence, combining an intricate diagnosis of language, Being, and the metaphysics of presence with a quasi-autobiographical epistolary account of Derrida's teaching sojourns in Oxford from 1977 to 1979. The book's structuring anecdote concerns the titular postcard itself, imprinted with an image of Plato and Socrates from a thirteenth-century manuscript of Matthew Paris's fortune-telling tracts held by the Bodleian (MS Ashmole 304). The image provided a jacket photo for the book and a point of philosophical departure for the epistolary narrator, who, having "stumbled across" the image at the Bodleian, "bought a whole supply of them," a stack of cards which, inscribed with his musings, imaginatively constitute the "Envois" section of *The Post Card*.[8] What struck Derrida about this postcard was, notoriously, the counterintuitive arrangement of the two philosophers: Plato dictates to Socrates, who inscribes the spoken words of his own historical pupil and auditor. This, Derrida avows, must be "Plato's dream: to make Socrates write, and to make him write what he wants, his last command, *his will*."[9] Alongside his speculation on what such a re-

4. Derrida, "How to Avoid Speaking: Denials," 73–74.
5. Derrida, "How to Avoid Speaking," 82, 78. Compare the discussion in Caputo, *Prayers and Tears*, 26–41.
6. Derrida, "Post-Scriptum: Aporias, Ways, and Voices," 299.
7. Hart, *The Trespass of the Sign,* from the Appendix to the second edition, 286.
8. Derrida, *The Post Card: From Socrates to Freud and Beyond,* 9–10.
9. Derrida, *The Post Card,* 52.

versal might imply for the Western metaphysics of writing, Derrida's narrator spends a good deal of the book ruminating on the past encountered in and through this mechanically reproduced image and its medieval original: he is "jealous of this Matthew Paris, whom I do not know. Want to wake him up to talk to him about all the sleepless nights between us," yet he also cannot help but admire the coded intricacy of the book's prognosticatory mechanism, which he works out patiently with the help of the manuscript catalogue and the Middle English inscriptions in the book itself ("ever first take your noumber in the Cerkelle sodenly thynkying on the question," as Derrida transcribes one of them).[10] The desire for an unmediated intimacy with Matthew Paris gets fulfilled in an ersatz sort of way months later, when Derrida sits in Duke Humfrey's Library (the manuscript room at the Bodleian) and finally gets a chance to peruse the auratic manuscript from which the postcard image has been lifted. The self-conscious archaeological rhetoric of *The Post Card*—with its playful invocations of the Bodleian and Duke Humfrey's Library itself, "sanctuary of the most precious manuscripts," as well as its obvious delight in the "Oxonian performativism" demanded in the recitation of The Oath—provides a kind of ingenuous counterpoint to Lacan's sober invocation of courtly love manuscripts in *The Ethics of Psychoanalysis*.[11] Derrida performs this medievalism not in the persona of the trained archivist such as Bataille, nor as the easily deflatable dilettante such as Lacan, but rather as the honest novice, the breathless amateur awed by the prestige and mystique of the medieval yet unwilling to cede its scrutiny to the claims of expertise.

In this respect, *The Post Card* functions as a retrospective allegory for the more occulted medievalism discernible in the first two decades of Derrida's writing career, from his earliest sense of the philosophical affiliations of Husserl's *Origins of Geometry* to a work like *Glas* (1980), with its visible dialectic of text and gloss and the deliberately Eucharistic "offering" it makes to its readers.[12] Particularly during the years of concern in the present book, Derrida often sought to contest the inscription of historical teleologies as such, along with the denials, elisions, and erasures that will always accompany the historical project and invisibly corrode its artifacts. Exposing false lineages and wrongly claimed genealogies, Derrida's 1960s archaeology was aimed above all at making crooked myr-

10. Derrida, *The Post Card*, 17.
11. Derrida, *The Post Card*, 216.
12. Derrida, "The Supplement of Copula: Philosophy before Linguistics"; and "Responses to Questions on the Avant-Garde." For Derrida's own accounting of the Eucharistic dimensions of *Glas*, see Derrida, "Passions: 'An Oblique Offering,'" 11 and 16.

iad straight lines of historiographical descent: "There is not one single history, a general history, but rather histories different in their type, rhythm, mode of inscription, intervallic, differentiated histories."[13] In taking *Of Grammatology* as Derrida's most precise delineation of the theoretical possibilities that such "differentiated histories" might generate, this chapter follows Paul de Man in reading *Of Grammatology* in large part as "a commentary on Rousseau," and in particular on the premodern liturgical archaeology of Rousseau's *Essay on the Origin of Languages*.[14] Liturgy performs as the unspoken object of archaeological provocation throughout *Of Grammatology*, motivating Derrida's explication of Rousseau and in some sense unifying his broader critical project vis-à-vis the metaphysics of presence. In the process, *Of Grammatology* provides a resounding if provisional *riposte avant la lettre* to a coterie of contemporary theologians who have staked their critiques of Derridean nihilism largely on their own liturgical inventions.

"Sophistry": Derrida and/in Radical Orthodoxy

Among the most visible movements in contemporary academic theology is the so-called Radical Orthodoxy, a Cambridge, U.K.–based collective of Christian thinkers (both Catholic and Protestant) whose aim is an anti-secularizing response to the culture of doubt and relativism they see as endemic to modernity. Radical Orthodoxy has continually presented itself as a form of theological mediation, one that "protests equally against assertions of pure reason and of pure faith; equally against denominational claims for a monopoly of salvation and against indifference to church order; equally against theology as an internal autistic idiolect, and against theology as an adaptation to unquestioned secular assumptions."[15] The group's mediating role in fact bases itself on a resolute anti-modernity: not a simplistic rejection of reason and rationalism, but a working recognition that the very notion of an autonomous sphere of reason divorced from faith is a *symptom* of modernity—and thus that post-Enlightenment forms of reason are hardly qualified to "save" the modern, as the Radically Orthodox propose to do.[16] Radical Orthodoxy "is a hermeneutic disposition and a style of metaphysical vision," writes Catherine Pickstock; "and it is not so much a 'thing' or

13. Derrida, *Positions*, 58; cited in Dosse, *History of Structuralism*, 2: 34.
14. de Man, *Blindness and Insight*, 111.
15. Milbank, "The Programme of Radical Orthodoxy," 33.
16. Milbank, "Programme," 45.

'place' as a 'task.'" [17] Salvation demands hard intellectual work, of course, and the Radical Orthodox writers have hardly abandoned the languages of high theory: their writings are characterized without exception by an adept and sometimes intimidating familiarity with the modern philosophical discourses they critique, and from the movement's inaugural text, Milbank's *Theology and Social Theory*, ancient Christian theologians from Augustine onward have been put in fecund dialogue with contemporary philosophers of language and of the gift (Heidegger, Derrida, Marion, and others).

Indeed, a central component of the Radical Orthodoxy's project has been a recovery of (a particular version of) the history and theology of pre-Reformation Catholicism in an effort to counter the decadence of the modern. This recovery has been described as "an extensive archaeology of patristic and medieval texts" very much in the spirit of the French *nouvelle théologie* and Henri de Lubac's *ressourcement* (to be discussed in chapter 5 below), though with quite different political and theological implications (Milbank himself has asserted that "Radical Orthodoxy considers that Henri de Lubac was a greater theological revolutionary than Karl Barth").[18] The titles of their books alone—*Cities of God, Truth in Aquinas,* and so on—register the group's will to revive the polemical spirit of their premodern interlocutors as part of a more general critique of contemporary secularisms. In the introduction to an eponymous 1999 essay collection, Radical Orthodoxy's three central figures have explained what they are up to with admirable clarity, foregrounding their mission to "reclaim the world by situating its concerns and activities within a theological framework" constructed out of the textual remains of the Christian past:

In what sense *orthodox* and in what sense *radical*? Orthodox in the most straightforward sense of commitment to credal Christianity and the exemplarity of its patristic matrix. But orthodox also in the more specific sense of reaffirming a richer and more coherent Christianity which was gradually lost sight of after the late Middle Ages. . . . Radical, first of all, in the sense of a return to patristic and medieval roots, and especially to the Augustinian vision of all knowledge as divine illumination—a notion which transcends the modern bastard dualisms of faith and reason, grace and nature. Radical, second, in the sense of seeking to deploy this recovered vision systematically to criticise modern society, culture, politics, art, science and philosophy with an unprecedented boldness. But radical in yet a third sense of realising that via such en-

17. Pickstock, "Radical Orthodoxy and the Mediations of Time," 63.
18. Reno, "The Radical Orthodoxy Project"; Milbank, "Programme," 35.

gagements we *do* have also to rethink the tradition. The fact of its late medieval collapse, the fact that such a collapse was *possible,* can sometimes point to even earlier
weaknesses.[19]

What Radical Orthodoxy seeks to offer us, then, can be characterized as
a methodology of corrective medievalism. By turning to the Christian
writings of the premodern era, beginning with the Augustinian theology
of late antiquity, these writers promise to redress the epochal splittings-
off—"disruptions," Milbank labels them in his contribution—of ontology from theology, reason from faith, nature from grace, that were the
inevitable result of the late medieval invention of a "reason-revelation
duality" absent from earlier Christian thought.[20] Importantly, as Milbank has pointed out, Radical Orthodoxy does not necessarily claim to
envision an orthodoxy "as perfected within pre-modernity" but entirely
lost to modernity, and it would be wrong to characterize the movement
as "conservative" in any unproblematized way (or even, as Pickstock has
averred, nostalgic).[21] Nevertheless, throughout a decade of combative
writing in the fields it embraces, the interventionist medievalism of the
Radical Orthodoxy group has worked energetically and pugnaciously to
make premodern Christian texts engage the secularist lapses of contemporary philosophy, social theory, and activism. Thus Graham Ward's
Cities of God reintroduces Augustine's vision of divine polity in order
to propose a new ethic of urban activism. Milbank and Pickstock's *Truth
in Aquinas* proposes what they envision as the forgotten centrality of
sacramental theology in Aquinas's understanding of truth as a corrective
to anachronistically epistemological modern approaches to the problem. And for David Moss, St. Anselm's writings on friendship provide a
model for a "radical" reclaiming of a "friendship with God" that has
been lost in antitheological notions of friendship since the early modern
period.[22]

The Radical Orthodoxy project thus posits the centrality of the medieval in the ongoing encounter between contemporary theology and the
theoretical discourses of poststructuralism and postmodernism. In this
respect, the movement's numerous claimings of the Middle Ages furnish
its most compelling textual artifacts for recovery and reengagement,

19. Milbank, Ward, and Pickstock, "Introduction: Suspending the Material: The Turn of Radical
Orthodoxy," in Milbank, Pickstock, and Ward, eds., *Radical Orthodoxy: A New Theology,* 2.
20. Milbank, "Knowledge: The Theological Critique of Philosophy in Hamann and Jacobi,"
23–24.
21. Milbank, "Programme," 44.
22. Moss, "Friendship: St. Anselm, *Theoria* and the Convolution of Sense."

from Augustine's *City of God* to Aquinas's *Summa theologiæ*. Such medievalisms have in turn served Milbank, Pickstock, and others as the most effective ammunition in what they clearly envision as an ongoing ethical battle against Continental theory, and in particular against the writings of Derrida. In *The Word Made Strange: Theology, Language, Culture*, Milbank, though admittedly influenced by poststructuralist theories of language, takes Derrida to task for a supposed "gnostic identification of creation with fall," an identification that leads to an impoverished view of history that is both disenchanted and incapable of redemption.[23] A more thoroughgoing response to Derrida has come from Catherine Pickstock, whose *After Writing: On the Liturgical Consummation of Philosophy* aims at a wholesale dismantling of Derrida's critique of Western logocentrism through a "recasting of the premodern" against what she sees as its pernicious recruitment by deconstruction. The most extended, argumentative, and universalizing appropriation of medieval theology among the Radically Orthodox, Pickstock's treatise also provides an engaging if often infuriating inquiry into the role of premodernity in Derrida's oeuvre, which she claims to have undermined by exposing its blindness to the imaginative role of liturgy in the history of metaphysics. The book thus provides an ideal point of entry into a consideration of Derrida's own views of liturgy and history as elaborated in an early work like *Of Grammatology*.

Pickstock begins her lengthy critique of poststructuralist nihilism with Derrida's essay "Plato's Pharmacy" (1972) and the grave misreading of the *Phaedrus* of which she accuses him. A *locus classicus* of binary-hunting deconstructive reading, "Plato's Pharmacy" views the *Phaedrus* through the lens of the Egyptian myth of Theuth and the invention of writing, a myth that Plato seems to include as an afterthought but that Derrida insists is an inevitable and necessary component of the dialogue. On one level, Derrida suggests, the invocation of the myth exposes the inability of Socratic philosophy to separate itself securely from the mythology it seeks to displace, and in particular that of the Sophists.

---

23. Milbank, *The Word Made Strange*, 62. See also Caputo, Dooley, and Scanlon, eds., *Questioning God*, which collects alongside specially commissioned writings the proceedings of the second Conference on Religion and Postmodernism in 1999. The transcription of the conference's roundtable, "On Forgiveness" (52–72), reprints the first direct encounter between Milbank and Derrida, though the tenor of their exchange conveys the impression more of ships passing in the night than of real intellectual dialogue. For an account of the implications of what Mark Dooley calls "this encounter between two movements which are currently battling it out for the minds and souls of many theological faculties throughout the United States and beyond," see Dooley's essay in the volume, "The Catastrophe of Memory: Derrida, Milbank, and the (Im)possibility of Forgiveness," 129–49 (citation from 131).

More crucially, though, Socrates' denigration of writing as artificiality, repetition, illegitimacy, and so on illustrates his wish to sustain "infinite self-presence," a wish that infuses the myth as a whole with the desire for the living immediacy of the spoken word against the artificiality of writing. For Derrida, Plato himself thus emerges as the "spitting image" of the Sophists, his denigration of writing an anxious and unspoken acknowledgment of his own philosophy's implication in sophistic reason.[24]

On Pickstock's reading, by contrast, it is Derrida who unknowingly aligns himself with the sophistic philosophies that are the object of Socrates' polemic. This alignment results from Derrida's misunderstanding of the Socratic critique of writing, which Pickstock sees not as advocating a "metapysical suppression of temporality, supplementarity, and difference in favour of self-presence, organlessness, and interior tranquillity," but as incarnational, rigorously dialectical, and doxological. Derrida overlooks the parodic elements of Socrates' critique, which in turn register the "parodic relation between sophistry and true dialectic."[25] And it is Derrida who, with the sophists, "hypostasize[s] writing so that it becomes an ideal science" against Socrates' own anti-fetishizing, anti-capitalist understanding of the oral. "Derrida simply does not *consider* the Platonic alternative that instead of being at once radical absence *and* original presence, the good might be an inaccessible and inexhaustible plenitude," Pickstock insists (11). Socrates' feints, figures, and traces when discussing the good signify not "capital's fear of itself," but rather his refusal to circumscribe the good with "ordinary, empirical data" or "technical knowing" (Pickstock's phrase), a refusal that stems from a deep-seated awareness—entirely lost on Derrida—that the good is transcendent and therefore not susceptible to immanentist propositions (11). The good's own mode of presence "is articulated through the gifts which it bestows"; the good proliferates through a Socratic *dissemination* that Derrida mistakes for *différance* and perpetual deferral.

Hand in hand with this Derridean neo-sophistic comes what Pickstock sees as "a denial of the living and dying physical *body*" that results directly from his "fixation with writing" (19, 23). While Derrida seeks to identify in the *Phaedrus*'s critique of sophistry a metaphysics of (oral, bodily) presence, again it is Derrida, not Socrates, who "suppresses the link between language and physicality, for in aligning writing with par-

---

24. Derrida, "Plato's Pharmacy," in *Dissemination*, 109, 117.
25. Pickstock, *After Writing*, 6; citations hereafter in text.

ricide or the absence of the father, and orality with a metaphysics of presence, he subtly denies the fact that language of any kind requires *bodily* presence" (21). On the most basic level, then, Derrida is misreading Socrates' critique of the myth of Theuth by his own flawed process of substitution and supplementation, which serves to maintain what to Derrida is "the all-important structural assimilation of capital, orality, the king etc." (26). And what this misreading erases most damagingly from the Platonic corpus is the liturgical understanding of language and the good that sustains it: "In the case of the myth of Theuth, therefore, supplementation is *not* construed as peculiarly written; nor, concomitantly, does this myth necessarily inscribe an unavoidable conflict between oral presence and written deferral. On the contrary, its promotion of *liturgy* tends to integrate writing with orality" (27).

Liturgy for Pickstock—and, she would maintain, for Socrates—is the very dialectical embodiment of the good. It is both an erotic, a loving gaze that is "neither totalizing nor rationalizing, since its 'object' cannot be seen once and for all," "an ontologically constitutive loss of self" (33); and a "doxologic," an orality of giving and devotion "in praise of what is good" (39).

According to Derrida's deconstruction of the *Phaedrus,* it is the sophists who are wedded to language and mediation through rhetoric and writing, whilst Socrates stresses the realm of unmediated truth before or beyond language. This opposition is the means by which Derrida accounts for Plato's hostility to poetry, rhetoric, and (written) language in general. However, there are intimations in the dialogue of an alternative configuration, in which Socrates is not hostile to signs as such, and construes the true language as doxological, that is to say, as ultimately concerned with praise of the divine. According to this view, he attacks sophistry not on the grounds of its linguistic mediation of truth, but because of its undoxological motivation. (37)

The "most pertinent" distinction for Socrates, then, is not that between the rule of language and the philosophical logos, but that between doxological and non-doxological language. "In an act of doxological expression," Pickstock argues, the provisional community defined by the act is "supremely centred and non-ironic, for genuine avowal involves commitment to such a degree that nothing can be held back or veiled." If, as we shall see, this resonates with Emmanuel Levinas's vision of liturgical expression, Pickstock would likely argue that what Levinas construes as a self-evacuating, death-anticipating loss, platonism discovered as a life-affirming ethic of plenitude: "Liturgy is . . . not a constative representation now and then of what is praise-worthy, but constitutes a whole way of life . . . doxology as a mode of life constitutes the supreme ethic" (39–40). Finally, then, Socrates' condemnation of sophistry entails a condemnation not of written language as such, but rather "of the separation of language from doxology, of art from liturgy, resulting in a sophistic 'virtual reality,' or realm of mere fiction which is manipulable, ironic, and uninhabited"—the realm, in a word, of deconstruction (42).

Deconstruction thus represents in *After Writing* an almost apocalyptic fulfillment of the separation of language from the liturgical. This divorce has unfolded diachronically rather than in ruptures, and the metaphor Pickstock prefers by which to capture its effects is that of spatialization. During the early modern period and its eventual denouement in Cartesianism, "the breakdown of the traditional religious order" came to be enacted in philosophy's "attempt to bypass the intervention of human temporality and subjectivity (which a liturgical knowledge and practice had embraced) via an apparently unmediated apprehension of 'objective' and 'given' facts"; this in turn led to the normalization of "sophistic spatialization," an anti-incarnational, often nihilistic sensibility that has become the dominant and pernicious symptom of modernity, "even to the extent that it has infiltrated the very structures of our language, almost obliterating its original liturgical character" (48); sophistic/modern spatialization is "an attempt to substitute a unicursal, abstract, and purely immanent ordering of reality for both eternity and time" (228). Particularly insidious here have been the "signs of death" that register the "necrophiliac" tendencies of modernity, tendencies especially visible in the death drives inspiring postwar French thought: "necrophilia and a life-death dualism is explicitly articulated in recent 'postmodern' and 'Levinasian' philosophy." Once again Pickstock's favorite target is Derrida, whose "theory of language as writing, not only sustains modern spatialization, but is also driven by the concomitant modern embrace of death" (103). From Cartesian *cogito* to Derridean *différance,* swept by Pickstock into the same antiliturgical dustpan, the myriad Enlightenment philosophies of death, destruction, and dualism collectively symptomatize the nihilistic death drive of modernity: "Hence the city which seeks to live only in spatial immanence is a necropolis defined by its refusal of liturgical life" (118).

The founding responsibility for this refusal falls squarely on the shoulders of late medieval philosophy and its debasement of liturgy, and in particular on those of Duns Scotus—not coincidentally a favorite of Gilles Deleuze, the intended subject of Heidegger's *Habilitationsschrift,* the central historical inspiration for Charles Sanders Peirce's theory of semiotics—in short, a human catalyst for the modernities Pickstock's treatise indicts. Such assessments of Duns Scotus have a long history in modern theology, of course, beginning with the proponents of the *nouvelle théologie* in interwar France and receiving their broadest treatment in the theological aesthetics of Hans Urs von Balthasar. For von Balthasar, Duns Scotus represented a "parting of the ways" by which God and creation became subsumed under a single (and neutral) concept of Being—leading ultimately to the "religion without religion" that has become the basis for certain strands of ethical reflection in recent postmodern theologies.[26] Following a number of other Radical Orthodox theologians who have raised the indictment of Scotism to an unprecedented level, Pickstock takes the writings of Duns Scotus as "perhaps the first definite theoretical symptom of the destruction from within of the liturgical city" (121). "Scotist politics" thus symptomatize a much broader secularization of communal life and the social body, a virtual poisoning of the well of liturgical life with the vial of secularism: "in the late Middle Ages the political emerges as a pseudo-liturgical power whose absolutist colonization of every realm of life parodies the traditionally sacramental structure of all forms of social interaction." Pickstock calls this colonizing process (in a wonderful phrase) "a soteriology of the State" (152), a newly secularized theology that was accompanied by concomitant changes in Eucharistic theology that severed the physical from the mystical in an "impoverishment of liturgical temporality" (166).

Yet *After Writing* is also prescriptive and remedial, an attempt to begin repairing the damage done by Duns Scotus and his postmodern progeny to what Pickstock calls the "Sacred Polis." This liturgical civilization existed in its purest form during the Western Middle Ages and achieved its most coherent expression as the liturgy of the Roman Rite, a liturgy of "impossibility" that "shatters all ordinary positions of agency and reception, especially as these have been conceived in the west since Scotus" (177). It is the resurrection of this liturgy—along with its models of subjectivity and human relationships between one another and God—to which *After Writing* ultimately aspires: indeed, "genuine subjectivity is to be attained through the redemptive return of doxological dispossession, thus ensuring that the subject is neither autonomously self-present, nor passively controlled from without," "the pendulum of 'choices' available to the citizen of the immanentist city" postulated by the sophists and reified by Derrida (170). For Pickstock, the very struc-

---

26. See especially Balthasar, *The Glory of the Lord,* vol. 5: *The Realm of Metaphysics in the Modern Age,* 16–19.

ture of the Roman Rite is "predicated upon a need for a constant re-beginning of liturgy because the true eschatological liturgy is in time endlessly postponed" (173). Pickstock proceeds through a minute dissection of the Rite, marshalling its language, its rhetoric, its apostrophic voice, its reconciliation of space and time, and the model of divine-human identification it promotes as part of a "liturgical and overtly ecclesial bestowal of peace" (228). Liturgy creates a unique chronotope that opens the way for "the liturgical gift," which in turn provides models of subjectivity, citizenship, and being for those willing to accept it.

The greatest such gift, of course, is the Eucharist, which transcends and conquers the boundary between life and death: "where death is not held as over against life, it is possible to restore meaning to language, and . . . the optimum site of this restoration is the integration of word and action in the event of the Eucharist" (252). Rather than fetish, the resurrected body in the Eucharist "is a completely imparted body, transmuted into a series of signs. Such constant dispersal turns body into gift" rather than fetishized fragment (266). Though the secular state has "parodically appropriated" the theology of the Eucharist toward its immanentist and nihilistic ends, the Eucharist can survive and be reappropriated against the antiliturgical city:

> its recommencements, invocations, permeations, and significations are situated within a construal of language as that which both signifies and provokes a beneficent mystery which is not wholly other from the sign, although it cannot be exhausted by the sign. Instead, the theological sign *includes* and *repeats* the mystery it receives and to which it is offered, and as such, it reveals the nature of that divine mystery as gift, relationality, and perpetuity. (267)

While the Platonic vision of language, unlike the sophistic, is clearly liturgical in inspiration, its "sacrifice of the body for a greater spiritual gain" contrasts with the resurrection of the body in Christianity (273), which outdistances its Hellenic predecessor through the power of divine incarnation. "With Christianity," Pickstock avows, "the optimum of meaningfulness and the optimum of living subjectivity coincide within the world—with all its temporality, space, and embodiment" (273). More emphatically, Pickstock claims to have "provided the articulations of a model of a liturgical attitude which *alone* offers a genuine restoration of both the subject and of language as such" (268; emphasis added).

The breathtaking confidence of *After Writing*, with its whirlwind tour of the Platonic and neoplatonic traditions, its antinecrophiliac assault on post-Scotus secularism, and its utter lack of rhetorical modesty (Pickstock's favorite words seem to be "only," "optimum," "alone," "genuine," "real," and their ilk), risks boxing out any dissent by insisting that its targets (and again, Derrida in particular) have misunderstood the intellectual foundations of their own epistemologies. *After Writing's* argumentative tactics register what many critics have identified as the (often amusing, always unexplained) ironies that suffuse Radical Orthodoxy's mission more generally: for example, its repeated claims to ecumenicalism that are constantly belied by the stridently evangelical Christianity (most often Catholic) at its core. Pickstock's prescription for a liturgical resurrection, too, is inseparable from her book's proselytizing for transubstantiation, a belief absent by definition from Protestant theologies —including Pickstock's own professed High Anglicanism. (Such ironies have led one commentator, writing for the *TLS*, to title his review article "On Not Seeing the Joke." [27])

The remainder of this chapter will set about correcting Pickstock's myopic recruitment of a particular liturgical medievalism against Derrida, whose writing during the 1960s actually had a surprising amount to say about precisely the doxological traditions and languages that Pickstock accuses him of annihilating. I have spent so much time summarizing Pickstock's treatise, though, in order to engage the specifically historical tenor of its argument, for it is on the terms of history that Pickstock, like so many of its other opponents, most vociferously rejects the Derridean project. For Pickstock, in fact, Derrida's gravest error is his failure to comprehend the medievo-liturgical presence at the core of the tradition he critiques, and thus it is no mistake that *After Writing* envisions itself as elaborating a specific premodern archaeology grounded in what is putatively the most "genuine" medieval artifact of all. "I have chosen as my paradigm of genuine liturgy," Pickstock tells us, "the mediaeval Roman Rite rather than more recent revised liturgies of the Anglican and Roman Church because the latter, although ostensibly the result of an attempt to interrupt the drift towards decadence characteristic of the liturgical practice of the seventeenth century, and to recover a purer and more ancient liturgical structure, nevertheless can be seen to have (unwittingly) incorporated the linguistic and epistemological structures of a modern secular order." The return of the "mediaeval Roman Rite," Pickstock insists, promises to "restore real language and action as liturgy" through a "revolutionary re-invention of language and

27. Jones, "On Not Seeing the Joke."

practice which would challenge the structures of our modern world."[28] Here, I think, is where the historical argument of *After Writing* is at its most vulnerable. For the liturgical text relied on throughout the book—Bernard Botte and Christine Mohrmann's *L'Ordinaire de la Messe*—is in fact an edition not of any "genuinely" medieval liturgical artifact, but of the post-Tridentine Rite, the uniform liturgy that the Catholic Church under Pius V imposed throughout its remaining jurisdictions (thus abolishing local performative traditions) following the convulsions of the Reformation. Far from a "real" medieval liturgy capable of challenging centuries of post-medieval reform, then, Pickstock's object of veneration is a counter-Reformation liturgy that was recorded, promulgated, decreed, and performed precisely in violent and conservative reaction to the liturgical innovations of sixteenth-century Protestantism.

The most philosophically disabling oversight in *After Writing*, by contrast, concerns Pickstock's failure to account for Derrida's own extended meditations on the metaphysics of Christian liturgical discourse, meditations that work powerfully against her repeated attempts to corner him as an anti-doxological secularist. This is a position Derrida was already rejecting in the mid-1960s, and largely through a considered negotiation of the liturgical boundaries of selfhood, ethics, and writing. The negotiation to which I refer here takes place in *Of Grammatology*, a text that bases its critique of logocentrism in part on a liturgical ecumenicalism that counters the Christian absolutism into which Pickstock's *After Writing* and the Radical Orthodox more generally constantly risk lapsing.

The Liturgical Trace

The Radical Orthodox theologians have largely avoided any extended engagement in print with the writings of the French-Lithuanian philosopher Emmanuel Levinas, whose corpus had such a deep impact on Der-

---

28. Pickstock, *After Writing*, 170–71: "The Vatican II reformers of the 1960s tended to assume that the text of the Roman Rite, which reached more or less its mature form in the Italian Mass Books of the eleventh and twelfth centuries, represents a corruption of an 'original liturgy,' a debasement of what went before. . . . [B]ecause the Vatican II reforms of the mediaeval Roman Rite failed to take into account the cultural assumptions which lay implicit within the text, their reforms participated in an entirely more sinister conservatism. For they failed to challenge those structures of the modern secular world which are wholly inimical to liturgical purpose: those structures, indeed, which perpetuate a separation of everyday life from liturgical enactment. So, the criticisms of the Vatican II revisions of the mediaeval Roman Rite, contained within this section, far from enlisting a conservative horror at change, issue from a belief that the revisions were simply not radical enough."

rida's early writings and indeed generated much of his work's central theological energies beginning in the 1960s. Levinas left Russia in 1923 for Strasbourg, where he met Maurice Blanchot; he then attended Edmund Husserl's 1928–29 lectures in Freiburg. After returning to France and naturalizing as a citizen in 1930, he became the first francophone exponent of Germanic phenomenology with his monograph *Théorie de l'intuition dans le phénoménologie de Husserl* (1930) and his translation of Husserl's *Cartesian Meditations* in 1931. Jean-Paul Sartre and many others credited Levinas with introducing France to phenomenology, a philosophical discipline Levinas would seek throughout his career to reconcile with the philological and theological enterprise of Talmud, one of his lifelong obsessions.[29] For Levinas, though, Judaism often functioned less as theology than as a kind of historical ethics of signification, an archaeological perceptiveness that was resolutely anti-Hegelian and emphatically anti-mystical (in this respect contrasting with the mystical scholarship of Gershom Scholem, who dedicated much of his career to the medieval tradition of Kabbalah).[30]

Derrida thus perceived in the work of Levinas a philosophy particularly suited to questioning the idealizing of historical epochs; like those of Walter Benjamin, Levinas's meditations on temporality provided some of the most eloquent modern arguments "against the immanent and impersonal laws of nineteenth-century historicism," as Susan Handelman has described them, in favor of "a theory of 'messianic time' to open history to redemption," yet without the risks of overly empathetic identifications of self and other.[31] More specifically, Levinas adumbrates in his 1960s writings on ethics what Derrida recognized as an indigenously premodern perspective on the nature of diachrony, a critique articulated most provocatively in his meditations on liturgical temporality.[32] This liturgical anti-teleology inspires Levinas's essay "On the Trail of the Other," published several years before *Of Grammatology* and cited there in Derrida's footnotes to Part I. Arguing against the "disinvested" visions of the past inspiring post-Hegelian historicisms, Levinas posits a distinctly devotional form of personal labor as an ethics of historical consciousness:

---

29. Handelman, *Fragments of Redemption: Jewish Thought and Literary Theory in Benjamin, Scholem, and Levinas*, 179.

30. Handelman, *Fragments of Redemption*, esp. chap. 10, "Talmudic Messianism," 306–36.

31. Handelman, *Fragments of Redemption*, 178.

32. Levinas's powerfully ethicizing influence on Derrida has been traced in detail by Critchley, *The Ethics of Deconstruction;* see 109–10 on "The Trace of the Other."

The work of the Self in the sense of a movement, without return of the Self, toward the Other, this I would encompass by the Greek term which in its original signification indicates the exercise of an office not merely gratuitously, but requiring on the part of the one who exercises it an investment with no strings attached. I want to circumscribe this idea with the term "liturgy" . . . the liturgy, the absolutely patient action, does not parallel works and the ethical in the form of cult. It is the ethical itself.[33]

The implications of the emphatic predicate nominative that inspires this passage—the liturgy *is* the ethical—have remained generally unexamined in the recent reception of Levinas, and I will not explore them here except as they relate to his influence on Derrida's own liturgical sensibility in *Of Grammatology*. What does seem worth emphasizing, though, is the extraordinary extent to which liturgy appears in this essay to encompass the entire domain of Levinasian relationality, with the absolute as much as with the neighbor.[34] The "liturgicality" of subjectivity, Levinas insists, does not "proceed from need"; implicitly challenging Lacan's "impatient" subject, suffering in his lack, Levinas proposes instead a "needless" subject—or rather, a subject-in-becoming instantiated most ideally in the liturgy. With its cyclical repetitions and its patient accumulations of past time into the lived present, liturgy provides a mechanism for creating and reproducing what Levinas terms a "non-allergic relation with alterity."[35]

Levinas returned frequently in this period to the liturgy as a mode of non-empathetic apprehension of the other; in the related essay "Meaning and Sense" (1964), liturgy constitutes "the exercise of a function which is not only totally gratuitous but requires on the part of him who exercises it a putting out of funds at a loss."[36] This is not a Lacanian loss, however: not a violent realization of lack that must be filled. Instead, this form of personal labor for the other is performed "without remuneration," and in this sense it resonates powerfully with Bataille's sovereign subject (though without the wasteful pathologies theorized by the latter). It may not be too much to say that the liturgical self is for Lev-

33. Levinas, "On the Trail of the Other," 38; the essay has also been translated as Levinas, "The Trace of the Other."

34. On this aspect of Levinas's ethics see Bloechl, *Liturgy of the Neighbor: Emmanuel Levinas and the Religion of Responsibility*, a book that leaves the liturgical largely on the level of metaphor. On liturgy as the unspoken ground of Levinas's critique of Heidegger, see Sikka, "Questioning the Sacred: Heidegger and Levinas on the Locus of Divinity," esp. 311–16; and, more directly, Purcell, "Liturgy: Divine and Human Service." Other critics have overlooked the liturgical tenor of Levinasian ethics, at least one of them going so far as to propose a liturgical corrective to its tenets; see Drabinski, "The Possibility of an Ethical Politics."

35. Levinas, *Otherwise than Being or Beyond Essence*, 49.

36. Levinas, "Meaning and Sense," in *Basic Philosophical Writings*, 50.

inas that self most passionately invested in the "responsibility for the other" that would become the ethical fulcrum of *Otherwise than Being* (1974). As such, liturgy shadows forth Levinas's ethical comprehension of temporality as such, "a diachrony refractory to all synchronization, a transcending diachrony" that forges a kind of liturgical historicism fully answerable to the claims of the past.[37]

Liturgical temporality thus constitutes for Levinas a means of discerning and living the past in its impossible totality within the present even as the lineaments of that past remain unknowable, incomprehensible, overwhelming. Liturgy defeats synchrony just as it swallows diachrony. Liturgy exists and is performed not in direct relation to God, but in the subject's relation of obligation to the neighbor who bears a trace of God and whose face the subject can recognize but never fully know. The presence of the past in all its demanding and often unanswerable fullness corresponds to the presence of God, a presence discernible only in *illeity,* Levinas's latinate neologism for that unnameable He who remains unrepresentable in the time of the subject yet fills the past with the traces of presence that make up both the subject's ethical relation to the neighbor and the language in which this intersubjectivity is expressed. Liturgy channels this strangely compelling relation of secular doxology and sacred diachrony in Levinas's thought, a relation that determines the shape of all ethical collectivities as they live out a constant renewal of human history.

Though Levinas's "On the Trail of the Other" does not address its own archaeological implications, the essay's liturgical vision of historical unfolding clearly anticipates the intersubjective doxologies of *Totality and Infinity* and *Otherwise than Being.* More importantly for the purposes of the present argument, the essay's liturgical sensibility exerted a powerful imaginative force upon its most influential successor text, *Of Grammatology.* Here Derrida directly credits Levinas's recent writings, and this liturgical essay in particular, for inspiring his own notion of the *trace,* the "absent presence" or "empty fullness" of the signifier that has constituted one of the central terms in the lexicon of deconstruction. In a crucial passage from *Of Grammatology*'s opening section, Derrida writes of the trace in language and the psyche as the haunting immanence of the past within the present:

there is no full speech, however much one might wish to restore it by means or without benefit of psychoanalysis. Before thinking to reduce it or to restore the meaning

37. Levinas, *Otherwise than Being,* 9.

of the full speech which claims to be truth, one must ask questions of meaning and of its origin in difference. Such is the place of a problematic of the trace. Why of the trace? What led us to the choice of this word? . . . I relate this concept of trace to what is at the center of the latest work of Emmanuel Levinas and his critique of ontology: relationship to the illeity as to the alterity of a past that never was and can never be lived in the originary or modified form of presence.[38]

"Illeity," again, is Levinas's latinism for the utter lack of equivalence or irreducible otherness in the neighbor that the subject will never overcome—in other words, that trace of God in the human. Illeity embodies the nature of liturgical time and its eternal propagation of the trace. For Levinas, awareness of the trace demands of the subject a constant self-abnegating, self-denying labor, a labor we might cast in recognizably premodern terms as the *opus non Dei,* the "work not of God" that is the ethical demand of the fully human Other. For Derrida, of course, the trace is also an effect of language and of writing; citing Heidegger, he insists upon the trace's function, in more familiarly deconstructive terms, as "the undermining of an ontology which, in its innermost course, has determined the meaning of being as presence and the meaning of language as the full continuity of speech" (70).

There is nothing inherently medieval about Levinas's writings on liturgy; indeed, given its roots in the philosopher's Talmudic scholarship, it would seem more accurate to recognize in his vision of liturgical subjection a temporality spanning thousands of years into a past that fully infuses the present. Yet Derrida's subsequent reflections on the trace in *Of Grammatology* integrate the Russian philosopher's theory of liturgy into a specifically Christian problematic that entails a critical appropriation of the Middle Ages as a nodal historical epoch.[39] This appropriation has important precedent very early on in *Of Grammatology,* when Derrida invokes the metonymic slide "from sign to sign" undergirding the semiotic project of Charles Sanders Peirce for its explicit continuity with medieval speculative grammar; here, Derrida isolates the conditions of signification at the "foundation" (Derrida's term) of every logical system: "the lowest level, the foundation of the possibility of logic (or semiotics) corresponds to the project of the *Grammatica speculativa* of Thomas d'Erfurt, falsely attributed to Duns Scotus. Like Husserl, Peirce expressly

38. Derrida, *Of Grammatology,* 69–70; citations hereafter in text.
39. The more general critical bibliography on Derrida's relationship with Levinas is already considerable; see, in addition to the studies cited above, Duncan, *The Pre-Text of Ethics: On Derrida and Levinas.*

refers to it. It is a matter of elaborating, in both cases, a formal doctrine of conditions which a discourse must satisfy in order to have a sense, in order to 'mean,' even if it is false or contradictory" (48). The late-medieval scholastics recognized that the "general morphology of that meaning . . . is independent of all logic of truth," for it arises exclusively in the relation of sign to sign. Inspired by (pseudo-)Duns Scotus, Derrida suggests, "Peirce goes very far in the direction that I have called the deconstruction of the transcendental signified" (49). One of the projects through the remainder of *Of Grammatology* will be to elaborate this premodern archaeology of deconstruction.

Gothic Inventions: Rousseau and the Liturgical Fall

As I have already suggested, *Of Grammatology* performs a sweepingly archaeological function vis-à-vis the ontology of the medieval by foregrounding the historicizing fallacies endemic to Enlightenment habits of periodization. This critique focuses on Jean-Jacques Rousseau's *Essai sur l'origine des langues* (*Essay on the Origin of Languages*), a fascinating but, until Derrida's treatment of it, little-read exposition of Rousseau's vision of language's role in the history of human civilizations. Derrida's much-discussed exegesis of Rousseau's *Essay* occupies nearly half of the text of *Of Grammatology,* slightly more than one hundred pages in Spivak's English translation: a commentary that is more than three times the length of its object, for the *Essay* is quite brief. Derrida's exhaustive reading of the eighteenth-century treatise has proved one of his most influential deconstructive engagements with Enlightenment rationality, providing a complement to his extended considerations of Saussurean linguistics and Lévi-Straussian ethnography earlier in the book. Though Derrida's engagement with the *Essay on the Origin of Languages* betrays all the intricacies and complexities of the author's work more generally, its archaeological stakes become clearly legible when this section of *Of Grammatology* is read alongside the plain-spoken polemic of the *Essay* itself.[40]

At the dawn of civilization, Rousseau contends, at that moment when one man was first recognized by another "as a sentient, thinking being similar to himself," the need to communicate led to the "institution of

40. See also Paul de Man's well-known and still clarifying essay, "The Rhetoric of Blindness," in *Blindness and Insight,* 102–41.

sensate signs for the expression of thought."[41] Though physical gesture rooted human communication naturally in the body, it was nevertheless a limited form of interaction, unable to express the emotions and the passions as effectively as speech, for "while visible signs can render a more exact imitation, sounds more effectively arouse interest" (9), and while "need dictated the first gestures . . . the passions stimulated the first words" (11). This initial distinction between need and passion is crucial for Rousseau: the satisfaction of basic human needs led to the dispersal of early populations around the world without the socializing glue of spoken language; the experience of love, pity, mourning, and anger, by contrast, would soon inspire "the invention of the most ancient words." And that, Rousseau contends, "is why the first languages were singable and passionate before they became simple and methodical" (12). Figurative, poetic language preceded literal, definitional discourse; if the "first tongue" still existed, he fantasizes, all its forms would have to be "in images, feelings, and figures," even its "mechanical part . . . correspond[ing] to its initial object" (14–15). The remainder of the *Essay* is devoted largely to assessing the moral implications of humanity's loss of this originary linguistic state.

The initial culprit, of course, was writing. The *Essay*'s fifth chapter, "On Script," outlines what Derrida will identify as Rousseau's Achilles heel: his belief that the emergence of script—and alphabetical writing in particular—exerted a deleterious effect upon the natural intimacy between speech and emotion. "Writing, which would seem to crystallize language," posits Rousseau, "is precisely what alters it. It changes not the words but the spirit, substituting exactitude for expressiveness. Feelings are expressed in speaking, ideas in writing. In writing, one is forced to use all the words according to their conventional meaning. But in speaking, one varies the meanings by varying one's tone of voice, determining them as one pleases" (21–22). Accordingly, Rousseau claims, Homer must be claimed as an oral rather than a scriptive poet: for centuries the *Iliad* and the *Odyssey* "were written only in men's memories," and Homer achieved his status as a rapture-inducing poet through the ancient musicality perduring in and inspiriting his surviving poems despite their written shell. While some would argue that modern poetry (the subject of the *Essay*'s chapter 7) registers the musical character of modern lan-

41. Rousseau, *Essay on the Origins of Languages*, 5; citations hereafter in text. O'Dea's helpful study *Jean-Jacques Rousseau: Music, Illusion and Desire* credits *Of Grammatology* with taking the *Essai* "out of its obscurity . . . at once establish[ing] the *Essai* as a major text in the Rousseau canon, and also help[ing] to stimulate the gradual growth of interest in all the musical writings that has taken place since" (46).

guages, for Rousseau this represents a naïve confusion between prosody and nature: "We have no idea of a sonorous and harmonious language, spoken as much according to sounds as it is according to words. . . . Any language, in which the same words can be set to several different melodies, has no determinate musical accent" (24–26). The original "social" human languages were those of "the southern climes" and are "children of pleasure rather than need" (46), products of the seasonal rhythms of agricultural communities as they gradually formed cultures and nations based on collectivity and consensus. The later, "Northern" languages—French, German, and English, for example—possess an innate barbarism determined by harsh climate and other uncomfortable facts of physical life in northern Europe, where men, "being more robust, are bound to have less delicate voices" (47). Languages of the south "are bound to be sonorous, accented, eloquent, and frequently obscure because of their power. Those of the north are bound to be dull, harsh, articulated, shrill, monotonous, and to have a clarity due more to vocabulary than to good construction" (49). The northern tongues, then— and this is a crucial point—are "better suited to writing than speaking," while the inherently more emotive southern languages "lose their life and warmth when they are written" (49). The *Essai* bemoans the triumph of north over south and, as a corollary, the defeat of melody by harmony: while melody provides an imitative medium of communication that once perfectly replicated human emotions and passions in language, European languages have lost the ennobling mimetic properties of the ancient tongues.

Indeed, before civilization and community, Rousseau argues, melody was the original binding force of language, for "the first grammarians subordinated their art to music and were professors of both." Rousseau argues that melody once had a mimetic function inextricably tied to the expression of the human emotions in language: "verse, singing, and speech have a common origin . . . the first discourses were the first songs" (50–51). Harmony, by contrast, represents the amalgamating decline of melodious language; if melody "expresses pity, cries of sorrow and joy, threats and groans" by "imitat[ing] the tones of languages," the addition of harmony "shackles melody, draining it of energy and expressiveness. It wipes out passionate accent, replacing it with the harmonic interval . . . in brief, it separates singing from speech, setting these two languages against each other to their mutual deprivation of all authenticity" (58). "Nature inspires songs, not accords," Rousseau contends; "she speaks of melody, not harmony" (62). The tone of the essay at this point becomes almost apocalyptic and suffused with moral implications: "In dropping its oral tone and sticking exclusively to the establishment of harmonics, music becomes noisier to the ear and less pleasing to the heart. As soon as it stops singing, it stops speaking. And then, with all its accord and all its harmony it will have no more effect upon us" (65). The entire course of human history for Rousseau is thus a gradual falling-off from the pristine unity of originary melodious speech toward an amalgamated and paradoxically cacophonous harmony (or, as de Man puts it, music for Rousseau "is the diachronic version of the pattern of non-coincidence within the moment"[42]). The ultimate result, the *Essay* maintains, is the loss of the persuasive arts in public discourse. "Societies have assumed their final form," he laments in the concluding chapter; "no longer is anything changed except by arms and cash" (72).

Even a cursory reading of the *Essay* reveals that the Middle Ages represent for Rousseau the great and disastrous Fall of musical language.[43] After tracing the gradual separation of music from speech during Greek and Roman antiquity, Rousseau—in the treatise's penultimate, culminating, and most polemical chapter ("How Music Has Degenerated")—casts the epoch between the fall of Rome and the Italian Renaissance as a thousand-year decline of melodious language from its ancient musical heights to its barbarous, Gothic depths:

Finally came the catastrophe that disrupted the progress of the human spirit without removing the faults that were its product. Europe, flooded with barbarians, enslaved by ignoramuses, lost at the same time her sciences, her arts, and that universal instrument of both: that is, harmoniously perfected language. Imperceptibly, every ear became accustomed to the rude voices of these coarse men engendered by the North. Their harsh, expressionless voices were noisy without being sonorous. . . . Singing soon became no more than a slow, tiresome sequence of drawling sounds and yells, without softness, without measure, and without grace. (70)

More disastrously still, the so-called Barbarian Invasions paved the way for the medieval invention of musical harmony, which Rousseau derides in a blistering image of liturgical polyphony as it arose from the "unlimited duration[s]" of medieval chant: "That singing was thus devoid of melody, consisting solely of volume and duration of the sounds, was bound to suggest at last a way of making it more melodious again, with

---

42. de Man, *Blindness and Insight*, 129.
43. On the "Fall-in-general" in *Of Grammatology*, see Hart, *Trespass of the Sign*, 15–21.

the help of the consonances. Several voices, ceaselessly drawling sounds of unlimited duration, in unison, happened upon some harmonies, which seemed pleasant to them because they added to the noise. And thus began the practice of descant and of counterpoint" (70). The "catastrophe" of the medieval is epitomized for Rousseau by Jean de Muris and the tedium of fourteenth-century Ars Nova writings on harmony and rhythm, with their obsessive treatment of intervals and note forms, signs of the arcane technicality that had triumphed over melody during the preceding millennium, when music was finally forced to submit to the medieval tyranny of writing. "Thus we see how singing gradually became an art entirely separate from speech, from which it takes its origin; how the harmonics of sounds resulted in forgetting vocal inflections; and finally, how music, restricted to purely physical concurrences of vibrations, found itself deprived of the moral power it had yielded when it was the twofold voice of nature" (71–72). In Rousseau's wonderfully paranoid view of history, the medieval is the privileged site of linguistic separation, deprivation, even immorality, the nadir of human communication whose legacy is the "final form" of eighteenth-century French opera. As he puts it wryly in his chapter 18, "It is known that our harmony is a Gothic invention" (66).

Rousseau's *Essay on the Origin of Languages* thus promotes an immense anti-medievalism as a central part of its argumentative tactics, historical assumptions, and moral consciousness. Though the *Essay* emerges as a vivid demonstration of the more general temporal and ethical partitionings in which any exercise in periodization inevitably engages, its theory and practice of periodization crystallize most anxiously around the specification of the medieval and its deleterious centrality to the historical trajectory recorded by Rousseau.[44] As such, the *Essay* registers the Enlightenment's obsessive construction of the Middle Ages as an era not simply of backwardness, darkness, and anti-individualism, but of linguistic degeneration, melodic impoverishment, and thus moral catastrophe. More specifically still, Rousseau invents the musical harmonies of the high medieval liturgy—"descant" and "counterpoint," terms that here denote the forms of liturgical polyphony that embellished the "ceaselessly drawling sounds" of Gregorian chant beginning in the twelfth century—as a convenient synecdoche for three millennia of linguistic denaturalization and moral regression that separate his own mo-

---

44. On periodization in the *Essay* and in *Of Grammatology*, see de Man's brief remarks in *Blindness and Insight*, 137–38.

ment from the "inventors of speech" and their melodious languages. Medieval liturgy embodies the barbaric essence of the process of historical degeneration diagnosed by Rousseau, assuming pride of place as the *Essay*'s favorite target of abjection—and, as Derrida will recognize, perhaps its most devastating vulnerability.

Rousseau's Regressions

It has never been a mystery why Derrida chose the *Essay on the Origin of Languages* as one of the three main prior texts in which to ground the larger project of *Of Grammatology*. For Derrida, the age of Rousseau occupies "a privileged place . . . in the history of logocentrism," a nodal moment along the trajectory that for thousands of years has been gradually subsuming the formal and phenomenological diversity of language under the domain of writing: "If the history of metaphysics is the history of a determination of being as presence, if its adventure merges with that of logocentrism, and if it is produced wholly as the reduction of the trace, Rousseau's work seems to me to occupy, between Plato's *Phaedrus* and Hegel's *Encyclopedia,* a singular position" (97). It is obvious already what this "between" represses, of course, a repression that Derrida's interrogation of Rousseau will do much to redress. The *Essay* in particular proves irresistibly symptomatic of this historical repression as it "opposes speech to writing as presence to absence and liberty to servitude" (168)—and it does so economically, with an argumentative efficiency that renders the historical unfolding of the world and its languages in a linear narrative that for Derrida is compromised from its inception. While Derrida only covertly addresses in *Of Grammatology* the question of periodization, the book's deconstruction of the *Essay on the Origin of Languages* focuses precisely on this putatively medieval historical problematic: the supposed separation of musicality from speech during the age of the barbarians, a degenerative "harmonizing" of human language almost apocalyptic in its Rousseauist guise.

Throughout *Of Grammatology* Part II, Derrida makes very clear the archaeological stakes of his critique of the *Essay,* which elaborates what he terms an "archeo-teleology of the nature of language and the language of nature" by which "the original and ideal essence of speech is song itself" (198). This underlying archeo-teleology inspires the historicism at work in the *Essay,* a punctuated troping of supplementarity, substitution, and accretion that Rousseau misrecognizes as a "gradual" process of decline and desolation. "It never varies: beginning with an origin or a center that divides itself and leaves itself, an historical circle is described, which is degenerative in direction but progressive and compensatory in effect" (202). The foundational contradiction that enables Rousseau's historical vision is the archaic inevitability of this degeneration, of "the desolating separation of song and speech" (199) that exists already at the origin of human speech—indeed, in some sense *constitutes* the origin:

> This then is the story. For the history that follows the origin and is added to it is nothing but the story of the separation between song and speech. If we consider the difference which fractured the origin, it must be said that this history, which is decadence and degeneracy through and through, had no prehistory. Degeneration as separation, severing of voice and song, has always already begun. . . . Rousseau's entire text *describes* origin as the beginning of the end, as the inaugural decadence. Yet in spite of that description, the text twists about in a sort of oblique effort to act *as if* degeneration were not prescribed in the genesis and as if evil *supervened upon* a good origin. As if song and speech, which have the same act and the same birthpangs, had not always already begun to separate themselves. (198)

Rousseau's historicist mission involves a rhetorical feint: a disingenuous insistence upon the "law of *geometric regression,*" as Derrida calls it, that would substitute inexorable decline for supplementary rupture. The "evil" Derrida identifies as the force of degeneration and decline in the *Essay* crops up at various points in the history of human language—yet the degeneration of language must be forcefully prescribed at the site of its origin. For Derrida, this archeo-teleological prescription is the "supplement," that paralysis of substitution and accretion that undermines the "fullness" of speech at its avowed origin, itself already suffused with "articulation," with "the becoming-writing of language." Rousseau "*declares* what he *wishes to say,* that is to say that articulation and writing are a post-originary malady of language; he says or *describes* that which he *does not wish to say:* articulation and therefore the space of writing operates at the origin of language." In short, Derrida proposes, the *Essay* reveals against its declarative confidence "that 'progress' takes place *both* for the worse *and* for the better. At the same time. Which annuls eschatology and teleology, just as difference—or originary articulation—annuls archeology" (229).

These annulments converge into what Derrida critiques as a kind of metaleptic historicism, one that condenses into the medieval a long chain of metonyms for the process of degeneration elaborated throughout the *Essay*. In an extended reading of the nineteenth chapter, where the *Essay* had posited a musico-linguistic catastrophe of epic proportions, Derrida turns with Rousseau to the epochal transition that initiated the final degenerative break with the melodious languages of the archaic past. While Rousseau regards the Middle Ages as "the catastrophe that disrupted the progress of the human spirit without removing the faults that were its product," a time when "harsh, expressionless voices were noisy without being sonorous," for Derrida this very abjection of the epoch exposes in the *Essay* the binary logic that undergirds Rousseau's historicism:

In addition to the system of oppositions that controls the entire Essay (servitude/politico-linguistic liberty, North/South, articulation/accent, consonant/vowel, capital/province//autarchic and democratic city), we may perceive here the strange workings of the historical process according to Rousseau. . . . It is thus, by destroying the "progress of the human spirit" that the anterior cycle had produced, that the invasion of the northern barbarians ushered in a new cycle of historical degeneration. The harmful and dissolving effects of philosophy had in fact been limited by themselves. (202)

The barbarian invasions, popularized in Rousseau's own century by Gibbon, mark the reified beginnings of the Middle Ages, which Rousseau imagines as violently severing language from its melodic "energy" (68). As read in *Of Grammatology*, by contrast, this epochal break provides the very foundation of Rousseau's entire theory of imitation and its putative loss; as Derrida puts it, "Spacing insinuates into presence an interval which not only separates the different times of speech and of song but also the represented from the representer. . . . Rousseau has need of imitation, he advances it as the possibility of song and the emergence out of animality, but he exalts it only as a reproduction adding itself to the represented though it *adds nothing,* simply supplements it."

A vast historical "interval" thus separates speech from song, just as an ideal musical mimesis will always elude human capacities. Rousseau's interval is the historical "trace," the surplus of musico-linguistic identity over which the *Essai* has no control. "This fissure is not one among others," Derrida posits. "It is *the* fissure: the necessity of interval, the harsh law of spacing. It could not endanger song except by being inscribed in it from its birth and in its essence" (200). This surplus or supplement is, very clearly in *Of Grammatology,* the trace of the medieval. Rousseau's construction of the Middle Ages serves as Derrida's most crucial point of attack against the Enlightenment's invention of the millennium it did so much to darken.

Derrida's intricate scrutiny of Rousseau's medievalism is not an isolated theme among his mid-1960s writings. It bears particular comparison with his anti-structuralist critique of Foucault's *Madness and Civilization* in "Cogito and the History of Madness," originally delivered as a
lecture at the Collège Philosophique in March 1963 and subsequently
published in *Writing and Difference*. (In a 1967 interview, Derrida proposed that *Of Grammatology* be read as a "bipartite work in the middle of
which one could insert *L'écriture et la différence*," further clarifying the
force of this apposition.)[45] Derrida's purpose as he relates it is to follow
Foucault's lead by "reinscribing an interpretation of the Cartesian Cogito within the total framework of *Madness and Civilization*."[46] The project of Foucault's book is "an archaeology of silence," an attempt to make
a certain history of madness speak against the emerging forces of repression—indeed, to make madness the very voice of this history, "its theme
and its first-person narrator."[47] Above all, Derrida contends, Foucault
aims to articulate (even while recognizing the impossibility of doing so)
"a purist, intransigent, nonviolent, nondialectical allegation" against
the Cartesian Cogito that would attempt to write a history of madness
not from the perspective of "the jailer," or classical scientific knowledge
that excluded and abjected madness from its domain (as Descartes himself sought to do in the *Meditations*), but from a position beyond the "objectivist project of classical reason." This "allegation" carries with it certain risks and entailments, for it "is often counterbalanced, equilibrated,
I should even say contradicted by a discourse in Foucault's book that is
not only the admission of a difficulty, but the formulation of *another*
project, a project that is not an expediency, but a different and more ambitious one, a project more effectively ambitious than the first one."[48]
And indeed, the ancillary project of *Madness and Civilization* raises what
Derrida insists are "prerequisite methodological or philosophical considerations" that go unacknowledged in the book yet have crucial bearing on its founding claims. This "other" project, Derrida suggests, is
diachrony.

"What is the historical responsibility of this logic of archaeology?"
Derrida asks of Foucault's book. "Where should it be situated?"[49] For the
nondialectical *beyond* that Foucault's structuralism inspires him to desire

45. Derrida, preface to *Writing and Difference*, x.
46. Derrida, "Cogito and the History of Madness," in *Writing and Difference*, 33.
47. Derrida, "Cogito and the History of Madness," 34.
48. Derrida, "Cogito and the History of Madness," 36.
49. Derrida, "Cogito and the History of Madness," 35.

depends utterly on a *before,* a precedent that will be arrested at the putative new beginning: "Because the silence whose archaeology is to be undertaken is not an original muteness or nondiscourse, but a subsequent silence, a discourse arrested by *command,* the issue is therefore to reach the origin of the protectionism imposed by a reason that insists upon being sheltered, and that also insists upon providing itself with protective barriers against madness." The issue for Derrida, then, is precisely that of historical delineation and the problems this would pose for a structuralist analytic. The Cogito symptomatizes a separation, the "Decision" (as Derrida characterizes Foucault's argument) in the early modern period to abject madness from and within the domain of reason, the Decision that "link[ed] and separate[d] reason and madness," the Decision that must be understood at once "both as the original act of an order, a fiat, a decree, and as a schism, a caesura, a separation, a dissection." Derrida prefers the term *dissension,* "to underline that in question is a self-dividing action, a cleavage and torment interior to meaning *in general.*"[50] Anterior to the Decision that divided reason against itself, Derrida posits, there must have been "a logos of free trade, that is . . . a logos that preceded the split of reason and madness, a logos which within itself permitted dialogue between what were later called reason and madness (unreason), permitted their free circulation and exchange, just as the medieval city permitted the free circulation of the mad within itself." Derrida's invocation of the "medieval city" here is more than a metaphorical convenience. The point of his critique is to exhume in *Madness and Civilization* "the virgin and unitary ground upon which the decisive act linking and separating madness and reason took root." I quote "Cogito and the History of Madness" at length here to illustrate the force of this point for the sort of critical archaeology of medievalism practiced by Derrida upon Foucault and, as we have seen, upon Rousseau:

The reason and madness of the classical age had a common root. But this common root, which is a logos, this unitary foundation is much more ancient than the medieval period, brilliantly but briefly evoked by Foucault in his very fine opening chapter. There must be a founding unity that already carries within it the "free trade" of the Middle Ages, and this unity is already the unity of a logos, that is, of a reason; an already historical reason certainly, but a reason much less determined than it will be in its so-called classical form, having not yet received the determinations of the "classi-

---

50. Derrida, "Cogito and the History of Madness," 38.

cal age." It is within the element of this archaic reason that the dissection, the dissension, will present itself as a modification or, if you will, as an overturning, that is, a revolution but an internal revolution, a revolution affecting the self, occurring within the self. For this logos which is in the beginning, is not only the common ground of all dissension, but also—and no less importantly—the very atmosphere in which Foucault's language moves, the atmosphere in which a history of madness during the classical age not only appears in fact but is also by all rights stipulated and specified in terms of its limits. In order to account simultaneously for the origin (or the possibility) of the decision and for the origin (or the possibility) of its narration, it might have been necessary to start by reflecting this original logos in which the violence of the classical era played itself out. This history of logos before the Middle Ages and before the classical age is not, if this need be said at all, a nocturnal and mute prehistory. Whatever the momentary break, if there is one, of the Middle Ages with the Greek tradition, this break and this alteration are late and secondary developments as concerns the fundamental permanence of the logico-philosophical heritage.[51]

On the terms of Foucault's argument, Derrida insists, the "founding unity" of the logos must be *pre*-medieval: even the crisis of late antiquity must antedate the "revolution . . . occurring within the self." The dissective revolution imputed to the early modern period is thus inherent to the "archaic reason" that hosts the very "dissension" that in turn makes Foucault's project plausible. This goes far beyond the commonplace that any historiographical insistence on change, transition, and innovation risks stabilizing and rendering monolithic the archaic it constructs as its ground. For Derrida, Foucault's refusal to account for the archaeology of dissension determines even his analytic language and his argumentative tactics; in Derrida's phrase, it pervades "the very atmosphere in which Foucault's language moves," an atmosphere that stipulates the limits of its subject rather than working against the structuralist synchronism that circumscribes the book's domain. Perhaps the most intriguing moment in Derrida's critique comes in that subordinate clause in the final sentence: "if there is one." Even if there *is* a "break . . . of the Middle Ages with the Greek tradition," Derrida proposes, "original logos" has a diachronic perdurance from which no decision of the Enlightenment can claim privileged distance. In short, the discourse of madness in the Age of Reason symptomatizes the period's own failure to know itself and suggests that it exists within a much longer *durée* than either Foucault or his subjects could have acknowledged: "this crisis in

51. Derrida, "Cogito and the History of Madness," 39.

which reason is madder than madness . . . and in which madness is more rational than reason . . . has always begun and is interminable. It suffices to say that, if it is classic, it is not so in the sense of the classical age but in the sense of eternal and essential classicism, and is also historical in an unexpected sense."[52]

As Derrida exposes them, then, while the ideological motivations behind the medievalisms of Rousseau and Foucault are quite distinct, their effects are remarkably similar. Rousseau invents the medieval as the barbaric epoch that infected melody with harmony, symbolizing the final incursion of writing into the domain of speech and its inexorable triumph over voice. Foucault, by contrast, envisions the Middle Ages as a millennium of "free trade" between madness and reason, an era of discursive flow that would only later be subsumed under the domain of the Cogito. What the Enlightenment *philosophe* and the postwar intellectual archaeologist both attempt to get away with, however, is a *deployment* of the medieval as an alibi for a refusal: a refusal of the "always already," of the archaic inherence of dissension and supplementarity, of the originary trace that—with Derrida's coaxing—erases the temporal distinctions upon which each project profoundly depends.

Derrida's reading of the *Essay on the Origin of Languages* reaches one of its culminating points in his treatment of Rousseau's polemic with his contemporary, Jean-Philip Rameau, the French composer, theorist, and philosopher who engaged in a long and often politically charged debate with Rousseau over the origins of melody, harmony, and musical understanding.[53] For Rameau, harmony, not melody, was to be understood as the "natural" or primary form of music, harmonic intervals the product of physical bodies in their natural vibrations; melody assumed a secondary or derivative role as an outgrowth of the primordial naturalism of harmony. (To simplify, for Rameau, harmony = nature, melody = culture; Rousseau, as we have already seen, holds exactly the reverse.) Rousseau, as Derrida points out, gave this dispute enormous ethical weight: "If Rameau is mistaken, his errings are moral faults before being theoretical errors" (211). Initially paraphrasing Rousseau in this regard, Derrida then turns Rousseau's demonizing polemic against Rameau on its head, suggesting that the theoretical scaffolding supporting his theory of melodic primacy rests on a devastatingly compromised ethnohistoricism:

52. Derrida, "Cogito and the History of Madness," 62.
53. The original context of this polemic is discussed in O'Dea, *Jean-Jacques Rousseau*, 28ff.

Rameau's aberration is a symptom. It betrays the sickness both of the history of the West and of European ethnocentrism. For harmony according to Rousseau is a musical perversion that dominates Europe (Northern Europe) alone, and ethnocentrism consists of considering it a natural and universal principle of music. The harmony that destroys the *energy* of music and shackles its *imitative* force—melody—is absent in the beginning of music (*in illo tempore*) and in non-European music (*alibi*). One wonders if Rousseau, conforming to a schema that we now know well, does not criticize ethnocentrism by a symmetrical counter-ethnocentrism and a profound Western ethnocentrism: notably by claiming that harmony is the evil and the science proper to Europe. (212)

The archaeology of Rousseau's ethnocentrism leads us back ultimately to its medieval impetus. Harmony for Rousseau is an invention of the Middle Ages, when the advent of liturgical polyphony served to corrupt once and for all the already degraded melodic speech inherited from antiquity. Rousseau's pathologizing invocation of the Gothic—as sickness, as perversion, as destruction, even as a kind of enslavement or "shackling" of mimesis—speaks volumes about the larger historical stakes for the Enlightenment in defining the medieval against itself. If Rousseau takes Rameau to the mat for his ethnocentric vision of harmony as universal and natural, Derrida exposes the sense in which Rousseau's own unacknowledged ethnocentrism—and thus the Enlightenment's, and thus the Western tradition's—must be indistinguishable from the medievalism that subtends it, a medievalism inspired by its moral rejection of "the evil and the science proper to Europe": namely, the liturgical harmonies of the medieval Church.

Neuming

As it comes to be dismantled in *Of Grammatology,* the Rousseauist theory of human language and its origins proves vulgarly historicist. Rousseau takes a kind of perverse delight in the inexorable decay of melody in which his own age's musical life vibrantly participates, and his medievalism should be understood in part (Derrida recognizes) as an individualized performance of cultural self-loathing. By way of concluding this chapter, though, I want to turn to *Of Grammatology*'s closing trajectory, which unfolds a vigorous rebuttal of Rousseau's medievalism by posing an implicit yet compelling liturgical posture against and within the history of logocentrism. With Levinas, though here without explicit acknowledgment, *Of Grammatology* argues that liturgy need not be coterminous with religiosity, that there may exist a realm of doxology unwedded to a specific theology yet emphatically not at the philosophical service of a nihilistic antiliturgicalism.

Nearing the end of his critique of the *Essay on the Origin of Languages,* Derrida begins to look elsewhere in Rousseau's writings for signs of the motivating fantasy of the *Essay:* the discovery of a pure language uninfected by the supplement. In Rousseau's diverse metalinguistic writings can be discerned a thoroughgoing desire for a language that will reconcile "the two contradictory possibilities that Rousseau wishes to retain simultaneously." Such a reconciliation would allow human languages a momentary recovery of what various historical catastrophes have sundered:

We shall, then, examine how Rousseau operates when, for example, he attempts to define the limit of possibility of the thing whose impossibility he describes: the natural voice or the inarticulate language. No longer the animal cry before the birth of language; but not yet the articulated language, already shaped and undermined by absence and death. Between the prelinguistic and the linguistic, between cry and speech, animal and man, nature and society, Rousseau looks for a limit "being born," and he gives it several determinations. There are at least two of them that have the same function. They relate to childhood and to God. In each, two contradictory predicates are united: it is a matter of language uncontaminated by supplementarity. (247)

The first of these fantasies, the fantasy of childhood, inspires Rousseau's *Emile,* where the child "has language" that nevertheless lacks "the power of *replacing itself,* of substituting one sign for another" (247). But this model falls far short of Rousseau's aim, for while "the child speaks without knowing how to speak," he also "speaks without knowing how to sing." What is needed, then, is a simultaneously "speaking and singing breath, breath of language which is nonetheless inarticulate." Where might such a paradoxically full yet inarticulate language—a language of non-supplementarity—be found? What historical practices model it, and how might they be recovered and reclaimed as a means of redressing the linguistic impoverishment of Rousseau's present?

For Rousseau, they are modeled—as Derrida reveals with breathtaking precision—in the liturgical culture of the medieval Catholic Church. They may be found in the liturgies of those same barbaric Middle Ages that represent the "final catastrophe" for the passionate musicality of language. *Of Grammatology* recognizes this irony, and its second part culminates in an incisive reading of the *philosophe's* almost mythical treatment of that most medieval of liturgical phenomena, the "neume" or *pneuma*. Rousseau's neume is not the inscribed, graphic note-form of medieval chant, but what Augustine and later writers on the liturgy described as the untexted melisma built on the last syllable of the Alleluia.[54] With Levinas clearly in mind, Derrida turns from the *Essay on the Origin of Languages* to Rousseau's entry on liturgical neuming from the *Dictionary of Music*. In the following extended passage from *Of Grammatology*, Derrida specifies the "spell of self-presence" that captivates Rousseau throughout the *Essay* as a historical blindness unknowingly cured in the *Dictionary*, from which the indented quotation in the middle of the Derridean passage derives:

Such a breath cannot have a human origin and a human destination. It is no longer on the way to humanity like the language of the child, but is rather on the way to superhumanity. Its principle and its end are theological, as the voice and providence of nature. It is on this onto-theological model that Rousseau regulates his repetitions of origin. With this exemplary model of a pure breath (*pneuma*) and of an intact life, of a song and an inarticulate language, of speech without spacing, we have, even if it is placeless [*atopique*] or utopian, a paradigm suitable to our measure. We can name and define it. It is the neume: pure vocalization, form of an inarticulate song without speech, whose name means breath, which is inspired in us by God and may address only Him. The *Dictionary of Music* defines it as such:

NEUME. S.f. A term in church-music. The neume is a kind of short recapitulation of the air in a mode, which is made at the end of an antiphon, by a simple variety of sounds, and without joining to them any words. The Catholics authorize this singular custom on a passage of St. Augustine, who says, that no words being possible to be worthy of pleasing God, it is laudable to address him in a confused music of jubilation. "For to whom is such a jubilation suitable, unless to an ineffable Being? and how can we celebrate this ineffable Being, since we cannot be silent, or find any thing in our transports which can express them, unless unarticulated sounds?"

To speak before knowing how to speak, not to be able either to be silent or to speak, this limit of origin is indeed that of a pure presence, present enough to be living, to be felt in pleasure [*jouissance*] but pure enough to have remained unblemished by the work of difference, inarticulate enough for self-delight [*jouissance de soi*] not to be corrupted by interval, discontinuity, alterity. Indeed, Rousseau thinks that this experience of a continual present is accorded only to God: given to God or to those whose hearts accord and agree with God's. (249)

54. On this vocabulary as it functions in medieval liturgical commentary, see Fassler, *Gothic Song: Victorine Sequences and Augustinian Reform in Twelfth-Century Paris*, 38–45.

Here is Rousseau's vision of "natural" language, returning this time as the wordless liturgical chant of the Christian Middle Ages—returning, in other words, as a "Gothic invention." And Rousseau's neumatic *jouissance,* Derrida argues, pervades the *Essay on the Origin of Languages:* the neume is "the spell of self-presence, inarticulate experience of time, tantamount to saying: *utopia."* Derrida ultimately exposes the Rousseauian *pneuma* as the fantasy of those pre-differentiated, pre-linguistic "gestures" and "inarticulate sounds" that Rousseau posits in the *Essay* as the Edenic state of human communication and commonality that the medieval will disastrously curtail. The result in Rousseau's text is what Derrida critiques as an impossibly metonymic theory of progress, "that continuous sliding, that slow transition from pure nature to the birth of society" (255). Even as the Middle Ages draw speech and song inexorably asunder, the era embodies the most idealized form of pure musical speech in its doxological performances.

The ultimate implications of Derrida's provocative unraveling of these liturgical aspirations in Rousseau become clear only in *Of Grammatology*'s closing pages, which serve to sum up the circuitous critique of the *Essay*'s "Theory of Writing" in Part II, chapter 4. Derrida titled this short final section "The Supplement of (at) the Origin," and it may be the least carefully read part of this massively influential book. By "least carefully read" I don't necessarily mean misunderstood: as the title that unifies them indicates, these pages in many ways most sharply articulate the negative read on Western grammatology adumbrated throughout the book. What I want to suggest is that they also embed a movingly recuperative stance toward the liturgical aura that Rousseau abjects. As Derrida writes of the *Essay,* "In the last pages of the chapter 'On Script,' the critique, the appreciative presentation, and the history of writing, declares the absolute exteriority of writing but describes the interiority of the principle of writing to language. The sickness of the outside . . . is in the heart of the living word, as its principle of effacement and its relationship to its own death" (313). Derrida's language here approaches the sacramental: if writing's exteriority to melodic language is the fallacy that sustains Rousseau's project, it remains nevertheless true that writing, that "scriptive contagion," is always already enshrined or consecrated in spoken language, the "living word" that must exist in intimate relation with the inscribed rem(a)inder of its own death.

It is of more than incidental interest here that, according to Derrida's intentionally pedantic overview of the dating of the works in question (*Of Grammatology,* 171–94), Rousseau would have developed the themes informing his entries on music for the *Encyclopaedia,* his own *Diction-*

naire de musique, and the *Essay* itself all within the span of his adult life as a Catholic convert, which did not come to an end until around 1754.[55] Despite his explicit denials, Rousseau envisions a world in which writing inhabits and in a sense comprises the purest doxologies of Christian liturgy: "As Saussure will do, so does Rousseau wish at once to maintain the exteriority of the system of writing and the maleficent efficiency with which one singles out its symptoms on the body of the language." This symptomatically inscribed liturgical *corpus* both corrodes and comprises language in its oral and written instantiations. Yet what emerges here cannot be reduced to a discourse of anti-doxological nihilism: it is, rather, a Levinasian attempt to find a foothold, to borrow resources, to refuse a simplistic ethics of separation and empathy in favor of a liturgy that casts its utterances in terms of concealment and deferral: "Thus," Derrida paraphrases Rousseau, "writing is always atonal. The place of the subject is there taken by another, it is concealed" (315).

If writing represents the "death" of language, then, it is death only in a liturgical sense, a death under erasure that will always and everywhere condition the linguistic renewals that writing comes to embody. Appropriately, then, *Of Grammatology* concludes with Rousseau's all-too-human dream of avoiding death as projected into his theory of speech and writing: "A speech without consonantic principle, what for Rousseau would be a speech sheltered from all writing, would not be speech; it would hold itself at the fictive limit of the inarticulate and purely natural cry. Conversely, a speech of pure consonants and pure articulation would become pure writing, algebra, or dead language. The death of speech is therefore the horizon and origin of language" (315). This is the originary contradiction on which Rousseau's project stumbles: that the demise of speech is fully yet mysteriously present at the origin of language, and thus that the death-like, inarticulate groans of the "natural cry" will mark both the beginning and the end—the very condition of possibility—of the life-giving liturgical neuming to which Rousseau's theory of the origin of languages aspires:

But an origin and a horizon which do not hold themselves at its exterior borders. As always, death, which is neither a present to come nor a present past, shapes the interior of speech, as its trace, its reserve, its interior and exterior differance: as its supplement.

But Rousseau could not think this writing, that takes place *before* and *within*

---

55. Derrida's *Of Grammatology* has since become a key player in the venerable dispute over this text's dating, for example in Bourdin, *Essai sur l'Essai,* 41–44.

speech. To the extent that he belonged to the metaphysics of presence, he *dreamed* of the simple exteriority of death to life, evil to good, representation to presence, signifier to signified, representer to represented, mask to face, writing to speech. But all such oppositions are irreducibly rooted in that metaphysics. Using them, one can only operate by reversals, that is to say by confirmations. The supplement is none of these terms. It is especially not more a signifier than a signified, a representer than a presence, a writing than a speech. None of the terms of this series can, being comprehended within it, dominate the economy of differance or supplementarity. Rousseau's *dream* consisted of making the supplement enter metaphysics by force. (315)

The clear evocation of Levinas in the phrase "mask to face" suggests the liturgical tenor of Derrida's final words in *Of Grammatology,* entering as they do into "the domain of the sacrament": "how we are present to each other." [56] The face of the Other is epiphanic, and if death provides the representational limit of the "metaphysics of presence," the writing that takes place "before and within speech" gives as much life as it takes away. Derrida almost seems to be suggesting that the *supplement* is itself a kind of sacrament, a liturgically enacted confirmation and reminder of the inspiriting presence of absent things: the supplement is not more "a representer than a presence."

It would thus be hard to imagine graver misreadings of Derridean critiques of Western metaphysics than those promoted within the Radical Orthodoxy. As Derrida himself avowed, deconstruction is itself a kind of analytical sacrament, "not destructive, not having the purpose of dissolving, distracting or subtracting elements in order to reveal an internal essence. It asks questions about the essence, about the presence, indeed about this interior/exterior, phenomenon/appearance schema." [57] In Milbank and Pickstock's view, however, "one cannot for Derrida ever present oneself, as oneself, to the Other, either with one's gifts, praise or prayer." [58] If Pickstock in *After Writing* holds Derrida accountable for promoting the "necrophilia" and "life-death dualism . . . explicitly articulated in recent 'postmodern' and 'Levinasian' philosophy," *Of Grammatology* in fact bases its concluding critique of Rousseau on the *philosophe's* Enlightenment investment in the "simple exteriority of death to life." If Pickstock's impassioned charter for a liturgical consummation aspires to a doxology "after writing," this doxology fails to account for that "writing beyond good and evil" that conditions the history of metaphysics

56. Beckwith, *Signifying God,* xv.
57. See Mortley, *French Philosophers,* 96–97.
58. Milbank and Pickstock, *Truth in Aquinas,* 91.

and, ultimately, of liturgical representation as such. And if *After Writing* finds in Derrida's oeuvre "the inevitably nihilistic conclusion of a rationalism indifferent to the specificities of human place, time, and desire," Derrida himself works throughout much of *Of Grammatology* to locate and specify the metaphysical desire of a particular eighteenth-century intellectual for the living presence of a pure speech untainted by the economy of script: a liturgical speech (only highlighting Pickstock's own ironic failure to distinguish between voiced and unvoiced prayers in the Tridentine Rite). As Derrida recognizes, the doxological inspiritings of liturgical language must always participate in (are a particularly forceful instantiation of) the same metaphysics of presence undergirding the self-comprehension of the Western tradition. In this sense, Derrida stages what is in effect a critique of the representational prerogatives of the very liturgical tradition that Pickstock claims to have recovered *against* deconstruction. One way to understand Part II of *Of Grammatology*, then, is for its status as a devastating response to the medievalism of the Radical Orthodoxy over a quarter of a century *avant la lettre*.

Of Grammatology may be more broadly claimed as one of the great twentieth-century interrogations of medievalism, the medievalism of Enlightenment rationality and its attendant ideology of periodization, the Enlightenment of Rousseau and his century's attempt to account for the legacy of the Dark Ages to European languages and cultures.[59] That Rousseau's abjection of the medieval returns in the form of liturgical supplement is not without a certain irony, as Levinas would surely have recognized. Asking nothing but endless patience from the subject, the liturgical trace will always exist as one of many "clues left behind," archaeological fragments from which "the historian will discover ancient civilizations as horizons for our world."[60]

59. In this sense, *Of Grammatology* has a kind of antiperiodizing sequel in *The Gift of Death*, with the latter's invocation of the Crusades and medieval Christian neo-Platonism in its discussion of Patočka on "the expansion of Europe" and the "failure to assume . . . the memory of [European] history *as* history of responsibility" (Derrida, *The Gift of Death*, 3–4).
60. Levinas, "On the Trail of the Other," 44.

FIVE

The Four Senses of Roland Barthes

Mutatis mutandis, the Middle Ages lived solely on rereading ancient texts, in Greek or Latin. Perhaps literature will now be precisely that: an object made of commentaries, a tutor of other languages, period. Who knows?

ROLAND BARTHES

In 1971, Roland Barthes sat for an interview with Stephen Heath on the subject of his latest work, particularly *S/Z*, which had appeared a year earlier. Throughout the interview, Heath continually tries to pin down the intellectual affiliations of his newly famous interlocutor. Is he a psychoanalyst, perhaps in the Lacanian school? A literary ethnologist in the tradition of Mauss and Lévi-Strauss? Perhaps a historian of culture seeking to take historical inquiry into the domain of the writerly? In typical fashion, Barthes opts for an antidisciplinary recursiveness, refusing to affiliate himself with a specific methodological or institutional program even while casting about for some sense of his own locatedness that will satisfy his interviewer. As Barthes explains in the session's most crystallizing moment, his work has been devoted above all to troubling distinctions between author and critic, writer and reader, text and commentary—distinctions historically specific to the modern epoch yet, Barthes fantasizes, perhaps not guaranteed the perpetuity they would seem to merit:

I don't exile criticism in C major, but I distinguish between critical roles and critical activity, which is no longer a critic's activity, but simply the activity of a writer. It's an activity of the text, of the intertext, of commentary, in that at bottom one can conceive of writing infinitely on past texts, or at least I can. Now, one could very well imagine a time when *works* in the traditional sense of the word would no longer be written, and the works of the past would be rewritten endlessly, "endlessly" in the sense of "perpetually": there would be an activity of proliferating commentary, branching out, recurrent, which would be the true writing activity of our time. After all, it's not unthinkable, since the Middle Ages did just that, and it would be better to go back to the Middle Ages, to what is called the barbarism of the Middle Ages, than to accept a barbarism of repetition; it would be better perpetually to rewrite *Bouvard and Pécuchet* than to stay in the unavowed repetition of stereotypes. Obviously I'm talking about a perpetual commentary that serious theoretical analysis would take beyond the stage of paraphrase to "crack" texts and obtain something else.[1]

If "proliferating commentary, branching out, recurrent" could indeed become the "true writing activity of our time," perhaps we would learn to forfeit our manifold investments in authorial originality. If "writing infinitely on past texts" could somehow corrode the reverence accorded to "*works* in the traditional sense of the word," we might escape the "barbarism of repetition" that mires literary and critical production in the quicksand of stereotypes. If, in short, we could just "go back to the Middle Ages," perhaps our era would invent its own "perpetual commentary" in lieu of the stale paraphrasing that passes for critical argument.

If the tone of Barthes's proposed medieval return seems offhand, its implied historical argument about the relation of text and commentary is actually quite precise; as I argue in this chapter, its inspiration is profound. For beneath Barthes's urbane investment in the so-called "barbarism of the Middle Ages" rests an awed devotion to the hermeneutical proliferations embodied in the exegetical culture of the medieval West as he understood it. By the time he came to write *S/Z*, Barthes had absorbed immense amounts from his study of premodern critical practices, though as the exchange above suggests, this process of interpretive osmosis more often remains uninterrogated and even abnegated than confronted head-on in the course of his self-reflections.

This avoidance is perhaps more surprising in Barthes's case than it might seem, for his institutional and intellectual relations with medieval studies represented a strong and vibrant force throughout his writing career.[2] As a fourth-form student at the Lycée Montaigne in Paris, he

1. Barthes, *The Grain of the Voice*, 148.
2. Most of the details about Barthes's life recounted in this chapter derive from three intellectual biographies of the critic: Stafford, *Roland Barthes, Phenomenon and Myth;* Calvet, *Roland Barthes: A Biography;* and Ette, *Roland Barthes: eine intellektuelle Biographie.*

was smitten with his French teacher, none other than the great Robert Grandsaine d'Hauterive, medieval lexicographer extraordinaire and compiler of the *Dictionnaire d'ancien français, moyen âge et renaissance,* whom Barthes would remember as one of the great "'conductors' of memory" linking the ancient French past to his early life and later years.[3] During the 1930s, moreover, while a student at the Sorbonne, Barthes participated frequently in dramatic revivals of ancient and medieval theater instigated by groups such as Gustave Cohen's *Théophiliens* (named for the thirteenth-century *Miracle de Théophile* by Rutebeuf), a group that also included the medievalist Paul Zumthor. As Helen Solterer has argued, such revivals argued for a "theatrical rapport between the living and dead" that brought the physical space of the interwar university into play as a crucial mediating site for the performative resurrection of the past.[4] If for Derrida the medieval inscribes the barbaric trace in the Enlightenment imagination, the Middle Ages of Roland Barthes deliver missiles of intellectual energy, both readerly and writerly, fissuring the confident façade of avant-garde critique.

Tel Quel Médiévale

Like the other premodernities treated in this book, Barthes's archaizing returns to the Middle Ages might be understood in relation to the often consuming medievalism inspiring the coterie of Parisian intellectuals associated with the journal *Tel Quel* during its first decade—a journal which, in Jean-Michel Rabaté's words, "embodied, summed up, or allegorized a whole state of mind; in short, stood for what is now seen with nostalgia and awe as 'the age of theory.'"[5] *Tel Quel* was launched in 1960 and supported by the full pantheon of left-leaning Parisian intellectuals, including Barthes, Kristeva, Lacan, Derrida, Foucault, Jean Baudrillard, Philippe Sollers, and many others. Though the journal's primary energies were directed toward a revitalization of literary studies with infusions of structuralism, psychoanalysis, and other theoretical currencies, *Tel Quel* was very much a historical enterprise as well, one that reached back enthusiastically to a Middle Ages it established as its *terminus a quo.* As its recent chronicler Patrick Ffrench notes, the stated project of the

---

3. Barthes, *Roland Barthes,* 108–9; see also Calvet, *Roland Barthes,* 17.
4. Solterer, "The Waking of Medieval Theatricality," 358.
5. Rabaté, *The Future of Theory,* 77.

journal was "a reframing of the history of literature from the time of Dante," a characterization that a survey of the complete run of *Tel Quel* strongly bears out.[6] In early volumes, Jean Starobinski reads the poetry of Rabelais through the lens of Spitzerian philology as a great medieval embracing of linguistic possibility, while Jean-Joseph Goux takes Augustine's *Confessions* as an attempt to negotiate the "speech of the other."[7] Volumes 11 and 12 printed a serial translation of Umberto Eco's long essay on the Middle Ages of James Joyce, "The Aesthetics of Chaosmos," which had appeared in Italian in 1962, shortly after the publication of Eco's thesis on the aesthetics of Thomas Aquinas.

The autumn 1965 issue features a Dante cluster, including a translated essay by Schelling, "Dante and the Philosophical Perspective"; a close reading of *Inferno* VIII by Edoardo Sanguineti; Bernard Stambler on Dante's three Purgatorial dreams and their status as privileged modes of narrative exposition; a short excerpt from the eighteenth-century polymath Giambattista Vico on Dante and the nature of "true poetics"; and an original piece by Sollers himself on Dante's works as symptomatic of a more general "crossing" or "traversing" of poetic writing. For Sollers, the *Commedia* remains "concealed in the depths of our culture like a blind spot, a limitless enigma whose very proximity seems to render us inattentive and verbose"—and whose revival among the avant garde thus has the potential to occasion a more rigorously historical attention "to language as an increasingly radical question."[8] The *Commedia* must be rescued from the jaws of its Renaissance and Enlightenment commentators, and in particular from Humanism, "which rapidly immobilized it, reduced it to a cultural reference whose torpor seems to have been disturbed solely by a painter, Botticelli."[9]

Though Julia Kristeva's later work on premodern cultures is well known to Anglo-American readers (the 1980 collection *Desire in Language,* for example, includes essays on Bellini and Giotto, while *Tales of Love* [1982] collects work on Bernard of Clairvaux, Thomas Aquinas, the literature of courtly love, and other topics), the medievalist archaeology of Kristevan semiology is already evident in her three earliest books:

---

6. Ffrench, *The Time of Theory,* 6. For a more historically minded account of the journal's relation to contemporary Left politics and its critique of "engagement," see Marx-Scouras, *The Cultural Politics of Tel Quel.*

7. Starobinski, "Saint Augustine et la parole de l'autre"; Goux, "Note sur Rabelais et le langage."

8. Sollers, "Dante et la traversée de l'écriture"; translated in Sollers, *Writing and the Experience of Limits,* 11–44.

9. Sollers, *Writing and the Experience of Limits,* 11.

Language the Unknown (*Le langage, cet inconnu,* 1969, published under the name Julia Joyaux), which includes a chapter on medieval speculative grammar and theory of vernacularity; Σημειωτικη *[Sēmeiōtikē]: Recherches pour une sémanalyse* (1969), in which the chapter titled "Le texte clos" (first written in 1966–67) attributes the change "from symbol to sign" in Occidental thought to "the second half of the Middle Ages (13th–15th centuries) . . . a period of transition for European culture"; and *Le texte du roman* (1970), which takes as its primary focus a little-known work by a magistrate and pedagogue affiliated with the House of Anjou during the middle decades of the fifteenth century.[10]

Antoine de La Sale's *Le petit Jehan de Saintré* (ca. 1455) is among a small collection of prose romances from the late Middle Ages that some have dubbed "proto-novels"; Kristeva claims *Le petit Jehan* as "perhaps the first writing in prose that could be called a novel (if one labels as such those works that depend on the ambiguous ideologeme of the sign)."[11] Kristeva wrote repeatedly on *Le petit Jehan de Saintré* during the years following her arrival in Paris in 1966, and the more condensed treatment of the novel in Σημειωτικη does much to explain why it was on this medieval text in particular she would choose to exercise her semanalytical ingenuity during the formative years preceding the completion of her dissertation, *Revolution in Poetic Language,* in 1974.[12] For Kristeva, *Jehan de Saintré*'s significance lies in its unique embodiment of a particular moment of transition in the history of textual understanding and production: "Literary history, immersed in referential opacity, has not been able to bring to light the *transitional structure* of this text, which situates it at the threshold of the two eras [of symbol and sign] and shows, through La Sale's naïve poetics, the articulation of this ideologeme of the sign, which continues to dominate our intellectual horizon."[13] The medieval novel's transitional status as a hallmark of the modern is apparent in ways both small and large: *Jehan de Saintré* "captures the blazon just before this splitting into praise and/or blame," introducing a new kind of

---

10. Kristeva, Σημειωτικη *[Sēmeiōtikē]: Recherches pour une sémanalyse,* 116.

11. Kristeva, *Le texte du roman,* translated in *Desire in Language,* 41–42.

12. Remarkably, none of the French medievalists who have edited or translated *Le petit Jehan* since 1970—and this includes producers of a critical edition, several French modernizations, and at least one English translation—have registered Kristeva's intervention into the text's long history of reception (see La Sale, *Little John of Saintré* and *Saintré*). Judging from the critical apparatuses accompanying the last three decades of editorial and critical scholarship on the work, one would never know that the writings of Antoine de La Sale provided the impetus for a crucial turn in the emergence of literary semiotics that was virtually founded on and in the text of this late medieval prose work.

13. Kristeva, *Desire in Language,* 42; *Sēmeiōtikē,* 120.

ambiguity into the blazon tradition, while also providing a point of origin for the modern textual management of narrative closure.[14] Indeed, if "medieval literature, dominated by the symbol," is predominantly "supported by the monolithic presence of signified transcendence," the epochal nature of La Sale's modest text haunts this monolithic culture with the very specter of modernity.[15] "Thus, at the close of the Middle Ages," Kristeva writes, "Antoine de La Sale doubly terminated his novel: as narrative (structurally) and as discourse (compositionally). This compositional closure, by its very naiveté, reveals a major fact later occulted by bourgeois literature": namely, the "double semiotic status" of the novel as "a linguistic (narrative) *phenomenon* as well as a discursive *circuit* (letter, literature)." So sweeping are the revisionary implications of this novel's cultural and semiotic work that Kristeva, near the end of her discussion in *Σημειωτική*, imputes to *Le petit Jehan de Saintré* nothing less than "the discursive origins of the literary event" ("les origines discursives du fait littéraire").[16]

As we shall see, Roland Barthes's contributions to *Tel Quel* only hint at such direct engagement with medieval writing practices. Even during his most avowedly structuralist decade, though, Barthes always regarded structuralism as itself a committedly historical enterprise. The synchronic locatedness of structuralism, in fact, had to be understood and somehow accounted for as part of a diachronic tide of avant-garde self-aggrandizement: "Revolutions in language, all exclusively literary, are very overstated; they boil down to waves of decency or of infatuation, with a bearing on certain minor literary procedures. They have been nothing but a tempest in a teacup."[17] Barthes's often ruthless comments on the rhetorics of avant-garde originality (though surely at times hypocritical, and perhaps intentionally so) go hand in hand with an enduring sense of the possibility of archaeological resurrections, as this précis of Vico's cyclical historicism articulates with a vague kind of longing: "According to Vico's image, history proceeds in a spiral, and things of the past return, but obviously not in the same place; thus, there are tastes, values, behavior, 'writings' of the past that may return, but in a very modern place."[18] The story of Barthes's *S/Z* is the story of just such a return, the resurgence of an archaic "behavior" in an unsuspecting corner of modernity.

14. Kristeva, *Desire in Language*, 53.
15. Kristeva, *Desire in Language*, 46; *Sēmeiōtikē*, 126.
16. Kristeva, *Desire in Language*, 57–58; *Sēmeiōtikē*, 139–41.
17. Barthes, *Œuvres Complètes* [hereafter *OC*] 1:80; cited in Stafford, *Roland Barthes*, 27.
18. Barthes, *Grain of the Voice*, 282.

Exegetical Culture

S/Z has long been regarded as Barthes's most influential and career-defining work. From the moment of its initial publication, this idiosyncratic analysis of Honore de Balzac's novella *Sarrasine* inspired reams of commentary from the French intelligentsia, which greeted its appearance as a kind of apotheosis not only of Barthes's career, but of the analytical habits that had dominated the critical scene in France over the preceding decade. In his massive history of French structuralism, François Dosse imputes an epochal status to the book, contending that the "rigorous method" of *S/Z* "radically broke with the first period of structuralism"; for Andy Stafford, Barthes's most recent intellectual biographer, *S/Z* is "perhaps the classic of 1960s French avant-garde writing." [19] *S/Z* remains the most studied and picked-apart text in Barthes's oeuvre, perhaps the one book of his most likely to be known beyond academic-critical circles. Surely the book's impact may be explained in part by the sheer muscularity of its project in purely formal terms: the radical ("from the roots up") displacement and commingling of the authorial text with a nonce commentary apparatus, in which the novella is fragmented into hundreds of lexias and parsed through five "codes" invented by the commentator specifically with *Sarrasine* in mind (an "anti-constructionist" approach to textuality, on Barbara Johnson's influential reading).[20] Published at the very end of the decade that has been the focus of this book, *S/Z* thus exercises something of a symbolic function as the sublime objectification of avant-gardiste ideology. At the same time, the book's deep-seated yet occluded medievalism renders it perhaps the most remarkable instantiation of the premodern condition that this book has examined.

If elsewhere Barthes is forthright about his impulse to take commentary "back to the Middle Ages," *S/Z* nowhere signals its critical affiliations with a medievalist practice whose influence I suggest suffuses its structure, critical sensibility, and mode of textual explication, and without which it would surely never have assumed the final form it did. In order to understand the nature of this unspoken debt, however, we must first appreciate Barthes's contemporaneous interest in the history and practice of biblical exegesis in French theology. In February 1971, roughly a year after the publication of *S/Z*, Barthes participated by invi-

19. Dosse, *History of Structuralism* 2:59; Stafford, *Roland Barthes*, 149. See also Culler, *Roland Barthes*, 88–90, on *S/Z* as an exemplification of the frequent indistinguishability between "structuralism" and "poststructuralism."

20. Johnson, "The Critical Difference: BartheS/BalZac," in *The Critical Difference*, 7.

tation in a two-evening colloquium on structural analysis and biblical exegesis sponsored by the Faculty of Protestant Theology at the University of Geneva, where he was a visiting member of the Faculty of Letters. In attendance were several of the present and future luminaries in literary criticism, exegetical studies, theology, and linguistics, including François Bovon, Jean Starobinski, Robert Martin-Achard, and Franz-J. Leenhardt. As its sponsor's sobriquet implies, this was clearly marked as a *Protestant* gathering, devoted to "scientizing" the study of biblical exegesis through a practical application of structuralist models to the analysis of biblical narrative ("The strength of Protestantism," Bovon avows in his introduction, "has always been to dare to take over into theology methods which were indispensable in the scientific world").[21] The invitations extended to Barthes and Starobinski (also a visiting lecturer that term in Geneva) signal the theology faculty's deliberate effort to affiliate new currents in Christian scholarship with what Bovon terms "a fad and an ideology," namely structuralism and the other modes of critical thought (psychoanalysis, Marxism, and so on) current in Parisian intellectual circles at the time. "One does not speak any more of historicity or of conscience," Bovon observes, "but of codes, arrangements, and systems. One quotes other names today: Lévi-Strauss, Barthes, Althusser, Foucault."[22]

The four published essays signal a will on the contributors' parts to explore structuralist ways of talking about scriptural discourse and exegetical ways of approaching structuralism without surrendering the intellectual specificity of the two critical modes, and Bovon's introduction registers a fair amount of ambivalence about the ideology of the "structuralist movement" in general (quoting Sartre, for example, on structuralism as the last intellectual bastion of the bourgeoisie). Nevertheless, what the colloquium does ultimately promote is an attempted escape in the name of structuralism from the specifically historical dimensions of exegetical research. "Turned too long towards diachrony," Bovon avows, "exegesis will find its bearings in synchrony"; in its putative jettisoning of "a preoccupation with history" that has plagued the course of twentieth-century exegetical studies (source study, *Formgeschichte*, redaction criticism, and so on), structuralism will serve accordingly as "a useful corrective to our present methods of exegesis because it restores to the text a horizontal reality, a synchronic truth. Thanks to structuralism, meaning becomes something else than this reference to a past, to

21. Barthes et al., *Structural Analysis and Biblical Exegesis: Interpretational Essays*, 20.
22. Barthes et al., *Structural Analysis and Biblical Exegesis*, 4.

the pre-history of the text."[23] Barthes's own paper, a close structuralist reading of Genesis 32:23–33, self-consciously risks "weakening the historical, economic meaning" of the text through analysis that seeks to reveal how the text becomes "unravelled, exposed, and disseminated" in the moment of its consumption.[24]

On one level, and despite its Protestant inspiration, this concern to rid exegesis of the taint of historical-critical methodologies speaks with some complexity to the legacy of the Second Vatican Council (1962–65), which had taken a strong stance on the value of historical criticism of the Bible.[25] While in 1964 John XXIII had gone so far as to dismiss several professors from the faculty of the Pontifical Biblical Institute in Rome for advocating these methods, by the issuance of Paul VI's *Instructio de historica Evangeliorum veritate* two years later, they were given qualified sanction as indispensable to the revelatory work of Catholic exegesis: "In order to bring out with fullest clarity the enduring truth and authority of the Gospels [the exegete] must, whilst carefully observing the rules of rational and of Catholic hermeneutics, make skilful use of the new aids to exegesis, especially those which the historical method, taken in its widest sense, has provided; that method, namely, which minutely investigates sources, determining their nature and bearing, and availing itself of the findings of textual criticism, literary criticism, and linguistic studies."[26] The papal instruction registers a good deal of caution, however, regarding the implications of this historical-critical Pandora's box for the promotion of biblical truth, for "the method in question is often found alloyed with principles of a philosophical or theological nature which are quite inadmissible, and which not infrequently vitiate both the method itself and the conclusions arrived at regarding literary questions." The participants in the 1971 Protestant colloquium were surely aware of the highly ambivalent status within Catholic exegetical circles of the methods several of them were rejecting in favor of structuralist synchrony: for Starobinski, the structuralist exegete is a "late comer" who "knows very well that his interpretation will be immediately confronted by all those before him, and he only makes the list longer"; Martin-Achard seemingly rejects structuralist synchrony wholesale, advocating a "diachronic reading of the Scriptures"

23. Barthes et al., *Structural Analysis and Biblical Exegesis*, 20, 7.

24. Barthes et al., *Structural Analysis and Biblical Exegesis*, 22.

25. See the discussion of Pius XII, John XXIII, and "modernity" in McCarthy, *The Catholic Tradition*, 49–55.

26. A usefully contemporaneous discussion of this instruction and its immediate context is Fitzmyer, "The Biblical Commission's Instruction on the Historical Truth of the Gospels."

that "seeks to describe the destiny of a biblical theme from its more remote origins."[27] It is tempting nevertheless to read the colloquium's proceedings as evidence of an implicit rejection of the modified historicism advocated by the papal letter: though Paul VI was unlikely to have been thinking about structuralism in the drafting of the *Instructio,* structuralism presents itself in the hands of the colloquium's practitioners as the very rejection of history writ large as a category of exegetical understanding.

I do not mean to suggest that this rejection of historical models of exegetical criticism can be explained as a critical anti-Catholicism, for this would misrepresent the self-conscious avant-gardisme prevalent within *Catholic* exegetical circles at the same moment. Less than two years prior to the Geneva gathering, in September 1969, Barthes had delivered a paper and participated in a round table as part of the second national congress of the Association catholique française pour l'étude de la Bible, held in Chantilly. Other notables at this gathering included Paul Ricoeur, the psychoanalyst of religion Antoine Vergote, and the great early modernist and semiotician Louis Marin. The colloquium's proceedings, published by Seuil in a 1971 volume titled *Exégèse et herméneutique,* emphasize both newly scientific approaches to the topic (most notably structuralism) and what Ricoeur in his opening keynote calls the "confrontation méthodologique," even the "champ polarisé par la constellation des méthodes" predominating in biblical exegesis, hermeneutics, and literature.[28] With considerably more sympathy toward historical methodologies than will be evident at the Geneva gathering two years later, the participants take historicism as an indispensable given as they map out the implications of their own methodological interventions: Ricoeur on the possible rapprochements between historical, structuralist, and hermeneutical methodologies virtually embodied in the first chapter of Genesis, Barthes on the structural analysis of Acts 10–11, Vergote on the "gift" of psychoanalysis to the study of exegesis, and so on. Here again, though, the history of exegesis proper represents a store of established, even official knowledge rather than a creative, revisionist force in its own right.

The problem is precisely archaeological. All of the speakers at both colloquia are consistently generous in their citations of the previous work that has inspired them, and the proceedings evidence a clear sense of mutual admiration and collective accomplishment. Nevertheless, in

27. Barthes et al., *Structural Analysis and Biblical Exegesis,* 57, 56.
28. Barthes et al., *Exégèse et herméneutique,* 35. For an overview of the conference by a Jesuit attender, see Léon-Dufour, "Exégètes et structuralistes."

the published collections that gather the contributions to the colloquia, there is one work of recent biblical scholarship that goes almost entirely unacknowledged, a multi-volume study published by a French theologian who had exerted a massive influence on the comprehension of premodern biblical interpretation in France throughout the previous decade. In this respect, the critical apparatuses of *Analyse structurale et exégèse biblique* and *Exégèse et herméneutique* become in effect a gathering of *auctoritates* studiously avoiding the exegetical elephant in the room no one wants to acknowledge. This elephant was a Jesuit theologian, activist, editor, historian of religion, and Cardinal named Henri de Lubac (1896–1991).

In the two decades following the end of World War II, French Catholicism endured a series of convulsions brought on by the massive social, political, and ideological upheavals caused by the war.[29] The Resistance aside, church and state in France had both proved grievously inadequate to the challenge of fascism and its apparatus, and lingering suspicions of the Church's general complicity in the Holocaust would continually crop up despite Rome's best efforts to quash them (as would painful memories of the complicity of the Action française, a very influential Catholic organization, before the war). As Liberation gave way to reconstruction during the mid-1940s, certain members of the French clergy emerged as leading intellectual voices in the ubiquitous effort to comprehend and address the nation's institutional and collective failures.

For some the solution was retrenchment: Henri-Irénée Marrou, an eminent scholar of late antiquity and a notable biographer of St. Augustine, called for the integration of denominational schools in the nation's public educational system. Others advocated internal transformation and renewal of the Church's mission and ritual. Marie-Dominique de Chenu, whose later work on neo-Platonism would transform the field of medieval intellectual history, was writing in 1947 for the journal of the Centre de Pastoral liturgique, an ecclesiastical organization dedicated to liturgical renewal at the levels of diocese and parish. For Chenu, liturgy modeled a form of activist community for the present-day faithful, even a "sociology" with its own political demands on its subjects: "The whole sociology of the community works in this sacred realm as well as on secular ground: its laws and techniques will have to be observed, beginning with the detection of natural communities (of neighborhood, of work, even of leisure) which will protect people from merely being part of a

---

29. Among the many works on postwar French Catholicism, especially pertinent is the fascinating 1967 study by Domenach and de Montvalon, *The Catholic Avant-Garde.*

crowd and help spur an active liturgy."[30] Still others searched for answers outside the traditional purview of theology, liturgy, and pastoral
education, turning instead to the realms of science and technology as solutions to the dogmatic failings of the institution. The writings of Pierre
Teilhard de Chardin (1881–1955), the visionary Jesuit paleontologist and
philosopher who had risked his career seeking to reconcile the theory
of evolution with the Christian theology of original sin, achieved a new
vogue during the 1950s, when his posthumously published magnum
opus, *The Phenomenon of Man,* gave French Catholicism a much-needed
response to the Church's history of antiscientific reaction. Liberation
theology, too, had strong intellectual and organizational roots in the
activist bent of postwar French Catholicism, as acknowledged by many
of its most prominent and active Latin American practitioners.[31] Diverse
and riddled with internal controversies though they were, the French
Catholic intellectual cultures of this period formed what has rightly
been termed a "Catholic avant garde," one deeply invested in harness-
ing various programs of social transformation to the unfolding of the
Church's own institutional history and in making such transformation
an explicit part of its public posture by writing for so-called engaged
journals such as *Esprit.*[32] It is striking (if, on reflection, unsurprising) how
many of these reformers were also prolific scholars of patristic and medieval Christianity, their theological and spiritual archaeologies inseparable from their ecclesiological activism.

One particularly influential archaeological strand of mid-century
Catholic reform—stretching back to the 1930s though gaining much
of its energy after the war—involved a purposeful return to the sources
and archives of the Christian tradition in a multifaceted attempt to redress what many perceived as a centuries-long forgetting of significant
dimensions of the Church's intellectual and spiritual origins. This self-
consciously historical movement within French Catholicism came to
be dubbed *ressourcement:* a rediscovery or redeployment of ancient theological, spiritual, and exegetical thought in contemporary reform. *Res-*

---

30. Domenach and de Montvalon, *The Catholic Avant-Garde,* 116.

31. See the pertinent discussions in Cleary, *Crisis and Change.*

32. Domenach and de Montvalon, *The Catholic Avant-Garde.* The definitive scholarly study of the
Catholic Church and the so-called crisis of modernism is Kurtz, *The Politics of Heresy.* On *Esprit,* see
(among others) Marx-Scouras, *The Cultural Politics of Tel Quel,* 15 and 29. For a fascinating contemporaneous view of "militant lay Catholicism" in France, see Ardagh, *The New French Revolution,* 379–
90, though the contrast drawn here between this milieu and that of the critical generation of the
1960s could not be stronger: "While intellectuals like Barthes and Lévi-Strauss have become in a
sense the anti-Christian theologians of the age, the Catholics in France have been turning from theology and ritual to social action" (379).

sourcement embraced numerous Catholic theologians in a still continuing effort to combat the post-Tridentine ossification of medieval theology manifest in twentieth-century neo-Thomism (anticipating in this respect the more polemical efforts of the Radical Orthodox school discussed in chapter 4, whose current practitioners claim strong affinity with de Lubac and other French Catholics associated with this earlier movement). Yet *ressourcement* also had quite practical results: the series Sources chrétiennes, the volumes of which now number more than four hundred, had its origins in occupied Paris during the war, and its first volume, a critical edition of Gregory of Nyssa's life of Moses, appeared in 1941, initiating a still continuing legacy of intellectual production that has included numerous editions of patristic and medieval homiletic, exegetical, and spiritual works, from the biblical commentaries of John Chrysostom to the sermons of Bernard of Clairvaux.[33]

Henri de Lubac's contributions to Sources chrétiennes included an introduction to Jean Daniélou's 1944 edition of the Genesis homilies of Origen, whom de Lubac had always regarded as the most brilliant and innovative premodern biblical interpreter. Of the series in general, de Lubac wrote in a 1959 report of his "conviction that the renewal of Christian vitality is linked, at least in part, to a renewed exploration of the period and works in which the Christian tradition is expressed with particular intensity."[34] This straightforward expression of de Lubac's affirmative historical sensibility, however, masks an unspoken bitterness regarding the damaging controversies that had been shadowing his career for more than a decade, which were part of a longstanding conflict between the Vatican and the Jesuit and Dominican orders of France. The trouble began with the publication of two books shortly after the war: *De la connaissance de Dieu* (1945), which stimulated such controversy when it was first published that de Lubac felt obligated to reissue the book with a reply to his critics as well as more expansive, explanatory footnotes in 1956 (as *Sur les chemins de Dieu*); and especially *Surnaturel* (1946), which argued that the understanding of grace informing modern neo-Thomism is gravely mistaken (and indeed miscomprehends Aquinas himself) in its insistence on a state of "pure nature" separate from Christian revelation.

The contentious reception of de Lubac's published works anticipated his public humiliation after the issue of the papal encyclical *Humani*

---

33. For a fascinating 1946 view of Sources chrétiennes and the problem of theological relativism, see Labourdette, "La théologie et ses sources."

34. De Lubac, *At the Service of the Church,* 93–94.

generis in 1950. While de Lubac and his supporters always maintained that the encyclical did not reference any of his writings directly, the results were equivalent: a number of his books were officially withdrawn from institutional libraries across the Catholic world, hundreds of copies of the just-published *Corpus mysticum* lay rotting in a Lyons warehouse, and from that point on any writing he produced on any subject had to pass through a censor approved by Rome. A devastating rumor mill and the machinations of high-level ecclesiastical officials conspired to get de Lubac banned from a nominal teaching position at Lyons, forced him to move several times, and made him something of a pariah among all but his closest allies for at least the first two-thirds of the decade. Rehabilitation came quickly, however: despite a "labyrinth of complications" from 1957 through 1959, soon after the elevation of Pope John XXIII in 1960 de Lubac was named by the new pope himself to the Preparatory Theological Commission for the coming Vatican Council. De Lubac would become one of the intellectual forces central to promoting the spirit of *aggiornamento* that shaped Vatican II in certain of its theological incarnations, the updating or renewal of Church teachings that blended the ancient with the reformist in an attempt to maintain the institution's strength in a swiftly changing modern world.

The long period of dissension that marked the middle years of de Lubac's career was thus just coming to an end when he published the first volume of his *magnissimum opus* in 1959. As he relates in his memoir, *Exégèse médiévale* was destined to become perhaps the least overtly controversial work of his career: "The Roman censor had given his agreement on the first part of *Exégèse médiévale* only on the express condition that a second part provide a critical restatement of what was as yet, he said, only the historical exposition of contestable views that both theology and science had since gone beyond."[35] The papal censors were initially worried about the work's unmediated historicism, its (perhaps overly appreciative) presentation of medieval source materials concerning the nature of scriptural revelation whose claims had since been corrected or surpassed by others working both within and without the Church. With his new institutional stature ensured, however, de Lubac could publish the three subsequent volumes without hedging his historical bets, and the censor's desire for a "critical restatement" was never fulfilled: the fourth volume appeared in 1964, at the precise midpoint of Vatican II, a point at which de Lubac's status as one of the Council's prime intellectual movers had become unambiguously clear. Over the

35. De Lubac, *At the Service*, 85.

next decade, *Exégèse médiévale* would prove one of the more influential works in the historical study of the Bible among French Catholics and non-Catholics alike, though its influence was more as a definitive reference book (a Purana, in de Lubac's own estimation) than as a critical intervention: if the Bolandist scholar Michel van Esbroeck could argue in 1968 that the "Christian synthesis" outlined in *Exégèse médiévale* served to reconcile the antithetical views of Ricoeur and Lévi-Strauss, of hermeneutics and structuralism, it was as a labyrinthine encyclopedia of the premodern history of biblical criticism that Roland Barthes likely came to know and absorb Henri de Lubac's "formless," "unmethodical," "whimsical" masterpiece.[36]

Yet the potential appeal of these volumes to a Protestant textophile such as Barthes lay precisely in their attention to form and method— particularly their own. In fact, the self-referential quality of *Exégèse médiévale* as a work of metatextual commentary can be glimpsed in the first paragraph of the introduction to volume one, which introduces the "four senses of scripture" as the defining paradigm of medieval exegetical practice. Here is de Lubac describing the inspiration and explicatory purpose of his book:

The distich with which our own Latin Middle Ages slowly established its doctrine relative to the senses of Sacred Scripture is well known. Its form was meant to act as an aid to memory and was at once popular and quasi-scholastic:

The letter teaches events, allegory what you should believe,
Morality teaches what you should do, anagogy what mark you should be aiming for.

Nicholas of Lyra cites it, around the year 1330, in his *Postilla* on the Letter to the Galatians, not to mention a passage of his celebrated Prologue to the *Glossa ordinaria*— a passage on which all of the present study will merely be a commentary [*page dont toute l'étude présente ne sera guère que le commentaire*].[37]

Its beguiling simplicity notwithstanding, this is a disconcertingly provocative passage, standing as it does at the very beginning of *Exégèse*

---

36. van Esbroeck, *Herméneutique, structuralisme et exégèse*. Compare de Lubac's assessment of the work in *At the Service*, 85.

37. De Lubac, *Medieval Exegesis: The Four Senses of Scripture*, vol. 1, 1; all citations to this work will be to this translation (and in a few instances to the French original) and will be given parenthetically in the text. The influence of *Exégèse médiévale* on twentieth-century critical thought extended as well to Fredric Jameson's *The Political Unconscious*, which works at some length with de Lubac's magnum opus and what Jameson terms "the striking and elaborate hermeneutic which is the patristic and medieval system of the four levels of scripture" in discussing Althusser's notion of expressive causality; see Jameson, *The Political Unconscious*, 29.

médiévale, and it is not hard to imagine Barthes's response to its almost perverse recursivity. For here de Lubac presents his multivolume study as consisting entirely of a commentary on a passage from the prologue to a commentary on a text: better yet, *Exégèse médiévale* describes itself as an exegesis of an exegetical directive (the distich from Nicholas of Lyra's Prologue) instructing its medieval readers in how to understand the exegesis performed in the text they are about to read (the *Glossa ordinaria*), which in turn constitutes a massive exegesis of its source text, the Holy Bible. If this elliptical description of the succeeding volumes as a commentary on a commentary on a commentary on a commentary—an "object made of commentaries," as Barthes would put it in the epigraph to this chapter—seems designed to rankle the curial censors hoping to pin de Lubac down to a particular (perhaps objectionable) theological position, it also adumbrates a way of understanding the nature of textual criticism that would find a natural home in the emergent language of literary poststructuralism, with its emphasis on textual inscrutability, indeterminacy, and play. As one of de Lubac's ancient witnesses puts it, "The eloquence of Sacred Scripture takes many shapes, and its meanings are many and varied. For this reason someone has said: He compares things that are celestial with things that are earthly, so that likenesses that we find well-known and familiar may provide a field of play for the things that incomprehensible greatness veils from our understanding" (1:31).

How to Speak of God

It is clear that Barthes himself was preoccupied with the four levels of scripture and their critical implications for structuralist reading practices during the years immediately preceding the publication of *S/Z.* I am referring to Barthes's now little-read discussion of the writings of Ignatius Loyola, the sixteenth-century Carmelite founder of the Jesuit order, which is included as a chapter of the 1971 book *Sade, Fourier, Loyola.* The chapter on Loyola was originally published as a separate essay with the title "Comment parler à Dieu?", and it appeared in volume 38 of *Tel Quel* in the summer of 1969—the year before the publication of *S/Z,* a draft of which Barthes was completing just as the essay went to press.[38] Barthes's inspiration for this turn to Loyola was almost certainly Bataille's meditations on Loyola from *Inner Experience,* where Bataille had

38. Barthes, "Comment parler à Dieu?"

recruited the *Exercises* as an example of mystical performance "in the dramatic mode" as opposed to the methodical—exhortative writing that commands its interpellant to "dissipate—extend for that reason your will—the absence, the dazed state, to which words are inclined."[39] For Bataille, Ignatius Loyola wrote "in absolute horror of discourse (of absence)," and the *Exercises* themselves "try to cope" with this absence "through the tension of discourse, and this artifice often fails."[40] Barthes takes up this thread, though he is much more interested in the technical means by which Loyola negotiates the anxiety of apophaticism through specific linguistic and rhetorical maneuvers.

Of particular interest to Barthes is the presence in the *Exercises* of what he envisions as an interlocutory performance, one that makes of its writing an open-ended *actio* (to adopt the most appropriate rhetorical term) limited only by its own ascetic imperatives. Opening the section called "The Multiple Text," Barthes outlines the multi-texted approach he will soon recruit vis-à-vis Balzac's *Sarrasine:*

Our reading habits, our very concept of literature, make every text appear today as if it were the simple communication of an author (in the present instance this Spanish saint who founded the Society of Jesus in the sixteenth century) and of a reader (in the present instance, ourselves): Ignatius Loyola wrote a book, this book was published, and today we are reading it. This outline, suspect for any book (since we can never definitively demonstrate *who* is the author and *who* is the reader), is assuredly false with regard to the *Exercises.* For if it is true that a text is defined through the unity of its communication, we are not reading *one* text, but rather *four* texts, disposed in the shape of the small book in our hands.[41]

The "four texts" that comprise Loyola's *Exercises* and create its web of legibility are described by Barthes as follows: (1) the ostensible "literal level" of the work, embodying "its objective, historical nature" (in this case instructions to the actual Jesuit directors of the exercises); (2) the "semantic text," the interlocutive exchange between director and exercitant that represents a sort of glue ("maniable material," in Barthes's phrase) that can be "elongated, shortened, softened, hardened" as it passes from one to the other: "if the first text constitutes the proper level of the discourse (as we read it), the second text is like the argument"; (3) the "al-

39. Bataille, *Inner Experience*, 13.
40. Bataille, *Inner Experience*, 14.
41. Barthes, *Sade, Fourier, Loyola*, 41; citations hereafter in text.

legorical" text, the text that is "written" by the exercitant once he receives the second text: "an *acted* text made up of the meditation, gestures, and practices given him by his director" and consecrated to God, who receives it as the "images and imitations" of allegory; and (4) the "strictly anagogic" text, the "reply from God, of which God is the donor and the exercitant the receiver": in and through this fourth text is promised an attainment of "the deepest meaning, the sign liberated by the Divinity" (41–42).

These are, more or less exactly, the "four senses of scripture" explicated by de Lubac in such loving detail throughout *Exégèse médiévale*. Barthes himself registers Loyola's debt to medieval exegetical practice (while giving remarkably short shrift to his own) just after describing the operation of the four texts: the *Exercises* is envisioned as "a structure of meanings" in which can be found "this diversity and this 'perspective' of languages which has marked the relationship established between God and His creation through the theological thinking of the Middle Ages and which can be seen in the theory of the four meanings of the Scriptures" (42). More important for Barthes is the "structure of interlocution" that involves the four speakers conversing through and among the four levels of the text. Each of these interlocutors assumes a "dual role" as sender and receiver, a role plagued (for its human agents, at least) by insecurity and incertitude, for the exercitant will never know whether his performed allegory will be accepted by God and thus reciprocated in anagogy. The "dramatic" character of the *Exercises* is the result of precisely this apophatic incertitude and its effects, which together create a "language of interrogation" that, according to Barthes, marks the originality of the work in the long history of Christian devotion.

The remainder of the chapter attempts to locate the four senses of Loyola's text—and particularly the third, the allegorical performance of the exercitant—within the "very material" contingencies of its social function as a mode of devotional praxis (47). Indeed, though Barthes argues more than once for the unprecedented character of the *Exercises* as an interrogative text, the chapter nevertheless outlines a compelling methodology for approaching the medieval tradition of contemplative asceticism that preceded Loyola. The linguistic "emptying out" of the subject inherent to all apophatic theology, for example, seems perfectly encapsulated in certain descriptions of Loyola's program: "All these protocols have the function of creating in the exercitant a kind of linguistic vacuum necessary for the elaboration and for the triumph of the new language: the vacuum is ideally the anterior space of all semiophany"

(49). At the same time, Barthes is adamant about separating Loyola's linguistic sensibility from those of his Christian antecedents. In a long footnote in the middle of the essay, the writings of the fourteenth-century Flemish mystic John Ruysbroeck furnish Barthes with a counterexample of a rich "image reservoir" that he opposes to the "very poor" one possessed by Loyola. Unlike Ruysbroeck, whose vision of hell (quoted from an 1869 translation by Ernest Hello) includes gluttons swallowing sulfur and molten sweat dripping from the fingers of corpses, Loyola views the underworld through a series of "intellectual cipher[s]" that signal an ascendancy of rhetoric over image. Likewise, Loyola's exhaustive "articulation" or "discernment" (*distinguo* in the Latin rhetorical tradition) in the *Exercises*, the paratactic enumerations and divisions that painstakingly separate units of time, exercises, and texts for the exercitant, operates not as the "condition, warranty, and fate of language," as it does for earlier mystics, but rather in pursuit of "the sign of God" rather than "knowledge of Him or His presence" (53). Even the genealogies of signification proliferate in Loyola's text to a degree not found (Barthes argues) in the ostensible "binary" rigidity of medieval systems of thought:

Ignatian discourse is made up of . . . extensions which, were they graphically projected, would have the appearance of a network of knots and branchings; a relatively simple network when the branchings are bifurcations (in the fourteenth and fifteenth centuries, the implied choice in a matter of conscience was called *binary*), but which can grow extremely complicated when the branchings are multiple.

These multiple branchings represent what Barthes eloquently terms the "continuous arborescence of Ignation discourse," its proliferation from the original fourfold text into a branching and "interlacing" tree ripe with the fruits of contemplation.

One possible explanation for Barthes's persistently unexamined denial of Loyola's continuity with medieval intellectual formations is that he saw the *Exercises* as among the first Christian reappropriations of the classical rhetorical tradition. The chapter repeatedly invokes Ciceronian terms such as *inventio, annominatio, distinctio, discretio, dispositio,* and so on, citing Loyola's incorporation of this vocabulary as a hallmark of "the beginning of the modern era in Ignatius's century" (65). In this respect, Barthes is simply reflecting the consensus among medievalists and historians of rhetoric contemporaneous with him in the 1960s, when it was still widely believed that the rhetorical tradition proper was largely dormant between the *Rhetorica ad Herennium* and the Italian Renaissance, surviving only in hypostatized form as part of the medieval trivium. Yet

Barthes held a quite capacious view of medieval rhetoric, having lectured on the trivium, the *ars praedicandi,* scholastic dialectic, and other medieval rhetorical traditions as part of his 1964–65 seminar at Hautes Études.[42]

For all its effort to "periodize" Loyola as *logothete,* as inventor of a particular language of vocative devotion, though, this long essay on the Jesuit father tugs irresistibly at the languages of medieval theology that lay behind the (ostensible) linguistic revolution he inspired. Thus, the dramatizations of the Passion in the *Exercises* take on "a theatrical quality which relates them to the medieval mysteries: they are 'scenes' the exercitant is called upon to live out, as in a psychodrama" (61). Loyola's radical departure from earlier modes of Christian visuality led him to reject medieval "mistrustings of the image" in favor of an "imperialism of the image"; at the same time, his "image linguistics," in Barthes's phrase, cannot be understood apart from the "positive theologies" that stood in stark opposition to the negatives propounded by his apophatic predecessors: "articulation permits the predication of God; every mystical effort is taken to reduce (or expand, as one will) God to His essence (Maimonides, through John of the Cross: 'Concerning God, we grasp nothing other than that *He is,* but not *What He is*'), and this effort already contains within itself the condemnation of all language; choosing the path of an exasperated punctuation, Ignatius opens to the Divinity a list, at once metaphorical and metonymic, of its attributes; it is possible *to speak* God." And wherever we see Barthes protesting too much about the originality of the *Exercises,* the curious gaps in his own knowledge of medieval religious discourses betray the historicism that fundamentally inspires his analysis: "the totally bookkeeping nature of sin as Ignatius's manual establishes it and which was little known in the Middle Ages, aware, above all, it seems, in a more cosmic way of original sin and of hell, cannot be completely foreign to the new capitalist ideology, articulated both on the individualist awareness of the person and on the inventorying of the good which, belonging to him personally, constitute him" (71). "The totally bookkeeping nature of sin": Barthes is describing nothing so much as the penitential discourses of the Middle Ages, the discourses that will inspire Foucault—just seven years later, in *La volonté de savoir*—to propose the medieval confessional as the fount and origin of the Occident's *scientia sexualis,* the obsessive naming, listing, and or-

---

42. See Barthes, *OC* 1:1562, as well as "L'ancienne rhétorique," 184–92. The continuation of the seminar the following year (1965–66) focused on nineteenth- and twentieth-century rhetorical systems; see *OC* 2:111.

dering of desires and perversions that surely inspired Loyola in his own paratactic approach to sin.[43]

Finally, if Barthes takes pains to demonstrate a "contrast . . . between Ignatian ascesis and Flemish mysticism" as embodied in Ruysbroeck (73), the conclusion of the essay locates as originary in the Jesuit hermeneutics of Loyola what was in fact one of the central paradoxes recognized in the apophatic tradition of Christian theology centuries before him:

Hearing turns into its own answer, and from being suspensive, the interrogation becomes somehow assertive, question and answer enter into a tautological balance: the divine sign finds itself completely absorbed in its hearing. Then the mantic act concludes, for, returning the deficiency from sign to sign, it has succeeded in including within its system this empty and yet significant place called the zero degree of the sign: restored to signification, the divine vacuum can no longer threaten, alter, or decentralize the plenitude which is part of every closed language. (75)

Pseudo-Dionysius the Areopagite would surely have agreed: God's inaccessibility to human language is not simply the result of his unknowability, but also of the specific nature of linguistic signification: our "closed language"—closed precisely *to divinity*—will inevitably fold in on itself when we attempt to win through its claustrophobic deficiencies. Far from a radical departure from a millennium of Ruysbroeckian "mystical intoxication," as they become in Barthes's late structuralism, Loyola's *Exercises* represent its apotheosis.

Roland Barthes, Scriptor

As I argue in chapter 4, Pierre Bourdieu's brief but intensive interest in the historiography of medieval art led directly to his initial formulation of the *habitus* and its subsequent deployment in his sociology of culture. And as I have begun to suggest here, a similarly concentrated preoccupation with medieval habits of mind inspired Barthes's working through of the notion of the "multiple text" over the closing years of the 1960s and, as we shall see, played a crucial role in the writing of *S/Z*. "Comment parler à Dieu?" appeared in *Tel Quel* in the summer of 1969, just after Barthes had completed his two-year seminar on Balzac's *Sarrasine*

---

43. On the paratactic aspects of medieval confessional discourses, see the discussions in Frantzen, *Before the Closet;* as well as the older study by Payer, *Sex and the Penitentials.*

at the École Pratique des Hautes Études. These were the same years in which Fernand Braudel's presence dominated the EPHE's Sixth Section (later the École des Hautes Études en Sciences Sociales), affording the Annales group regular interaction with figures such as Lévi-Strauss of the Fifth Section (with whom Braudel had a longstanding and contentious relationship) and Bourdieu (a main rival in the Sixth beginning in the late 1960s).[44] It would be largely inaccurate, in fact, to view the Annales historians as discrete from the emergent postwar avant garde; the two critical subcultures shared many intellectual agendas and were at times mutually constitutive, whether within or without the official university establishment.[45] As far back as 1950, in a review of André Joussain's *La loi des révolutions* for *Combat,* Barthes himself had yoked his desire for "multiple dimensions" of historical understanding and the "recovery of syntheses" in historical writing to the work of Marc Bloch and Lucien Febvre, the Annales intellectuals whose work had created its own kind of revolution in French historical writing over the course of the preceding decades.[46] And Barthes—along with Bourdieu, Kristeva, Michel de Certeau, Lévi-Strauss, and several other notables of the Parisian avant garde —contributed regularly to the journal *Annales* during these years, a period in which cutting-edge medievalists and avant-garde coteries such as the Tel Quel group inhabited intersecting spheres of influence in the centralized academic culture of modern France. Braudel himself, the historian par excellence of the *longue durée,* was forced to identify himself as a "structuralist by temperament," if not by profession or intellectual commitment.[47] And the editorial offices of the journal that Braudel launched in 1960, *Études rurales,* were housed in Lévi-Strauss's "laboratory of social anthropology" at the Collège de France; Georges Duby served as one of the founding editors. The mutual enchantment enjoyed by premodern historians and avant-garde cultural critics such as Barthes during this antidisciplinary decade took many forms (for example, a forum on the work of Lévi-Strauss published in *Annales* in 1965, to which Barthes contributed an essay on the synthetic challenge the ethnologist had provoked to the writing of history and ethnology) and endured long after its initial burgeoning: as late as 1979, commenting on Michelet and historiography, Barthes credited "the entire Annales school of history, and the 'living history' school of Georges Duby, Emmanuel Le Roy

44. Burke, *The French Historical Revolution,* 43.
45. See further the comments in Ganim, "The Literary Uses of the New History," 211.
46. Barthes, "Les révolutions suivent-elles des lois?" *OC* 1:85–86.
47. Dosse, *New History in France: The Triumph of the Annales,* 91–92.

Ladurie, and Jacques Le Goff," for recognizing "what history owes to Michelet, who reexamined and rethought the body within history, with its suffering, its humors, blood, physiologies, and foods."[48]

Barthes's affinities with this historical movement hint at his more general investment in the Middle Ages as the discernible yet always hazy horizon of modernity, an investment registered very clearly in Barthes's piece on Duby and Mandrou's two-volume *Histoire de la civilisation française,* published in *Annales* in 1960. After a fairly descriptive overview of the project, Barthes offers some closing speculations on historiography and periodization in a concluding paragraph appended as a kind of afterthought to the review proper. The passage is worth quoting at length for its anticipation of the many ambivalences that will shape Barthes's medievalist sensibilities over the succeeding decade:

The acquisition of a new body of knowledge (and that is indeed the project of Duby and Mandrou's book) always implies going against, or challenging, an old body of knowledge. There is no such thing as an ideally empty mind. Now, in the case of a history of French civilization, this former (and as it were innate) body of knowledge with which the new author must struggle, come to terms, or collaborate is in no way homogeneous. In matters of civilization, the further a reader goes back in time, the less he or she knows, so that what one could call the didactic status of the Middle Ages is very different from that of modern times. Entirely condensed upon itself as it is through its very remoteness, medieval civilization spontaneously appears as much more structured than the civilization in which we still live. The four centuries of the Middle Ages form a sort of natural synchrony and consequently a civilization much more than a history. Conversely, the further one moves forward in time, the more extensive "spontaneous" knowledge becomes, the more disseminated the very notion of civilization, and the more difficult the synthesis. In other words, there is, with respect to the average reader, a sort of didactic law that one could call *the acceleration of knowledge.* I wonder (and this is really just a thought) if this acceleration of knowledge does not require in the same proportions an acceleration of the narrative, in other words if the narrative should not become denser and denser and aim at synthesis as it gets closer to our times. Duby and Mandrou have deliberately tried to divide almost evenly their chapters into the ten centuries of our History. With respect to old biases, it is already quite daring to grant as much importance to the Middle Ages as to modern times. Perhaps one should go even further, that is to say expand the former and condense the latter, so as to emphasize even more the "historical" dimension

48. Barthes, *Grain of the Voice,* 337. On Barthes's often appreciative stance toward the Annales school of history see Stafford, *Roland Barthes,* 35 and elsewhere.

of the Middle Ages, a period that we "synchronize" too readily, and the "synchronic" dimension of a modernity whose unity only a very dense synthesis can render.[49]

In the Middle Ages, Barthes contends, there existed an underlying cultural spontaneity, a "natural synchrony," between all regimes and modes of knowledge production, a synchrony that does not obtain in the modern epoch, with its fractured knowledges, its competing epistemologies, its divided subjects. The audacity of Duby and Mandrou's project in according equal importance to medieval and modern centuries, then, only highlights the disjunction between the two epochs, one of which appears as a "civilization," the other of which possesses a "history." The unintended but fruitful consequence, according to Barthes, is that the coauthored *Histoire de la civilisation française* emphasizes the historical dimension of the Middle Ages that modernity synchronizes too easily. The "acceleration of knowledge" (but not, at least in the same proportions, of *récit*) that follows the Middle Ages provides the historian with a homology for the process of reconstruction necessary to historical understanding, as well as a way to comprehend the mutually constitutive relation between *savoir nouveau* and *savoir ancien,* especially if the latter exhibits the kind of totalizing habits attributed here to medieval epistemologies. A crucial subtext to this discussion may be the fact that Barthes, Duby, Lévi-Strauss, Braudel, and so many other figures in this milieu were part of an institutional and extra-institutional effort dedicated to (re)producing just such a critical totality: as Duby later described it, "We were convinced that the only way to study a subject as vast as rural society around the world was to implement what was by far the most fruitful part of the *Annales* program, namely, the goal of bringing all the sciences of man together in a cooperative effort"[50]—an effort perhaps not so far removed from the "natural synchrony" of knowledge imputed by Barthes to the culture of medieval France.

Throughout the 1960s, in fact, Barthes often cast his writerly aspirations in just these terms: as a revivification of the totalizing character of a premodern milieu of textual collaboration and collective knowledge production. One can perceive in Barthes's writing from this period a sense of "practicing" the Middle Ages as itself a kind of "response to the plural of the text," as he often described his broader critical mission. In an interview with Raymond Bellour in *Les lettres françaises,* published in

49. Barthes, review of Duby and Mandrou, *Histoire de la civilisation française,* 999.
50. Duby, *History Continues,* 60.

May 1970, Barthes is asked about the traditional distinctions in literary history and criticism between reading and writing, distinctions which a work like *S/Z* seems intended to blur. Does this not then suggest, Bellour asks, "that the operation of commentary aims to permit a kind of rehierarchization of literary values insofar as the commentary constitutes in itself a literary experience, or, in your words, a discourse of reading, a writing-reading?" Barthes responds with the sentences I have chosen as the epigraph to this chapter: "Yes, and that's nothing to be afraid of. Mutatis mutandis, the Middle Ages lived solely on rereading ancient texts, in Greek or Latin. Perhaps literature will now be precisely that: an object made of commentaries, a tutor of other languages, period. Who knows?"[51]

Rather than following up Barthes's provocative suggestion—namely, that the critical project of *S/Z* and of late structuralism as a whole might be considered a revival of the archaic rather than a radical invention of the new—Bellour steers the interview toward *Empire of Signs,* and Barthes's medievalism goes unexamined. A year later, though, in the interview with Heath discussed in the opening section of this chapter, Barthes goes further still, calling for a revival of medieval exegesis as a salve to modernity's poverty of imagination, with its endless recyclings of the same: a revival that would properly establish "proliferating commentary" as the "true writing activity of our time." As the trajectory of his own career might suggest, Barthes remains always ambivalent regarding the possible institutional sites that might produce such a medieval revival, on the one hand calling for a cultivation of the "amateurism" that infused the reading habits of "monarchical or even feudal societies" trying to ward off alienation, on the other longing for the "savor of a regulated life, of a strict schedule, as in a monastery: a disturbing phenomenon that pursues me even today."[52]

This ambivalence may evoke as well Barthes's self-consciousness regarding his imaginative debts to his fellow travelers in the French avant garde, many of whom inhabited similarly marginal academic positions during these years (Barthes never took his *agrégation* exam and did not occupy an official university post until his election to the Collège de France).[53] When pressed by Bellour on his unacknowledged appropria-

---

51. Barthes, *Grain of the Voice,* 82. Thus Barthes would likely have been in perfect agreement with Alexandre Leupin's glibly stern suggestion that Geoffrey of Vinsauf "exemplifies the utopic dissolution or fusion of theorist and writer promoted by Roland Barthes more than seven centuries after the *Poetria nova*" (*Barbarolexis,* 21).

52. Barthes, *Grain of the Voice,* 217, 260.

53. On this institutional aspect of the avant garde see the many sharp assessments in Bourdieu, *Homo Academicus.*

tions of psychoanalytic and other critical languages, Barthes defends himself by imputing his refusal of scholarly citation in *S/Z* to the practice of *compilatio*, one of the most prevalent models of authorial activity in medieval literary theory:

My recourse to psychoanalytic language, as to all other idiolects, is ludic in nature, citatory—and I'm convinced that everyone does this, in more or less good faith. One never owns a language. A language can only be borrowed, it "passes around," like an illness or currency. In *S/Z* you could see that, in spite of all deontology, I did not "list my sources" . . . if I neglected to mention my creditors (Lacan, Julia Kristeva, Sollers, Derrida, Deleuze, Serres, among others)—and I know they have understood this—it's to emphasize that in my eyes it's the entire text, through and through, which is citatory. I indicated this in my presentation when I recalled the roles of *compilator* and *auctor* in the Middle Ages.[54]

The presentation Barthes refers to here may be either the Hautes Études seminar itself, in which the argument of *S/Z* was presented in skeletal form over an extended period, or a public lecture that preceded the Bellour interview. In either case, Barthes is here casting his own intellectual relationship with the avant-garde coterie of late-1960s Paris (Lacan, Kristeva, Sollers, Deleuze, Serres, and others) in terms of medieval, collaborative modes of authorial production. The avant garde is a culture of *compilatio*, in the medieval understanding of this rhetorical term: a book-making coterie whose members all contribute in their own ways to the confection of the text.[55] While the *auctor* will be accorded at least some of the cultural capital generated by this collaborative enterprise, the text that results will be relatively untainted by an author-function constraining its significance as collective rather than individual production. As Barthes suggests in "From Work to Text" (1971), Georges Bataille was an avatar of this textualist sensibility: "How do you classify a writer like Georges Bataille? Novelist, poet, essayist, economist, philosopher, mystic? The answer is so difficult that the literary manuals generally prefer to forget about Bataille who, in fact, wrote texts, perhaps continuously one single text." Yet this "single text" of Bataille, despite the prolific and varied career of its scribe, commands no homage from its readers: "no vital 'respect' is due to the Text: it can be *broken* (which is just what the Middle Ages did with two nevertheless authoritative texts—Holy Scrip-

---

54. Barthes, *Grain of the Voice*, 78.
55. On the role of *compilatio* in medieval literary theory, see Minnis, *Medieval Theory of Authorship*, esp. 191–210.

ture and Aristotle); it can be read without the guarantee of its father, the restitution of the inter-text paradoxically abolishing any legacy."[56]

Barthes was not alone in recalling the authorial lexicons of the Middle Ages as a precedent for avant-garde textual practices. In a review of *S/Z* published in *Le Monde* in May 1970, Raymond Jean praised Barthes for deliberately reviving the fourfold model of textual production as it was understood in medieval theory of authorship:

A method which is so exciting, so clever, and also so rigorous that one finishes this book with the feeling that the Ancients were quite right to consider the *commentary* as the most "active" form of criticism. For it is indeed a commentary that Barthes intends to offer us here. He justifies this by saying that he has tried to be the *scriptor, compilator, commentator,* and *auctor* of the past all at once—an attempt that gives back to "the critical analysis of a text" an original, efficient and dynamic dimension that one had long lost hope of ever seeing in it again, considering how obsolete that type of exercise had become.[57]

What is fascinating about this description of *S/Z*, appearing as it did in the leading French daily newspaper (and thus likely seen by more readers than any other review of the book), is Jean's will to anchor the newness of a particular avant-garde production in its resurrection of the old. That is, the reviewer's hyperbolic praise results not from the character of *S/Z* as a unique and unprecedented mode of textual commentary, but from the book's archaism: its revival of a seemingly "obsolete" medieval sensibility that found commentary "the most 'active' form of criticism." As an embodiment of a new kind of "explication de texte," *S/Z* performs this revisionist function well, working to subsume the four levels of medieval textual production—authorship, inscription, compilation, commentary—within a single "exercice," in Jean's term.

In *S/Z* itself Barthes only rarely hints at his awareness of the book's medievalism, though I am inclined to believe that he wrote with its implications fully in mind. The author's preoccupation with the premodern explains much of the analytic dynamism of *S/Z* in ways both small and large. A particularly heated exchange between Sarrasine and La Zambi-

56. Barthes, *Image-Music-Text,* 157, 161; on this passage see Richman, *Reading Georges Bataille,* 2. Compare Peter Haidu, writing just three years later in a review essay on Paul Zumthor's *Essai de poétique médiévale:* "The Middle Ages knew that a text began to signify between the lines, only in the writing of another text, even if it were commentary. Augustine is the mark of this: Scripture [*l'Écriture*] being revelation, it must endlessly be repeated, systematically intra- or intertextualized, for that is the condition of its life; all of medieval writing will be the perverse commentary on/of this relation to the only possible Book" ("The Middle Ages, the Other," 29).

57. Jean, "Le 'commentaire' comme forme 'active' de la critique," III.

nella, for example, taken as a "volley of codes" that multiply, constitutes the proairetic register at one point in the novella: "A society aware of the —in some sense—linguistic nature of the world, as was medieval society with its *Trivium* of the arts of speech [*des arts de la parole*], believing that it is not the truth which brings an end to the confrontation of languages, but merely the force of one of them, can then, in a ludic spirit, attempt to encode this force, to endow it with a protocol of results: this is the *disputatio,* the function of certain of whose terms was to close off, arbitrarily but necessarily, the infinite repetition of dialogue."[58] Barthes understands dialogue, then, in part as scholastic disputation; in its performative dimension, Balzac's text as a whole makes use of the premodern trivial arts of grammar, logic, and rhetoric in calling its fictional world into being through the interplay of the five codes. Throughout *S/Z*, the artist, too, has the power to conjure within and against the symbolic, for it "is he who knows the code, the origin, the basis, and thus he becomes the guarantor, the witness, the author (*auctor*) of reality: he has the right to determine the difference between the sexes, against the very protestation of the interested parties" (167–68). Here again medieval theory of authorship and *auctoritas* serves to channel the semantic undercurrents of modern fiction, suggesting the extent to which *S/Z* can often seem inseparable from the medieval domain of textuality that inspirits it.

From Sense to Code: The Biblical Multiplicity of S/Z

How, then, might we begin to comprehend the epistemological status of *S/Z* as an archaeological endeavor, a methodological and formal revival of medieval exegetical practice rather than a nonce excrescence of avant-garde originality? First, I want to make it clear that I am not insisting on a series of one-to-one correspondences between moments in Henri de Lubac's *Exégèse médiévale* and specific passages in *S/Z*, though as we shall see in the remainder of this chapter, I do think a number of such correspondences might be drawn. What I want to suggest, rather, is that a knowledge of *Exégèse médiévale* will give us a more interesting and in some sense more fulfilling way to read *S/Z*, a text central to the avant garde's self-fashioning yet rooted formally and spiritually in a Catholic tradition of biblical scholarship. The extent to which this relationship is counterintuitive is a measure of the extent to which even the most at-

---

58. Barthes, *S/Z*, 155; all page references to *S/Z* hereafter will be internal and keyed to the Miller translation and, in a few instances, to the 1970 Seuil edition.

tentive critical readers of *S/Z* have missed the premodern forest for the postmodern trees.[59]

We should begin, then, with the forest. The interpretive practice Barthes appropriated most transparently from de Lubac was the simple but crucial decision to enumerate the various levels of textual meaning into five discrete and named "codes": the proairetic, the semantic, the cultural, the hermeneutic, and the symbolic. Even the most searching commentators on *S/Z* have taken this foundational decision on Barthes's part practically for granted, as if it required no comment beyond the author's own somewhat circular explanations: "I did in fact distinguish five main semantic fields or codes," he remarked in 1970. "Admittedly, I don't know if this selection has any theoretical stability; similar experiments would have to be done on other texts to find out."[60]

But why five? Why such a small and arbitrary number, when one could easily imagine twelve, twenty, or a thousand levels of meaning contributing to the "multiple text" of Balzac's novella? In the initial delineation presented in *S/Z* itself—the naming of "the five major codes under which all the textual signifiers can be grouped" (19)—we can find no stated explanation or inspiration for the seemingly arbitrary enumeration of the five governing codes, and it is not at all clear that five was the original number chosen: as Barthes remarked after the book's publication, "This division has the essential function of defining units through which pass a reasonable number of meanings: one, two, three, four meanings."[61] Here again Barthes credits the more general stylistic "mutation" from his earlier work apparent in *S/Z* to the Parisian avant garde of which he was a central part: "change is often brought about by others: it's because I was surrounded by 'formulators,' writers like Derrida, Sollers, Kristeva (always the same names, of course), who taught me things, persuaded me, opened my eyes."

---

59. When I conceived and began writing this chapter, in fact, I fully expected to discover that *S/Z*'s reworking of the four senses of scripture would be a widely held assumption in the study of Barthes, and that my own contribution would be to fill out more intricately the affinities between *S/Z* and *Exégèse médiévale*. To my real surprise, however, not one of the sixty-odd critical studies of *S/Z* published from the year of the book's appearance through 1994 and listed in Philippe's comprehensive bibliography *Roland Barthes* (77–85, items 467–527) so much as mentions fourfold exegesis as an inspiration for the interpretive practice adopted by Barthes in this book (though see the discussion in Sarrazin, "Plaisir du texte biblique," 21, which seems to hint at Barthes's engagement with the "sens plénier des Saintes Écritures," though without elaboration).

60. Barthes, *Grain of the Voice*, 74.

61. Barthes, *Grain of the Voice*, 71. Another number system in *S/Z* was professedly arbitrary; according to Calvet, *Roland Barthes*, 182, "the whole of Barthes's text is organized into ninety-three sections or chapters. 'Why ninety-three?' a friend once asked him. 'Because that's the year my mother was born,' he replied with a smile." A useful explication of the five codes and their role in *S/Z* can be found in Moriarty, *Roland Barthes*, 120–28.

Always the same names indeed. A more searching appraisal of his critical debts would surely have led Barthes to account for the rootedness of his intepretive practice in *S/Z* in the fertile soil of biblical exegesis. For when Barthes in *S/Z* outlines the "five major codes under which all the textual signifiers can be grouped," he cannot help but evoke the "scholasticism of the four senses" that Christian theology had for a millennium located in the text of the Bible, the "doctrine of the fourfold sense" that had long been familiar to modern historians of theology and that *Exégèse médiévale* had revived for new generations of French intellectuals. As Henri de Lubac had put it in the first volume, "it would be wrong to attach importance to just any aberrant list" (82), while Barthes insists that in *S/Z*, "there will be no other codes throughout the story but these five, and each and every lexia will fall under one of these five codes" (19).

As the Loyola essay shows, Barthes was exploring the interpretive currency of the fourfold sense in his own work while working out the structure of *S/Z*. Once we graph the permutations of these various levels through the three relevant works (see table 1), we can begin to understand how the hermeneutical universe of medieval exegesis inspires the overarching critical modality of *S/Z* (in the case of *S/Z* itself, the table reproduces the sequence given by Barthes in the Bellour interview, in which he enumerates them in perceived order of significance). Barthes would define the first code delineated for *S/Z* in Aristotelian terms as the "succession of actions," that which allows the text (in this case *Sarrasine*) to be read, quite simply (and "empirically," in Barthes's account), "as a story." The "historical" or "literal" sense of Scripture as it was known to medieval exegetes performs the same function captured in the distich that opens *Exégèse médiévale* ("The letter teaches events"; see above) and characterized in *Sade, Fourier, Loyola* as the text's "objective, historical nature" (41). Things get a bit more complicated after this, but I think it is beyond question that the four senses delineated by de Lubac have metamorphosed into the five codes inspiring *S/Z*. This is hard to see without the intervening treatment of Loyola, of course, which perhaps explains why Barthes's explicators have overlooked what seems such an obvious trajectory.

The first step in the metamorphosis was to jettison the moral sense of scripture; thus, in *Sade, Fourier, Loyola,* where Barthes is forthright about the structural role of the fourfold sense in Loyola's *Exercises,* the original moral sense of Scripture—"the part through which a rule of life is maintained" (2), as one of de Lubac's witnesses had described it in the early seventeenth century—yields to the more purely semantic interlocutions

TABLE 1 The Levels of Meaning, Henri de Lubac to Roland Barthes

Exégèse médiévale (1959–63)			
1. HISTORICAL	2. ALLEGORICAL	3. MORAL	4. ANAGOGICAL

"Comment parler à Dieu?" (Tel Quel, 1969)/Sade, Fourier, Loyola (1971)			
1. LITERAL	2. SEMANTIC	3. ALLEGORICAL	4. ANAGOGICAL

S/Z (1970)				
1. PROAIRETIC	2. SEMANTIC	3. CULTURAL	4. HERMENEUTIC	5. SYMBOLIC

between the director and the exercitant. Next, the medieval allegorical sense (level 2 for de Lubac, level 3 for Barthes's Loyola) maintains its status as the most powerfully meaning-producing of the four levels, but it changes from de Lubac's "deep waters" of Scripture that are "hard to swim," in the words of Geoffrey of Saint Victor, into Loyola's "acted" text that constitutes a performed reading of the literal and semantic senses. The anagogical sense remains a constant here, though this level too experiences an important transformation: from a biblical mode of individualized eschatology ("an object of your hope") to a purely semiotic liberation within the closed space of Ignatian discourse.

From de Lubac's writings on medieval hermeneutics to Barthes's essay on Loyola, then, the textual levels or codes remain roughly the same; self-consciously modeled on the four senses of Scripture, the four levels of Loyola's *Exercises* strongly retain their medieval character as the underlying webs of meaning that generate reader response and the assignation of meaning. From *Sade, Fourier, Loyola* to *S/Z*, on the other hand, the codes are augmented by one while losing the ethical sheen of anagogy. The "historical" or "literal" level of the biblical or Ignatian text becomes the proairetic code of Balzac, the sequential progression of plot-action-dialogue that forms the bare surface of the novella. Next, Barthes tears the veil of medieval allegory in two, yielding the codes of culture and hermeneutics. From its primal status as the "part that is played amid the long-lost, ancient shadows," allegory—the rhetorical master trope of meaning—branches into cultural context and hidden meaning within the textual field of *S/Z*. And finally, in a brazen act of theological corrosion, anagogy becomes symbol. Reordering and reprioritizing the four senses of scripture, Barthes robs allegory of its theologized mysteries while divesting scripture's anagogical level of its eschatological promise.

What we are seeing in this gradual appropriation is a process I would characterize as a secularization of interpretation, one that entails a fundamental reliance on a medieval exegetical habit of mind the religious dimensions of which have been excised. That this excision was an enabling one for Barthes seems clear given the intellectual capital that has been invested in *S/Z* and its role in defining French theory over the last three decades. The incongruity of proposing the influence of *Exégèse médiévale* on one of the hallmark texts of the 1960s avant garde is obvious, for today many share the same attitude toward the "scholasticism of the four senses" voiced by the many historians of theology whom de Lubac himself had attacked: that it imposes a dry, inflexible interpretive apparatus upon its tutor text, embodying in its hopelessly dense levels of reading "a senseless game," "a mania," even "an exercise in bad taste" (xviii). Among Anglo-American scholars, the prevailing bias against this sort of criticism is due in large part to the influence of D. W. Robertson, whose so-called Exegetical method has tended over the last several decades to dominate discussions of the relationship between biblical exegesis and literary criticism. Robertson's magnum opus, *A Preface to Chaucer,* was published in 1962 and made extensive use of the first volume of *Exégèse médiévale*, particularly in the chapter on "Allegory, Humanism, and Literary Theory." [62] In Robertsonian criticism, the four levels of scripture do indeed become a bastion of interpretive constraint, promoting what Lee Patterson once termed a "catalogue of totalizings" at the service of a "conservative, universalist, and institutional view of the Middle Ages." [63] For Henri de Lubac, by contrast, the four levels are precisely what lend the biblical text its malleable and proliferative character and produce the "universally and teemingly abundant" (42) meanings it holds eternally in store for its readers.

Of course, structuralists of Barthes's generation loved tables, graphs, lists, and charts, and the one I have constructed above risks conveying its own inflexibility in the exegetical scheme that was by no means present in Barthes's avant-garde refraction of its possibilities. Yet for both Barthes and de Lubac, the crossing and interpenetration of textual levels and codes could be understood as the very fiber of the text, creating a constant tension between structural rigidity and semiotic multiplicity. De Lubac identifies this tension as "an organic and specified multiplicity of meaning" in the biblical text that would always exceed the bounds of the four levels while remaining perceptible only through the collective

---

62. Robertson, *A Preface to Chaucer,* 286–303.
63. Patterson, *Negotiating the Past,* 32–33.

lens they provided: "this idea of 'various, multiple styles of speech in the Sacred Literature' is not at all adequate when it comes to constituting a doctrine of spiritual understanding. Spread out visibly along the surface, like the colors of the light spectrum [*Etalée en surface, comme les couleurs du spectre solaire*] . . . the infinity of meanings established by this idea does not yet constitute a structure. It is the traditional theory of the triple or quadruple sense that gives us this structure" (82). In strikingly similar language, Barthes envisioned the text's meanings as "spread like gold dust on the apparent surface of the text [*répandue comme une poussière d'or sur la surface apparente du texte*]" (9), but gold that could be gathered only through the economy of the five codes. And if for de Lubac the text's "infinity of meanings" can be grasped by "passing tier by tier through different degrees of depth," for Barthes the text's sequential connotations are the mechanism by which "meaning proliferates by layering [*marcottage*]" (8). Endless varieties of meanings, multiple codes, intrications of metaphor, allegory, and textual surface: if the "five codes" Barthes selects to decipher the text of *Sarrasine* are in effect a retooling of the "four senses" of Scripture as studied by de Lubac, *S/Z* might be reimagined as a kind of *Glossa Ordinaria* on Balzac, an attempt to enlist the structural mechanics of premodern exegesis as part of an avant-garde interrogation of textual multiplicity.

Apparent throughout *S/Z* and *Exégèse médiévale* is an obsession shared by de Lubac and Barthes that might be described as a passionate love of textual metaphor. The Jesuit theologian and the Protestant avant-gardiste share a deep-seated will to delineate and exploit as many metaphors and similes for the writing, reading, and meaning of texts as they can find. "The excess of metaphor," Barthes contends, "is a game played by the discourse . . . an attempt to exhaust the nonetheless infinite variety and inventiveness of synonyms, while repeating and varying the signifier, so as to affirm the plural existence of the text, its return." This hermeneutic game "consists in presenting, acrobatically, for as long as possible, the plural diversity of possibilities within a singular syntagm" (58–59). For de Lubac, of course, the text's acrobatic metaphoricity is no game at all but an exegetical impulse that serves the purposes of the postwar *ressourcement* of pre-Enlightenment Catholic thought: by recognizing the boundless diversity of premodern biblical exegesis, the Church can recover the richness in its theologies, liturgies, and sacraments and thereby help the faithful address more rigorously the complex political issues of their day. Barthes wants to establish this metaphorical self-consciousness as an integral part of *nouvelle critique* in an attempt to wrest structuralist criticism from the rigid formalisms of its less skilled practitioners. Yet who can read the following passages side by side—the first appearing in volume 1 of *Exégèse médiévale* in 1959, the second in the closing pages of *S/Z* eleven years later—and not wonder at the intimate proximity of these two hermeneutic systems?

Scripture is like the world: "undecipherable in its fullness and in the multiplicity of its meanings." A deep forest, with innumerable branches, "an infinite forest of meanings": the more involved one gets in it, the more one discovers that it is impossible to explore it right to the end. It is a table arranged by Wisdom, laden with food, where the unfathomable divinity of the Savior is itself offered as nourishment to all. Treasure of the Holy Spirit, whose riches are as infinite as himself. True labyrinth. Deep heavens, unfathomable abyss. Vast sea, where there is endless voyaging "with all sails set." Ocean of mystery. Or raging torrent. . . . (1:75)

[T]he text is replete with multiple, discontinuous, accumulated meanings, and yet burnished, smoothed by the "natural" movement of its sentences: it is an egg-text . . . we can say that any classic (readerly) text is implicitly an art of Replete Literature: literature that is replete: like a cupboard where meanings are shelved, stacked, safeguarded (in this text nothing is ever lost: meaning recuperates everything); like a pregnant female, replete with signifieds which criticism will not fail to deliver; like the sea, replete with depths and movements which give it its appearance of infinity, its vast meditative surface; like the sun, replete with the glory it sheds over those who write it, or finally, acknowledged as an established and recognized art: institutional. (200–201)

For all their differences in inspiration, ideology, and religiosity, what movingly unites *Exégèse médiévale* and *S/Z* is their authors' common sense of awe in the face of the text in its laborious intricacy and immensity.

I use the term "laborious" advisedly here, for throughout *S/Z* one of Barthes's most insistent metaphors for textual production and reception is that of work: "To read . . . is a labor of language," the text itself "a nomination in the course of becoming [une *nomination en devenir*], a tireless approximation, a metonymic labor" (11). The Barthesian text recuperates the "labored" text with all its premodern connotations as both a product and an embodiment of work or *opus,* a secularizing revision of the *opus Dei* that de Lubac constantly invokes as the human foundation of biblical exegesis. The two writers share as well a particular investment in the tropes of classical rhetoric as sites of textual labor. Barthes called throughout his career for a more general *ressourcement* of "the several hundred figures propounded by the art of rhetoric down through the centuries," which in section XIV of *S/Z* he collectively terms "a labor of classification intended to name, to lay the foundations for, the world" (26); with an expert's eye for detail, Barthes even evokes prosopography as "a rhetorical genre particularly in favor in the neo-rhetoric of the second century A.D." (56). De Lubac, too, ever aware of the classical sources of medieval exegetical vocabularies, is quite frank about his subject's debts to the history of rhetoric, debts owed by the moral imperatives of tropology: "In the most general acceptation, a trope was a figure, a mode, or a *turn* of phrase (*tropos, conversio*), by which one turns some expression to designate some object other than the one naturally meant. *Tropologia,* accordingly, was a 'speech turned around' or 'turning' something else 'around'; it was a 'turned' or 'turning manner of speech.' There was nothing in it that might suggest an idea of moral conversion" (129).

Barthes cast his own predilections for textual "work" in intriguingly medieval terms during an interview for *Le Monde* conducted three years after the publication of *S/Z.* The overall subject of the interview was Barthes's actual writing habits, the daily routines, methods, and practices surrounding his typical workday: "it seems so important to me to ask a writer about his writing habits, putting things on the most material level, I would even say the most minimal level possible."[64] Early on in the interview he revealed something of the ritualistic ceremonial that shaped his quotidian engagement in the writing process:

When writing is placed in its historical or even anthropological context, it can be seen that for a long time writing was attended by great ceremony. . . . In certain Christian monasteries of the Middle Ages, the copyists began their work only after a day of meditation. Personally, I call the set of those "rules" (in the monastic sense of the word) which predetermine the work . . . the "protocols" of work. The etymology is clear: it means the first page glued to a manuscript in preparation for writing.[65]

The monastic analogy employed here reveals the same fascination with medieval textual culture that inspires the Loyola essay. The material text figures importantly in the "metonymic labor" sustaining textual production: resuscitating the lost codicological sense of "protocol" from the medieval Latin *protocollum* (ultimately from the Late Greek *protokollon*), Barthes signals the premodern sensibility that inspires his own set of artistic conventions as a revival of a medieval scribal *habitus.*

If writing and reading are labor, then of course the text is the material product of that labor, a textile or needful thing that the exegetical

---

64. Barthes, *Grain of the Voice,* 177.
65. Barthes, *Grain of the Voice,* 178.

craftsman renders useful. In the words of one of de Lubac's eleventh-century witnesses, the senses of scripture collectively "make an inter-woven pattern," one furnished "with a moral sense and a spiritual sense [joined] together in an interconnected way" (95). "It is written that a rope with three strands is hard to break," writes another: "For surely it is true that Scripture, which has usually been interpreted in an historical, allegorical, and moral sense, is too strong to be ruptured by any distor-tions of heretics or pagans" (107). This biblical notion of the "woven" text, its elements intricately entwined and inseparable, inspires Barthes to analogize the networks of signification making up *S/Z* to embroidered finery:

The text, while it is being produced, is like a piece of Valenciennes lace created before us under the lacemaker's fingers: each sequence undertaken hangs like the temporar-ily inactive bobbin waiting while its neighbor works; then, when its turn comes, the hand takes up the thread again, brings it back to the frame; and as the pattern is filled out, the progress of each thread is marked with a pin which holds it and is gradually moved forward . . . This process is valid for the entire text. The grouping of codes, as they enter into the work, into the movement of the reading, constitute a braid (*text, fabric, braid:* the same thing); each threat, each code, is a voice; these braided—or braiding—voices form the writing: when it is alone, the voice does no labor, trans-forms nothing: it *expresses;* but as soon as the hand intervenes to gather and inter-twine the inert threads, there is labor, there is transformation. (160)

What interests Barthes here, following de Lubac, is not the text as fin-ished product of scribal labor, but the continual re-creation or "braiding" of meaning by the "movement of the reading." Initially the braided or woven text can be known by the reader only in its individual strands, which, when gathered together in the reading experience, yield the text in its diaphanous fullness.

The reader, too, can be "filled" with text until sated—or, better, un-til hungry for more. To de Lubac, who loved the ancient notion of the "edible" text, the medieval vocabulary of *ruminatio* (which, as I argue in chapter 2, also influenced Lacan) was a favorite source of metaphorical abundance, as signaled in a passage that casts the Bible, in de Lubac's paraphrase, as a "bountiful vineyard where there are always some grapes to pick after the vintage": "the words of Sacred Scripture," as one medi-eval writer had mused, "when they have been gleaned for a first and sec-ond vintage, can be squeezed so as to yield a rich and intoxicating liq-uid, as if it were usual for them, laden with sacred meanings as they are, to flow again even as if they had never been touched in the first place"

(79). For Guerric of Igny, cited further on in de Lubac's text, the Bible is "ample and refreshing fare in the form of the three loaves of history, allegory, and morality" (93). The text as delineated in *S/Z* is similarly edible: speaking of the ways certain works invent the notion of character, Barthes notes the verbal "complexity" that "determines the character's 'personality,' which is just as much a combination as the odor of a dish or the bouquet of a wine" (67). By contrast, a text too saturated in cultural convention risks the fate of all bad food: "the Balzacian text is clotted with it [*tout empoissé*]: because of its cultural codes, it stales, rots, excludes itself from writing . . . it is the quintessence, the residual condensate of what cannot be rewritten" (98). And finally, the referential codes "have a kind of emetic virtue, they bring on nausea by the boredom, conformism, and disgust with repetition that establishes them." The "remedy" for this textual emesis, Barthes suggests, "is to make them ironical, i.e., to superimpose on the vomited code [*code vomi*] a second code which expresses it at a distance" (139).

No metaphorical register seems to have appealed more consistently to both de Lubac and Barthes than the musical. Early on in *S/Z* Barthes goes so far as to propose that the "area of the (readerly) text" is "comparable at every point to a (classical) musical score"; Barthes in fact inscribes such a score in the body of the text, where the progression of semes, cultural codes, enigmas, and so on are assigned whole, half, quarter, and eighth notes in the "tonal text" that makes up *Sarrasine* (28–29). This musical analogy holds a great allure for Barthes, who elsewhere in *S/Z* captures the musical "texture" of the writing by imagining it as a chorus of multiple and often clashing voices:

> The best way to conceive the classical plural is then to listen to the text as an iridescent exchange carried on by multiple voices, on different wavelengths and subject from time to time to a sudden dissolve, leaving a gap which enables the utterance to shift from one point of view to another, without warning: the writing is set up across this tonal instability (which in the modern text becomes atonality), which makes it a glistening texture of ephemeral origins [*une moire brillante d'origines éphémères*]. (41–42)

To "listen" to the text as a kind of carefully staged musical performance demands a literalization of the *vox* in the text, the deployment of "voice" that lends writing, in Barthes's own deliberately synaesthetic terms, its iridescence, its glitter, its gaps, shifts, and instabilities.

For de Lubac, too, the choral character of the scriptural text perfectly reproduces its unified diversity. Treating the "harmony" between the Old and New Testaments, he envisions a "convergence" of dissimilar things as the key to a musical reading of the text:

Such agreement is something unique, which no example could properly account for, although the vocabulary with which it is defined is borrowed from music and receives certain elucidations from it. This agreement does not consist of a simple parallelism, or of a simple hierarchy, but of a veritable unity. But a unity of this kind is not, to be sure, a confusion. What we are dealing with is a consonance, that is to say, a harmony that is realized by a convergence between things that are at first glance dissimilar and recognized as such. (1.245)

Here again we are seeing the tense interplay between regulating structure and semiotic multiplicity. Far from paradoxical, this musical interplay furnishes the very condition of the experience of reading, in which "consonance" and "convergence" can be achieved only through an acknowledgment of ostensible dissimilarity.[66] Swept up in the musicality of the readerly text, the reader will locate the difference and dissension produced by the intercalation of manifold codes and senses as part of an exegetical *symphonia,* an incompletely scored performance in which readerly desire sings the *cantus firmus* to the celestial harmonies resonating from the sacred words of scripture.

Beautiful Captives

The "classical plural" of the text, then, the final triumph of its written unity over the instabilities and dissimilarities that draw the reader astray, resounds as a deep musical structure holding the text together by its roots. If for Barthes and de Lubac such musical grounds undergird texts at their foundations, the textual surface (to invoke their own lovingly mixed metaphors) is best likened to a thin veil, an *integumentum* that can be pushed aside to reveal the alluring body of writing beneath. Barthes first elaborates these corporeal metaphors in *S/Z,* though he treats them more extensively three years later. As Barthes would pose the question of the incarnational text in *The Pleasure of the Text* (1973), "Does the text have human form, is it a figure, an anagram of the body? Yes, but of our erotic body. The pleasure of the text is irreducible to physiological need.

---

66. "Harmony from dissonance" was a particularly common metaphor in medieval canon law; see Kuttner's classic lecture, *Harmony from Dissonance.*

The pleasure of the text is that moment when my body pursues its own ideas—for my body does not have the same ideas I do."[67]

Such gendered images of the "body as text" with all their erotic implications have become familiar to the point of banality in criticism of the last thirty years, though in *S/Z* we can sense the theoretical excitement generated by the homological proximity of textual consumption and sexual delectation (an analogy that would of course serve very different purposes in some of the central texts of French feminism in the succeeding decade).[68] The body in *Sarrasine* is "the biological chromosomatic Book," Barthes suggests in an explicitly biblical analogy, even "a duplicate of the Book: the young woman originates in the Book of Life" (37). Codes and bodies are continually and simultaneously "unveiled" in the lexias structuring *S/Z,* a book that makes much of the seductive delays and suspensions inherent to the reader's experience of the classic text: "Perhaps a special morpheme should be constituted for this final hesitation of the discourse in beginning a story, a suspense which is purely discursive, analogous to the final moments of a striptease" (88). In *S/Z* this productive analogy sustains a number of more intricate approaches to the paratactic flow of narrative:

Striptease and blazon refer to the very destiny of the sentence (both are constructed like sentences), which consists in this (doomed thereto by its structure): the sentence can never constitute a *total;* meanings can be listed, not admixed: the total, the sum are for language the promised lands, glimpsed *at the end* of enumeration, but once this enumeration has been completed, no feature can reassemble it—or, if this feature is produced, it too can only be *added* to the others. (114)

The "partiality" of the text emerges most clearly in its "unveiling": in the hermeneutic undressings that allow the reader to gradually "unfold" (another of Barthes's favored images) its various layerings yet which never quite permit satiation. The reading subject, caught up in a hopeless desire for the culmination of this sexual-textual performance, "knows the female body only as a division and dissemination of partial objects: leg, breast, shoulder, neck, hands. Fragmented Woman is the object offered to Sarrasine's love. Divided, anatomized, she is merely a kind of dictionary of fetish objects" (112).

Textual unveilings, eroticized but readable flesh, violently fragmented and luxuriously fetishized body parts: for those invested in the original-

67. Barthes, *The Pleasure of the Text,* 5–6.
68. See, among many others, Moi, *Sexual/Textual Politics: Feminist Literary Theory.*

ity of twentieth-century critical vocabularies, the polymorphously erotic nature of textual reception as theorized by Barthes will likely seem far removed from the sober language of premodern biblical exegesis. Medievalists, to the contrary, have long been aware of the kinkier side of medieval hermeneutics: the fascination with the literal skin that makes up the parchment manuscript, the sexual connotations of "glossing" that inspire the Wife of Bath's bookish eroticism, the monastic desire to peer beneath the *integumentum* that covers the alluring body of the scriptural text.[69] Henri de Lubac unearthed many original contributions to this exegetical subgenre, though he hardly framed them with the approvingly eroticizing language favored by Barthes. The most spectacular of these analogies occupies his long section in volume 1 of *Exégèse médiévale* on the interpretive tradition of the so-called Beautiful Captive, which took its inspiration from a passage in Deuteronomy that issues a set of instructions to victors in war who come upon a beautiful woman they desire among their vanquished enemies: "you shall bring her home to your house," the Bible demands, "and she shall shave her head and pare her nails. And she shall put off her captive's garb, and shall remain in your house and bewail her father and mother a full month; after that you may go in to her, and be her husband, and she shall be your wife" (Deut. 21:10–13).[70]

For countless medieval exegetes, the passage served as an allegory for the proper Christian approach to pagan letters (i.e., the "beautiful captive"), which had to be pared and purged of their morally questionable aspects before they could be reconciled with scriptural tradition. The originator of this interpretive approach to the Beautiful Captive episode, according to de Lubac, was Origen (not Jerome, as is commonly supposed), who glossed the passage as follows:

I too have often gone forth to war against my enemies, and I have found among my spoils a beautiful woman. For even among our enemies we find things that are good and proper. If, therefore, we read wise and knowledgeable words in one of them, we must purify them, we must remove and cut away everything in this knowledge that is deadly and vain. This is just like the hair and nails of this woman who was taken when the enemy was plundered. Thus we shall make her our wife, when she no longer has anything that has the appearance of infidelity, anything that smacks of death on her head or on her hands, so that she no longer bears anything impure or deathful either

69. See, most influentially, Dinshaw, *Chaucer's Sexual Poetics,* esp. 3–27; and more recently the essays collected in Frese and O'Keeffe, eds., *The Book and the Body.*

70. On this passage, see in particular Dinshaw, *Chaucer's Sexual Poetics,* 22–24, which draws heavily on the Beautiful Captive discussion in de Lubac's first volume.

in her sentiments or in her actions. For the women of our enemies have no purity about them, seeing that there is no wisdom in them that is not mingled with some impurity. (213)

For de Lubac this "beautiful image" (!) of a "purified" habit of reading demands that pagan texts be approached as a tempting but sullied female body, a textualized *corpus* that must undergo a vigorous process of scraping, purging, refashioning, and rewriting before it is suitable for Christian consumption. The homosocial model of textual encounter proposed here undergoes numerous revisions during the Middle Ages, and de Lubac cites dozens of writings exemplifying the misogynist creativity that this horrifying gloss provoked. "Firstly," Saint Augustine demands, "all the uncleanness of *superstition* should be removed and cut off from her, and so she should be adopted for the study of truth" (216). Once the feminine text has been cleansed, avows the biographer of Saint Maieul of Cluny, it willingly subjects itself to the desire of its captor: "When her head had been made bare and she had had her nails clipped and her hair shorn, and had been cleansed of all her filth, she came to embrace the one by whom she had been captured. Drawing on this simile, [Maieul] found it worthwhile to remember what was found useful in the books of the philosophers" (217). Even Pope Gregory IX, warning the Franciscans against the "worldly knowledge" embedded in classical letters, cautions that the "captive" text should yield with little resistance to the Christian reader: "The girl who was captured from the enemy, who has had her hair shorn and her fingernails clipped and who is joined to a man of Israel, should not be dominated by him, but should rather submit to him as a subject" (221).

When read alongside this and the many other violently gendered models of textual reception discussed in *Exégèse médiévale*, Barthes's account of the "anatomized" and "fragmented" body postulated in Balzac's *Sarrasine* seems positively tame. Yet Sarrasine's readerly act of "undressing" this body sounds very much like the moral purging of the Beautiful Captive in the exegetical tradition. As Barthes describes this process:

This sundered, dissected body (we are reminded of the boy's games at school) is reassembled by the artist (and this is the meaning of his vocation) into a whole body, the body of love descended from the heaven of art, in which fetishism is abolished and by which Sarrasine is cured. However, without the subject's realizing it as yet, and although the finally reassembled woman is actually there before him, near enough to touch, this redeeming body remains a fictive one, through the very praises Sarrasine addresses to it . . . an object whose *underneath,* whose *insides* will continue to arouse his concern, his curiosity, and his aggression: undressing La Zambinella (by drawing), questioning her and himself, and ultimately breaking the hollow statue, the sculptor will continue to whittle the woman (just as he whittled his pew in church as a child) thereby returning to its (fragmented) fetish condition a body whose unity he supposed he had discovered in such amazement. (112)

Sarrasine's performance of a simultaneously bodily and textual "whittling" eerily reenacts the ritual of shearing, clipping, shaving, and cleansing undergone by the Beautiful Captive of Deuteronomy. The artist (a rebellious Jesuit himself, we must remember, in Balzac's *Sarrasine*) becomes de Lubac's Christian reader, receiving an unsuitable body from the perverse realm of castration that he must "sunder" and "dissect" before reassembling it into the "redeeming body" that nevertheless remains a fetish object even after it is carved into submission. The narrative striptease theorized in *S/Z* thus exhibits a specifically exegetical sensibility, recruiting for late structuralism a staged encounter with the erotic body of an ultimately redemptive text.

For both Henri de Lubac and Roland Barthes, though, the gendering of commentary is finally too limiting an interpretive operation to exercise upon a text destined to achieve a kind of universality embracing its boundless community of human readers. This text stretches to its metaphorical apogee in the heavens themselves, which it covers with a writing surface so wide and ubiquitous that migrating birds can travel through its channels of codes, senses, citations, and zones: "The text, in its mass, is comparable to a sky, at once flat and smooth, deep, without edges and without landmarks; like the soothsayer drawing on it with the tip of his staff an imaginary rectangle wherein to consult, according to certain principles, the flight of birds, the commentator traces through the text certain zones of reading, in order to observe therein the migration of meanings, the outcropping of codes, the passage of citations" (*S/Z,* 14). For Barthes the celestial limitlessness of the text grants it an all-encompassing semiotic mass, an inexhaustible ability to produce meaning on the page and in the reader. This imagery derives most famously from Augustine, and specifically from a passage in the *Confessions* that inspires many of the writers cited by de Lubac: "You know, O Lord, how you clothed men with skins when by sin they became mortal. In the same way you have spread out the heavens like a canopy of skins, and these heavens are your Book, your words in which no note of discord jars, set over us through the ministry of mortal men. Those men are dead, and by their death this solid shield, the authority of your words delivered to us through them, is raised on high to shelter all that lies beneath it." [71] The Augustinian notion of the Book as a celestial "skin," a writing surface that wraps the mortal universe in its embrace, serves as one of the most poignant metaphors for the "marvelous depths" of the biblical text, as one of de Lubac's chapter titles terms it. The Bible has been written for us and can be read for us, but we as individual readers remain utterly insignificant beneath what de Lubac calls "the intelligible heavens that it unfurls before our eyes" (76). The "ideal text," Barthes avows in the same spirit of interpretive humility, "is a galaxy of signifiers, not a structure of signifieds; it has no beginning; it is reversible; we gain access to it by several entrances, none of which can be authoritatively declared to be the main one; the codes it mobilizes extend *as far as the eye can reach*" (5–6, emphasis in original). Writing at the end of a decade breathlessly invested in its own interpretive innovations, Barthes imputes to the text the same celestial boundlessness that provided medieval biblical exegesis with its justifying purpose.

71. Augustine, *Confessions,* 13.15.16; see Jean-François Lyotard's strange rhapsody from 1997 on this passage. Originally presented under the title "The Skin of the Skies," this work is reprinted as the second part of the long essay comprising most of Lyotard's *The Confession of Augustine* (discussed below in the Epilogue).

Epilogue

Nous n'avons jamais été modernes. For the most part, the epistemological segregations that defined modernity and its regimes of knowledge production over the course of the twentieth century were resolutely opposed to the kinds of historical self-scrutiny demanded by the acceptance or even the entertainment of Bruno Latour's corrosive proposition. Claims of avant-garde originality are always vulnerable, of course, particularly the claims of what Latour calls those "modernizing avant-gardes" who have allegedly "broken with their own pasts" yet whose vocabularies, philologies, and cosmologies remain firmly rooted in the bygone eras they have forgotten. "The moderns have a peculiar propensity for understanding time that passes as if it were really abolishing the past behind it," Latour writes. "They all take themselves for Attila, in whose footsteps no grass grows back. They do not feel that they are removed from the Middle Ages by a certain number of centuries, but that they are separated by Copernican revolutions, epistemological breaks, epistemic ruptures so radical that nothing of the past survives in them—nothing of the past ought to survive in them."[1] The irony in Latour's invocation of Attila as a trope of avant-garde radicalism is as easy to miss as it is revealing: for Attila embodies all the violence, darkness, and ignorance imputed to the barbarian invasions that gave grotesque birth to the very Middle Ages that modernity has so often sought to abject. The postwar French avant garde studied in this book, though, was less a

1. Latour, *We Have Never Been Modern,* 68.

marauding band of fifth-century Huns than a rhetorical community of fourth-century Romans, performing their metaleptic relation to a bygone era that continued to surround them in both archaic and residual forms. The dramatic genre embraced by this community was neither, to invoke the "Eighteenth Brumaire," the decimating tragedy of an Attila nor the schizoid farce of an Augustine, but a comedy in the classic sense of *commedia:* the domain of coincidence and improbability, of the surprise ending and the fortuitous meeting of minds—a theater of history that absorbed the languages, rhetorics, and epistemes of an epoch that its actors felt themselves to be at once conserving, surpassing, and reliving.[2] For Henri Bergson, writing in the year 1900, an event enters the domain of the comic "when it belongs simultaneously to two altogether independent series of events and is capable of being interpreted in two entirely different meanings at the same time." This "reciprocal interference of series," as Bergson termed it, will create its effects most powerfully through precisely the kinds of juxtapositions and equivocations that are the hallmark of avant-garde medievalism in its most provocative forms.[3]

An equally indigenous term that captures the complex tenor of the premodern condition might be *translatio studii,* a medieval phrase connoting the long, incremental (and indeed often quite comical) process of cultural osmosis that enabled the Christian cultures of the Middle Ages to retain the classical knowledges of antiquity without the apparent taint of polytheism or paganism. The avant-garde premodern was nothing if not a large-scale translation project, entailing a series of discrete acts of cultural appropriation that together define this era in part as an efflorescence of critical neomedievalism. Central to this *translatio* of the medieval in French critical thought of the 1960s was the consistent tension between the transparency of the translative process within certain reflections on method (as in Bourdieu's postface, which is explicit about its debts to Panofsky, or Barthes's circa-1970 interviews) and its occlusion within specific critical artifacts (*S/Z* does not once mention the four senses of scripture despite its clear reliance on their mechanism, while Bataille's *La somme athéologique* never names Thomas Aquinas, though of course his presence is everywhere). The medievalism of the French avant garde appears in this light remarkably ecumenical, if not voracious. To invoke Umberto Eco's useful typology of the "ten little Middle Ages" ob-

2. See Bynum's comments on "history in the comic mode" in *Fragmentation and Redemption,* 24–25.

3. Bergson, "Laughter," in Sypher, *Comedy,* 123.

taining in postmodern culture, the premodern condition entails both the *philosophia perennis* of the neo-Thomists and the "philological attitude" of the *Annales;* it exploits the speculative urbanity of "ironical revisitation" while flirting at moments with the neo-fascist implications of "occult philosophy" and its Will to Power.[4] The sheer density of the premodern condition can thus suggest only a provisional and partial answer to the question that has centrally motivated this book: how is it that the most consistently abjected era in the Western tradition came to assume such a formative role in avant-gardiste theorization of language, culture, and society?

We might begin to consider this question simply by recalling the truism that much of what gets embraced under the rubric of *theory* has been dedicated to a critique of the master narratives and social practices of the Enlightenment—or, in the words of Jean-François Lyotard, "that severe reexamination which postmodernity imposes on the thought of the Enlightenment."[5] The self-knowing Cartesian subject was dismantled by the models of the unconscious proposed in Freudian and, later, Lacanian psychoanalysis; Kantian "instrumental reason" and the idealist Hegelian dialectic of History came under withering critiques at the hands of the Frankfurt School critics, particularly Theodor Adorno and Max Horkheimer (and, from a very different direction, in the work of Foucault); the neat binaries underpinning Rousseau's models of language and writing dissolved in the early years of Derridean deconstruction; the continuing ideological and historical legacy of European expansionism has received decades of theoretical scrutiny from the perspective of postcolonial studies; the consolidation of the modern bourgeois family in the eighteenth century remains a source of critical engagement for feminist and queer theory and historicism; and the list goes on. If the Middle Ages represent a semiotically rich site of transgression, perversion, and fanaticism for contemporary popular culture, for the 1960s avant-garde, the medieval provided above all an archive of cultural and intellectual production that seemingly escaped the moral compass of the Enlightenment—and (in this reading) without the baggage of humanism, capitalism, colonialism, and triumphalist individualism represented by the Renaissance. The general critique of the European Enlightenment in the second half of the twentieth century drew some of its most critically imaginative energy from an era both historically and genealogically prior to the Enlightenment, the epoch of "our infancy" (in Eco's ironic char-

4. Eco, "Dreaming of the Middle Ages," in *Travels,* 68–72.
5. Lyotard, "What Is Postmodernism?" in *The Postmodern Condition,* 73.

acterization) that allowed those who turned to it the momentary fantasy that the particular modernity they both inhabited and lamented was inevitable yet noncompulsory, of the avant garde's own making. While such an idealized Middle Ages could often provoke nostalgia for a lost age of "natural" social relations and transparent hierarchies of power, it nevertheless provided postwar critical thought with an almost inexhaustible source of intellectual sustenance in its assault on postmedieval legacies to the Western tradition.

Nostalgia, in fact, often seems beside the point for this particular intellectual formation, and it is in this sense that the avant-garde premodern might perform a considerable corrective function in relation to other modes of critical neomedievalism that have gained some currency in recent decades. (Or even in its own decade: when Marshall McLuhan published *The Gutenberg Galaxy* in 1962, the year of Georges Bataille's death, he could not have known that his postulation of the postmodern age's oblique return to the tribalism and diversity of the premodern was already a critical assumption among certain of his French contemporaries.[6]) It may in fact be their resistance to idealizing nostalgia and historical essentialism that most distances Bataille and the 1960s avant garde from the flattening effects of many other forms of theoretic medievalism over the final decades of the twentieth century. At the same time, the premodern condition as this book has understood it was less interested in promoting philologically precise accounts of the medieval world from a circumscribed archive than it was in deriving critically useful medievalisms from a boundless field of residual memories, archaic artifacts, and cultural continuities. If the medievalist's worn-on-the-sleeve erudition is as often performed as it is practiced among the French avant garde, this only seldom dilutes the theoretical energy that the Middle Ages infused at every level into the subculture that gave us French theory. What comes across in many avant-garde writings (and often movingly so) is the sheer depth of admiration these thinkers held for both premodern writers themselves and the contemporary scholars accounting for their legacy to modern thought. Lacan gasps with an only barely ironized amazement at a poem by Arnaut Daniel that exemplifies the "paradoxes of sublimation" for his seminar auditors. In *Of Grammatology,* Derrida makes quite clear his conceptual debt to St. Augustine's description of melismatic singing as a crucial moment in the philosophy of language to be marshaled against Rousseau and the En-

---

6. On McLuhan's relation to French thought of the 1960s, see the provocative essay by Theall, "Marshall McLuhan, Canadian Schizo-Jansenist."

lightenment. In a short published lecture by an art historian musing on the conceptual edifice of the Gothic cathedral, Bourdieu finds what will prove perhaps the most significant keyword in his sociological lexicon.

Given the critique of modernity that motivates them, of course, the languages of premodernism among the avant garde often risked lapsing into rhetorics of *anti*modernism, frequently without the self-consciousness that would be required to render such moments in any way useful. Antimodernism presents its own set of problems, particularly in its difficult role within the postmodern, however the latter is circumscribed (as a movement, a sensibility, a *habitus,* and so on). The frequent convergence of the premodern and the antimodern has had important bearing on the many attempts among contemporary critics to define the postmodern at least since Jean-François Lyotard's 1979 manifesto *The Postmodern Condition,* which was received as both a diagnosis and a symptom of its subject. As Lyotard himself recognized, though, the advent of a discernible postmodernism could be properly understood only in complex relation to its management of the various modes of antimodernism that have attempted to corrode it. "Antimodern" was and remains a rallying cry for various forms of radical theological conservatism, from the rise of French neo-Thomism in the late nineteenth century to the Radical Orthodoxy at the turn of our own; the word served as the title of the most straightforwardly polemical work of Jacques Maritain, published in 1922 for *La Revue des Jeunes.* It was in *Antimoderne* that Maritain first sought to articulate a post-Leonine neo-Thomism as a specifically intellectual intervention against the rising tide of modernity. For Maritain, "the conditions required for the success of a scholastic renaissance" were self-evidently premodern conditions, yet with an emphatically avant-garde twist: the reconciliation of Bergsonism and Catholicism in the service of a metaphysics that would yield "un monde nouveau" for the faithful and the apostate alike.[7] As Maritain puts it more strongly in his preface, the paradoxical character of "modern antimodernity" is that which allows his own polemical treatise to draw from St. Thomas Aquinas the radicalism required to change the future: "Anti-moderne *contre les erreurs du temps présent, elle est* ultramoderne *pour toutes les vérités enveloppées dans le temps à venir.*"[8]

Le temps à venir: rhetorically, at least, Maritain's antimodernism approaches the eschatological. That such an avowedly conservative pro-

---

7. Maritain, *Antimoderne,* 115, 113.

8. Maritain, *Antimoderne,* 16. On Maritain as "anti-modernist in the marketplace" of twentieth-century Thomisms, see John, *The Thomist Spectrum,* 16–31.

motion of the *anti*modern can present itself boastfully as the only truthful way to be *ultra*modern suggests the difficulty of discerning the precise relation between the *pre*modern and the *post*modern. Indeed, if the premodern condition possesses one unifying element, it may lie in this capacity as archaizing provocation: as that channel through which modernity is incited to confront and stage its own historical and ontological limits. In this respect, Latour's *We Have Never Been Modern* can be read less as an Archimedean critique of those "modernizing avant-gardes" he urbanely dismisses than as the belated jeremiad of the premodern condition.

In the same spirit, Lyotard himself would eventually turn away from the legitimation crises attending the new technocracy and toward what he saw as an earlier mode of global inscription, the "skin of the skies." His final project, in fact, was to be a book on St. Augustine (whom he would elsewhere place in the pantheon of the "moderns," alongside Nietzsche, Freud, and Heidegger).[9] Uncompleted during Lyotard's lifetime, *La Confession d'Augustin* survives as two essays and numerous fragments recording the author's quasi-devotional meditations upon a text that he had come to see as formative of his own self-understanding as a philosopher. "We mumble our way through the traces left by the absolute that you are," Lyotard writes to God; Augustine, he contends, bequeathed to humanity a world of such "traces" rooted only in the absent object of their devotion.[10]

La Confession d'Augustin is far from a theological abnegation of the postmodern, however. Throughout its scattered passages, Lyotard adopts the persona of the Augustinian confessant as he engages in a continuing quest to discern the archaic genealogy of the phenomenological *habitus,* which binds modern critical thought inexorably to the temporal and linguistic imaginings of the bishop from Hippo: "Augustine complains that the present flies so rapidly from future to past that the slightest pause is excluded, *ut nulla morula extandatur.* So much so that none of the three temporal states in which a sign is successively presented truly *is.* Writing tails off between two abysses. Modern phenomenological thought has made these analyses famous."[11] The book lingers in particular over a handful of passages from *Confessions* book 10, in which Lyotard sees an influential paradigm of temporal reflection that survives as the "lived present" of his own philosophical inheritance.

9. Lyotard, *The Postmodern Explained,* 43.
10. Lyotard, *Confession of Augustine,* 40.
11. Lyotard, *Confession of Augustine,* 44–45.

The "chase after your voice" comes to an end in book X. Or rather, the chase is pursued in the direction not of the narrative of the past, but of the point from which this narrative is made possible. No longer in the narration of external events, but in the epiphany of the consciousness of time. The agitated movement of things is succeeded by the dizziness of the soul meditating on the peaceful umbilic of this movement, the motif of which will be resumed by Descartes with the Cogito. The prose of the world gives place to the poem of memory, or more exactly the phenomenology of internal time. The whole of modern, existential thought on temporality ensues from this meditation: Husserl, Heidegger, Sartre.

The past is no longer, the future is not yet, the present passes by, but as things (*opera*). And yet, I am aware of their nothingness, since I can think them in their absence. There is therefore a present of the past, and this present, as long as I think it, does not pass. It is this present that Husserl will call the *Living Present,* oddly. In Augustine, this present, immanent to internal consciousness, this umbilic, from which signs become readable to me, this present, then, is like the echo in temporality of the divine Present, of his eternal today.[12]

The spirit of Augustine lives and breathes, Lyotard contends, in the existentialism of Sartre and the philosophy of Husserl and Heidegger, whose invention of phenomenology gave the twentieth century its most powerful critique of Cartesian rationalism. The "present of the past" signifies for Lyotard not a cliché of diachrony, but a kind of temporal immanence that puts Augustine's epiphany in the *Confessions* and Husserl's dismantling of Descartes in the *Cartesian Meditations* into a transmillennial dialogue that speaks across the fraught ideological divide of the Enlightenment.

More provocative, perhaps, is the Augustinian idiom of sacrament that Lyotard discerns in the founding texts of phenomenology: most prominently, the "living present" of Husserl, which functions as a transhistorical "umbilic" embracing history, divinity, and the philosophical inheritance itself. Lyotard is not so far here from Derrida's meditation on the liturgical supplement at the end of the *Grammatology:* that inspiriting presence made manifest in the differential nature of language "in the heart of the living word."[13] Yet given the attention to the materiality of language in *La Confession*, Lyotard clearly has in mind as well the codicological sense of *l'ombilic*. The Latin *umbilicus* denoted a decorated sphere adorning each end of the rod on which a papyrus scroll was rolled. Anchoring the scene of writing (the site "from which signs be-

12. Lyotard, *Confession of Augustine,* 73–74.
13. Derrida, *Of Grammatology,* 313.

come readable to me," in Lyotard's words), the *umbilicus* both maintains the readability of the Book and decodes its language through a sacramental consumption: "So autobiography (if it is one) changes into cryptography: the last books of the *Confessions* devour this encrypting of the atemporal in the temporal, eat the Word become flesh and single out within the three temporal ecstasies in which it has been sacrificed and, as it were, dispersed, the kernel of permanence in which they are recollected." [14]

Just before his death, it seems, Lyotard confessed his own abiding investment in the premodern condition. The "kernel of permanence" adumbrated in Augustine's *Confessions* embodies for Lyotard what I posited in the introduction as the sacramental character of the avant garde's relation to the medieval past, and thus might serve here as an appropriate concluding metaphor. Understood in its critical fullness, this sacrament need not be a religious one (certainly not a Christian one), for its sacralizing function embraces the historical totality of critical thought as its very medium of miraculous transformation. Modes of critique, habits of mind, and means of subjection are not simply inherited from the medieval past, nor patiently reconstructed out of its ruins; rather, they are invoked, called into being, summoned from another place, translated from isolated fragments into whole systems of thought that maintain the dialectic of belief and doubt that characterized the sacramental culture of the Middle Ages. Jacques Lacan watches the entire tradition of ethical philosophy play itself out in the crystal ball of courtly love. Pierre Bourdieu isolates a phrase from Aquinas and emerges with a defining sociological paradigm. Jacques Derrida interprets a medievalizing passage from an eighteenth-century dictionary of music as one of the most revealing moments in Enlightenment thought. Roland Barthes discovers in the ostensibly monolithic textual culture of the medieval West a cornucopian epitome of free play and multiplicity. And Georges Bataille emerges from the ruins of Rheims to translate medieval nonsense poetry, write the life of a medieval child murderer, and reimagine the *Summa Theologiæ* as a pagan catechism of Nietzschean modernity. The premodern condition is in part a performative condition, then, yet one with an overriding investment in the enduring consubstantiality of those thinkers, writings, and artifacts it makes present to one another across centuries of critical reflection.

14. Lyotard, *Confession of Augustine*, 74.

A Note on the Appendices

Though obviously tied to this book's argument, the two essays that follow are intended for consultation as discrete critical works by Georges Bataille and Pierre Bourdieu, and both are translated here for the first time. In order to facilitate their use by others, we have retained the full bibliographical information provided by these two critics in the notes rather than keying shorter author-title references to this book's bibliography, which does not list the sources cited in the footnotes to the appendices (unless they are themselves cited in the preceding chapters). Our own notes and emendations appear in brackets, though full bibliographical information—first names of authors, publishers, etc.—has been added silently to citations where necessary.

Medieval French Literature, Chivalric Morals, and Passion

—from *Critique* 38 (1949)

GEORGES BATAILLE | *Translated by Laurence Petit*

The Romantic appeal (as well as the Romantic temperament) of the Middle Ages most obviously originates in its
composite nature. Christianity undoubtedly derives from
Greek philosophy—it is the popular form moral philosophy took when grounded in reason. However, medieval
Christianity, which was indistinguishable from the whole
culture of the time, is not merely the subjection of reason
that the entire society had to endure. In medieval Christianity, reason is nothing less than the contrary of the
subjection of society. If one considers, in particular, the
dominant moral ethic of that era, two opposite trends can
readily be distinguished: the Christian values of the ecclesiastical elite, on one hand, and those of the military aristoc-
racy, on the other. It is interesting to follow the obstinate
efforts that were made to mask this opposition and create synthetic forms. And yet, in doing so, one discovers
a general failure of those efforts. Christian moralization
undoubtedly contributed to giving chivalric traditions the
idealizing, deceitful, and pretentiously empty form that
Don Quixote denounced. On the other hand, a remarkable

adaptability to Catholic life led to the impasse—and abuse—that gave birth to the Reformation.

———

Literature gave its form—and sometimes its impulse—to these transformations of the moral idea. The dominant moral ethic of the Middle Ages is conveyed to us just as much through the *chansons de geste* or the romances of the Round Table as through the theologians' treatises. Hence the interest of the work that the medievalist Gustave Cohen has just published on the institution of chivalry, which he studied mainly in French literary texts.[1]

In principle, few medieval institutions are more familiar to us than that of chivalry; and yet, this does not mean that it is well known. This is what emerges most clearly from reading the book we have just mentioned. It actually emerges in two different ways: first of all, from the fact that an author as learned as Cohen should not really be able to tell us about the origin of chivalry, and especially, from the half legendary and half idealizing nature of the texts employed.

The origin of chivalry is certainly Germanic, and radically foreign to the origins of Christian or Roman institutions. One may also assume that it is the survival, in the Christian world, of a secret society of a relatively primitive nature. Let us add here, as a personal remark, that it is not absurd to recall those organizations of young people described by Georges Dumézil, whose members distinguished themselves by their wild and savage antics. The (strictly speaking) savage and frenzied character has subsided, if not disappeared, but it must be noted that even though the quality of knight was not lost with age, the meaning, or rather the prestige of the word, remains closely associated with the idea of youth. Without dwelling on it, the author still mentions, on several occasions, this principle that is in contradiction to the very form of the institution. For that matter, what remains, at least, of the traditions of violence of the Germanic tribes is the knight's ideal obligation to devote his life to adventure, that is to say to combat. The knight who marries out of love, or the one who lives for too many years without trying to

---

1. [Gustave Cohen, *Histoire de la chevalerie en France au Moyen Age* (Paris: Richard-Masse, 1949). Bataille cites page numbers parenthetically from Cohen's book throughout this review article, including those pages on which Cohen is citing medieval works, for which we have in turn provided English translations.]

show his value through violence, is *recreant,* and *recreance,* although followed by no formal decline, remains irreconcilable with the fundamental aspect of the chivalric ideal.

It seems here that an old tradition was in opposition with the actual facts. At the time explored by Cohen, that is to say primarily from the eleventh to the thirteenth century, a knight was a man of noble origin who, because he possessed a horse and armor, was entitled to be *dubbed.* *Dubbing* seems to be a survival from an initiation ceremony of a relatively widespread type: it could even well be that Marcel Griaule, whose opinion Cohen cites, was right in believing that the *colée,* the blow inflicted by the hand of the initiator on the neck of the initiated, could originally have signified a mystical decapitation as well as a change of personality (*History of Chivalry,* 45). The *colée* was the crucial moment in a ceremony that seems to have been usually performed without much reverence and without any preparation other than military education. Yet its importance probably had more to do with the vague memories of its origins than with a de facto attention that might often have been missing.

The actual prestige of the chivalric condition seemingly goes hand in hand with the memory of a much greater poetic prestige.

That is how, I would suggest, we ought to understand this passage from Chrétien de Troyes's *Perceval* in which the young hero, who lives in a wild forest, suddenly sees, on a beautiful spring day,

venir cinq chevaliers armés
et parés de toutes leurs armes.
Et très grande noise menaient
les armes de ceux qui venaient
car souvent se heurtaient à leurs armes
les branches de chênes et charmes
et tous les hauberts frémissaient. . .

[five armed knights coming through the woods, in armor from head to toe. And the approaching knights' armor made a great racket, for the branches of oak and hornbeam often slapped against the metal. Their hauberks all clinked. . .[2]]

The naive young man believes that they are angels, and that their leader is God himself, because of his beauty, and he prostrates himself to wor-

2. [Chrétien de Troyes, *Perceval,* lines 100–107; translated by William Kibler (New York and London: Garland, 1990).]

ship him: "Êtes-vous Dieu ?—Eh! Non, ma foi.— Qui êtes-vous donc?— Chevalier suis" (104–5) ["Are you God?"—"No, by my faith."—"Who are you, then?"—"I am a knight"]. Without any actual prestige, this would not have been intelligible. However, literary expression, carried by the tide of reminiscence, made it possible, to this degree, to transcend the realm of facts. In truth, the prestige these knights have in Perceval's eyes recalls the *sacred,* inhuman impression that the initiated young men of the Germanic tribes may have—and ritually must have—given of themselves.

———

Moral treatises sometimes disregard the importance, in the order of values, of prestigious characters whose acts and behavior determine the favorable or unfavorable judgment of all those who are subjected to this prestige. It is not always apparent that such cases have to do with an essential modality of value, which confers prestige on whoever has it. The dominant moral ethic is always the one that endows with irrefutable prestige the person who abides by its conditions and follows the commandments it implies. What maintains this fundamental aspect of social life beyond the confines of a theoretical ethic has to do with the fact that the seduction to which one is subjected possesses the irrational nature of passion. The initiated member of the Germanic tribes had to acknowledge the value of passion, without which there is no boundless war frenzy. The only moral ethic to which he was introduced stemmed from the privilege of a stronger and more appealing passion over lesser, degraded passions.

The medieval knight, who was well integrated into Christian society and could not give himself over to this exclusive cult of one passion, was nonetheless, morally speaking, a perfect vehicle for seductive passion. We shall see, later on, that he became, unlike the frenzied young German, a man of sometimes contradictory passions who yet never lost that characteristic of being, in the moral game, above all a passionate man as well as an object of passion, and forever a creature of prestige.

Hence the exceptional interest of a partially twofold evolution. The Church tried to subordinate the knight's prestigious passion to a rational moral ethic, and at the same time European civilization, breaking with a Germanic tradition, associated erotic passion with passion for war.

The institution of chivalry in the *chansons de geste* is still completely separate from both moralizing concerns and erotic prestige. The passages cited by Cohen, in which the trouvère can be seen raising religious or

moral concerns, *do not connect them in any way with the chivalric condition.*
What emerges from Cohen's analyses, moreover, is that the spirit of the
chansons de geste was at times contrary to that of the chivalry of pure passion, in that their authors, even though they glorify the hero's wild and
frantic valor, sometimes condemn it from the point of view of reason—
or piety, endowed with the feelings dictated by reason. *The Song of Roland*
has its hero say, through the wise Olivier: "Vaillance sensée n'est point
folie. / Modération vaut mieux qu'outrecuidance. / Français sont morts
par votre faute. [. . .] / Votre prouesse, c'est pour notre malheur que nous
l'avons vue! / Vous en mourrez et France en recevra honte" (64) [There
is wise valour, and there is recklessness: / Prudence is worth more than
foolhardiness. / Through your o'erweening you have destroyed the
French. [. . .] / Your prowess, Roland, is a curse on our heads / Now you
will die, and fair France will be shent"³]. This may not be the opinion of
the poet or of those who took pleasure in listening to him. In short, the
chansons de geste bear witness to a world in which the warrior's immediate inclination, as it existed in the Germanic tradition, was being called
into question. However, it was being called into question in the name
of Christianity or reason, in that Christianity and reason were no longer
foreign to the knights. Cohen does not specify what emerges from the
texts he is bringing to the fore, that is to say, that this inclination was
not being questioned then *in the name of chivalry itself.* The songs stage
blameworthy knights, such as Isembart or Raoul de Cambrai, both rebellious, driven by a spirit of excess, turning themselves into outlaws.
However, it was the general law of society, feudal law or human law, that
these knights flouted; it was not yet the chivalric law. For that matter, it
is not without pride or complacency that Raoul de Cambrai's excessiveness is portrayed: an indomitable pride, a persistently frenetic spirit and
an obstinate determination drive this knight to violate both religious
piety and filial devotion. However, the author (and therefore the listener)
is content with a last-minute conversion and sympathy is openly expressed for the abominable hero.

In short, the *chansons de geste* give the impression of a world in which
persisted, *without explicitly asserting itself,* a spirit of warlike passion still
connected with a sort of divine and sacred grandeur, without which, for
that matter, there would have been no prestige. Such a spirit, within the
sphere of moral ethic, undoubtedly represented a fundamental source
of attraction. In the dominant class, it is certain that a decisive value was
still attributed to *passion,* which gives combat immediate efficiency, to

---

3. [*The Song of Roland,* lines 1724–35, trans. Dorothy L. Sayers (Baltimore: Penguin, 1957).]

such an extent that the dominant and clear-cut moral truth could not be separated from it. Moral truth can indeed be based only on the indisputable dictates of the man of prestige, divinely driven by irrational passion; it is the durable truth of what is unquestionably divine. . . . Reasoned moral ethic would have no strength, would obtain no *sanction* if it did not partake of a general assumption of its evidently, albeit logically unmotivated, sacred nature. The work of moralizing reason thus consists not only in defining acts that accurately meet the demands of common interest, but also in linking them to the prestige of a sacred appearance.

Hence the paradox of war prestige, which was belatedly tied, in the Middle Ages, to the moral attitude defined by Christianity. It was difficult for the Church to sanctify a condition that was so little in keeping with the spirit of the Gospel. A scholastic saying cited by Cohen (173) indeed identified chivalry with evil: *militia malitia,* as people would say (in medieval Latin *miles* is often the translation for knight). However, the seduction of such evil was so great that, instead of cursing it, the clergy decided to redefine it as good. Not, it goes without saying, in the sense of an exaltation of the life that the knights actually led, but by discerning, in the seductive character of their condition, the sign of an ideal vocation. This shift is not ordinarily given the attention it deserves, and yet it reveals the innermost forces at work in the judgments that found good and evil. The position of good is inherently given in a determination of worldly life (*sacred* life). Consequently, if such determination is contrary to good as defined rationally, it becomes necessary to lie. Although what is *sacred* is not in the least identical with good, it must nonetheless now become good. Hence the possibility of a *sacred* status from the other world defined by its identity with good, or that of a *sacred* essence from this world that is being substituted by an *ideal*. In both cases, lying is inevitable, and it is introduced at the moment of transcendence.

God is not the *sacred* given in worldly life in the form of contagion, immanence, or more exactly active immanence, dangerous and ruinous for the personal (and separate) being. What is *sacred* is that which denies and destroys the separation to which we cling in the fear of death, that which merges us directly (mystical fusion is an example of this) into the immanence of man and the world. On the contrary, it is the *thing* that is transcendent, this particular object that presents itself from the start as a limit to any possibility of fusion (God is the *sacred*, or infinite, character, granted to the transcendence of the finite object, of the separate object).

This shift is, for that matter, given from the start in the operation that limits the *sacred* within the world of things, and situates it in a clear-cut manner outside this world in which we spend our lives catching hold of finite objects. It is through a sort of inversion that the *sacred,* immanence itself, has taken on the value of transcendence. In this *order of things* that is our world, the *sacred* transcends what is close to us, the familiar: it is the unusual. Hence the instability of the categories of immanence and transcendence—immanence itself becoming, in its opposition to the world of things, of minor transcendences, transcendence itself (major transcendence).

If I now return to the *sacred* nature of the knight, this nature is directly conveyed in the violence of arms, which is not immediately different from that of murder or of the slaughter of animals. Nasty brawls, knife fights, and foul crime partake of the *sacred,* but in a petty manner, which places the murderer at the level of an indistinct and, as it were, infinite human misery—a misery that corresponds to the absence of rules and laws, the dirty immanence that no command can dominate. In principle, war carnage, which easily slips into the massacre of prisoners, of disarmed men and women, partakes of the same horror, immanent in mankind.

However, for a number of reasons, the military condition is maintained within the established order, within peace: the soldier who walks through the streets of the city therefore retains his violent nature, but it is inactive, and thus deeply separated from the nonviolent world in which he walks. One can say, under these conditions, that the military condition, in so far as it refers to carnage, transcends civilized life. It can be added that, unlike the common law murderer, who also walks through the streets and may just possibly possess his own transcendence, the soldier is not put at the bottom of the ladder by organized society: he may sometimes even dominate society. The sort of transcendence of the military condition that corresponds to this domination is called nobility. Indeed, nobility is a *sacred* nature that separates the nobleman from the common man. In a sense it is a *participation,* an immanence, and this nature in which all noblemen *participate on equal terms* has a universal value, a meaning that endures in all the spheres of the possible. However, it is defined in relation to what it is not, what it transcends— in relation to the peasant, the bourgeois, or the commoner.

Now, it must be said that any prestigious character given to sacred horror, which frightens and seduces at the same time, is driven by this transcendence into a fundamental difficulty. The essential point is the fact that this character seduces. However, if the seduction of the senses leads to political power, this seduction can be induced, it is necessarily induced, to justify this domination through reason. In other words, if one defines as transcendent what is *sacred,* this notion will still have to be grounded in reason. Anything that affirms any superiority has to assert itself, sooner or later, on all the fronts where a superiority is being defined. Men may for a long period of time regard as superior that which seduces them, but this obliges the forces of seduction, or oppression, to answer a demand for valor in the field of reason: by this, I am not saying to answer as required, but merely to answer.

The reaction of the Church toward chivalry did not respond to the letter of the Gospel so much as to a more general principle. Essentially, the Christian Church represented the fusion of the *sacred* and the good. It was based upon the postulate that that which in the world had the appearance of the divine was justified through reason, that it was fundamentally good. It is in this sense that it took responsibility for the obligation, implied in the military condition, to identify blatant opposites: fighting and good, violence and reason. The Crusades made that task easier (they even gave rise to "religious chivalry": Templars, Hospitallers). As early as the second half of the twelfth century, the bishop of Chartres, John of Salisbury, defined the duties and meaning of organized chivalry. It was to defend the Church, fight and even attack the infidels, pacify the country and protect the poor against insult (174–75). Chivalry was thus organized for doing good, and it had an understanding of the notion of good. Similarly, toward the end of the thirteenth century, the blessed Ramon Llull wrote a sort of breviary of nobility: the *Book of the Order of Chivalry.* For Llull, the common people had to support the knight so that he would be able to devote himself entirely to chivalric exercises, hunting and tournaments (John of Salisbury was still condemning the latter). He was responsible for maintaining divine and human laws and imposing them on the common people through terror and faith. However, he also had to protect this common people; he was to protect the Church, and consequently, all those protected by the Church: women, widows, orphans, and more generally, the weak, the deprived, and the needy (176–77).

For that matter, the role of the Church would be difficult to understand if one failed to perceive, between these two authors, the entire development of a secular literature. Between John of Salisbury and Ramon Llull, strictly *chivalric* literature proliferated and came to play a prominent role in the elaboration of the dominant moral ethic. John of Salisbury clearly defined the position of the Church, but in any case, the facts (that is to say the evolution of value judgments) went beyond the simple definition of a prelate. It is actually the life of Christian society, in its multiple aspects, that elaborated the new moral ethic. It mingled with the legends of the Round Table in a manner that is difficult to specify, and yet that obviously imposed itself in every aspect.

It is important to note that the moralizing action of the Church did not exert itself directly. If moral commandments were tied to the chivalric condition, it was hardly because of the intervention of the theologians (such as John of Salisbury). The medieval, and partially moralizing, laws of chivalry that finally came to be dominant seem to have been formulated in literature first. A fictitious, legendary world was necessary to introduce them into real life. This is perfectly normal if one remembers that they became operative in the world of passion, which necessarily expresses itself through images and myths, and which, unlike the limits of the real world, requires the unlimited games of fiction. One could make the general assertion that the ethic of passion is romantic (if not mythical), that the prestige that paves the way for it was expressed in more ancient times through the creation of mythical beings, and nowadays through the creation of heroes of novels (in this respect, the Knights of the Round Table have a transitional value, by being less endowed with specific beliefs than the gods or demigods of the Germanic tribes, and yet less vague than the pure inventions of the modern novel). For that matter, the shift from the ethic of passion to that of reason requires in and of itself that one resort to the limitlessness of fiction. Thus it was in the forest of Brocéliande, in the kingdom of Logres, in the place where King Arthur used to gather his knights around a round table and where those very knights lived possessed and tormented by the desire to seek adventure, that moralizing reason and frenetic excitement gradually merged.

In the most ancient form that is known, the romances of the Round Table are, indeed, far from the Christian moral ethic. And even though they introduce into chivalric savagery the element we call humanity, it is at first supported less by piety than eroticism. In Chrétien de Troyes's *Perceval*, the first aspect of a moral law linked to chivalric dignity is conveyed through this recommendation by the hero's mother:

Vous serez chevalier d'ici peu,
fils, s'il plaît à Dieu, et je le permets.
Si vous trouvez près ou loin
dame qui d'aide ait besoin
ou pucelle dans le malheur
que votre aide prête
leur soit, si elles vous en requièrent
car tout honneur leur est dû.

Qui aux dames honneur ne porte
son propre honneur il voit périr. (108)

[Before long you'll be a knight, son, so I believe, if it pleases God, and I grant it. Should you encounter, near or far, a lady in need of aid, or a maiden in distress, make yourself ready to aid them, if they ask for your help, for it is the most honorable thing to do. He who fails to honor the ladies finds his own honor dead within. (513–22)]

This is at the very least ambiguous, since it is seemingly more about obliging the ladies than assisting the needy.

The central passage from the same romance, based on a link between moral ethic and chivalry, tends, it is true, to resolve the ambiguity by leaning toward good. Cohen is right to insist on this essential passage, which refers to Perceval's dubbing by Gornemant de Goort: "le preud'homme," says Chrétien de Troyes, "a pris l'épée / il la lui ceint et le baisa / et dit qu'il lui a donné / avec l'épée le plus haut Ordre / que Dieu a fait et commandé / c'est l'Ordre de Chevalerie / qui doit être sans vilenie" (113) [the gentleman took the sword, girded it on him and kissed him, and said that with the sword he had given him the highest order that God had set forth and ordained, that is, the order of knighthood, which must be maintained without villainy (1612–18)]. It is all explicitly about sparing the vanquished enemy who begs for mercy, helping women in distress, going to church and praying. This time, it is specified, regarding those precepts, that the young knight should refrain from saying, on every occasion: "So my mother taught me." Gornemant adds: "Vous pouvez dire que le chevalier / qui vous chaussa votre éperon / vous l'apprit et vous l'enseigna. / A quoi Perceval répond en lui promettant / que jamais il ne sonnera / mot, tant qu'il sera vivant / si ce n'est de lui, car il lui semble / que c'est le bien qu'il lui enseigne" (114) ["You can say that the vavasor who attached your spur taught and instructed you." And the boy promised that he would never again as long as he lived speak a word of any master but him, for he thought that that was good advice (1666–73)].

In the atmosphere of contemplation, mystery, and symbolic piety which is that of the quest for the *grail,* this takes on a particular importance. It is undoubtedly not really about the Christian ethic. However, along with passion's dreamy nature, which has come to replace mere frenzy, appears a tendency toward good, which is at first naive and vague, but which the Church inevitably had to use.

Regarding this aspect, Cohen makes only one simple allusion to the *Prose Lancelot,* which, following as it did the romances in verse by Chrétien de Troyes, was undoubtedly of considerable importance in the diffusion of the legends of the cycle of Arthur.[4] The main thing about this text is that it was the work of a cleric, who introduces into the legend the elements of an ever firmer theological construction. He introduces what is undoubtedly the weakest character in the cycle, the knight Galahad, purified from the carnal passions that still drive Perceval or Lancelot. By doing so, he removes part of the seductive value from a legend whose ambiguity is one of its fundamental meanings. However, from our perspective, this is only of secondary importance. The link between the chivalric condition and the practice of good is indeed condemned in the *Prose Lancelot,* which highlights moral teachings given by the arming knight during the dubbing ceremony. We are, from then on, in the realm of pious symbolism, which connects the arms of the new knight to God's intentions for him. For that matter, the arming scene in the *Prose Lancelot* recalls another highly significant text from about the same period that was quite widespread in France and England.

Although the *Ordene de chevalerie* [5] has nothing to do with the cycle of Arthur, it also takes the form of a legend. It is the story of one episode in the wars of the Crusaders against Saladin, at the end of the eleventh century. Saladin imprisoned Hugues de Saint-Omer, Lord of Tibériade. He treated him courteously and, before releasing him, asked him how knights were armed. The Latin lord first refuses to answer, but soon has to yield to the orders of his jailer. In the end, it is not clear whether or not this fictitious episode had a historical counterpart, but the fact remains that these kinds of stories must have entertained their listeners. This particular one was the vehicle for a long moralizing speech in which, this time, the chivalric condition took on the value of a pious consecration. In the story of the *Ordene de chevalerie,* the initiator lays out the initiated on a bed, then "dresses him in white linen cloth, to hold the body well, then gives him a vermilion robe whose color indicates the defense of the Church, brown shoes which herald the earth to which he will return, and a white belt to preserve him from lust. He adds the two golden spurs to serve God, the sword that he has buckled on

---

4. Regarding this immense romance, see Ferdinand Lot's masterly work, *Étude sur Le Lancelot en prose* (Paris: Champion, 1918). Lot dates this text to the period between the end of 1221 and the end of 1225.

5. Cohen cites this text from the Barbezan edition (Paris: Chaubert et C. Herissant, 1759). There is a more recent edition, albeit less readily available, by Roy Temple House, *L'Ordene de Chevalerie,* University of Oklahoma Bulletin no. 162 (Norman, Oklahoma, 1919).

him, whose blade will protect him against the enemy, and whose two sharp edges are Rectitude and Loyalty to defend the weak against the powerful. The white headdress protects him against sin" (144). This symbolic teaching, which goes with the ceremony, is accompanied, after the *colée* (which is not delivered, but only described in the present case), by a small number of moral prescriptions: not to take part in a wrong judgment or in a betrayal, to help women ("Car femmes doit-on honorer / et pour leurs droits grand faix porter"), to fast on Good Friday and hear mass every day. The virtue of generosity, of *largesse,* is also put forward by the author of the poem.

The mere fact of mentioning the daily obligation to attend mass shows that this was not at all a system that was as yet taken for granted. The encounter between the Latin lord and Saladin could well have taken place, and, in any case, this is in no way about the customs of actual chivalry, but about those of an ideal chivalry. It was in literature that the new moral ethic was organized, but we must insist here on some specific aspects of its diffusion.

The romances of the Round Table were certainly quite widespread in the dominant class, whose staple diet they most probably were. The clerics used the possibilities for moralization that they represented and sketched out by themselves, without too much commitment, a synthesis of the chivalric spirit and Christianity. The *Ordene de chevalerie* represents a later stage and is probably more important than Cohen reckons. Thanks to their geographic distancing, it does seem that the clerics themselves introduced an ideal, and yet systematic, proposition for their noble congregation. What Cohen does not say about this short poem is that it was probably preached and used by preachers. Its theme can be found in sermon *models* (which were used by the orators to pepper their teaching with short tales), and the text's numerous manuscripts seem to have been, in most cases, collections of morally edifying poems.

It is certain that such an effort had some impact, undoubtedly superficial, in the transforming action it had on mores. However, the very idea of chivalry, because of this, had to be tied to behaviors where the terms *noble* and *moral* coincided. This must have been how the connection was established, since the memory of it has come down to us. The term "chivalric" thus became endowed with proud and generous fervor, and even with a poetic intention affecting the conduct of one's life.

However, this character of piety which is emphasized, after the *Prose Lancelot,* by the *Ordene de chevalerie* must have contributed to maintaining the world of chivalry within that of fables. What is striking, if one considers the chivalric ethic as a whole, is its power, usually acquired by the world of morality, to institute inaccessible ideals. The young Germanic warrior may not have lived up exactly to the mythical image that was offered to him, but it was mainly a quantitative difference, in the form of a lesser audacity, or lesser strength, or even, generally speaking, lesser passion. And yet, it is unlikely that, had he given free rein to his passion, he would have desired to be what he was not, something other than what he was, whereas *chivalry* never offered the knight anything but a dream whose reality at once warned him discreetly that he would turn away if he were not a fool. Be it the pious knight, or the adventurous knight, the knight-errant or the passionate lover, we are constantly presented with fables aimed at nourishing a dreamy childhood, or a late childishness. True piety necessarily had other sources. Tournaments alone, that is to say the athletic feats, fit the frantic pace of the quest for the Holy Grail. And passionate love could only be sincere if it laughed at the models provided by fiction. This left the *comedy* of passions, which this ethic of passion offered at all levels. It is thus clear that, in the world of moral ethic, formal rules and a freedom of determination gradually develop, which are based just as much on the comedy of virtue, in opposition to passions, as on the comedy of passion.

––––––

Opening it up to the concerns of moral ethic deeply perverted a system of sacred conducts, justified only by the authenticity of a savage frenzy. However, it would be wrong to view this opposition too simply. First of all, it probably gave rise to the birth, if not of passionate love, at least of a great narrative literature of passionate love.

Cohen reverently quotes a term that might sound detestable. While referring to love, Charles Seignobos, his master, apparently used the following expression: "This French invention from the twelfth century." First of all, it is truly pretentious to say of love that it was an invention, for if it is true that literature plays a part in the diffusion of the forms that love takes on, it makes no sense to say that literature, and not the violence of passion, generates these forms. But even if one ponders these literary origins, it is absurd to give so much importance to the versions of the romances of the Round Table that have come down to us. Without mentioning the poetry of the *langue d'oc,* which, in those days, could not legitimately be called French, Arabic poetry, among others, had already expressed passionate love, following a tradition that dates back to the pre-Islamic tribes.

For that matter, this simplification makes it necessary, when discussing chivalry and the new moral ethic it introduced into the dominant society, to emphasize possible influences of various kinds. The *Ordene de chevalerie* is not only remarkable in that it provides the most significant expression of the chivalric ethic. The narrative upon which it is based is situated precisely at a remarkable meeting point of the civilized forms of the Middle Ages. Now, it does seem that the Muslims had institutions similar in some respect to the chivalry of Christianity, at least in that they had "secret societies" of combatants, of which at least one, that of the Assassins (of the Old Man in the Mountain), is well known to us. The Muslims' "secret societies" differed from the primitive initiatory societies such as chivalry in that they were *elective,* and did not result merely from the division of society into age groups or sects. As in Freemasonry, one became a member as a result of a deliberate choice that had not been predetermined by birth, as was the case with nobility based on parentage, which turned the knight into a knight more than dubbing did. Apparently, these Muslim societies must have had a formal reality and a spiritual consistency sharper than that of chivalry. What is more, regarding the short poem on the arming of Saladin, it is possible to assume that these kinds of symbolic interpretations about the pieces of the clothing as well as the arms could have had oriental antecedents. In any case, they appear in the *History of Habib and Dorothil-Goase* in the passage relating the story of an initiatory arming.[6] This is just one direction for possible research, but if one considers that Freemasonry has retained a sort of ritual linked to symbolic interpretations of the same nature as those we are discussing, one could conclude at least that we know very little about the history of initiatory orders in the Middle Ages and of their relation to modern orders.

––––––

In this respect, it may be assumed that the history of chivalry is all the more interesting as, in the formal sense, it had no reality of its own, as the literary testimonies merely convey a desire either in the nostalgia for the past, or in fiction, or even, perhaps, in the reflection of foreign institutions. However, it should not follow that it had no influence on the development of a moral ethic, for that matter independent from the formal institution. The world of honor, as both religion and moral code,

6. Cited by F.T.B. Clavel, *Histoire pittoresque de la franc-maçonnerie* (Paris: Pagnerre, 1843), 351–52.

originates in what chivalry represented, whether it be as a real caste or as mythical chivalry. At this point, we leave chivalric or clerical literature per se to re-enter the realm of facts. And we return from the construction of dreams to the clear-cut determinations of passion.

It remains to be seen if honor itself, as the dominant moral ethic— for instance in the seventeenth century—was not deeply perverted by the multiple contradictions it presented to the classical moral ethic, for these contradictions were the source of confusions and compromises. It remains to be seen if, in the religion of honor, the ethic of passion did not reach its weakest and most reconcilable form, in spite of its irrational ardor, with the reign of laws justified by both pure ethic and reason. This religion could even be subtly presented as being the profound betrayal of passions: for does it not reduce pride and original frenzy to the geometric point? Does it not have as its ultimate goal to annihilate and annul precisely what it seems to defend? And has the *evil* in it not taken on the saddest form, that of the defense of a reserve no longer justified, against the law, by any surpassing of the self or outburst of passion?

And yet, we all know the reason why we cannot renounce this survival, within us, of a moral ethic that was formed by no intellectual speculation and came down to us merely as a fire, the result of the naïve ardor of a timeless passion.

The reason is that, through a considerable attenuation, by means of brakes opposed to the animality of our most common violent impulses, passion reached, in one fixed point, its preferred object, which is, for man, a woman, or for woman, a man. There is no doubt that this woman or this man did not have the power to condense in themselves the promises the world brings, at birth, to the being in the process of coming to life. But luckily, for a man, a particular woman suddenly has the power to be an opening onto the totality of the world. The reverse is also true, but what irradiates the privileged man and designates him as such is the fact that he is, in any case, a prey to passions, lost in the world like a flame in fire. Hence the necessity for a life that frenzy consumes through endless adventures and perpetually renewed fights.

This is the starting point of a dialectic of personality and consummation, which precisely brings to light the brakes without which violence would be lost in the immediate animal deflagration. Thus, honor, which maintains, through a diluted yet irreducible attention, a thin core of pride, is not necessarily the sign of a renunciation, the reduction to an empty form. It is also, *perhaps,* the sign of a categorical refusal: by preserving honor, we *perhaps* maintain the sovereignty without which we would no longer be the flame in the fire and would merely be the thing subordinated to the function. Who knows?

It is quite remarkable to see, at the origin of honor's erotic dance, in which we still take part, the passion of man for woman make a point of specifying that it had to surpass itself and had to drive, if need be, the honor fanatic to dishonor.

In Chrétien de Troyes's *Lancelot,* whose second title is *The Tale of the Knight with the Cart,* Lancelot, while looking for Queen Guinevere, whom he loves, is asked, in order to find her, to climb onto a cart: "The cart," says Cohen, "was then similar to the pillory and was only used by thieves, bandits and murderers: it was a sinister cart. A dwarf of low birth, standing under the shafts, invites Lancelot to climb onto it, if he wants to be reunited with the queen, and after hesitating for two seconds . . . he accepts the gnome's invitation."

Lancelot, who enters a town in this equipage, is booed by the crowd in the streets, but

Le chevalier de la charrette songe
en homme qui défense ni force
n'a envers amour qui le gouverne;
et son penser est de telle sorte
qu'il s'en oublie lui-même,
ne sait s'il est ou s'il n'est point;
il ne lui souvient de son nom,
ne sait s'il est armé ou non,
ne sait où il va, d'où il vient;
de rien ne lui souvient
si ce n'est d'une seule chose et pour elle
il a oublié toutes les autres.
A celle-là il pense tant
qu'il ne voit et qu'il n'entend. (83)

[The Knight of the Cart was lost in thought, a man with no strength or defense against Love, who torments him; his meditation was so deep that he forgot his own identity; he was uncertain whether he truly existed or not; he was unable to recall his own name; he did not know if he were armed or not, or where he went nor whence he came. He remembered nothing at all save one creature, for whom he forgot all others; he was so intent upon her alone that he did not hear, or see, or attend to anything.[7]]

7. [Chrétien de Troyes, *Lancelot,* lines 711–24, trans. William Kibler (New York and London: Garland, 1981).]

Admittedly, honor is the result of passion, is in itself a passion and the indication of a violence that nothing could reduce. And yet, the man of passion, who affirms that life is the realm of seduction—that it is worth living only insofar as, while being itself driven by passion, it still has the power to inspire passion, and itself driven by seduction, it still has the power to seduce—can still put above honor the possibility of a passion that is greater, more absorbing, and capable of consuming his whole being. Honor itself, at that moment, does not count: it is the lover's weakness to have hesitated "two seconds." No doubt such consummation is impossible from the immediate impulsion, which rushes the course of life in cruder outbursts. It presupposes a softening of the original ferocity and it is logical that it should have followed the moral anguish and awareness that irrational frenzy holds little power. And yet, it provides one certainty: that passion is the only thing that does not deceive us, and that calculated moves opposing the exercise of sheer violence come to an end as soon as fury is replaced by an awareness of the promise that the universe belongs to the open being.

This by no means signifies that nothing has ever been promised to the reasonable and appeased being but death.

Postface to Erwin Panofsky,
Gothic Architecture and Scholasticism

PIERRE BOURDIEU | *Translated by Laurence Petit*

Gothic Architecture and Scholasticism is undoubtedly one of those books that most effectively challenges positivism. To claim that the *Summa* and the cathedral can be compared, as intelligible bodies built according to identical rules including, among other traits, a strict separation between the parts, a strict and explicit clarity of formal hierarchies, and a harmonious reconciliation of contraries, is indeed to run the risk of accepting, at best, the respectful and cautious tribute that a "fascinating, yet purely theoretical, view"[1] rightly deserves.

The idea that, between the different aspects of a historic totality, there should exist, as Max Weber puts it, a kinship of choice (*Wahlverwandtschaft*), or, as linguists say, a structural affinity, is not new. However, the search for the geometric locus of all the symbolic forms of expression of a particular society or a particular time has stemmed from a metaphysical or mystical inspiration more often than from a purely scientific intention. For that matter, it is undoubtedly not a coincidence that Gothic architecture should have been, for a long time, one of the preferred objects of intuitionistic fervor. Thus, to quote but one example among the many questions raised by the "spiritual structure" of the Gothic cathe-

---

1. Cf. Louis Grodecki, review of *Gothic Architecture and Scholasticism*, in *Diogène* 1 (1952): 134–36; Ernst Gall, in *Kunstchronik* 6 (1953): 42–49; Jean Bony, in *Burlington Magazine* 95 (1953): 111–12; Robert Branner, "A Note on Gothic Architects and Scholars," *Burlington Magazine* 99 (1957): 372; reviewed anonymously in *Times Literary Supplement*, January 24, 1958. (I borrow these references from Erwin Panofsky.)

dral, Hans Sedelmayr, enthralled by the magic of the "ideal cathedral," contrasts a systematic study of the architectural elements and a methodical examination of the technical characteristics and visual qualities of the cathedral with a "phenomenology" that reinterprets the concrete characteristics of the forms according to their alleged meanings. He sees in Gothic architecture and its associated arts the figurative expression of a certain liturgy or, better yet, of an original, "Augustinian" manner of understanding traditional liturgy.[2] If the deciphering of "meanings" always runs the risk of being nothing but a "projective test," and if the critic is right in observing that analyses such as Sedelmayr's lay themselves open to falling into a vicious circle on account of the fact that the phenomena interpreted—whether the "principle of the baldaquin," mural "diaphanousness" or "form suspension" (*das Schweben*)—can be in accordance with the significance discovered by the author only because they were constituted and named according to these meanings[3]—must one, for all that, renounce, in the name of a positivist definition of the scientific fact and evidence, all interpretive attempts that refuse to limit themselves to the face value of the phenomena?

Indeed, to affirm by postulate the comparability of the different orders of social reality would not make any sense if the conditions under which the comparison becomes possible and legitimate were not simultaneously defined: "When one undertakes to establish how mental habits produced by primitive and classic scholasticism may have affected primitive and classic Gothic architecture, one must *leave aside* the notional contents of the doctrine and focus one's attention on its *modus operandi.*" Thus, to have access to the comparison while avoiding that curious mixture of dogmatism and empiricism, mysticism and positivism that characterizes intuitionism,[4] one must abandon the idea of finding, in the data given by intuition, the principle capable of truly unifying them, and must submit the compared realities to a treatment that makes them available to comparison in an identical manner. The objects that are the focus of the comparison are not given by a mere empirical and intuitive apprehension of reality. They must be mastered above and be-

2. Hans Sedelmayr, *Die Entstehung der Kathedrale* (The Creation of the Cathedral) (Zurich: Atlantis Verlag, 1950). Cf. Grodecki, "L'interprétation de l'art gothique," *Critique* (October 1952): 847–57; and "Architecture gothique et société médiévale," *Critique* (January 1955): 25–35.

3. Grodecki, "L'interprétation de l'art gothique," 856.

4. In its haste to attain the unifying principle of the various aspects of social totality, intuitionism cuts corners and, whether it be a question of comparing distinct societies or the distinct subsystems within the same society, it claims to concentrate immediately, as if by force, on the geometric locus of the various structures without the preliminary effort necessary to bring out the structures of the various domains.

yond immediate appearances and constructed through a methodical analysis and an abstract approach. It is only if one avoids being taken in by superficial, purely formal and sometimes accidental analogies that one can isolate from the concrete realities in which they both express themselves and hide the structures among which can be established the comparison that is intended to reveal common properties.

Panofsky has shown elsewhere that the work of art can reveal meanings at different levels depending on the interpretive perspective applied to it, and that the lower-level (that is to say, the most superficial) meanings remain partial and degraded, and therefore erroneous, as long as the upper-level meanings that encompass and transform them remain elusive. The most naïve experience first encounters "the primary layer of meanings that we can penetrate on the basis of our existential experience," or, in other words, the "phenomenal meaning which can be subdivided into the meaning of things and the meaning of expressions" (or, according to a more recent essay, into "factual meaning" and "expressive meaning," defined as "primary or natural meaning" of forms).[5] Such an understanding is laden with "demonstrative concepts" that, as Panofsky observes, designate and apprehend only the sensory properties of the work (for instance, when one describes a peach as velvety or a lace fabric as diaphanous) or the emotional experience that such properties evoke in the spectator (when one speaks of stern or joyful colors).[6] In order to have access to "the layer of meanings, this one being secondary, which can only be deciphered if based on a knowledge transmitted in a literary manner" and that may be called "the area of the meaning of the *signified*,"[7] we must have at our disposal "specifically characterizing concepts" that go beyond the mere designation of sensory qualities and, apprehending the stylistic qualities of the work of art, constitute a veritable "interpretation" of the work.[8] Within this secondary layer, Panofsky makes a distinction: on the one hand, there is the "secondary or conventional subject," that is to say "the themes or concepts that manifest themselves through images, stories or allegories" (as, for example, when a group of characters sitting around a table in a particular arrangement represents the Last Supper), whose deciphering falls under the domain

5. Erwin Panofsky, "Zum Problem der Beschreibung und Inhalsdeutung von Werken der bildenden Kunst," *Logos* 21 (1932): 103–19; "Iconography and Iconology: An Introduction to the study of Renaissance Art," *Meaning in the Visual Arts* (New York: Doubleday and Co., 1955), 28.

6. Panofsky, "Ueber das Verhältnis der Kunstgeschichte zur Kunsttheorie," *Zeitschrift für Aesthetik und allgemeine Kunstwissenschaft* 18 (1925): 129–61.

7. Panofsky, "Zum Problem der Beschreibung und Inhaltsdeutung von Werken der Bildenden Kunst."

8. Panofsky, "Ueber das Verhältnis der Kunstgeschichte zur Kunsttheorie."

of iconography. On the other hand, there is "the intrinsic meaning or content" that can be apprehended again—in an iconological interpretation that is to iconography what ethnology is to ethnography—only on the condition that one treats the iconographic meanings and the methods of composition as "cultural symbols," as the expressions of the culture of a nation, an epoch, or a class, and endeavors to isolate "the fundamental principles that underlie the choice and presentation of motifs as well as the production and interpretation of images, stories, and allegories and give the formal composition and the technical processes their very meaning" by relating "the intrinsic meaning of the work, or group of works, to the largest possible number of cultural documents historically connected with this work or group of works."[9] Thus, without delving into the particulars of the analysis, one can see that an interpretive approach based on the expressive, and, if one may say, "physiognomic" qualities of the work of art—on which a certain romantic representation of the aesthetic experience bases the entire comprehension of the work—is but an inferior and degraded form of the aesthetic experience when it is not supported, controlled, and corrected by the history of the style, the types, and the "cultural symptoms." The inferior acts of deciphering are radically different depending on whether they represent the entire aesthetic experience or are integrated in a unitary apprehension (artificially broken by the analysis), because, in this case, they receive their full significance from the upper-level act that encompasses and surpasses them in a more adequate and more specific interpretation. It is only through an iconological interpretation that the formal arrangements and technical properties (and, through them, the formal and expressive properties) take on their *meaning*, and that, as a result, the gaps of a pre-iconographic and pre-iconological interpretation are revealed: "In the fourteenth and fifteenth centuries, for instance . . . the traditional type of Nativity with the Virgin Mary reclining in bed or on a couch was frequently replaced by a new one which shows the Virgin kneeling before the Child in adoration. From a compositional point of view this change means, roughly speaking, the substitution of a triangular scheme for a rectangular one; from an iconographical point of view, it means the introduction of a new theme to be formulated in writing by such authors as Pseudo-Bonaventure and St. Bridget. But at the same time it reveals a new emotional attitude peculiar to the later phases of the Middle Ages. A really exhaustive interpretation of the intrinsic meaning or content might even show that the technical procedures characteristic of a cer-

9. Panofsky, "Iconography and Iconology," 30–31 and 38–39.

tain country, period, or artist, for instance Michelangelo's preference for sculpture in stone instead of in bronze, or the peculiar use of hatchings in his drawings, are symptomatic of the same basic attitude that is discernible in all the other specific qualities of his style."[10] The various levels of meaning are thus *linked together,* like the levels of language, to form a hierarchical system in which the includer becomes in turn the included, the signified in turn the signifier, and that the analysis explores through its ascending or descending operations.

If it is true that the work reveals different levels of meaning depending on the cipher that is applied to it, it follows that a degraded representation of the cipher inevitably entails a degrading deciphering. For this reason, it does not suffice to acknowledge, with Emile Mâle, that "the art of the Middle Ages is highly symbolic" to discover the whole truth of medieval symbolism. According to Mâle, "Artists were as clever as theologians in spiritualizing matter. For instance, they gave the great chandelier of Aachen the shape of a city defended by towers. What is this city of light? The inscription informs us that it is the Celestial Jerusalem. The Beatitudes of the soul promised to the Chosen are represented between the crenelations, next to the Apostles and the Prophets who guard the Holy City. Is this not a magnificent way of rendering St John's vision? The artist who surmounted a thurible with the image of the three young Hebrews in the blazing fire turned a beautiful thought into a sensory experience. The fragrance that rose from the furnace seemed to be the very prayer of the martyrs. These pious workmen put all the tenderness of their souls into their works."[11] The discovery of the iconographic significance of these representations cannot be fully satisfying—instead of appearing as the manifestation of something else, the signified being in turn the signifier— unless one admits the philosophy of artistic creation and the epistemology of the science of the cultural object that is objectively engaged in a purely iconographical research. The intention of the work conceived not as symbol but as mere *allegory,* as sensory translation of a concept or an "iconographical program," would boil down to the conscious intention of its creator: it would not convey anything that its author had not expressly meant to convey, or meant for it to convey. Its meaning would therefore be completely exhausted as soon as the inspiring influence emerged, whether it be an iconographic model such as the miniatures of the *Apocalypse* of Beatus

10. Panofsky, "Iconography and Iconology," 30–31.
11. Emile Mâle, *L'art religieux du XIIe au XIIIe siècles* (Paris: Club du libraire, 1960 [1st edition Paris, 1896]), 53.

or a certain Oriental fabric, a literary document, like Vincent de Beauvais's *Mirror,* or the philosophical and aesthetic ideas of such an important individual as Suger. This representation of the work of art and its creation comes to express itself explicitly, either in a praise of allegory,[12] or in an exaltation of creative individuality such as the following: "We readily believe that the great art of the Middle Ages is a collective work, and one must admit that there is in such a notion a great deal of truth, since the art of the time expresses the thought of the Church. However, this very thought is incarnate in a few superior men. It is not the crowds who create, but the individuals."[13] To contrast individuality with community so as to better safeguard the rights of creative individuality and the mystery of individual creation is to forgo discovering community at the very heart of individuality in the form of culture—in the subjective sense of *cultivation* or *Bildung*—or, to speak the language used by Panofsky, in the form of the *habitus* through which the creator partakes of his community and time, and that guides and directs, unbeknownst to him, his apparently most unique creative acts.

It is therefore also an "artistic program," but one for whose signs historiographical positivism is searching in vain, because this program, by its very essence, eludes the consciousness of both its creator and those who partake of the same culture. Indeed, it does not need to be intentionally expressed by anybody to *express itself* and can express itself without expressing an individual and conscious desire for expression (unlike what certain psychologistic interpretations of the ambiguous notion of *Kunstwollen* suggest). "When we wish to get hold of those basic principles which underlie the choice and presentation of motifs, as well as the production and interpretation of images, stories and allegories, and which give meaning even to the formal arrangements and technical procedures employed, we cannot hope to find an individual text which would fit those basic principles as John 13:21 ff. fits the iconography of the Last Supper. To grasp these principles we need a mental faculty comparable to that of a diagnostician—a faculty which I cannot describe better than by the rather discredited term 'synthetic intuition.'"[14] This just shows that the epistemologically founded intuition of iconological science is the outcome of a methodical approach and therefore has nothing in common with the hasty and uncontrolled intuition of intuitionism. It also shows that such a science must give up the hope of discerning the

---

12. Mâle, *L'art religieux,* 218–22.
13. Mâle, *L'art religieux,* 17.
14. Panofsky, "Iconography and Iconology," 38.

detailed and palpable evidence of its discoveries. Whereas iconography fulfills, as if effortlessly, the methodological ideal of positivism—since it sometimes happens that things, such as this chandelier of Aachen, provide it with the very cipher according to which they need to be deciphered—iconology is condemned, in essence, to the *methodological circle* that is only too easily reduced to a vicious circle. Forced, by necessity of method, to apprehend each particular object through its relationships with the objects of the same class, to "correct," as Panofsky puts it, the interpretation of a specific work by a "history of style" that can be constructed only from particular works, iconological analysis, like any structural science, must expect no other evidence of the truth of its discoveries than the truths that these discoveries enable it to discover.

Whether we deal with historical or natural phenomena, the individual observation assumes the character of a "fact" only when it can be related to other, analogous observations in such a way that the whole series "makes sense." This "sense" is, therefore, fully capable of being applied, as a control, to the interpretation of a new individual observation within the same range of phenomena. If, however, this new individual observation definitely refuses to be interpreted according to the "sense" of the series, and if an error proves to be impossible, the "sense" of the series will have to be reformulated to include the new individual observation. This *circulus methodicus* applies, of course, not only to the relationship between the interpretation of motifs and the history of style, but also to the relationship between the interpretation of images, stories and allegories and the history of types, and to the relationship between the interpretation of intrinsic meanings and the history of cultural symptoms in general.[15]

Where positivism wants to see nothing but the imprudent audacity of an approach devoid of rigor, Panofsky enables one to glimpse the added demands that are imposed by an increased demand for accuracy. Far from being able, like positivist interpretation, to hide behind an indefinite accumulation of minor true facts, structural interpretation involves all the acquired truth in each truth in order to attain its object, because the whole truth lies in the truth of the whole.

One can appreciate the audacity of a research that, by breaking out of a methodological choice with the most phenomenal level of meaning, at once avoids resorting in any way to the palpable and tangible evidence with which the positivists, those "friends of the Earth," are satisfied—since the documents can testify to the truth of an interpretation only in so much as they let themselves be interpreted according to

---

15. Panofsky, "Iconography and Iconology," 35 n. 1.

the same principles of interpretation as those to which they testify—and exposes itself fully, and at any time, to the partial and specific questions of positivist false rigor. It is with a modesty that is a striking contrast to the positivist's *certitudo sui* ("The inscription tells us that . . .") that Panofsky presents what he calls "an element of proof," the *inter se disputando* of Villard de Honnecourt's *Album*. In fact, this proof, which is in perfect accordance with the positivist ideal of iconographic historiography, cannot be fully satisfying unless one agrees to enter the game of structural interpretation as a system that is to itself, as such, the one and only proof of its own truth. And nothing, in a good method, permits one to distinguish between this particular proof and the whole system of evidence that has been put forward throughout the book and that is valid because of its coherence. However, it is easy to understand why Panofsky has given it this prominent place: in this case, indeed, the "sense of the series" is not just capable of "including the new observation," but also of constituting it as such, of *creating* literally, while informing it beforehand, a reality to which positivism, lacking in interpretive schemes, had remained blind.[16] And yet, because it assesses this evidence by the coherence of the system of evidence with a definition of experience as a yes-or-no answer to an isolated question, positivism can still refuse to see, in the systematic construction of facts, anything other than the result of a manipulation of the facts inspired by a taste for analysis and founded, as a last resort, on *petitio principii*. And it is easy for positivism, since the scientist who breaks with the positivist conception of fact and proof must also give up the positivist hope that the subjects or documents they have left behind may come and testify in favor of the truth of an interpretation of their behavior and of their works that has always eluded their consciousness and that can be obtained only indirectly, by making the assumption of their unconsciousness.

---

16. It seems significant that the "critique" of this evidence should play a prominent role in Ernst Gall and Robert Branner's reviews (see above). Gall sees in the fact that this inscription was added later (cf. Hans R. Hahnloser, *Villard de Honnecourt* [Vienna: A. Schroll, 1935]—which Panofsky specifies explicitly (note 61), by insisting on the highly significant fact that this expression was preferred over the much more common *inter se colloquendo*, and was used by an architect about other architects—a formal denial of the book's thesis, concluding that the builders of cathedrals could not have had a clear idea of what they were doing. However, Panofsky was content with saying that "some French architects of the thirteenth century acted and thought according to a strictly scholastic logic," which in no way implies that they were consciously aware of the schemes of thought and action defining this logic.

Thus, it is the *formulation* of a problem that, as he reminds us, had already been posed before him that Panofsky renews radically. Indeed, the intuition—already expressed by Gottfried Semper (who saw in Gothic art a "mere expression in stone of Scholastic philosophy"[17]) and by Dehio ("*Gothik ist eine steinerne Scholastik*")—that there exists a relation between plastic art and theology had led specialists to search for the direct and, if one may say so, tangible "influences" that, through "iconographic programs," according to Mâle, or symbolics, according to Sauer,[18] would enable one to explain the parallel observed in the evolution of Gothic art and scholastic thought. If Panofsky reminds us of these similarities (chapter 1) while showing, for the earlier and later epochs that will no longer be examined afterwards, the signifying whole that they reveal, it is to ask a truly original question: the chronological similarities become significant and meaningful only if they point toward logical, or, better yet, iconological correspondences that can be accounted for in the order of sense and whose causes can be manifested. In this respect, the central period for the evolution of Gothic art and Scholastic thought constitutes a special case (hence its special place in the book), since one can both highlight structural homologies perfectly irreducible to these kinds of literal (and therefore consciously performed) translations of the theological language into the architectural language, such as those Mâle and Sauer saw, and discover their determining principle in the scholastic institution as a "habit-forming force." It is therefore both a questioning and a solution that apply well beyond this particular, though highly significant, case formulated by Panofsky. While the structural method is generally content (and that is a lot already) with establishing the homologies between the structures of the various symbolic systems of a society and an epoch and the principles of formal conversion that enable one to shift from those of one to those of another, each of them being considered in itself and for itself, in its relative autonomy, Panofsky endeavors to discover the "concrete . . . connection" that will account, completely and concretely, for the logic and existence of these homologies. And, with this end in view, he is not content to invoke a "unitary vision of the world" or a "spirit of the time" and thus give as an expla-

17. Gottfried Semper, *Der Stil in den technischen und tektonischen Kuensten,* vol. 1 (Frankfurt: Verlag für Kunst und Wissenschaft, 1860), 19.

18. In his work *Symbolik des Kirchengebaudes und seiner Ausstattung in der Auffassung des Mittelalters* (Freiburg-in-Brisgau, 1902; 2nd edition Herder, 1924), Joseph Sauer endeavored to highlight the liturgical and iconological meanings of the various parts of the Gothic church by relying on texts by Honorius of Autun, Sicard of Cremona, and Durandus of Mende.

nation the very phenomenon that needs to be explained,[19] nor even the concrete individual—in this particular case, such-and-such architect—as the site for the coincidence or coexistence of structures, which often plays, in such a case, the role of refuge for ignorance. He offers the apparently most naïve explanation (simply perhaps because it takes some of the mystery out of these correspondences). In a society in which the transmission of culture is monopolized by a school, the profound affinities that bind together human works (and, obviously, behaviors and thoughts) find their principle in the scholastic institution vested with the function of transmitting, consciously and also, in part, unconsciously, a subconscious knowledge, or, more exactly, of producing individuals endowed with this system of subconscious (or deeply buried) schemes that constitute their culture or, better yet, their *habitus;* in short, of transforming the collective heritage into an individual and collective subconscious. To relate the works of a period with practices derived from a school of thought is to give oneself one of the means to explain not only what they *claim,* but also what they *betray* in so far as they partake of the symbolics of an epoch and a society.

It would undoubtedly be naive to end at this point the search for an explanation, as if the school were an empire within an empire, as if culture encountered with it its absolute beginning. However, it would be just as naïve to ignore the fact that, through the very logic of its functioning, the school modifies or defines the contents and spirit of the culture it transmits. This is never as true, or so it seems, as in the case of scholastic thought, a school of thought that owes its most essential characteristics to the schools of thought in which it was constituted.[20] If it is true that, as Martin Grabmann observes, the very works of Thomas Aquinas that were not directly "born from the school and in the school," like the *Summa,* were nevertheless "written, for the most part, for the school,"[21] it follows that the method of presentation and thought that is so brilliantly asserted in the *Summa* probably owes its most characteristic traits to the organization and pedagogical traditions of the Parisian university of the thirteenth century as well as to the pedagogical functions Thomas Aquinas expressly assigned to it. Thus, for instance, how not to see in the principle of clarification the transposition of a purely

19. However, Ernst Gall, in his review, wishes to return from the *modus operandi* to the *Zeitgeist.*
20. "The thirteenth century," Gordon Leff writes, "is the century of rival schools. The most eminent thinkers can be linked to the Augustinians, Aristotelians or Averroists" (*Medieval Thought* [Harmondsworth: Penguin Books, 1958; 2nd ed. 1962], 170).
21. Martin Grabmann, *La somme théologique de Saint Thomas d'Aquin,* trans. Edmond Vansteenberghe (Paris: Nouvelle Librarie Nationale, 1925), 13.

pedagogical imperative that must impose itself with a particular rigor on an educational system aiming, before anything else, at *making explicit* the meaning confined in the "authorities"? The *"modus dicendi compendiosus, apertus et facilis"*—according to the expression William of Tocco uses to characterize the oral teachings of Thomas Aquinas[22]—is the mode of presentation that "is appropriate for the initiation of beginners" (*congruit ad eruditionem incipientum*), as Thomas Aquinas writes in the Prologue of the *Summa*. Indeed, to the "ever increasing questions, articles and useless arguments," to the lack of order and coherence characteristic of a presentation left to be ruled by the fortunes of discussion, Thomas Aquinas intends to substitute, at the price of a constant simplification, the clarity of a plan "in accordance with the order of discipline," a plan that manifests itself, as it were, in the work itself and that excludes both the pointless, overlong passages and the well-phrased but unnecessary repetitions that "generate boredom or confusion in the minds of the listeners." However, beyond the attention given to the plan, which shows in the desire to make it manifest and patent, it is the very structure of the presentation that betrays the very organization of the scholastic practice through the system of thought shaped by the scholastic exercise that *quaestio* represents as the "minutes" of the *disputatio*. One should see, or so it seems, in this system of thought that is at the same time a pedagogical technique an "invention" related to the development (interdependent with a certain type of urban life) of the cathedral schools and the universities.

From the tenth to the twelfth century, there occurs a shift of the center of knowledge and, as a result, of the school, to which corresponds a profound change in the preoccupations and style of intellectual life. Culture expands beyond the monasteries, which remain isolated in rural areas, while the new school organizes itself in bishops' palaces and urban centers, meeting new demands, entering new debates, in short mirroring in its organization and activity all the characteristics of the towns.[23] Although they are very close in time, a whole world separates the great school of Bec, in Normandy, from the school of Abelard at Sainte-Geneviève. On the one hand, with the monastic school of a great abbey, we have a rigorously organized educational system, subjected to a single rule and dominated by the values of piety, which has as its center the *lectio*, as a reading, commentary, and meditation on the consecrated texts.

22. Guilelmus de Tocco, *Vita s. Thomae Aquinatis*, ed. Prümmer, 86; cited in Grabmann, *La somme théologique*, 86.

23. Cf. Gérard Marie Paré, Adrien Marie Brunet, and Pierre Tremblay, *La renaissance du XIIe siècle, les écoles et l'enseignement* (Paris and Ottawa: J. Vrin, 1933), 21.

On the other hand, we have the first form of the Parisian university where rivalries between competing specialized schools endow the *disputatio,* the dialectic, with an essential function. It is therefore hardly surprising that to such different situations should correspond extremely different types of intellectual interest, methods of thinking, and productions of the mind. *Monachi non est docere, sed lugere.* The mystic and antidialectic tradition of the monasteries contrasts with the scholastic inclination for the rationalization of faith, inseparable, as Max Weber has shown, from a routinization of traditional knowledge and the methods of transmission of such knowledge. Scholastic thought might thus derive many of its characteristics from the logic peculiar to the functioning of the scholastic institution through which and for which it was produced and perhaps even to the functioning of the scholastic institution in its universality. Therefore, whether its origin was the process of the *Sic et non* that Peter Abelard, after the canonists, had introduced in academic practice, or the Aristotelian writings, and in particular the *Topics,*[24] the *disputatio* as a method aiming at reconciling contraries is undoubtedly the most typical product of the scholastic institution—which, as soon as it constitutes itself as such, with a specific function and a specialized body of masters, must propose a consistent doctrinal corpus, be it at the price of fictitious conciliations, for instance those allowed by this typically professorial philosophy of philosophy and of the history of philosophy that *philosophia perennis* represents.

In order to show the full impact of this analysis (and Panofsky paves the way for such an extension when he remarks that "mental habits" similar to those of the scholastics or the Gothic architects are at work in any civilization), one must first observe that the schemes that organize the thoughts of cultured men in the societies endowed with a scholastic institution (for example, the organizing principles of speech that the treatises of rhetoric called figures of words and figures of thought) probably fulfill the same purpose as the unconscious schemes the ethnologist discovers, through the analysis of creations such as rites or myths, in the individuals living in societies devoid of such institutions, the same purpose as these "primitive forms of classification," to speak the language of

24. Cf. Grabmann, *Geschichte der scholastischen Methode,* vol. 2 (Freiburg: Herdersche Verlagshandlung, 1911), 219.

Durkheim and Mauss, which could not be the subject of a conscious understanding and of an explicit and methodical transmission. However, in addition to this, by using the scholastic concept of *habitus* to designate the culture instilled by school, Panofsky shows that culture is not just a common code, or even a common repertoire of answers to common problems, or a set of particular and particularized forms of thought, but rather a whole body of fundamental schemes, assimilated beforehand, that generate, according to an art of invention similar to that of musical writing, an infinite number of particular schemes, directly applied to particular situations. This *habitus* could be defined, by analogy with Noam Chomsky's "generative grammar," as a system of internalized schemes that have the capacity to generate all the thoughts, perceptions, and actions characteristic of a culture, and nothing else. What Panofsky is trying to draw from these concrete and particular discourses that Gothic cathedrals or general theological *summas* represent is perhaps, at the end of the day, this "interior form," to speak the language of Wilhelm von Humboldt, that is to say the *modus operandi,* capable of generating both the thoughts of the theologian and the designs of the architect, that founds the unity of thirteenth-century civilization.

It is therefore natural that one could observe, in domains that are worlds apart at the phenomenal level, the expression of this general tendency, which generates particular schemes that can be applied to various domains of thought and action. Thus, Robert Marichal, referring explicitly to the interpretation of Gothic architecture proposed by Panofsky, establishes a set of striking homologies between Gothic handwriting and Gothic architecture and their respective evolution:[25] "The break of the diagonal rib starts very early, as of the eleventh century; the diagonal rib, in the Western world, appears around 1075; it is in England and the duchy of Normandy that archeologists have encountered the first uses of the intersection of the ribs. It is in the Île-de-France that it 'determined a style'; it is in England and in the duchy of Normandy that the break first appears and . . . it is also in the Île-de-France and in Picardy that Gothic handwriting seems to have been canonized."[26] The *modus ope-*

25. [At this point Bourdieu cites the first of several plates reprinted in the postface from a number of discrete secondary sources; these plates (not reproduced here), which include photographs of cathedral façades and buttresses, sketches of rose windows, and manuscript facsimile pages, may be found in Bourdieu's French translation following pp. 136, 152, and 154.]

26. Robert Marichal, "L'écriture latine et la civilisation occidentale," in Centre international de Synthèse, *L'Écriture et la Psychologie des Peuples, XXIIe semaine de Synthèse* (Paris: Armand Colin, 1964), 232–33.

randi that, according to Panofsky, is at work in the Gothic cathedral is also expressed in the graphic composition of the manuscripts:

Anybody who has once opened any *Summa* has noticed that the author always took great care in leading his readers from proposition to proposition and in enabling him to have present in his mind the progression of his reasoning. Saint Thomas, at the beginning of the *Summa,* enumerates the parts of which it is composed: each part, each treatise, each question is preceded by a summary; each article has, as its title, a question beginning with *utrum.* It starts with the presentation of the objections, the first one being announced by *videtur quod non,* and each of the following ones by *praeterea;* then, after the stereotyped formula *sed contra,* an opposing argument, usually the only one of its kind, gives the answer to the question, explained and justified by the *corpus articuli,* thus placed at the center of the system and introduced by the equally stereotyped sentence *respondeo dicendum;* finally, there follow, numbered *ad primum, ad secundum,* etc., the replies to each of the objections presented at the beginning. When a scribe has copied this pattern some ten thousand times, how could he not, no matter how absent-minded or stubborn one may like to imagine him, have acquired the habit of thus conducting his own thought?

However, if an uninformed reader compares a manuscript from the ninth, tenth, or eleventh centuries, a beautiful manuscript, it goes without saying, of a work in prose, to a manuscript equally as neat of the *Summa theologiæ,* he will have the impression, I think, that the former is clearer and less daunting than the latter, and yet if he takes a closer look at them, he will notice that the latter enables one to follow the author's thought much more easily.

In the manuscripts of the ninth, tenth and eleventh centuries, he will find sometimes a full page, sometimes two compact columns, without any white space; no division, a punctuation blended in the text; discrete capital letters that do not stop the gaze, even if, at a few major breaks, they stick out slightly in the margin; in short, a layout that is remarkably regular, dense, and yet attractive, open thanks to the delicate handwriting, the independent letters and the large space between the lines. The page has the cold elegance and the beautiful trappings of those large blind arcades of the steeple of the Abbaye-aux-hommes, in Caen, or those "Lombard stripes" on the façade of Marmoutier. It is, as it were, this "impenetrable space" that the Romanesque edifice represents; in no way does it express the order of discourse.

Admittedly, a few, less numerous, manuscripts, as well as some technical books (Cicero's *Partitiones,* for instance) that are sometimes in the form of dialogues, such as the *De Oratore,* also by Cicero, present, like our modern printed books, pages divided into small paragraphs whose last line is more or less blank. They are easy to read and even study. However, beside the fact that the breaks are often arbitrary, all the paragraphs follow the same pattern: the logical progression of the thought and the subordination of the parts to one another do not exist . . . and for a good reason, since some manuscripts, such as the Pliny (*Hist. Nat.,* Paris, Bibl. Nat., lat. 6796), are but a series of isolated notes, and, in the others, literary preoccupations have led the author to conceal, rather than emphasize, his structure.

Scholastic Gothic manuscripts are no less dense than the manuscripts of the ninth, tenth, or eleventh centuries. On the contrary, copyists are more than ever afraid of emptiness: if a line ends with a word that is too short to fill in the justification, they add, in the blank space, one or several random letters, which are annulled, that is to say crossed out. If, by a chance happening that has to do with the very nature of the task, a notebook happened to end with several blank lines, they copy the last previous lines while framing them with a *va . . . cat* that annuls them; the space between the lines has been reduced; the writing is more dense. And yet, the copyists have succeeded, like the philosophers, in reconciling the two contradictory demands that they have to meet, *pro et contra*: a taste for density, and the need to proceed by hierarchically grouped "parts of parts." Let us take the manuscript (Paris, Bibl. Nat., lat. 15783) of the *Summa theologiæ:* each "question" starts with a large dropped initial, half-blue and half-red over a red and fairly complex watermark: each article starts with an A— that of *Ad primum, Ad secundum,* etc., alternately blue and red, smaller and with a watermark simpler than the dropped initial of the "question." In order to show clearly each of the divisions of the article, booksellers invented the large "pied-de-mouche," alternately red and blue. In the text, the "questions" are not numbered, but they are numbered at the top of the page, in the standard title, and, naturally, in the table of contents. Whatever the page to which the book opens, one glance is enough for an expert reader to know where he stands.[27]

It is therefore an entire system of expression, of a totally different nature, that is integrated in the system of interpretation proposed by Panofsky. Moreover, Marichal's analysis reveals not only how, in the copyist's daily activity, the *habitus,* defined by the interiorization of the principles of clarification and reconciliation of contraries, is constituted, but also how this *habitus* is concretely actualized in the specific logic of a particular practice.

It can be assumed that the "masters" collaborated with the booksellers in the elaboration of a bookish architecture that so clearly "showed" their thought processes, but the booksellers and the copyists are imbued with the same methods: within the sentence, they carried the "division" of the text to the smallest logically conceivable unit by separating words from each other permanently . . . to the point of re-creating veritable ideograms. What is more—and it is most unlikely that the "masters" intervened in these technical details—within the very words, inside each letter, prompted by an

27. Marichal, "L'écriture latine," 236–40.

inveterate *habitus,* they highlighted irreducible elements: the Gothic break, indeed, "divides" the letter while "composing" it. To substitute one or several acute angles for a curve is to decompose a movement into its "elementary" stages as do military rules for the use of weapons. Now, through a singular encounter, in the same way that the seed of the entire development of Gothic architecture lies in the intersection of the ribs of a vault—this "footing" of the groined vault—similarly, it is not the origin . . . but also the systematic use of the break that seems to me, if not to result from, at least to have been particularly favored by, the presence of the footings [*empattements*] at its base. By introducing angles in the letter, that is to say a decomposition of the haste, these "footings" or "serifs," as they are called in typography, caused, by symmetry, a similar decomposition of the upper curves that the random size of a quill nib had started.[28] A sign, I dare not say a proof, of the accuracy of this interpretation could be found in the fact that the Italian Gothic cathedrals, which have, so to speak, no "break," have never had "footings" either, and it is, at any rate, certain that it is indeed the footings, or serifs, that have permitted the definitive distinguishing of the words.[29]

Thus, a respect of the very principles that defined the processes of theological thought or the layout of the architectural space leads to solutions and achievements that are both original and reducible to more general schemes. In addition, the application to writing of the principles that rule any production of cultural works in turn respects a principle that the scholastics could not name—unlike the others, since it is, in a sense, the principle defining the way to respect principles, a principle that claims that the operations constitutive of the *habitus* be carried— by a sort of indefinite reduplication of which Gothic architecture also provides examples—to the limits of the possible (as if the *habitus,* this grammar that generates behaviors, tended to produce all the concrete sentences whose virtuality it contains), and that no conscious program, especially if imposed from the outside, would ever be able fully to predict.

———

It is understandable that Panofsky should have found in the scholastic *habitus* the principle enabling him to explain not only a state in Gothic architecture but also an "apparently erratic though in reality obstinately

28. [Marichal uses the word *empattement* for both "footing" in architecture and "serif" in typography.]

29. Marichal, "L'écriture latine," 240–41.

consistent" evolution, as revealed in the minute analysis of the solutions that have been successively brought to three architectural *quaestiones*. When, regarding the evolution of the organization of the nave wall, Harry Bober disputes the pertinence of the "dialectic" scheme proposed by Panofsky and suggests, instead, discerning in the different stages of such an evolution "a succession of individual solutions that are ingenious, original, but independent,"[30] he is merely mistaken about the logic according to which the *modus operandi* is actualized. Indeed, there is no doubt that the solutions of Pierre de Montereau or Hugues Libergier represent inventive and creative acts and are, in this respect, as original and ingenious as one would have them; the fact remains, nonetheless, that one can find the principle that enables one to explain what was a creation of unpredictable novelty. To this end, it suffices to note that each of these *quaestiones,* or, even better, each of the successive forms that it may have taken over the course of its history (let us remember, for instance, the opposition between the search for clarity and the concern to fill in the handwritten page), was able to exist as such only for minds well-equipped with a certain problematics, that is to say a certain customary way of questioning reality. Moreover, each of the successive solutions that led to the final solution can be understood by reference to the scheme of fundamental thought that caused the question to arise at the same time that it directed the search for a solution irreducible to the scheme and, as a result, unpredictable—as, in another domain, the slightest speech act—and yet in accordance *a posteriori* with the rules of grammar. As a result, it is understandable that the *modus operandi* could be revealed in the *opus operatum* and only there.

It is undoubtedly in the same direction that one must look in order to transcend the opposition between the "functionalist" thesis and the "illusionistic" thesis. Let us consider, for instance, the homology between the intersection of the ribs and the break of Gothic writing: there is no relation between the two technical inventions and it is quite by chance that they should both end up marking the predominance of the Gothic arch over the Roman arch. "It appears therefore that the English scribes probably beveled their quills quite by accident while the masons were building their vault over the intersection of the ribs, but it is not by accident that the two processes became so popular and gave birth to a style: they were both the answer to a certain taste for angular forms, stretched-out heights and even perhaps picturesque perspectival effects

30. Harry Bober, review of Panofsky, *Gothic Architecture and Scholasticism,* in *Art Bulletin* 35 (1953): 310–12.

and plays of light and shadow that can be found both in the naves or the aisles of cathedrals and in the pages of manuscripts."[31] The ultimate truth of a style is not contained in embryo in an original inspiration, but is continuously defined and redefined as a constantly evolving meaning, which constructs itself in accordance to itself and in reaction to itself. It is the continued exchange between questions that exist solely for and by a mind well-equipped with a predetermined type of schemes and more or less innovative solutions, obtained by applying the same schemes but capable of transforming the initial scheme, that constitutes this unity of style and meaning that, at least afterwards, may seem to have preceded the works heralding the final success and that retrospectively transforms the various moments of the temporal series into mere preparatory sketches. If the evolution of a style appears neither as the autonomous development of an essence that is unique and always identical to itself, nor as a continuous creation of unpredictable novelty, but as a progression that excludes neither forward leaps nor backward glances, it is because the creator's *habitus* as a system of schemes directs in a constant manner choices that, although not deliberate, are no less systematic, and that, although not ordered and organized expressly with respect to an ultimate end, carry nonetheless a sort of finality that will only be revealed *post festum*. This self-constitution of a system of works linked by a set of significant relationships is accomplished in and through the association of contingency and meaning that is continuously created, destroyed, and created again according to principles that are all the more constant as they elude the mind more completely, in and through the permanent transmutation that introduces the accidents of the history of techniques into the history of style by raising them to the order of meaning, and in and through the invention of obstacles and difficulties that appear to be created in the name of the very principles of their solution and whose counter-finality in the short term may conceal a higher finality.

It is definitely the genesis of a meaning from an accident that managed to become the *origin* of a process oriented toward a final meaning only because it was perceived, questioned, and treated according to the logic of a certain system of schemes of thought, perception, and action that Panofsky reveals when he observes that the pointed arches of Caen and Durham started to speak before they acted, whereas the flying buttresses started to act before they spoke, other elements of the edifice having never ceased to speak and act at once. These human works that the

31. Marichal, "L'écriture latine," 233.

rib vault, the break of Gothic handwriting, or the flying buttress represent have, to use the language of scholasticism, an *intention*[32] that is ambiguous in that they can be apprehended and appreciated either for their mere technical function or for their "optical value," which supposes a "special interest in form."[33] This objective intention, which can never be reduced to the creator's intention,[34] depends on the schemes of thought, perception, and action the creator owes to his belonging to a society, an epoch, and a class:[35] it follows that it is from the concrete system of significant relations that defines the object that must be drawn the categories of interpretation of the object whose validity is assessed according to the heuristic fecundity and the coherence of the system of interpretation. If one fails to relate a style to its own norms of perfection, one is indeed condemned to sterile interrogations or to those fictitious debates of which the conflict between the "functionalists" and the "artificialists" is a good example. Even more precisely, Panofsky suggests that the French custom of labeling as "classic Gothic" the central period of the Gothic has often led interpreters to apply unconsciously to Gothic architecture the plastic norms of the Greeks and Romans instead of endeavoring to define the specific norms of Gothic "classicity." The same analysis would undoubtedly apply for the concept of "rationalism": the "medieval rationalism" of which Panofsky is speaking is to "rationalism" as Viollet-le-Duc understood it, as well as to Pol Abraham's "illusionism," what Gothic "classicity," defined according to its own criteria of perfection, is to the concept of "classic" when it is unconsciously or consciously credited with transhistorical validity. In order to account for the division of cathedral architecture into so many hierarchies of homologous elements, Viollet-le-Duc proposes a strictly technical explanation: the repetition of the same forms and the use of the same generating lines have the capacity, he suggests, to reduce the number of "traits" (that is to say, working drawings) given as models to the workmen. Panofsky's argument integrates this explanation: Thomas Aquinas's "*nam et sensus ratio quaedam est*" is the most adequate expression of a "visual logic" based on

---

32. Panofsky, "The History of Art as a Humanistic Discipline," in *Meaning in the Visual Arts*, 11.

33. Panofsky, "The History of Art," 12.

34. Panofsky, "Der Begriff des Kunstwollens," *Zeitschrift für Aesthetik und allgeime Kunstwissenschaft* 14 (1920): 321–39.

35. "Classical taste demanded that private letters, legal speeches and the shields of heroes should be 'artistic' (with the possible result of what might be called fake beauty), while modern taste demands that architecture and ash trays should be 'functional' (with the possible result of what might be called fake efficiency)"; Panofsky, "The History of Art," 13.

the intrinsic ambiguity of the objective intention that dwells in all the cultural works of the twelfth and thirteenth centuries.

––––––

However, does not the philosophy of art that is implied in the notion of *habitus* as generative grammar adjust itself only too well, and therefore too exclusively, to those periods in which a style achieves its own perfection and that exploit, to the point of accomplishing them and, perhaps, exhausting them, the possibilities given by an inherited art of inventing, rather than inventing, strictly speaking, a new art of inventing? Indeed, it all works as if the chronological order could be, so to speak, deduced from the logical order, history being merely the place where the tendency to self-completion of the system of logical possibilities (those that define a style, for instance) is accomplished. But what about those periods of rupture and crisis in which a new generative grammar is being formed? In the presence of those innovators who, like Abbot Suger, break with the aesthetic traditions of their time and milieu, is it necessary, this time, to accept the irreducibility of creative individuality?

In fact, in order to explain this creation of creative schemes, one must treat the creator's singular *habitus* as such, that is to say as a principle of unification and explanation of this set of apparently disparate conducts that constitute a life as one. Such a systematic biography causes one right away to invert the relation traditional iconography establishes between the works and the creator's aesthetic or philosophical principles. The reading of the iconographic clarifications Suger provides to the historian in the *Liber de Rebus in Administratione Sua Gestis* and in the *Libellus Alter de Consecratione Ecclesiae Sancti Dyonisii* reveals that this innovator has found in Pseudo-Dionysius and John Scotus Eriugena's "metaphysics of light" the ideology that miraculously came to consecrate (that is, to sanction and sanctify) his "avant-garde" taste for an aesthetics of light and bedazzlement. Therefore, one could not, in this case, hold philosophical representations as the principle of artistic creations, and one must search elsewhere, for fear of not finding the explanation, for the source of a taste that is expressed as much in the style of the writings as in the choice of the materials, the objects, and the forms. In order to show the strength of an analysis that is valid because of its determination to hold as well as hold together all the aspects of reality, it suffices to recall the relationship it establishes between the aesthetic positions of Suger and St. Bernard of Clairvaux and various sociologically significant aspects of their biographies. On the one hand, the ascetic, in whose personality the radical rejection of all material beauty appears, in its very excess, as a "negative aesthetics" rather than an indifference to art; on the other hand, the aesthete who indulges in a frantic passion for all that bedazzles. On the one hand, the child of a poor family, destined from an early age for the Church that makes him all that he is; on the other hand, a young nobleman who chooses, at the end of adolescence, to devote himself to the monastery and imposes on it his absolute rigorism. This would undoubtedly be sufficient to understand the systematic differences that oppose Suger and St. Bernard in every aspect and in every domain—in the style of their faith, in their image of religious life, in their temporal action, and in their relationship to beauty that is but one dimension of a more general attitude toward existence—if Panofsky did not endeavor to define, moreover, the peculiar nature of the relationship Suger maintains with his social condition (and, inseparably, with the Church). Consequently, although Panofsky never does so explicitly, one cannot help but establish a relation between the taste for splendor and luxury that Suger dares to affirm and impose against the sophisticated people in his entourage, and other aspects such as his taste for the company of men in high places and the somewhat pretentious preciosity of his style. And if, with Panofsky, one adds a last trait, Suger's small stature, one can see in his liberated attitude toward physical and, above all, social "smallness" the generating and unifying principle of this singular personality and, as a result, the principle that enables one to understand and explain the singular form of his innovative action. There is therefore no contradiction in putting forward, in the study of a period of transition and rupture, and regarding one of the main agents of the invention of a new style, some forces that created habits other than that which the analysis of Gothic architecture at its peak favored. And undoubtedly, systematic biographies of the creators of the classic period, architects or scholastics, would even enable one to give a full account of the remarkable variations that no academic indoctrination can fully abolish.

If one wanted to render in its entirety the system of causes that explain the historical success of Abbot Suger's innovations, one would undoubtedly have to reintroduce some of the facts that Suger puts forward to justify his enterprise and that have been set aside out of a choice of method. Thus, for example, it seems indisputable that, with the growing urbanization and the large gatherings due to markets, fairs, and pilgrimages, the need for larger churches could only have intensified. Moreover, there is no doubt that Suger's position in the political and ecclesiastical hierarchy as well as the special significance of his abbey gave his initiatives an exceptional *legitimacy,* even in the aesthetic field, in such a way that, at least in the ever-changing royal scene, architects were obliged, as Panofsky observes, to pay careful attention to the difficulties, however problematic these might have been, that they had inherited from him —for instance with respect to the west façade—and that they took a century to resolve. However, they had to reject for a while, as mere rationalizations, the reasons given by Suger: that is to say, just as much his references to the "metaphysics of light" as the justifications coming from the increasing number of followers of the Church, because they tended to establish relations of simple and direct dependence where there were, to paraphrase Cournot, "independent causal series within the order of causality" whose "combination or encounter" generated this fortunate accident that the Gothic style represents.

––––––

Faced with such exercises of methodological virtuosity, one cannot help recalling a sentence from *Iconography and Iconology:* "The art historian differs from the 'naïve' spectator in that he is conscious of what he does."[36] One should, Saussure wrote likewise, "show the linguist what he does," that is to say, as Emile Benveniste comments, highlight "what preliminary operations he engages in unconsciously when he tackles the linguistic facts."[37] Just as much as and undoubtedly better than he did in the theoretical writings to which we have referred in order to justify our analysis of the epistemological presuppositions involved in this book, Erwin Panofsky reveals here, in a striking manner, that he can do what he does only on the condition that, at any given moment, he should know what he is doing and what it takes to be doing it, because both the most humble and the most noble scientific operations are worth the full value of the theoretical and epistemological conscience that accompanies these operations.

36. Panofsky, "Iconography and Iconology," 31.
37. Emile Benveniste, "Saussure après un demi-siècle," in *Problèmes de linguistique générales* (Paris: Gallimard, 1966), 38.

Works Cited

Abelard, Peter. *Ethics*. Edited and translated by D. E. Luscombe. Oxford: Clarendon Press, 1971.

———. *Historia Calamitatum*. In *The Letters of Abelard and Heloise*. Translated by Betty Radice. New York: Penguin, 1974.

Aers, David. Preface, "Historical Inquiries/Psychoanalytic Criticism/Gender Studies." *Journal of Medieval and Early Modern Studies* 26 (1996): 199–208.

———. "A Whisper in the Ear of Early Modernists; or, Reflections on Literary Critics Writing the 'History of the Subject'." In *Culture and History, 1350–1600: Essays on English Communities, Identities and Writing*, ed. David Aers, 177–203. Detroit: Wayne State University Press, 1992.

Aichele, George et al./The Bible and Culture Collective. *The Postmodern Bible*. New Haven, Conn.: Yale University Press, 1995.

Angela of Foligno. *Le livre de l'expérience des vrais fidèles*. Edited by M.-J. Ferré. Paris: Droz, 1927.

Antliff, Mark. *Inventing Bergson: Cultural Politics and the Parisian Avant-Garde*. Princeton, N.J.: Princeton University Press, 1993.

Ardagh, John. *The New French Revolution: A Social and Economic Study of France, 1945–1968*. New York: Harper and Row, 1968.

Armstrong, Nancy, and Leonard Tennenhouse. *The Imaginary Puritan: Literature, Intellectual Labor, and the Origins of Personal Life*. Berkeley: University of California Press, 1992.

Arraj, James. *Mysticism, Metaphysics and Maritain*. Chiloquin, Ore.: IGB, 1993.

August, Marilyn, and Ann Liddle. "Beyond Structuralism: The Cerisy Experience." *Sub-Stance* 5–6 (1973): 227–36.

Balthasar, Hans Urs von. *The Glory of the Lord: A Theological*

Aesthetics, vol. 5: *The Realm of Metaphysics in the Modern Age.* Translated by Oliver Davies et al. San Francisco: Ignatius Press, 1991.

Barthes, Roland. "L'ancienne rhétorique." *Communications* 16 (1970): 172–229.

———. "Comment parler à Dieu?" *Tel Quel* 38 (1969): 32–54.

———. *The Grain of the Voice: Interviews 1962–1980.* Edited by Stephen Heath, translated by Linda Coverdale. New York: Hill and Wang, 1985.

———. *Image-Music-Text.* Translated by Stephen Heath. New York: Hill and Wang, 1977.

———. *Œuvres complètes.* Edited by Eric Marty. Paris: Éditions du Seuil, 1993– . [Three volumes published to date.]

———. *The Pleasure of the Text.* Translated by Richard Miller. New York: Noonday Press, 1975.

———. Review of Duby and Mandrou, *Histoire de la civilisation française. Annales* 15 (1960): 998–99.

———. *Roland Barthes.* Translated by Richard Howard. New York: Hill and Wang, 1977.

———. *Sade, Fourier, Loyola.* Translated by Richard Miller. New York: Hill and Wang, 1976.

Barthes, Roland, et al. *Structural Analysis and Biblical Exegesis: Interpretational Essays.* Translated by Alfred M. Johnson Jr. Pittsburgh, Pa.: The Pickwick Press, 1974.

———. *Exégèse et herméneutique.* Paris: Éditions du Seuil, 1971.

Bataille, Georges. *The Accursed Share: An Essay on General Economy.* Volume 1: *Consumption.* Translated by Robert Hurley. New York: Zone Books, 1991.

———. *The College of Sociology 1937–39.* Edited by Denis Hollier, translated by Betsy Wing. Minneapolis: University of Minnesota Press, 1988.

———. *Erotism: Death and Sensuality.* Translated by Mary Dalwood. San Francisco: City Lights, 1986.

———. "Fatrasies." *La Révolution Surréaliste* 6 (1926): 2–3.

———. *Guilty.* Translated by Bruce Boone. San Francisco: Lapis Press, 1988.

———. *The History of Eroticism.* Volume 2 of *The Accursed Share.* Translated by Robert Hurley. New York: Zone Books, 1991.

———. *Inner Experience.* Translated by Leslie Anne Boldt. Albany: State University of New York Press, 1988.

———. *Œuvres complètes.* 12 volumes. Paris: Gallimard, 1971–88.

———. *On Nietzsche.* Translated by Bruce Boone. New York: Paragon House, 1992.

———. *Sovereignty.* Volume 3 of *The Accursed Share.* Translated by Robert Hurley. New York: Zone Books, 1991.

———. *The Trial of Gilles de Rais.* Translated by Richard Robinson. Los Angeles: Amok, 1991.

———. *The Unfinished System of Nonknowledge.* Edited and translated by Michelle

Kendall and Stuart Kendall. Minneapolis: University of Minnesota Press, 2001.

———. *Visions of Excess: Selected Writings 1927–1938.* Edited by Allan Stoekl. Translated by Allan Stoekl with Carl R. Lovitt and Donald M. Leslie Jr. Minneapolis: University of Minnesota Press, 1985.

Bauman, Zygmunt. *Postmodern Ethics.* Oxford: Blackwell, 1993.

Beauvoir, Simone de. *Tous les hommes sont mortels.* Paris: Gallimard, 1946.

Beckwith, Sarah. *Signifying God: Social Relation and Symbolic Act in the York Corpus Christi Plays.* Chicago: University of Chicago Press, 2001.

Benjamin, Walter. *The Origin of German Tragic Drama.* Translated by John Osborne. London and New York: Verso, 1998.

Bennington, Geoffrey, and Jacques Derrida. *Jacques Derrida.* Chicago: University of Chicago Press, 1993.

Bergson, Henri. *Laughter.* In *Comedy,* ed. Wylie Sypher, 61–90. Garden City, N.Y.: Doubleday, 1956.

Bernard of Clairvaux, Saint. *Sermons on the Song of Songs,* vol. 2. Translated by Kilian Walsh. In *The Works of Bernard of Clairvaux* vol. 2. Shannon, Ireland: Irish University Press, 1971.

Bhabha, Homi K. "DissemiNation: Time, Narrative, and the Margins of the Modern Nation." In *Nation and Narration,* ed. Homi K. Bhabha, 291–322. London: Routledge, 1990.

Biddick, Kathleen. *The Shock of Medievalism.* Durham, N.C.: Duke University Press, 1998.

Bloechl, Jeffrey. *Liturgy of the Neighbor: Emmanuel Levinas and the Religion of Responsibility.* Pittsburgh, Pa.: Duquesne University Press, 2000.

Bloch, R. Howard, and Stephen G. Nichols. *Medievalism and the Modernist Temper.* Baltimore and London: Johns Hopkins University Press, 1996.

Bloom, Harold. *Shakespeare: The Invention of the Human.* New York: Riverhead Books, 1998.

Booth, Wayne C. *The Company We Keep: An Ethics of Fiction.* Berkeley and Los Angeles: University of California Press, 1988.

Borch-Jacobsen, Mikkel. *Lacan: The Absolute Master.* Translated by Douglas Brick. Stanford, Calif.: Stanford University Press, 1991.

Bourdieu, Pierre. "The Genesis of the Concepts of Habitus and of Field." *Sociocriticism* 2 (1991): 11–24.

———. *Homo Academicus.* Translated by Peter Collier. Stanford, Calif.: Stanford University Press, 1988.

———. *In Other Words: Essays towards a Reflexive Sociology.* Translated by Matthew Adamson. Stanford, Calif.: Stanford University Press, 1990.

———. *Language and Symbolic Power.* Translated by Gino Raymond and Matthew Adamson. Cambridge: Harvard University Press, 1991.

———. *The Logic of Practice.* Translated by Richard Nice. Stanford, Calif.: Stanford University Press, 1990.

———. *Outline of a Theory of Practice*. Translated by Richard Nice. Cambridge: Cambridge University Press, 1977.

———. *Pascalian Meditations*. Translated by Richard Nice. Stanford, Calif.: Stanford University Press, 2000.

———. "Postface." In Erwin Panofsky, *Architecture gothique et pensée scolastique*, translated by Pierre Bourdieu, 135–67. Paris: Les Éditions de Minuit, 1967.

Bourdieu, Pierre, and Jean-Claude Passeron. *Reproduction in Education, Society, and Culture*. Translated by Richard Nice. London: Sage Publications, 1977.

Bourdin, Dominique. *Essai sur l'Essai sur l'origine des langues de Jean-Jacques Rousseau: Pour une approche pragmatique du texte*. Geneva and Paris: Editions Slatkine, 1994.

Bové, Paul. "Dante, Gramsci and Cultural Criticism." *Rethinking Marxism* 4 (1991): 74–86.

Bowie, Malcolm. *Lacan*. Cambridge: Harvard University Press, 1991.

Brennan, Teresa. *History after Lacan*. London and New York: Routledge, 1993.

Breton, André. *Manifestoes of Surrealism*. Translated by Richard Seaver and Helen R. Lane. Ann Arbor: University of Michigan Press, 1969.

Brownlee, Marina, Kevin Brownlee, and Stephen G. Nichols, eds. *The New Medievalism*. Baltimore and London: Johns Hopkins University Press, 1991.

Buell, Lawrence. "In Pursuit of Ethics." *PMLA* 114 (1999): 7–19.

Burke, Peter. *The French Historical Revolution: The Annales School, 1929–1989*. Stanford, Calif.: Stanford University Press, 1990.

Butler, Judith. *Antigone's Claim*. New York: Columbia University Press, 2000.

Butler, Judith, John Guillory, and Kendall Thomas, eds. *What's Left of Theory? New Work on the Politics of Literary Theory*. New York and London: Routledge, 2000.

Bynum, Caroline Walker. *Fragmentation and Redemption: Essays on Gender and the Human Body in Medieval Religion*. New York: Zone Books, 1991.

Calvet, Louis-Jean. *Roland Barthes: A Biography*. Translated by Sarah Wykes. Bloomington: Indiana University Press, 1994.

Camic, Charles. "The Matter of Habit." *American Journal of Sociology* 91 (1986): 1039–87

Caputo, John. *The Prayers and Tears of Jacques Derrida: Religion without Religion*. Bloomington: Indiana University Press, 1997.

Caputo, John D., Mark Dooley, and Michael J. Scanlon, eds. *Questioning God*. Bloomington: Indiana University Press, 2001.

Caserta, Ernesto G. "Croce's Essay on Dante." *Italian Culture* 8 (1990): 121–36.

Cazelles, Brigitte, and Charles Méla, eds. *Modernité au Moyen Âge: Le défi du passé*. Geneva: Droz, 1990.

Certeau, Michel de. *The Practice of Everyday Life*. Translated by Steven Rendall. Berkeley: University of California Press, 1984.

———. *The Writing of History*. Translated by Tom Conley. New York: Columbia University Press, 1988.

Champagne, Roland. *Georges Bataille*. New York: Twayne, 1998.

Cohen, Sande. "Critical Inquiry, *October,* and Historicizing French Theory." In *French Theory in America,* ed. Sylvère Lotringer and Sande Cohen, 191–215. New York and London: Routledge, 2001.

Cleary, Edward L., O.P. *Crisis and Change: The Church in Latin America Today.* Maryknoll, N.Y.: Orbis Books, 1985.

Cole, Andrew. "What Hegel's Master/Slave Dialectic Really Means." *Journal of Medieval and Early Modern Studies* 34 (2004): 577–610.

Coletti, Theresa. *Naming the Rose: Eco, Medieval Signs, and Modern Theory.* Ithaca and London: Cornell University Press, 1988.

Colish, Marcia. *Medieval Foundations of the Western Intellectual Tradition, 400–1400.* New Haven and London: Yale University Press, 1997.

Conner, Peter Tracey. *Georges Bataille and the Mysticism of Sin.* Baltimore and London: Johns Hopkins University Press, 2000.

Copeland, Rita. "Gender, Space, Reading Histories." Introduction to *New Medieval Literatures* 2 (1998): 1–8.

Corbellari, Alain. "Joseph Bédier, Philologist and Writer." In R. Howard Bloch and Stephen G. Nichols, *Medievalism and the Modernist Temper,* 269–285. Baltimore and London: Johns Hopkins University Press, 1996.

Coward, Harold, and Toby Foshay, eds. *Derrida and Negative Theology.* Albany: State University of New York Press, 1992.

Critchley, Simon. *The Ethics of Deconstruction: Derrida and Levinas.* Oxford: Blackwell, 1992.

Culler, Jonathan. "The Literary in Theory." In *What's Left of Theory?* ed. Judith Butler, John Guillory, and Kendall Thomas, 271–92. New York and London: Routledge, 2000.

———. *Roland Barthes.* New York: Oxford University Press, 1983.

Cunningham, Valentine. *Reading after Theory.* Oxford: Blackwell, 2002.

Cusset, François. *French Theory: Foucault, Derrida, Deleuze & Cie et les mutations de la vie intellectuelle aux États-Unis.* Paris: Le Decouverte, 1993.

Daly, Mary. *Gyn/Ecology: The Metaethics of Radical Feminism.* Boston: Beacon Press, 1978.

Damico, Helen, and Joseph B. Zavadil, eds. *Medieval Scholarship: Biographical Studies in the Formation of a Discipline.* 3 vols. New York: Garland, 1995.

Daniel, Arnaut. *Poetry.* Edited and translated by James J. Wilhelm. New York and London: Garland, 1981.

Dean, Carolyn. *The Self and Its Pleasures: Bataille, Lacan, and the History of the Decentered Subject.* Ithaca and London: Cornell University Press, 1992.

Deferrari, Roy, and Sister M. Inviolata Barry. *A Lexicon of St. Thomas Aquinas Based on the* Summa Theologica *and Selected Passages of His Other Works.* Washington, D.C.: Catholic University of America Press, 1948.

Deleuze, Gilles. *Bergsonism.* Translated by Hugh Tomlinson and Barbara Habberjam. New York: Zone Books, 1991.

Deleuze, Gilles, and Félix Guattari. *Anti-Oedipus: Capitalism and Schizophrenia.* Translated by Robert Hurley, Mark Seem, and Helen R. Lane. New York: Viking, 1977.

de Man, Paul. *Allegories of Reading: Figurative Language in Rousseau, Nietzsche, Rilke, and Proust.* New Haven, Conn.: Yale University Press, 1979.

———. *Blindness and Insight: Essays in the Rhetoric of Contemporary Criticism.* 2d ed. Minneapolis: University of Minnesota Press, 1983.

Dennehy, Raymond. "The Philosophical Catbird Seat: A Defense of Maritain's *Philosophia Perennis.*" In *The Future of Thomism,* ed. Deal W. Hudson and Dennis Moran, 65–76. Notre Dame, Ind.: University of Notre Dame Press for the American Maritain Association, 1992.

Derrida, Jacques. *Archive Fever: A Freudian Impression.* Translated by Eric Prenowitz. Chicago: University of Chicago Press, 1996.

———. *Circumfession: Fifty-nine Periods and Periphrases.* In Geoffrey Bennington and Jacques Derrida, *Jacques Derrida.* Chicago: University of Chicago Press, 1993.

———. *De la grammatologie.* Paris: Éditions de Minuit, 1967.

———. *Dissemination.* Translated by Barbara Johnson. London: Athlone Press, 1981.

———. "Faith and Knowledge: The Two Sources of 'Religion' at the Limits of Reason Alone." Translated by Samuel Weber. In *Religion,* ed. Jacques Derrida and Gianni Vattimo, 1–78. Stanford, Calif.: Stanford University Press, 1998.

———. "How to Avoid Speaking: Denials." In *Derrida and Negative Theology,* ed. Harold Coward and Toby Foshay, 73–142. Albany: State University of New York Press, 1992.

———. *The Gift of Death.* Translated by David Wills. Chicago: University of Chicago Press, 1995.

———. *Of Grammatology.* Corrected edition. Translated by Gayatri Chakravorty Spivak. Baltimore and London: Johns Hopkins University Press, 1997.

———. "Passions: 'An Oblique Offering.'" In *Derrida: A Critical Reader,* ed. David Wood, 5–35. Oxford: Blackwell, 1992.

———. *Positions.* Translated by Alan Bass. Chicago and London: University of Chicago Press, 1988.

———. *The Post Card: From Socrates to Freud and Beyond.* Translated by Alan Bass. Chicago and London: University of Chicago Press, 1987.

———. "Responses to Questions on the Avant-Garde." *Digraphe* 6 (1975): 152–53.

———. "The Supplement of Copula: Philosophy before Linguistics." In *Textual Strategies: Perspectives in Post-Structuralist Criticism,* ed. Josué V. Harari, 28–120. London: Methuen, 1979.

———. *Writing and Difference.* Translated by Alan Bass. Chicago: University of Chicago Press, 1978.

Derrida, Jacques, and Gianni Vattimo, eds. *Religion.* Stanford, Calif.: Stanford University Press, 1998.

Descombes, Vincent. *Modern French Philosophy*. Translated by L. Scott-Fox and
   J. M. Harding. Cambridge: Cambridge University Press, 1980.
Dianteill, Erwan. "Pierre Bourdieu et la religion: Synthèse critique d'un synthèse
   critique." *Archives des Sciences Sociales des Religions* 118 (2002): 5–19.
Dinshaw, Carolyn. *Chaucer's Sexual Poetics*. Madison: University of Wisconsin
   Press, 1989.
———. *Getting Medieval: Sexualities and Communities, Pre- and Postmodern*. Dur-
   ham, N.C.: Duke University Press, 1999.
Doering, Bernard E. *Jacques Maritain and the French Catholic Intellectuals*. Notre
   Dame, Ind.: University of Notre Dame Press, 1983.
Dooley, Mark. "The Catastrophe of Memory: Derrida, Milbank, and the (Im)pos-
   sibility of Forgiveness." In *Questioning God*, ed. John Caputo, Mark Dooley,
   and Michael J. Scanlon, 129–49. Bloomington: Indiana University Press,
   2001.
Domenach, Jean-Marie, and Robert de Montvalon. *The Catholic Avant-Garde:
   French Catholicism since World War II*. Translated by Brigid Nelson et al.
   New York: Holt, Rinehart and Winston, 1967.
Donneaud, Henry. "Une vie en service de la théologie." *Revue Thomiste* 92 (1992):
   17–51.
Dosse, François. *A History of Structuralism*. 2 vols. Translated by Deborah Glass-
   man. Minneapolis: University of Minnesota Press, 1997.
———. *New History in France: The Triumph of the Annales*. Translated by Peter V.
   Conroy Jr. Urbana: University of Illinois Press, 1994.
Drabinski, John. "The Possibility of an Ethical Politics: From Peace to Liturgy."
   Philosophy and Social Criticism 26 (2000): 49–73.
Dreyfus, Herbert L., and Paul Rabinow. *Michel Foucault, Beyond Structuralism and
   Hermeneutics*. Chicago: University of Chicago Press, 1992.
Duby, Georges. *History Continues*. Translated by Arthur Goldhammer. Chicago:
   University of Chicago Press, 1994.
Duncan, Diane Moira. *The Pre-Text of Ethics: On Derrida and Levinas*. New York:
   Peter Lang, 2001.
Eagleton, Terry. *After Theory*. New York: Basic Books, 2003.
Eco, Umberto. *Travels in Hyperreality: Essays*. Translated by William Weaver. San
   Diego: Harcourt Brace Jovanovich, 1986.
Esposito, Constantino, and Pasquale Porro, eds., *Heidegger e i medievali*. Special
   issue of *Quaestio* 1 (2001).
Ette, Ottmar. *Roland Barthes: eine intellektuelle Biographie*. Frankfurt: Suhrkampf,
   1998.
Fassler, Margot. *Gothic Song: Victorine Sequences and Augustinian Reform in Twelfth-
   Century Paris*. Cambridge: Cambridge University Press, 1993.
Ferretti, Silvia. *Cassirer, Panofsky, and Warburg: Symbol, Art, and History*. Trans-
   lated by Richard Pierce. New Haven and London: Yale University Press,
   1989.

Ferry, Luc, and Alain Renaut. *French Philosophy of the Sixties: An Essay on Antihumanism.* Translated by Mary H. S. Cattani. Amherst: University of Massachusetts Press, 1990.

Fitzmyer, Joseph A. "The Biblical Commission's Instruction on the Historical Truth of the Gospels." *Theological Studies* 25 (1964): 386–408.

Ffrench, Patrick. *The Time of Theory: A History of Tel Quel (1960–1983).* Oxford: Clarendon Press, 1995.

FitzGerald, Desmond J. "Gilson, *Aeterni Patris* and the Direction of Twenty-First Century Catholic Philosophy." In *The Future of Thomism,* ed. Deal W. Hudson and Dennis Moran, 83–90. Notre Dame, Ind.: University of Notre Dame Press for the American Maritain Association, 1992.

Foucault, Michel. *The Archaeology of Knowledge.* Translated by A. M. Sheridan Smith. New York: Pantheon, 1972.

———. *Discipline and Punish: The Birth of the Prison.* Translated by Alan Sheridan. New York: Pantheon, 1977.

———. *Ethics.* Volume 1 of *The Essential Works of Michel Foucault, 1954–1984.* Edited by Paul Rabinow, translated by Robert Hurley et al. New York: New Press, 1997.

———, ed. *I, Pierre Rivière, Having Slaughtered My Mother, My Sister, and My Brother . . . : A Case of Parricide in the 19th Century.* Translated by Frank Jellinek. Lincoln: University of Nebraska Press, 1975.

———. *Language, Counter-Memory, Practice: Selected Essays and Interviews.* Edited by Donald F. Bouchard, translated by Donald F. Bouchard and Sherry Simon. Ithaca, N.Y.: Cornell University Press, 1977.

———. "Les mot et les images." *Le Nouvel Observateur* 154 (October 25, 1967): 49–50.

———. "Le 'non' du père: Jean Laplanche, Holderlin et la question du père." *Critique* 178 (March 1962): 195–209.

———. "Préface à la transgression." In *Hommages à Georges Bataille.* Special issue of *Critique,* no. 195–196 (August-September, 1963): 751–69.

Fradenburg, Louise. "'So That We May Speak of Them': Enjoying the Middle Ages." *New Literary History* 28 (1997): 205–30.

Frantzen, Allen. *Before the Closet: Same-Sex Love from* Beowulf *to* Angels in America. Chicago: University of Chicago Press, 1998.

———, ed. *Speaking Two Languages: Traditional Disciplines and Contemporary Theory in Medieval Studies.* Albany: State University of New York Press, 1991.

Gadamer, Hans-Georg. *Truth and Method.* Translated by W. Glen-Doepel, edited by John Cumming and Garrett Barden. New York: Seabury Press, 1975.

Ganim, John. "The Literary Uses of the New History." In *The Idea of Medieval Literature: New Essays on Chaucer and Medieval Culture in Honor of Donald R. Howard,* ed. James M. Dean and Christian K. Zacher, 209–26. Newark: University of Delaware Press, 1992.

Gibbs, Robert. *Correlations in Rosenzweig and Levinas.* Princeton, N.J.: Princeton University Press, 1992.

Gill, Carolyn Bailey, ed. *Bataille: Writing the Sacred*. London and New York: Routledge, 1995.

Gilson, Etienne. *The Mystical Theology of St. Bernard*. Translated by A.H.C. Downes. New York: Sheed and Ward, 1940.

Goux, Joseph. "Note sur Rabelais et la langage." *Tel Quel* 15 (1963): 79–81.

Guerlac, Suzanne. *Literary Polemics: Bataille, Sartre, Valéry, Breton*. Stanford, Calif.: Stanford University Press, 1997.

———. "'Recognition' by a Woman! A Reading of Bataille's *L'Erotisme*." In *On Bataille*, ed. Allan Stoekl. Special issue of *Yale French Studies* 78 (1990): 90–105.

Gutting, Gary. *French Philosophy in the Twentieth Century*. Cambridge: Cambridge University Press, 2001.

Haidu, Peter. "Making It (New) in the Middle Ages: Towards a Problematics of Alterity." *diacritics* 4 (1974): 2–11.

Halpern, Richard. *Shakespeare's Perfume: Sodomy and Sublimity in the Sonnets, Wilde, Freud, and Lacan*. Philadelphia: University of Pennsylvania Press, 2002.

Handelman, Susan. *Fragments of Redemption: Jewish Thought and Literary Theory in Benjamin, Scholem, and Levinas*. Bloomington: Indiana University Press, 1991.

Hanna, Ralph. "Will's Work." In *Written Work: Langland, Labor, and Authorship*, ed. Steven Justice and Kathryn Kerby-Fulton, 23–66. Philadelphia: University of Pennsylvania Press, 1997.

Harasym, Sarah, ed. *Levinas and Lacan: The Missed Encounter*. Albany: State University of New York Press, 1998.

Harpham, Geoffrey. *The Ascetic Imperative in Culture and Criticism*. Chicago and London: University of Chicago Press, 1987.

———. *Shadows of Ethics: Criticism and the Just Society*. Durham, N.C.: Duke University Press, 1999.

Hart, Kevin. *The Dark Gaze: Maurice Blanchot and the Sacred*. Chicago and London: University of Chicago Press, 2004.

———. *The Trespass of the Sign: Deconstruction, Theology and Philosophy*. 2d edition. New York: Fordham University Press, 2000.

Hawley, Daniel. *Bibliographie annotée de la critique sur Georges Bataille de 1929 à 1975*. Geneva: Librairie M. Slatkine, 1976.

Hegel, Georg Wilhelm Friedrich. *Medieval and Modern Philosophy. Lectures on the History of Philosophy: The Lectures of 1825–1826*, volume 3. Edited by Robert F. Brown, translated by J. M. Stewart. Berkeley and London: University of California Press, 1990.

Heidegger, Martin. *Frühe Schriften*. Edited by Friedrich-Wilhelm von Herrmann. Part 1, volume 1 of *Gesamtausgabe*. Frankfurt: Vittorio Klostermann, 1978.

Heimonet, Jean-Michel. *Politiques de l'écriture, Bataille/Derrida: Le sens du sacré dans la pensée française du surréalisme à nos jours*. Chapel Hill: University of North Carolina Press, 1987.

Hemming, Laurence Paul, ed. *Radical Orthodoxy? A Catholic Enquiry*. Aldershot: Ashgate, 2000.

Hoagland, Sarah. *Lesbian Ethics: Toward New Value*. Palo Alto, Calif.: Institute of Lesbian Studies, 1988.

Hollier, Denis. *Against Architecture: The Writings of Georges Bataille*. Translated by Betsy Wing. Cambridge, Mass. and London: MIT Press, 1989.

———. *La prise de la concorde: Essais sur Georges Bataille*. Paris: Gallimard, 1993.

———. "'La tragédie de Gilles de Rais' au 'Théâtre de la cruauté'." *L'Arc* 32 (1967): 63–70.

Hollier, Denis, ed. *Georges Bataille après tout*. Paris: Editions Belin, 1995.

Holly, Michael A. *Panofsky and the Foundations of Art History*. Ithaca, N.Y.: Cornell University Press, 1984.

Hollywood, Amy. *Sensible Ecstasy: Mysticism, Sexual Difference, and the Demands of History*. Chicago: University of Chicago Press, 2002.

Hommages à Georges Bataille. Special issue of *Critique*, no. 195–196 (August–September 1963).

Horkheimer, Max. *Critical Theory: Selected Essays*. Translated by Matthew J. O'Connell et al. New York: Continuum, 1995.

House, Roy Temple. *L'Ordene de Chevalerie: An Old French Poem*. Chicago: University of Chicago Libraries, 1918.

Huchet, Jean-Charles. *Littérature médiévale et psychanalyse: Pour une clinique littéraire*. Paris: Presses Universitaires de France, 1990.

Hudson, Deal W., and Dennis Moran, eds. *The Future of Thomism*. Notre Dame, Ind.: University of Notre Dame Press for the American Maritain Association, 1992.

Hult, David. "Gaston Paris and the Invention of Courtly Love." In *Medievalism and the Modernist Temper*, ed. R. Howard Bloch and Stephen G. Nichols, 192–224. Baltimore and London: Johns Hopkins University Press, 1996.

Irwin, Alexander. *Saints of the Impossible: Bataille, Weil, and the Politics of the Sacred*. Minneapolis: University of Minnesota Press, 2002.

Jameson, Fredric. *The Political Unconscious: Narrative as a Socially Symbolic Act*. Ithaca, N.Y.: Cornell University Press, 1981.

———. *Postmodernism, or, The Cultural Logic of Late Capitalism*. Durham, N.C. and London: Duke University Press, 1991.

———. *A Singular Modernity: Essays on the Ontology of the Present*. London: Verso, 2002.

Jauss, Hans Robert. *Alterität und Modernität der mittelalterlichen Literatur: Gesammelte Aufsätze 1956–1976*. Munich: W. Fink, 1977.

———. "The Alterity and Modernity of Medieval Literature." *New Literary History* 10 (1979): 181–227.

———. "Literary History as a Challenge to Literary Theory." *New Literary History* 2 (1970): 7–37.

———. *Literaturgeschichte als Provokation der Literaturwissenschaft*. Constance: Universitätsverlag, 1967.

———. *Toward an Aesthetic of Reception.* Translated by Timothy Bahti, with an introduction by Paul de Man. Minneapolis: University of Minnesota Press, 1982.

Jay, Martin. *Cultural Semantics: Keywords of Our Time.* Amherst: University of Massachusetts Press, 1998.

———. *Downcast Eyes: The Denigration of Vision in Twentieth-Century French Thought.* Berkeley, Los Angeles, and London: University of California Press, 1993.

———. "Lafayette's Children: The American Reception of French Liberalism." *SubStance* 31 (2002): 9–26.

Jean, Raymond. "Le 'commentaire' comme forme 'active' de la critique." *Le Monde* (May 9, 1970, supplement): III.

John, Helen James, S.N.D. *The Thomist Spectrum.* New York: Fordham University Press, 1966.

Johnson, Barbara. *The Critical Difference: Essays in the Contemporary Rhetoric of Reading.* Baltimore: Johns Hopkins University Press, 1981.

Jones, Gareth. "On Not Seeing the Joke." *Times Literary Supplement,* 2 April 1999.

Judt, Tony. *Past Imperfect: French Intellectuals, 1944–1956.* Berkeley: University of California Press, 1992.

Juranville, Alain. "Ethics with Psychoanalysis." Translated by Denise Merkle. In *Levinas and Lacan: The Missed Encounter,* ed. Sarah Harasym, 121–38. Albany: State University of New York Press, 1998.

Kaelber, Lutz. "Weber's Lacuna: Medieval Religion and the Roots of Rationalization." *Journal of the History of Ideas* 57 (1996): 465–85.

Kastan, David Scott. *Shakespeare after Theory.* New York: Routledge, 1999.

Kauppi, Niilo. *French Intellectual Nobility: Institutional and Symbolic Transformations in the Post-Sartrian Era.* Albany: State University of New York Press, 1996.

———. *The Making of an Avant-Garde: Tel Quel.* Berlin and New York: Mouton de Gruyter, 1994.

Kay, Sarah. *Courtly Contradictions: The Emergence of the Literary Object in the Twelfth Century.* Stanford, Calif.: Stanford University Press, 2001.

Kaeuper, Richard W. *Chivalry and Violence in Medieval Europe.* Oxford: Oxford University Press, 1999.

Kerr, Fergus. *After Aquinas: Versions of Thomism.* Oxford: Blackwell, 2002.

Kessler, Michael, and Christian Sheppard, eds. *Mystics: Presence and Aporia.* Chicago and London: University of Chicago Press, 2003.

Kisiel, Theodore. *The Genesis of Heidegger's* Being and Time. Berkeley and London: University of California Press, 1995.

Kojève, Alexandre. *Introduction to the Reading of Hegel: Lectures on the Phenomenology of Spirit.* Edited by Allan Bloom, translated by James H. Nichols Jr. Ithaca, N.Y. and London: Cornell University Press, 1980.

Krauss, Rosalind. *The Originality of the Avant-Garde and Other Modernist Myths.* Cambridge, Mass.: MIT Press, 1985.

Kristeva, Julia. *Desire in Language: A Semiotic Approach to Literature and Art.* Translated by Thomas Gora, Alice Jardine, and Leon S. Roudiez. New York: Columbia University Press, 1980.

———. *Σημειωτικη: Recherches pour une sémanalyse.* Paris: Éditions du Seuil, 1969.

———. *Tales of Love.* Translated by Leon S. Roudiez. New York: Columbia University Press, 1987.

Kurtz, Lester R. *The Politics of Heresy: The Modernist Crisis in Roman Catholicism.* Berkeley: University of California Press, 1986.

Kuttner, Stephan. *Harmony from Dissonance: An Interpretation of Medieval Canon Law.* Wimmer Lecture 10. Latrobe, Pa.: Archabbey Press, 1960.

Labourdette, M.-M., O.P. "La théologie et ses sources." *Revue Thomiste* 46 (1946): 353–71.

Lacan, Jacques. *Écrits: A Selection.* Translated by Alan Sheridan. New York and London: W. W. Norton, 1977.

———. *The Ethics of Psychoanalysis: The Seminar of Jacques Lacan Book VII, 1959–1960.* Edited by Jacques-Alain Miller, translated by Dennis Porter. New York: Norton, 1997.

———. *L'éthique de la psychanalyse: Le Séminaire de Jacques Lacan Livre VII.* Ed. Jacques-Alain Miller. Paris: Seuil, 1986.

———. "Kant avec Sade." *Critique* 191 (September 1962): 291–313.

———. *On Feminine Sexuality: The Limits of Love and Knowledge. The Seminar of Jacques Lacan Book XX, 1972–1973: Encore.* Translated by Bruce Fink. New York: Norton, 1998.

Land, Nick. *Thirst for Annihilation: Georges Bataille and Virulent Nihilism: An Essay in Atheistic Religion.* New York and London: Routledge, 1992.

Langland, William. *The Vision of Piers Plowman.* Edited by A.V.C. Schmidt. London: J. M. Dent, 2001.

La Sale, Antoine de. *Little John of Saintré/Le Petit Jehan de Saintré.* Translated by Irvine Gray. London: Routledge, 1931.

———. *Saintré.* 2 volumes. Edited by Mario Eusebi. Paris: Libraire Honoré Champion, 1993–94.

Latour, Bruno. *We Have Never Been Modern.* Translated by Catherine Porter. Cambridge: Harvard University Press, 1993.

Lavin, Irving, ed. *Meaning in the Visual Arts: Views from the Outside: A Centennial Commemoration of Erwin Panofsky (1892–1968).* Princeton, N.J.: Institute for Advanced Study, 1995.

Le Boulier, Jean-Pierre. "Georges Bataille et la Société des anciens textes français: Deux 'échecs sinistres' (1925–26)." *Revue d'histoire littéraire de la France* 91 (1991): 691–703.

Leclercq, Jean. *The Love of Learning and the Desire for God: A Study of Monastic Culture.* Translated by Catharine Misrahi. New York: Fordham University Press, 1961.

Lefebvre, Henri. *The Production of Space.* Translated by Donald Nicholson-Smith. Oxford: Blackwell, 1991.

Lehman, David. *The Last Avant-Garde: The Making of the New York School of Poets.* New York: Doubleday, 1998.

Leiris, Michel. "De Bataille l'impossible à l'impossible 'Documents'." In *Hommage à Georges Bataille.* Special issue of *Critique,* no. 195–196 (August–September, 1963): 685–93.

Léon-Dufour, X. "Exégètes et structuralistes." *Recherches de science religieuse* 58 (1972): 5–15.

Lerer, Seth, ed. *Literary History and the Challenge of Philology: The Legacy of Erich Auerbach.* Stanford, Calif.: Stanford University Press, 1996.

Leupin, Alexandre. *Barbarolexis: Medieval Writing and Sexuality.* Translated by Kate M. Cooper. Cambridge: Harvard University Press, 1989.

———. "The Middle Ages, the Other." Translated by Frances Bartkowski. *diacritics* 13 (1983): 21–31.

Levinas, Emmanuel. *Basic Philosophical Writings.* Edited by Adriaan T. Peperzak, Simon Critchley, and Robert Bernasconi. Bloomington: Indiana University Press, 1996.

———. "On the Trail of the Other." Translated by Daniel J. Hoy. *Philosophy Today* 10 (1966): 34–44.

———. *Otherwise than Being or Beyond Essence.* Translated by Alphonso Lingis. Martinus Nijhoff Philosophy Texts 3. The Hague: Martinus Nijhoff, 1981.

———. "The Trace of the Other." Translated by Alphonso Lingis. In *Deconstruction in Context: Literature and Philosophy,* ed. Mark C. Taylor, 345–59. Chicago: University of Chicago Press, 1986.

Lochrie, Karma. "Desiring Foucault." *Journal of Medieval and Early Modern Studies* 27 (1997): 3–16.

Lorau, René. *Autodissolutions des avant-gardes.* Paris: Galilée, 1980.

Lotringer, Sylvère. "Artaud, Bataille et le matérialisme dialectique." *Sub-Stance* 5–6 (1973): 207–225.

Lotringer, Sylvère, and Sande Cohen, eds. *French Theory in America.* New York and London: Routledge, 2001.

Lubac, Henri de. *At the Service of the Church: Henri de Lubac Reflects on the Circumstances that Occasioned His Writings.* Translated by Anne Elizabeth Englund. San Francisco: Ignatius Press, 1993.

———. *Exégèse médiévale: Les quatre sens de l'écriture.* 4 volumes in 2 parts. Paris: Aubier, 1959–64.

———. *Medieval Exegesis: The Four Senses of Scripture.* 4 volumes. Translated by Mark Sebanc. Grand Rapids, Mich.: Eerdmans, 1998–.

Lyotard, Jean-François. *The Confession of Augustine.* Translated by Richard Beardsworth. Stanford, Calif.: Stanford University Press, 2000.

———. *The Postmodern Condition: A Report on Knowledge.* Translated by Geoff Bennington and Brian Masumi. Minneapolis: University of Minnesota Press, 1984.

———. *The Postmodern Explained: Correspondence 1982–1985.* Translated by Don Barry et al. Minneapolis: University of Minnesota Press, 1993.

Macksey, Richard, and Eugenio Donato. *The Structuralist Controversy: The Languages of Criticism and the Sciences of Man.* Baltimore and London: The Johns Hopkins University Press, 1970.

Maillet, Christine. "L'amour courtois." *Lettres de l'École freudienne* 14 (1975).

Marichal, Robert. "L'Écriture latine et la civilisation occidentale du Ier au XVIe siècle." In *L'Ecriture at la psychologie des peuples: XXIIe Semaine de Synthèse,* ed. Marcel Cohen, 199–247. Paris: Armand Colin, 1963.

Maritain, Jacques. *Antimoderne.* Paris: Desclée, 1922.

———. *Bergsonian Philosophy and Thomism.* Translated by Mabelle L. Andison with the assistance of J. Gordon Andison. New York: Philosophical Library, 1955.

———. "Commentaire au livre de G. Dandoy, *L'Ontologie du Vedânta.*" In Jacques and Raïssa Maritain, *Oeuvres Complètes* vol. 4. Freiburg: Éditions Universitaires, 1983.

Marx-Scouras, Danielle. *The Cultural Politics of Tel Quel: Literature and the Left in the Wake of Engagement.* University Park, Pa.: Pennsylvania State University Press, 1996.

Masson, André. "Georges Bataille." *Bulletin des Bibliothèques de France* 7 (1962): 475–77.

Mathy, Jean-Philippe. *Extrême-Occident: French Intellectuals and America.* Chicago: University of Chicago Press, 1993.

Mattheus, Bernd. *Georges Bataille: Eine Thanatographie.* 3 volumes. Munich: Matthes & Seitz, 1984–95.

Mauss, Marcel. "Techniques of the Body." In *Incorporations,* ed. Jonathan Crary and Sanford Kwinter, 455–475. New York: Zone Books, 1992.

Mazzoni, Cristina. *Saint Hysteria: Neurosis, Mysticism, and Gender in European Culture.* Ithaca, N.Y.: Cornell University Press, 1996.

McCarthy, Timothy G. *The Catholic Tradition: The Church in the Twentieth Century.* Second edition. Chicago: Loyola Press, 1998.

McCool, Gerald A., S.J. *From Unity to Pluralism: The Internal Evolution of Thomism.* New York: Fordham University Press, 1989.

———. *The Neo-Thomists.* Milwaukee, Wis.: Marquette University Press, 1994.

McLuhan, Marshall. *The Gutenberg Galaxy: The Making of Typographic Man.* Toronto: University of Toronto Press, 1962.

Menocal, María Rosa. *Shards of Love: Exile and the Origins of the Lyric.* Durham, N.C.: Duke University Press, 1994.

Métraux, Alfred. "Rencontre avec les ethnologues." *Critique* 195–196 (1963): 677–84.

Milbank, John. "Knowledge: The Theological Critique of Philosopy in Hamann and Jacobi." In *Radical Orthodoxy: A New Theology,* ed. John Milbank, Catherine Pickstock, and Graham Ward, 23–24. London: Routledge, 1999.

———. "The Programme of Radical Orthodoxy." In *Radical Orthodoxy? A Catholic Enquiry,* ed. Laurence Paul Hemming, 33–45. Aldershot: Ashgate, 2000.

———. *The Word Made Strange: Theology, Language, Culture.* Oxford: Blackwell, 1997.

Milbank, John, and Catherine Pickstock. *Truth in Aquinas.* London and New York: Routledge, 2001.

Milbank, John, Catherine Pickstock, and Graham Ward, eds. *Radical Orthodoxy: A New Theology.* London: Routledge, 1999.

Miller, Jacques-Alain. "Ethics in Psychoanalysis." Translated by Jorge Jauregui and Marguerite Laporte. *lacanian ink* 5 (1992): 13–27.

Minnis, A. J. *Medieval Theory of Authorship: Scholastic Literary Attitudes in the Later Middle Ages.* London: Scolar Press, 1984.

Moi, Toril. *Sexual/Textual Politics: Feminist Literary Theory.* London: Methuen, 1985.

Monson, Don A., and William D. Paden. "The Troubadour's Lady: An Exchange." *Exemplaria* 14 (2002): 485–517.

Moriarty, Michael. *Roland Barthes.* Stanford, Calif.: Stanford University Press, 1991.

Mortley, Raoul. *French Philosophers in Conversation: Levinas, Schneider, Serres, Irigaray, Le Doeuff, Derrida.* London and New York: Routledge, 1991.

Moss, David. "Friendship: St. Anselm, theoria and the Convolution of Sense." In *Radical Orthodoxy: A New Theology,* ed. John Milbank, Catherine Pickstock, and Graham Ward, 127–42. London: Routledge, 1999.

Mowitt, John. *Text: Genealogy of an Antidisciplinary Object.* Durham, N.C.: Duke University Press, 1992.

Nichols, Aidan, O.P. "Thomism and the Nouvelle Théologie." *The Thomist* 64 (2000): 1–19.

Nichols, Stephen G. "Modernism and the Politics of Medieval Studies." In *Medievalism and the Modernist Temper,* ed. R. Howard Bloch and Stephen G. Nichols, 25–56. Baltimore and London: Johns Hopkins University Press, 1996.

Nordquist, Joan. *Georges Bataille: A Bibliography.* Santa Cruz, Calif.: Reference and Research Services, 1994.

———. *Jacques Lacan: A Bibliography.* Santa Cruz, Calif.: Reference and Research Services, 1987.

———. *Pierre Bourdieu: A Bibliography.* Santa Cruz, Calif.: Reference and Research Services, 1997.

O'Dea, Michael. *Jean-Jacques Rousseau: Music, Illusion and Desire.* New York: St. Martin's Press, 1995.

O'Keeffe, Katherine O'Brien, ed. *The Book and the Body.* Notre Dame, Ind.: Notre Dame University Press, 1997.

Panofsky, Erwin. *Architecture gothique et pensée scolastique.* Translated by Pierre Bourdieu. Paris: Les Éditions de Minuit, 1967.

———. *Korrespondenz 1910–1968: eine kommentierte Auswahl in fünf Bänden.* Edited by Dieter Wuttke. Wiesbaden: Harrassowitz, 2001.

———. *Gothic Architecture and Scholasticism.* Latrobe, Pa.: St. Vincent Archabbey Press, 1951.

Patterson, Lee. *Negotiating the Past: The Historical Understanding of Medieval Literature.* Madison: University of Wisconsin Press, 1987.

———. "On the Margin: Postmodernism, Ironic History, and Medieval Studies."
Speculum 65 (1990): 87–108.

Payer, Pierre. *Sex and the Penitentials: The Development of a Sexual Code, 550–1150.*
Toronto: University of Toronto Press, 1984.

Pègues, R. P. Thomas, O. P. *La somme théologique de Saint Thomas d'Aquin en
forme de catéchisme pour tous les fidèles: Ouvrage honoré d'un Bref de Sa Sainteté
le Pape Benoît XV.* Toulouse: Librairie Édouard Privat, 1919.

Perloff, Marjorie. *The Futurist Moment: Avant-Garde, Avant Guerre, and the Language of Rupture.* Chicago and London: University of Chicago Press, 1986.

Philippe, Gilles. *Roland Barthes.* Bibliographie des Ecrivains Français no. 3. Paris
and Rome: Memini, 1996.

Pickstock, Catherine. *After Writing: On the Liturgical Consummation of Philosophy.*
Oxford: Blackwell, 1998.

———. "Radical Orthodoxy and the Mediations of Time." In *Radical Orthodoxy?
A Catholic Enquiry,* ed. Laurence Paul Hemming, 63–75. Aldershot: Ashgate,
2000.

*Position des thèses soutenues per les élèves de la promotion de 1922 pour obtenir le
diplôme d'archiviste paléographe.* Paris: Picard, 1922.

Purcell, Michael. "Liturgy: Divine and Human Service." *Heythrop Journal* 38
(1997): 144–64.

Rabaté, Jean-Michel, ed. *The Cambridge Companion to Lacan.* Cambridge: Cambridge University Press, 1993.

———. *The Future of Theory.* Oxford: Blackwell, 2002.

———. *Jacques Lacan: Psychoanalysis and the Subject of Literature.* New York: Pal-
grave Macmillan, 2001.

Rajchman, John. "Lacan and the Ethics of Modernity." *Representations* 15 (1986):
42–56.

———. *Truth and Eros: Foucault, Lacan, and the Question of Ethics.* New York:
Routledge, 1991.

Ragland, Ellie. *Essays on the Pleasure of Death: From Freud to Lacan.* New York:
Routledge, 1995.

Renard, Jean-Claude. *L'"Expérience intérieure" de Georges Bataille ou la négation du
Mystère.* Paris: Seuil, 1987.

Reno, R. R. "The Radical Orthodoxy Project." *First Things* 100 (2000): 37–44.

Richardson, Michael. *Georges Bataille.* London and New York: Routledge, 1994.

Richman, Michele. *Reading Georges Bataille: Beyond the Gift.* Baltimore: Johns
Hopkins University Press, 1982.

Robbe-Grillet, Alain. *For a New Novel: Essays on Fiction.* Translated by Richard
Howard. New York: Grove Press, 1965.

Robertson, D. W. *A Preface to Chaucer: Studies in Medieval Perspectives.* Princeton,
N.J.: Princeton University Press, 1962.

Roudiez, Léon. "Présentation du Colloque Artaud/Bataille." *Sub-Stance* 5–6
(1973): 199–206.

Roudinesco, Elizabeth. *Jacques Lacan.* Translated by Barbara Bray. New York: Columbia University Press, 1997.

Rousseau, Jean-Jacques. *Essay on the Origins of Languages.* Translated by John H. Moran and Alexander Gode. In Moran and Gode, eds., *On the Origin of Language.* Chicago: University of Chicago Press, 1966.

Said, Edward W. *The World, the Text, and the Critic.* Cambridge: Harvard University Press, 1983.

Saler, Michael T. *The Avant-Garde in Interwar England: Medieval Modernism and the London Underground.* Oxford and New York: Oxford University Press, 1999.

Sarrazin, Bernard. "Plaisir du texte biblique: l'illisible et l'illimité." *Textuel* 15 (1984): 20–29.

Sartre, Jean-Paul. *What Is Literature?* Translated by Bernard Frechtman. New York: Philosophical Library, 1949.

Schaffer, Scott. Review of Alain Badiou, *Ethics. Bad Subjects* 8, no. 13 (2002).

Schinkel, Willem. "Pierre Bourdieu's Political Turn?" *Theory, Culture, and Society* 20 (2003): 69–93.

Sells, Michael. *Mystical Languages of Unsaying.* Chicago: University of Chicago Press, 1994.

Shoaf, R. A. "Medieval Studies after Derrida after Heidegger." In *Sign Sentence Discourse: Language in Medieval Thought and Literature,* ed. Julian N. Wasserman and Lois Roney, 9–30. Syracuse, N.Y.: Syracuse University Press, 1989.

Sikka, Sonia. "Questioning the Sacred: Heidegger and Levinas on the Locus of Divinity." *Modern Theology* 14 (1998): 299–323

Sollers, Philippe. "Dante et la traversée de l'écriture." *Tel Quel* 21 (fall 1965): 12–33.

———. "Pourquoi Artaud, pourquoi Bataille?" *Sub-Stance* 5–6 (1973): 9–12.

———. *Writing and the Experience of Limits.* Edited by David Hayman, translated by Philip Barnard and David Hayman. New York: Columbia University Press, 1983.

Sollers, Philippe, ed. *Bataille: Vers une Révolution culturelle.* Paris: Union Générale d'Éditions, 1973.

Solterer, Helen. "The Waking of Medieval Theatricality: Paris 1935–1995." *New Literary History* 27 (1996): 357–90.

Spiegel, Gabrielle. *The Past as Text: The Theory and Practice of Medieval Historiography.* Baltimore and London: Johns Hopkins University Press, 1999.

Stafford, Andy. *Roland Barthes, Phenomenon and Myth.* Edinburgh: Edinburgh University Press, 1998.

Starobinski, Jean. "Saint Ausutine et la parole de l'autre." *Tel Quel* 21 (1965): 67–75.

Staten, Henry. *Eros in Mourning: Homer to Lacan.* Baltimore: Johns Hopkins University Press, 2002.

Stock, Brian. "Tradition and Modernity: Models from the Past." In *Modernité au Moyen Âge: Le défi du passé,* ed. Brigitte Cazelles and Charles Méla, 33–44. Geneva: Droz, 1990.

Stoekl, Allan. *Agonies of the Intellectual: Commitment, Subjectivity, and the Performative in Twentieth-Century French Tradition.* Lincoln: University of Nebraska Press, 1992.

———. *Politics, Writing, Mutilation: The Cases of Bataille, Blanchot, Roussel, Leiris, and Ponge.* Minneapolis: University of Minnesota Press, 1985.

Stoekl, Allan, ed. *On Bataille.* Special issue of *Yale French Studies* 78 (1990).

Strohm, Paul. *Theory and the Premodern Text.* Minneapolis: University of Minnesota Press, 2000.

Surya, Michel. *Georges Bataille: La mort à l'oeuvre.* Paris: Séguier, 1987.

———. *Georges Bataille: An Intellectual Biography.* Translated by Krzysztof Fijalkowski and Michael Richardson. London: Verso, 2002.

Swartz, David. *Culture and Power: The Sociology of Pierre Bourdieu.* Chicago: University of Chicago Press, 1997.

Taylor, Charles. *The Ethics of Authenticity.* Cambridge: Harvard University Press, 1992.

Taylor, Mark C. *Altarity.* Chicago: University of Chicago Press, 1987.

———. *Deconstructing Theology.* New York: Crossroad Publishing Company, 1982.

Taylor, Mark C., ed. *Deconstruction in Context: Literature and Philosophy.* Chicago: University of Chicago Press, 1986.

Theall, Donald F. "Marshall McLuhan, Canadian Schizo-Jansenist and Pseudo-Joycean Precursor of and Preparer for the Dissemination of French Theory in North America." In *French Theory in America,* ed. Silvère Lotringer and Sande Cohen, 111–23. New York and London: Routledge, 2001.

Thomas Aquinas, Saint. *Dieu.* Volume 1 of *La somme théologique.* Translated by A. D. Sertillanges, O.P. Paris: Société Saint Jean l'Évangeliste/Desclée & Cie, 1925.

van Buren, John. *The Young Heidegger: Rumor of the Hidden King.* Bloomington: Indiana University Press, 1994.

van Esbroeck, Michael. *Herméneutique, structuralisme et exégèse: Essai de logique kérygmatique.* Paris: Desclée, 1968.

Vance, Eugene. "The Modernity of the Middle Ages in the Future: Remarks on a Recent Book." *Romanic Review* 64 (1973): 140–51.

Wallwork, Ernest. *Psychoanalysis and Ethics.* New Haven, Conn.: Yale University Press, 1991.

Ward, Graham. *Cities of God.* London: Routledge, 2000.

Warren, Michelle. "Joking with the Enemy: Beyond Ritual in the *Ordene de chevalerie.*" *Exemplaria* 15 (2003): 263–296.

Webb, Stephen H. "The Rhetoric of Ethics as Excess: A Christian Theological Response to Emmanuel Levinas." *Modern Theology* 15 (1999): 1–16.

Weber, Max. *The History of Commercial Partnerships in the Middle Ages.* Translated by Lutz Kaelber. Philadelphia: Rowman and Littlefield, 2003.

Weingrad, Michael. "Parisian Messianism: Catholicism, Decadence, and the Transgressions of Georges Bataille." *History and Memory* 13 (2001): 113–32.

Wycliffe, John. *The English Works of Wyclif Hitherto Unprinted.* Edited by F. D.

Matthew. Early English Text Society, original series 74. London: Trübner, 1880.

Wyschogrod, Edith. *An Ethics of Remembering: History, Heterology, and the Nameless Other.* Chicago and London: University of Chicago Press, 1998.

———. *Saints and Postmodernism: Revisioning Moral Philosophy.* Chicago: University of Chicago Press, 1990.

Zink, Michel. *The Enchantment of the Middle Ages.* Translated by Jane Marie Todd. Baltimore and London: Johns Hopkins University Press, 1998.

Žižek, Slavoj. *Enjoy Your Symptom! Jacques Lacan in Hollywood and Out.* New York: Routledge, 2001.

———. *For They Know Not What They Do: Enjoyment as a Political Factor.* London: Verso, 1991

———. *The Metastases of Enjoyment: Six Essays on Women and Causality.* London: Verso, 1994.

———. *The Sublime Object of Ideology.* London: Verso, 1989.

Zumthor, Paul. "Comments on H. R. Jauss's Article." *New Literary History* 10 (1979): 367–76.

———. *Essai de poétique médiévale.* Paris: Seuil, 1972.

———. "Médiéviste ou pas." *Poétique* 31 (1977): 306–321.

———. *Speaking of the Middle Ages.* Translated by Sarah White. Lincoln: University of Nebraska Press, 1986.

Zupančič, Alenka. "Ethics and Tragedy in Lacan." In *The Cambridge Companion to Lacan,* ed. Jean-Michel Rabaté, 173–90. Cambridge: Cambridge University Press, 1993.

———. *Ethics of the Real: Kant, Lacan.* London: Verso, 2000.

Index

Lightning Source UK Ltd.
Milton Keynes UK
UKOW06f1142030615

252821UK00001B/124/P